GCSE English
Language & Literature

All right, so the new Grade 9-1 English GCSEs are pretty challenging...
but with this brilliant CGP book by your side, they won't seem so tough.

It's packed with clear study notes, example answers and essential practice questions.
We've even included a realistic practice exam at the end of the book,
plus plenty of advice to help you score top marks in the real tests.

So why choose someone else's dreary English book when you can have CGP?
Go on, you deserve it.

Complete
Revision & Practice
Everything you need to pass the exams!

Contents

Published by CGP

Editors:
Claire Boulter
Emma Crighton
Jack Perry

With thanks to Glenn Rogers for the proofreading
and Ana Pungartnik for the copyright research.

Acknowledgements:

With thanks to iStockphoto.com for permission to use the image on page 157

Letter on page 20 to Princess (later Queen) Victoria from King Leopold I of Belgium,
August 1832, from The Letters of Queen Victoria, Volume 1 (of 3), 1837-1843.

Page 134: 'Ghosts' by Robert W. Service used by courtesy of Mrs Anne Longepe.

Page 137: 'At Sea' by Jennifer Copley.

Article entitled 'Confessions of a Nanny' on page 159 © Guardian News & Media Ltd 2016.

Page 168: 'For a Five-Year-Old' by Fleur Adcock from 'Poems 1960-2000' (Bloodaxe Books, 2000)

Page 169: 'The Beautiful Lie' is from 'The Beautiful Lie' by Sheenagh Pugh (Seren, 2002)

Every effort has been made to locate copyright holders and obtain permission to reproduce sources.
For those sources where it has been difficult to trace the copyright holder of the work, we would be grateful
for information. If any copyright holder would like us to make an amendment to the acknowledgements,
please notify us and we will gladly update the book at the next reprint. Thank you.

ISBN: 978 1 78294 368 6

Clipart from Corel®
Printed by Elanders Ltd, Newcastle upon Tyne.

Based on the classic CGP style created by Richard Parsons.

Text, design, layout and original illustrations © Coordination Group Publications Ltd. (CGP) 2016
All rights reserved.

How To Use This Book

This book tells you how to deal with even the trickiest English questions that might come up in your GCSEs.

Check whether you're doing **one** English GCSE or **two**

1) <u>Everybody</u> has to study <u>English Language</u> at GCSE. Page 7 tells you more about what you'll have to do in the exam, and what the <u>examiners</u> will be looking for in your answers.

2) You might also take a GCSE in <u>English Literature</u>. If you do, you'll have to read and analyse a range of <u>prose</u>, <u>drama</u> and <u>poetry</u> — page 73 gives you more information on what you'll study and what you need to do to get a <u>great mark</u> in the exam.

Learn how to write great **exam answers**

1) <u>Section One</u> of this book gives you advice on how to <u>plan</u> and <u>write</u> answers for English Language and English Literature. It includes extracts from <u>sample answers</u> to show you how to approach the different types of questions you're likely to come across.

2) Accurate <u>grammar</u>, <u>punctuation</u> and <u>spelling</u> is vital — you can pick up extra marks for writing well in both English Language and English Literature. <u>Section Eleven</u>, near the end of the book, gives you loads of tips on how to make sure your answers are <u>accurate</u> and <u>well written</u>.

3) To get a top grade, you need to know the correct <u>technical terms</u> (rhetoric, alliteration, stanza etc.) There's a handy <u>glossary</u> at the back of the book that defines all the terms you'll need.

Get to grips with the **English Language** course

1) <u>Sections Two to Four</u> of this book are about English Language:

- <u>Section Two</u> is all about how to <u>read</u>, <u>understand</u> and <u>select information</u> from the different types of texts that might come up in the exams.

- <u>Section Three</u> digs deeper into the <u>techniques</u> that writers use — it shows you how to pick out different features of language and structure and analyse their effects.

- <u>Section Four</u> guides you through how to <u>write</u> your own creative and non-fiction texts — it gives you advice on how to <u>structure</u> your writing, the sort of things to <u>include</u> and what <u>language</u> to use.

2) You'll also be assessed on your <u>spoken language</u>, but for most exam boards this won't count towards your GCSE. <u>Section Twelve</u> gives you some pointers on how to do well in the <u>spoken language</u> assessment.

Get ready for the **English Literature** exams

There's no replacement for knowing your <u>set texts</u> really well, but <u>Sections Five to Ten</u> of this book will give you a helping hand to get a top grade in your English Literature exams:

- <u>Section Five</u> gives you advice on what to look out for when you're studying a <u>prose</u> or <u>drama</u> text.

- <u>Section Six</u> is all about the specific things you need to think about if you're reading a <u>play</u>, and <u>Section Seven</u> covers the different elements of <u>prose</u> texts.

- <u>Section Eight</u> talks you through analysing <u>poetry</u>, including how to <u>compare poems</u>.

- <u>Section Nine</u> shows you how to get to grips with the poems in your <u>Poetry Anthology</u>, and <u>Section Ten</u> is all about how to understand and analyse a poem you <u>haven't read</u> before.

Planning Answers

We've all been there — you turn over your exam paper, read the question, notice that time's slipping away and start scribbling your answer. But I promise, if you take a few minutes to plan, you won't regret it.

Read the questions **carefully** and **calmly**

1) Give yourself time to read through the <u>questions</u> and any <u>texts</u> or <u>extracts</u> at the start of the exam.

2) Always <u>read the questions</u> before the texts or extracts — that way, you'll know what to look out for.

3) Make sure you're clear about what the questions are <u>asking</u> you to do by <u>underlining</u> the <u>key words</u>.

> How does Brontë <u>present</u> the <u>changing relationship</u> between <u>Jane</u> and <u>Mr Rochester</u>?

4) Once you've read the questions, carefully <u>read</u> through any <u>texts</u> or <u>extracts</u> you've been given. It's a good idea to <u>highlight</u> key <u>words</u> or <u>phrases</u> that will help you to answer the questions — but don't spend ages doing this.

Remember, it's your exam paper and you can write on it if it helps you.

Jot down your **main ideas** before you start writing

1) You <u>don't</u> need to make a plan for <u>short-answer questions</u>.

2) For each <u>long-answer question</u> (e.g. those that require you to write an essay or a piece of descriptive writing), spend a few minutes planning your answer.

3) Don't go into too much <u>detail</u> — just get your <u>main ideas</u> down, and <u>outline</u> the <u>structure</u> of your answer.

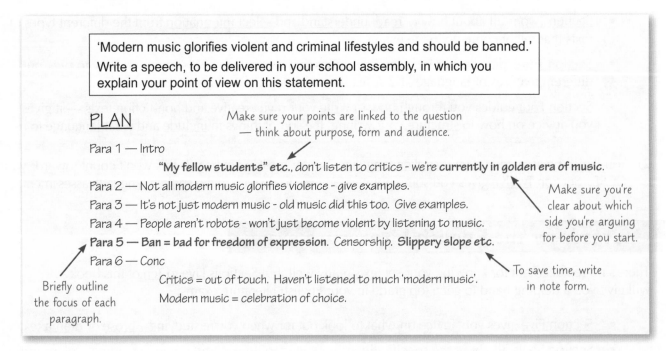

'Modern music glorifies violent and criminal lifestyles and should be banned.'
Write a speech, to be delivered in your school assembly, in which you explain your point of view on this statement.

PLAN

Make sure your points are linked to the question — think about purpose, form and audience.

Para 1 — Intro
"My fellow students" etc., don't listen to critics - we're **currently in golden era of music**.
Para 2 — Not all modern music glorifies violence - give examples.
Para 3 — It's not just modern music - old music did this too. Give examples.
Para 4 — People aren't robots - won't just become violent by listening to music.
Para 5 — **Ban = bad for freedom of expression**. Censorship. **Slippery slope etc.**
Para 6 — Conc
Critics = out of touch. Haven't listened to much 'modern music'.
Modern music = celebration of choice.

Briefly outline the focus of each paragraph.

Make sure you're clear about which side you're arguing for before you start.

To save time, write in note form.

You might not need to plan every answer...

You probably won't need to plan every answer in your exams, but you should make a brief plan to help you with any question that requires a longer answer. Leave some time to check your work at the end, too.

P.E.E.D.

To get good marks, you need to explain and develop your ideas properly. That's why P.E.E.D. is useful.

P.E.E.D. stands for **Point, Example, Explain, Develop**

To write good English essays about texts you've read, you must do <u>four</u> things:

1) Make a <u>point</u> to answer the question you've been given.

2) Then give an <u>example</u> from the text (see page 4 for more on this).

3) After that, <u>explain</u> how your example backs up your point.

4) Finally, <u>develop</u> your point — this might involve saying what the <u>effect on the reader</u> is, saying what the <u>writer's intention</u> is, <u>linking</u> your point to another part of the text or giving your <u>own opinion</u>.

The <u>explanation</u> and <u>development</u> parts are very important. They're your chance to show that you <u>really understand</u> and have <u>thought about</u> the text. Here are a couple of <u>examples</u>:

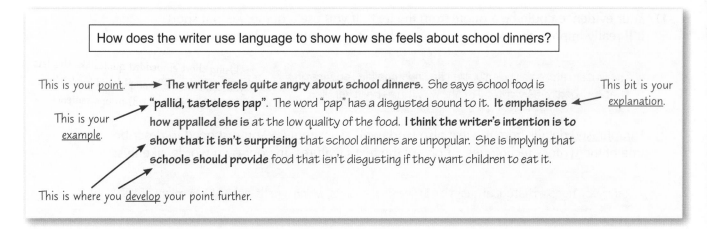

> How does the writer use language to show how she feels about school dinners?

This is your <u>point</u>. → **The writer feels quite angry about school dinners.** She says school food is "**pallid, tasteless pap**". The word "pap" has a disgusted sound to it. **It emphasises** ← *This bit is your <u>explanation</u>.*

This is your <u>example</u>. → how appalled she is at the low quality of the food. **I think the writer's intention is to show that it isn't surprising** that school dinners are unpopular. She is implying that **schools should provide** food that isn't disgusting if they want children to eat it.

This is where you <u>develop</u> your point further.

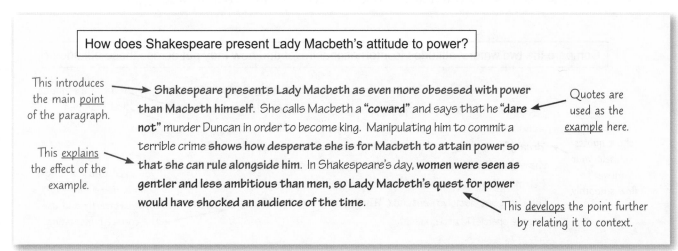

> How does Shakespeare present Lady Macbeth's attitude to power?

This introduces the main <u>point</u> of the paragraph. → **Shakespeare presents Lady Macbeth as even more obsessed with power than Macbeth himself.** She calls Macbeth a "**coward**" and says that he "**dare** ← *Quotes are used as the <u>example</u> here.*

not" murder Duncan in order to become king. Manipulating him to commit a

This <u>explains</u> the effect of the example. → terrible crime **shows how desperate she is for Macbeth to attain power so that she can rule alongside him.** In Shakespeare's day, **women were seen as gentler and less ambitious than men, so Lady Macbeth's quest for power would have shocked an audience of the time.**

This <u>develops</u> the point further by relating it to context.

P.E.E.D. should help you to explain and develop your points...

Other versions of P.E.E.D. also focus on explaining and developing — P.E.E.R. (Point, Example, Explain, Relate), P.E.E.C.E. (Point, Example, Explain, Compare, Explore) and so on. Use the one you've been taught.

Using Examples

However fabulous the point you make in your answer is, it won't get you top marks unless you can back it up with examples from the text. Cue a page that shows you how it's done...

Use **details** from the text to **back up** your points

Whenever you make a <u>point</u> about a text, you need to use short pieces of <u>evidence</u> to <u>back it up</u>.

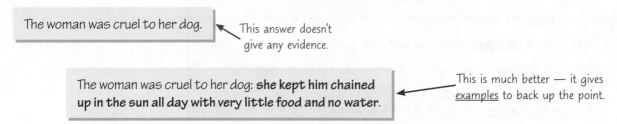

The woman was cruel to her dog.

This answer doesn't give any evidence.

The woman was cruel to her dog: **she kept him chained up in the sun all day with very little food and no water**.

This is much better — it gives <u>examples</u> to back up the point.

Your evidence can be **quotes** or **examples**

1) Your evidence could be a <u>quote</u> from the text. If you use a quote, keep it <u>short</u>. It'll really impress the examiner if you <u>embed</u> it in a sentence, like this:

> The writer refers to the situation as "indefensible", suggesting that he is extremely critical of the way it has been handled.

Using short embedded quotes like this lets you combine the 'example' and 'explain' parts of P.E.E.D. (see p.3) in one sentence.

2) <u>Paraphrased details</u> from the text also work well as examples. You just need to describe one of the <u>writer's techniques</u>, or one of the <u>text's features</u>, in your own words, like this:

> Tennyson uses a rhetorical question in the final stanza, which emphasises the heroism of the Light Brigade.

3) Here's an <u>example</u> to show you how to work your evidence into your answer:

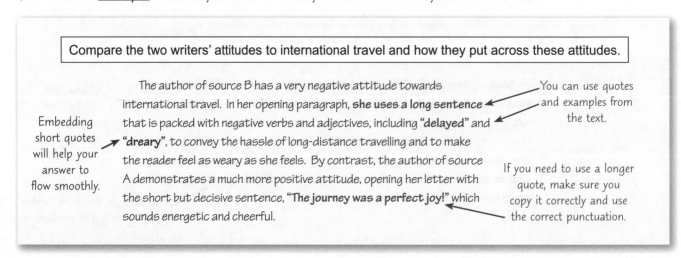

Compare the two writers' attitudes to international travel and how they put across these attitudes.

The author of source B has a very negative attitude towards international travel. In her opening paragraph, **she uses a long sentence** that is packed with negative verbs and adjectives, including **"delayed"** and **"dreary"**, to convey the hassle of long-distance travelling and to make the reader feel as weary as she feels. By contrast, the author of source A demonstrates a much more positive attitude, opening her letter with the short but decisive sentence, **"The journey was a perfect joy!"** which sounds energetic and cheerful.

You can use quotes and examples from the text.

Embedding short quotes will help your answer to flow smoothly.

If you need to use a longer quote, make sure you copy it correctly and use the correct punctuation.

Use examples to support your ideas...

Whether you paraphrase or use a quote, backing up your points with evidence from the text is really crucial in your English exams. Just make sure that you then explain how the evidence supports your point.

Reading with Insight

To get the top grades, you need to show that you can 'read with insight' — you've got to make it clear that you understand more than just the obvious things. You can think of it as 'reading between the lines'.

You need to look **beyond** what's **obvious**

Looking beyond what's obvious will help you to make sure you've done the 'D' part of P.E.E.D. — look back at p.3 for more on this.

1) You may understand what <u>happens</u> in a text, or what it's <u>about</u>, but you'll need to write about <u>more</u> than just that in your answers.

2) You can show <u>insight</u> if you work out what the writer's <u>intentions</u> are and how they want the reader to <u>feel</u>.

3) Here are a couple of <u>examples</u> of the kinds of things you could write:

> *The rhetorical questions make the reader doubt whether homework is a good thing. The writer seems to want to make readers feel guilty.* Think about the reasons <u>why</u> the writer has included certain features — show you've understood their <u>intended effect</u> on the reader.

4) Remember to include <u>examples</u> from the text to <u>support</u> your interpretation:

> *Darcy is portrayed as an unlikeable character in this extract. He is described as "above being pleased", hinting at his arrogance and haughtiness. However, the swiftness with which the ball-goers change their opinion of him shows their fickleness and hints that their judgement is not to be trusted.* Try to explain <u>how</u> the writer creates a particular impression of a character or event. Examiners love it if you can give <u>alternative interpretations</u> that go beyond the obvious.

Inference means working things out from clues

1) Writers don't usually make things obvious — but you can use <u>evidence</u> from the text to make an <u>inference</u> about what the writer <u>really</u> wants us to think.

2) You need to analyse <u>details</u> from the text to show what they <u>reveal</u> about the writer's intentions:

> *The writer uses words like "endless" and "unoriginal", which imply that he did not enjoy the film.* The writer's <u>language</u> indicates their <u>emotions</u> and <u>attitude</u>.

> *The writer sounds sarcastic when she calls the contestants "the finest brains the country could scrape together".* The writer will often use <u>tone</u> (see page 25) to <u>imply</u> what they really mean — look out for <u>sarcasm</u> (see page 34) or <u>bias</u> (see page 36).

3) You could use <u>phrases</u> like these to show that you've made an <u>inference</u>:

> The writer gives a sense of...

> The writer appears to be...

> This suggests that...

Think about the effect the writer wants to create...

Everything in a text has been carefully crafted by the writer, so look for clues that reveal their intentions. Demonstrate that you understand what the writer is showing you, not just what they're telling you.

Revision Summary

At the end of most sections in this book, you'll find pages like this one. They're important, so don't skip them. Do all these questions, then go back and look up the bits you didn't know. Check them, then do the whole lot again until you get 100% correct.

1) If you're given any texts or extracts in the exam, you should:
    a) Read them before you read through the questions.
    b) Read them after you read through the questions.

2) True or false?
    You should make a detailed plan for every question in your exams.

3) What are the two main things that you should include in a plan?
    a) Your main ideas
    b) Lots of detailed evidence from the text
    c) The exact wording of your answer
    d) The structure of your answer

4) Give one way that you can save time when writing a plan.

5) What does P.E.E.D. stand for?

6) Give three ways that you could develop a point.

7) In your longer answers, how many of your points should be backed up with evidence from the text?
    a) A few of them
    b) About half of them
    c) Some of them
    d) All of them

8) Quotes from the text should usually be:
    a) short.   b) long.

9) Give one reason why you should embed your quotes into your answers.

10) Choose two answers.
    When using a longer quote, make sure that you:
    a) copy it correctly.
    b) include a capital letter.
    c) don't include quotation marks.
    d) use the correct punctuation.

11) Give two examples of things you could comment on to show that you are reading with insight.

12) What does 'inference' mean?

13) Give an example of a phrase you could use to show that you've made an inference.

Introduction to English Language

English Language is a <u>compulsory</u> GCSE — everyone has to do it. This page gives you a quick overview of what to expect from your English Language exams, so when the time comes they won't be quite as scary.

GCSE English Language assesses your **Reading** and **Writing**

1) The English Language GCSE is designed to test your <u>reading</u> skills. In the exams you'll probably have to:

- read and answer questions on <u>two non-fiction</u> texts you haven't studied before. The two texts will be from <u>different centuries</u> (e.g. one from the 19th century and one from the 21st century).
- <u>read</u> and answer questions on one or two <u>fiction</u> texts you haven't studied before.

Sections Two and Three of this book tell you how to pick out information and analyse texts.

2) You'll also be tested on your <u>writing</u> skills. In the exams you'll probably have to:

- <u>write your own</u> piece of <u>non-fiction</u> — e.g. a newspaper article or a speech.
- do some <u>creative writing</u> — e.g. a short story or description.

Section Four of this book gives you advice on how to write a range of text types.

3) Your <u>speaking and listening</u> will also be assessed, but this <u>won't</u> count for your GCSE. (See pages 151-153.)

Each **Assessment Objective** refers to a **Different Skill**

The <u>assessment objectives</u> are the things you need to <u>do</u> to get good marks in the exam — they're the same for all exam boards. Here's a brief description of the <u>English Language</u> assessment objectives (AOs):

AO1
- <u>Pick out</u> and <u>understand</u> pieces of <u>explicit</u> and <u>implicit</u> information from the texts.
- <u>Collect</u> and <u>put together</u> information from different texts.

AO2
- <u>Explain</u> how writers use <u>language</u> and <u>structure</u> to achieve their <u>purpose</u> and <u>influence</u> readers.
- Use <u>technical terms</u> to support your analysis of language and structure.

AO3
- <u>Identify</u> different writers' <u>ideas</u> and <u>perspectives</u>.
- <u>Compare</u> the <u>methods</u> used by different writers to convey their ideas.

AO4
- <u>Critically evaluate</u> texts, giving a <u>personal opinion</u> about how successful the writing is.
- Provide detailed <u>evidence</u> from the text to <u>support</u> your opinion.

AO5
- Write <u>clearly</u> and <u>imaginatively</u>, adapting your tone and style for various <u>purposes</u> and <u>audiences</u>.
- <u>Organise</u> your writing into a clear <u>structure</u>.

AO6
- Use a range of <u>sentence structures</u> and <u>vocabulary</u>, so that your writing is <u>clear</u> and <u>purposeful</u>.
- Write <u>accurately</u>, paying particular attention to spelling, punctuation and grammar.

Make sure you understand how your exams work...

Don't worry if all this seems a bit overwhelming — the key is to know what you have to do, then get lots of practice doing it. That way, when the exam comes round, answering the questions will be second nature.

Information and Ideas

This page will help you with assessment objective 1 (see p.7).

Information and ideas can be **Explicit** or **Implicit**

1) The first thing you need to be able to do in order to <u>analyse</u> a text is to <u>understand</u> the basic things it's <u>telling you</u>.

2) The information and ideas you need to pick out will either be <u>explicit</u> or <u>implicit</u>.

3) <u>Explicit</u> information is <u>clearly written</u> in the text.

> *Last weekend, it rained a lot.* The text states that it rained, so we <u>know</u> that it rained. We also know <u>how much</u> it rained — "a lot."

4) <u>Implicit</u> information needs a little more <u>detective work</u> — you'll need to work it out from what is said in the text.

> *The castle was dark, decrepit and freezing cold.* → In this sentence, it is <u>implied</u> that the author doesn't like the castle very much, but this isn't stated outright.

You'll also need to **Summarise** information

1) You might be asked to pick out information and ideas on the <u>same topic</u> from two <u>different texts</u> and to <u>summarise</u> the <u>similarities</u> or <u>differences</u> in what you've picked out.

> **Source A**
>
> *What a miserable afternoon. Daddy shouted at me just for being late to school. "You should be more responsible now you're <u>thirteen</u>, Andrew!" he yelled. He said he had half a mind to stop wasting his money on my private education. I know he's angry, but <u>I think it was a bit of an overreaction</u>.*
>
> **Source B**
>
> *Today was not a happy day, even though it was Richard's <u>16th</u> birthday party. Richard sat quietly, his hands folded in his lap, as Father ranted about how the party was a waste of the little money we have. <u>Richard only broke his silence to acknowledge Father's tirade with a respectful "Yes, Sir"</u>.*

Look for <u>explicit</u> differences, such as the boys' ages...

...and <u>implicit</u> differences, such as what the boys' reactions tell you about their personalities and attitudes.

2) Make sure you <u>back up</u> your points with examples from the text.

3) Use <u>linking words</u> to write about similarities and differences — they show you've made a <u>comparison</u>.

To show similarities:	
• Similarly	• Likewise
• Equally	• Also

To show differences:	
• Whereas	• Although
• However	• But

These are a few examples of linking words, but there are plenty more.

If you master these skills, you can pick up some easy marks...

You'll need good observation skills to answer these kinds of questions. Comment on the explicit similarities or differences between the texts, but don't forget to dig a bit deeper and write about implicit ideas too.

Audience

In the exams, you'll need to think about the audience — the intended readers of the text.

Writers aim their work at **General** or **Specific** audiences

1) The writer will always have a <u>group of people</u> in mind when they write — this is their <u>audience</u>.

2) The audience of a text can be quite <u>general</u>, e.g. adults, or more <u>specific</u>, e.g. parents with children under the age of 3.

3) Some texts will have <u>more than one</u> audience, e.g. children's books will try to appeal to the <u>kids</u> who read them, but also to the <u>parents</u> who will <u>buy</u> them.

Look for **Clues** about the target audience

1) Sometimes you can work out <u>who</u> the target audience is by the text's <u>content</u> (subject matter):

> *This latest model is a beautiful car. Its impressive engine can send you shooting from 0-60 mph in less than 8 seconds.* This text is clearly aimed at someone who's interested in <u>high-performance cars</u>.

2) The <u>vocabulary</u> (choice of words) can tell you about the target audience, e.g. about the <u>age group</u>:

> *Today, we witnessed a discussion on fox hunting. As one can imagine, this issue, although it has been debated for many years, still managed to elicit mixed emotions from all concerned.* The <u>sophisticated vocabulary</u>, like 'elicit', rather than 'bring out', and the <u>complex sentences</u> show that this text is aimed at <u>adults</u>.

> *Dungeon Killer 3 is the hottest new game of the year! There are 52 awesome levels and 6 cool new characters — don't miss out on the wildest gaming experience of your life!* This one uses modern <u>slang</u> and <u>simple sentences</u>, so it's clear that this text is aimed at <u>younger people</u>.

3) The <u>language</u> can also give you clues about the target audience's <u>level of understanding</u>:

> *The object of a game of football is to get the ball in the opposing team's goal. Sounds easy, but the other team has the same thing in mind. Also, there are eleven players on the other team trying to stop you.* The <u>simple</u>, <u>general</u> explanations in this text show that it's written for people who <u>don't know much</u> about football.

> *The next hole was a par 3 and I hit my tee shot directly onto the green. Sadly, my putting let me down badly, and I ended up getting a bogey.* The <u>technical vocabulary</u> here shows that this is for people who know <u>quite a bit</u> about golf.

The audience is one of the first things you should look for in a text...

You need to work out who the intended audience of a text is so that you can discuss the writer's purpose, the techniques they use and how successful they are. Keep the audience in mind throughout your answer.

Purpose and Viewpoint

Every text you come across in your English Language exams will have been written for a reason.

There are **Four Common Purposes** of writing

1) The <u>purpose</u> of a text is the <u>reason</u> that it's been written — what the writer is <u>trying to do</u>.

2) Most texts are written for <u>one</u> of these reasons:

To Argue or Persuade
- They give the writer's <u>opinion</u>.
- They get the reader to <u>agree</u> with them.

To Advise
- They <u>help</u> the reader to <u>do something</u>.
- They give <u>instructions</u> on what to do.

To Inform
- They <u>tell</u> the reader about something.
- They help the reader to increase their <u>understanding</u> of a subject.

To Entertain
- They are <u>enjoyable</u> to read.
- They make the reader <u>feel</u> something.

Pages 11-14 tell you how to spot a text's purpose.

3) Lots of texts have <u>more than one</u> purpose, though. E.g. a biographical text could be written to both <u>inform</u> and <u>entertain</u> its audience.

4) In the exams, read the texts carefully and make sure that you think about <u>what</u> the writers are trying to <u>achieve</u> (and <u>how</u> they're achieving it).

5) Look out for helpful exam questions that actually <u>tell you</u> the writer's purpose. E.g. if the question asks you about how the writer uses language to <u>influence</u> the reader, you know it's about <u>persuading</u>.

Viewpoint and **Attitude** are **Different** to **Purpose**

1) A writer's purpose is what they're trying to <u>do</u>, but their <u>viewpoint</u> (or attitude) is what they <u>think</u> about the <u>topics</u> that they're writing about. For example:

Use the highest-quality olive oil you can find to ensure the best taste possible. This text's <u>purpose</u> is to <u>advise</u> its audience about cooking. The <u>writer's viewpoint</u> is that good-quality olive oil improves the <u>taste</u> of the food.

2) You can work out what a writer's viewpoint might be by looking for clues in the <u>language</u>, <u>tone</u>, <u>style</u> and <u>content</u> of a text. For example:

I urge you to visit this truly unique and hidden valley — you must see such beautiful scenery at least once in your life. This text's <u>purpose</u> is to <u>persuade</u> its audience to visit a place. The <u>writer's viewpoint</u> is their <u>belief</u> that the valley is beautiful and that it should be visited. The writer uses <u>emotive adjectives</u> and an <u>upbeat tone</u> to convey their viewpoint.

You need to know the purpose and viewpoint to write a good answer...

Always make sure you consider a text's purpose and the writer's viewpoint. If there's more than one purpose to a text, write about them both. Show the examiner that you really understand the text.

Informative Texts

Informative texts (like this book, in fact) always have something they're trying to tell you. Have a look at this page to find out some ways that you can spot informative texts.

Informative writing **Tells** you something

1) When writing an informative text, the writer's aim is to pass on <u>knowledge</u> to the reader as <u>clearly</u> and <u>effectively</u> as possible.

Have a look back at p.9 for more on audience.

2) They will adapt their <u>language</u> to match their intended <u>audience</u>, e.g. they <u>might</u> need to write for different <u>age groups</u>, or for people with different <u>levels of understanding</u>.

3) Purely informative texts will present information in a <u>balanced</u> and <u>factual</u> way. They will contain lots of <u>facts</u> and <u>figures</u>, but no <u>opinions</u>.

Labradoodles were initially bred as guide dogs for people with allergies due to their low-shedding coats. They are a relatively small breed, rarely growing above 70 cm in height.

Informative texts often contain <u>facts</u> such as dates and statistics, and use <u>clear</u>, <u>direct</u> <u>language</u> and a <u>formal</u> tone.

4) Some informative texts might also be <u>arguing</u> a particular viewpoint, though. For example:

Many newspapers <u>carefully pick</u> information that supports a particular political party. Even though a newspaper article may not say outright what its opinion is, it can still be <u>biased</u>.

Bias is when a piece of writing is influenced by the opinion of its author — see page 36.

Here's an **Example** of an **Informative** text

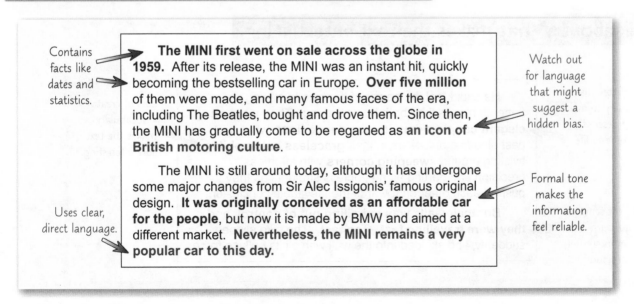

Contains facts like dates and statistics.

Uses clear, direct language.

The MINI first went on sale across the globe in 1959. After its release, the MINI was an instant hit, quickly becoming the bestselling car in Europe. **Over five million** of them were made, and many famous faces of the era, including The Beatles, bought and drove them. Since then, the MINI has gradually come to be regarded as **an icon of British motoring culture**.

The MINI is still around today, although it has undergone some major changes from Sir Alec Issigonis' famous original design. **It was originally conceived as an affordable car for the people**, but now it is made by BMW and aimed at a different market. **Nevertheless, the MINI remains a very popular car to this day.**

Watch out for language that might suggest a hidden bias.

Formal tone makes the information feel reliable.

Look at some examples of informative writing as practice...

You need to be able to recognise informative writing and explain how it's being used. If the information is biased, make sure you comment on that. It will show the examiner you've really thought about the text.

Entertaining Texts

Entertaining texts make you feel something. You need to be able to explain how they do this.

Entertaining writing aims to be Enjoyable to read

1) Entertaining writing is the sort of thing you'd read for <u>pleasure</u>, e.g. literary fiction.

2) Unlike informative texts, they contain <u>few facts</u>. Instead, they try to make you <u>feel</u> something, like <u>scared</u>, <u>excited</u>, or <u>amused</u>.

3) Entertaining writing is often very <u>descriptive</u> (see p.37), and uses <u>narrative techniques</u> to make texts more enjoyable to read (see p.41).

4) Writers also use <u>structural techniques</u> to create entertaining texts (see pages 42-45). E.g. lots of <u>short</u>, <u>punchy</u> sentences can be used to make a text feel more <u>exciting</u>.

<table>
<tr>
<td>I'm drawn towards it. The pull is magnetic. I risk half a step closer, and another, until my bare toes line up like soldiers against the dry soil of the cliff edge.</td>
<td></td>
<td>Texts written to entertain often use <u>imagery</u> and <u>interesting vocabulary</u>, and <u>sentence lengths</u> tend to vary.</td>
</tr>
</table>

5) Writers might use entertaining writing to <u>engage</u> a reader when they have <u>another</u> purpose in mind. E.g. travel books are <u>entertaining non-fiction</u>, but they're also <u>informative</u>.

<table>
<tr>
<td>Polidori Island has several miles of unspoilt beaches that are reliably, blissfully empty, regardless of the season. For a misanthropic fellow like myself, it is sheer perfection.</td>
<td></td>
<td>This text <u>informs</u> the reader about Polidori Island, but it uses interesting <u>adjectives</u> and <u>adverbs</u> to <u>entertain</u> the reader.</td>
</tr>
</table>

Think about What makes the text entertaining

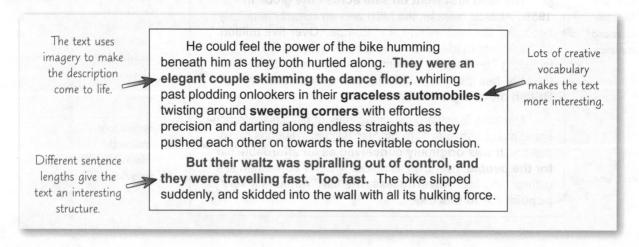

The text uses imagery to make the description come to life.

He could feel the power of the bike humming beneath him as they both hurtled along. **They were an elegant couple skimming the dance floor**, whirling past plodding onlookers in their **graceless automobiles**, twisting around **sweeping corners** with effortless precision and darting along endless straights as they pushed each other on towards the inevitable conclusion.

    But their waltz was spiralling out of control, and they were travelling fast. Too fast. The bike slipped suddenly, and skidded into the wall with all its hulking force.

Lots of creative vocabulary makes the text more interesting.

Different sentence lengths give the text an interesting structure.

Many entertaining texts also have other purposes...

Entertaining writing really helps to keep readers interested. So even if a writer's main purpose is to inform, argue, persuade or advise, they might still want to make their writing entertaining so the reader enjoys it.

Texts that Argue or Persuade

When you're writing about a text that argues or persuades, you need to be able to say exactly how it does it.

Arguing and Persuading are Similar

1) When people write to <u>argue</u>, they want to make the reader <u>agree</u> with their <u>opinion</u>. They use <u>clear</u> and <u>forceful</u> language to get their points across, and they might use <u>facts and figures</u> to back up points.

2) <u>Persuasive</u> writing tries to get the reader to <u>do something</u>, such as support a charity. It does this with techniques including <u>emotive language</u> that aims to make the reader <u>sympathise</u> with their cause.

3) When writing to <u>persuade</u>, writers might sometimes be <u>more subtle</u> about their aims and opinions. For example:

It is clear that this is a good school, and that people who attend it do well. →	This writer uses the phrase 'It is clear' to make their <u>opinion</u> sound like <u>fact</u>. This can make the writing sound more <u>informative</u>, when actually it's <u>persuasive</u>.

4) When writing to argue or persuade, writers often use <u>rhetorical devices</u> such as <u>hyperbole</u>, <u>repetition</u> or <u>rhetorical questions</u> (see p.35).

Consider the Effects of the writer's choice of Language

The writer uses statements to make their point clearly and forcefully.

Uses rhetorical questions.

Uses emotive language.

WHY BOTHER WITH BREAKFAST?

David Barowsky, *nutritional analyst*

Eating breakfast improves mental and physical performance.

This is a well-known and incontrovertible fact. And yet **20 million of us** Britons regularly skip this essential refuelling opportunity. Why is this the case?

Are we too busy commuting, getting the kids ready for school, blow-drying our hair? Do you often feel frantic and harassed in the morning? Well, the time has come to change your ways. Breakfast does not have to be an elaborate or time-consuming meal. Allow ten minutes extra for a nutritious bowl of porridge or granola every morning, and the benefits will be noticeable almost immediately.

Another troubling trend is the rising number of children and teenagers who don't eat breakfast before leaving for school or college. **Allowing your kids to skip breakfast is reckless and irresponsible. You** are simply not providing them with the energy they need to face the day. Set a good example by eating breakfast yourself, and make sure you build a morning meal into your children's daily routine as soon as possible.

Facts and figures are used to back up their argument.

Addresses the reader directly using the pronoun 'you'.

Think about how the writer is trying to persuade the reader...

If a writer is trying to argue a point or persuade you to do something, they're trying to make you see things from their point of view. It'll be one-sided, with carefully chosen evidence to support their point of view.

Texts that Advise

When writing to advise, a writer uses reassuring and easily understandable language to guide their reader.

Writing to **Advise** sounds **Clear** and **Calm**

1) When writing to <u>advise</u>, writers want their readers to <u>follow their suggestions</u>.

2) The tone will be <u>calm</u> and <u>less emotional</u> than writing that argues or persuades.

3) The advice will usually be <u>clear</u> and <u>direct</u>. For example, it might use:

> • <u>Vocabulary</u> that matches the audience's <u>subject knowledge</u>.
> • <u>Second person</u> pronouns (e.g. 'you') to make the advice feel <u>personal</u>.
> • A <u>logical structure</u> that makes the advice <u>easy to follow</u>.

4) The register (see p.25) may be <u>formal</u>, e.g. in a letter from a solicitor offering legal advice...

> *To proceed with your claim, you must first contact the company's head office.* This uses a <u>formal register</u>, but it still uses the <u>pronoun</u> 'you' to appeal to the reader.

5) ... or <u>informal</u>, e.g. in a magazine advice column.

> *Whatever you decide, make sure you're following your head as well as your heart.* This uses a <u>colloquial phrase</u> ('follow your heart') to help <u>advise</u> the reader.

Writing to **Advise** looks **Like This**

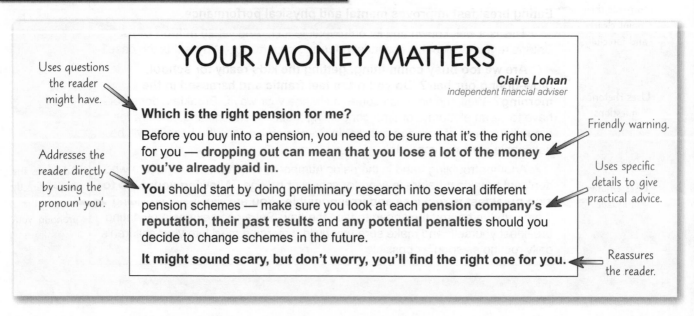

Uses questions the reader might have.

Addresses the reader directly by using the pronoun 'you'.

YOUR MONEY MATTERS

Claire Lohan
independent financial adviser

Which is the right pension for me?

Before you buy into a pension, you need to be sure that it's the right one for you — **dropping out can mean that you lose a lot of the money you've already paid in.**

You should start by doing preliminary research into several different pension schemes — make sure you look at each **pension company's reputation, their past results** and **any potential penalties** should you decide to change schemes in the future.

It might sound scary, but don't worry, you'll find the right one for you.

Friendly warning.

Uses specific details to give practical advice.

Reassures the reader.

Learn to spot the common features of texts that advise...

Texts that advise can be written for many different audiences, but a lot of the features will stay the same. Look at whether the language is formal or informal — it'll vary depending on the subject and audience.

Warm-Up Questions

To help you digest everything you've read so far, here's a page of warm-up questions. The questions shouldn't take you too long, but try to write a few sentences for each one. You can check your answers in the back of the book to see how you're getting on. Then, when you're ready, have a look at page 16.

Warm-Up Questions

1) Read the short passage below.

> "We're going to be late, Samuel," warned Rita, biting her thumbnail nervously.
> "We'll be fine!" insisted Samuel from the depths of his wardrobe. After a moment he emerged, triumphantly holding his favourite leather jacket aloft.
> Rita glared pointedly at her watch, then at Samuel, who grinned.
> "We'll be fine," he repeated, trying on the jacket and admiring his reflection in the full-length mirror.
> "It's bad enough that we have to go to this reunion at all, and now we're going to show up late too," complained Rita. "This is all your fault."

   a) Which character is reluctant to go to the reunion?
   b) Which character cares most about time management?
   c) Who is the more confident character in the passage?
   d) Write down a quote from the passage to support each of your answers to parts a) to c).

2) For each sentence, write down the word which best describes its intended audience.

   a) *"Do you yearn for a simpler, more reliable way of managing your finances?"*   **children / adults**

   b) *"When buying a used car, try to get as much information from the dealer as you can."*   **experts / novices**

3) Briefly summarise the differences between the attitudes of these two writers.
   Writer A: *"I've always considered mixed schools to be a barrier to educational progress. We should all stick with traditional, single-sex education."*

   Writer B: *"Mixed-sex schools are clearly superior, but parents should have a choice."*

4) Is the purpose of the following sentences to entertain, persuade or advise?
   Briefly explain each of your answers.
   a) Shop around for the best quote — some insurers are much more expensive than others.
   b) As the train moved south, first crawling, then increasing to a steady gallop, the scenery gradually changed from the flat and drab to the dramatic and beautiful.
   c) Who could disagree with the fact that children should eat healthily?

Exam-Style Questions

Now you've learnt some theory, it's time to put it into practice with these exam-style questions. They're similar to the ones you might see in your GCSE English Language exams. You should try to do them without looking back at this section for help. You can mark yourself using the answers in the back of the book.

Q1   Read the following extract from a novel.

List **four** facts from the text about George.

> The doorbell rang. Someone must have answered it, because moments later I heard George's nasal tones in the hallway.
> "So lovely to be here!" he cried, his voice carrying easily across the living room.
> "Did you invite him?" I hissed, staring desperately at Rosa.
> "I could hardly leave him out," she said coolly. "It would have been too obvious."
> He entered the room. His garish purple suit and elaborate hairstyle made him stand out sharply from the other guests. "George, darling," Rosa cooed. "You made it."
> "Rosa!" he said, presenting her with a bottle of cheap-looking wine. "And Freddie," he said to me with a smirk, extending a greasy hand adorned with several gaudy rings. "Good to see you."
> "You too," I said, forcing a smile and letting go of his hand quickly. "Drink?"
> "Oh, go on then," said George, "I'd love a nice whisky, if you have any?"
> "Nothing but the best for you, George," I replied through gritted teeth.

Q2   Read the following extract from an advice leaflet about an election.

How does the writer use language to advise the reader?

> ## It's Decision Time — But Who Do I Vote For?
> Unless you've been living under a rock for the past month, you'll probably have noticed that there's an election coming up. Deciding who to vote for can be a daunting task, but it's also an important one. Luckily, there's plenty of help out there.
> Firstly, you need to be well-informed on the principles and policies that each party stands for. If you start to feel overwhelmed by all the political lingo in their leaflets, don't panic — have a look online, where there are plenty of websites that break it down for you.
> It's also a good idea to look into the candidates in your constituency. They represent you in parliament, so you'll want to vote for someone who has a strong voice, and who will stand up for what your area needs.
> It's true — choosing who to vote for isn't easy. However, if you take the time to do a bit of research, you will be able to make the right decision for you.

Literary Fiction

In the exam, you'll have to read and analyse a literary fiction text — here's what you need to know...

Literary fiction **Entertains** the reader

1) Literary fiction, such as a novel or short story, is written to entertain. It might do this by affecting the reader's emotions, describing the atmosphere of a place, using an intriguing structure or developing the personality of a character.

2) All literary fiction has a narrator. It's most often either a first-person (uses 'I' and 'we') or third-person (uses 'he', 'she' and 'they') narrator.

3) Literary fiction uses lots of descriptive and figurative language (e.g. metaphors, similes, analogy and personification) to capture the reader's imagination.

4) Literary fiction is also structured to interest the reader — texts will often build the tension towards a dramatic climax, or they might use repetition and varied sentence structures to change the pace of a text.

5) Dialogue is also often used to move the plot along and give insight into the thoughts and feelings of different characters.

See Section Three for more on all these language and structural features.

Look Closely at the **Language** used in a text

These adjectives set the scene as an uninviting place.

The use of the emotive verb 'drowned' shows that the writer doesn't like that the fields have been covered in concrete.

The writer uses Dorine's surroundings to tell the reader about her personality.

The word 'flicker' implies that there isn't much hope, which creates tension.

Edward hurried down the **dark**, **smog-filled** alley. The place had become almost completely unrecognisable: the green fields he remembered from his childhood had long since been **drowned in concrete**. The alley became darker, and its bends and turns were increasingly disorientating. **A creak. A whisper.** Every noise put him on edge. **But he pressed on.**

Eventually, Edward found himself at Dorine's lab. He walked in, stooping to avoid hitting his head on the low door frame. The lab was a large circular room; the walls were lined with **hundreds of tattered books, and half-finished research papers** lay strewn across the many desks.

The books seemed to whisper quietly to each other, as if disconcerted by the presence of an outsider. Edward felt as though they were watching him.

Dorine was poring over some papers in front of her, and hadn't noticed that Edward had arrived. After a few moments, she looked up from her desk and saw Edward waiting. **She could see** the **flicker of hope** glimmering in his eyes — the hope that they might still be able to turn back the clock.

"I'm afraid it's not looking good, Ed," Dorine murmured.

My God, thought Edward in disbelief. ***How could we have let this happen?***

The use of very short sentences adds to the feeling of unease and suspense.

The fact that Edward carries on even though he is scared makes him seem admirable to the reader.

Personification makes it clear that Edward feels uncomfortable in the lab.

The narrative is third person, so the reader can see from the perspective of both Edward and Dorine.

This rhetorical question makes the reader want to know what has happened, which creates suspense.

You need to practise writing about extracts from literary fiction...

You'll always have to write about a piece of literary fiction in your English Language exam, so make sure you get plenty of practice. You could start by looking at question 2 in the exam-style questions on p.23.

Literary Non-Fiction

Now it's time for literary non-fiction — literary writing that's based in fact.

Literary non-fiction is **Entertaining** but **Factual**

1) Literary non-fiction texts use <u>literary styles</u> and <u>techniques</u>, but they are based on <u>facts</u> or <u>real events</u>.

2) Non-fiction texts such as <u>biographies</u>, <u>autobiographies</u>, and <u>travel writing</u> will often be written in a similar style to literary fiction.

3) They are written to <u>inform</u> the reader about something, but the writer uses a literary style to make it <u>entertaining</u> too. For example, they might use <u>descriptive</u> language and <u>dialogue</u> to make the information more <u>interesting</u> to the reader.

4) Literary non-fiction is almost always written in the <u>first person</u>, which adds a sense of <u>personality</u> to the text, helping to <u>engage</u> the reader.

Have a look back at the previous page to remind yourself about literary style.

Literary non-fiction tries to **Engage** the **Reader**

Directly addresses the reader, making them feel more involved.

Dearest reader — I wish today to impart to you some recollections of my summer spent in Paris, a city which over time has played host to a multitude of great thinkers and artists. A hundred years may have passed since the French Revolution, but Paris remains a shining beacon of revolutionary spirit.

The text uses lots of emotive adjectives to clearly show the writer's viewpoint. Purely informative non-fiction wouldn't use adjectives like these.

Contains facts and refers to real places to inform the reader.

The city of Paris has some **spectacular** specimens of architecture. One bright evening, I took a particularly enjoyable stroll down **the Champs-Élysées**, and was quite amazed by the **stunning** curvature of its **Arc de Triomphe**. **The arch incited within me the strongest feelings of awe and wonderment; it is truly a structure built to inspire.**

The writer's viewpoint gives the description a positive tone.

The language used in this text is quite formal, which makes the writer seem more authoritative.

Paris has been ever-popular with the gentleman traveller, but this year the city **captures one's imagination** more than ever before, as it hosts the annual 'World's Fair'. There I saw many wonderful artefacts, including a magnificent replica of the Bastille, the famous site of the rebellion which began France's Revolution. The replica was incredibly lifelike, **from the gloomy outer stonework to the banquet hall within**.

This description adds detail, which helps things come to life for the reader.

Although the fortress was a truly thrilling diversion, it was far from the real star of the fair — that honour belonged to the newly-erected 'Eiffel Tower', said to be the largest building on Earth. The new tower amazed fair-goers with its enormous metallic form (although some were not altogether thrilled by its brash modernity). Whether one marvels at this remarkable feat of engineering, or recoils from its audacious magnitude, **the new tower is assuredly a sight to behold**.

Ends with a strong, memorable statement that will stay in the reader's mind.

This sentence creates suspense by not revealing what the 'real star' is right away.

Literary non-fiction is not as complicated as it might sound...

You might not have heard of it before, but don't let the phrase "literary non-fiction" worry you — it's just a category that's used to describe any text that is factual, but is written in an entertaining, literary way.

19th-Century Texts

In the exam, you'll have analyse a 19th-century text. Here's some useful information about the period.

19th-century Writing is often quite Formal

1) 19th-century texts can sound a bit <u>different</u> to more modern texts, but you should still be able to <u>understand</u> what's going on.

2) A lot of the texts will use a more <u>formal register</u> (see p.25) than modern writing, even if the <u>audience</u> is quite <u>familiar</u> (see next page for an example of this).

3) The sentences may be <u>quite long</u> and the <u>word order</u> can sometimes be different to modern texts. Try not to worry about this — just <u>re-read</u> any sentences you can't make sense of at first. Here are a couple of examples:

In the exam, any words in the text that aren't used today will be defined for you in a glossary.

Then, Albert being gone and we two left alone, Edward enquired as to whether I might accompany him on a stroll in the garden.	This sentence is written using a <u>formal</u> register, e.g. it uses 'enquired' instead of 'asked'. It might seem a bit <u>confusingly phrased</u> too, but 'Albert being gone and we two left alone' is just <u>another way</u> of saying 'Albert had gone and the two of us were left alone.'

I believe it necessary to abandon this foul enterprise.	Sometimes it can seem as if a word has been <u>missed out</u> — modern writers would probably put 'is' after 'it' in this sentence.

19th-century society was Different to today

1) Knowing about 19th-century <u>society</u> will help you to <u>understand</u> texts from the period better.

2) It will also help you to compare the <u>viewpoints</u> and <u>perspectives</u> of writers from different <u>time periods</u>.

Social Class

- Early 19th-century society was <u>divided</u> between the rich <u>upper classes</u> (who owned the land) and the poorer <u>working classes</u>.
- Throughout the 19th century, the <u>Industrial Revolution</u> was creating opportunities for more people to make more <u>money</u>.
- This meant that the <u>middle classes</u> grew in <u>size</u> and <u>influence</u> throughout the century.

Education

- In the <u>early</u> 19th century, <u>few</u> children went to school. Children from poor families often <u>worked</u> to help support their families instead.
- In the <u>late</u> 19th century, <u>education reforms</u> made school <u>compulsory</u> for all young children.
- <u>Rich</u> families often sent their children to <u>boarding school</u>, or hired a <u>governess</u> to live with the family and teach the children at <u>home</u>.

Women

- After they got married, most women were expected to be in charge of looking after the <u>home</u> and <u>children</u>.
- Women didn't have as many <u>rights</u> as men — they couldn't <u>vote</u> in elections and they often didn't <u>control</u> their own money and property.

Religion

- <u>Christianity</u> had a big influence — most of the <u>middle</u> and <u>upper classes</u> attended <u>church</u> regularly.
- However, <u>science</u> was beginning to challenge religious ideas, e.g. Darwin's theory of <u>evolution</u> questioned the Bible's account of <u>creation</u>.

19th-Century Texts

Have a look at this piece of 19th-century Writing

This is a letter written to Princess (later Queen) Victoria of the United Kingdom by her uncle, King Leopold I of Belgium. In it, Leopold describes his new wife, Louise Marie.

The tone is affectionate but the register is formal — this is common in 19th-century letters.

Being 'virtuous' was an important quality in 19th-century society — it means having strong morals.

This shows the 19th-century viewpoint of what was valued in upper class women.

You might come across a tricky phrase or sentence. Use the context and the rest of the sentence to work out what's going on. Here, Leopold suggests that Louise Marie doesn't try very hard at playing the harp.

19th-century texts often phrase things differently — here, a modern writer might have said "I should end this letter here."

Laeken, 31st August 1832.

MY DEAREST LOVE,—You told me you wished to have a description of your new Aunt. I therefore shall both mentally and physically describe her to you.

She is extremely gentle and amiable, her actions are always guided by principles. She is at all times ready and disposed to sacrifice her comfort and inclinations to see others happy. She values goodness, merit, and **virtue** much more than beauty, riches, and amusements. With all this she is highly informed and very clever; **she speaks and writes English, German and Italian**; she speaks English very well indeed. In short, my dear Love, you see that I may well recommend her as **an example for all young ladies**, being Princesses or not.

Now to her appearance. She is about Feodore's* height, her hair very fair, light blue eyes, of a very gentle, intelligent and kind expression. A Bourbon** nose and small mouth. The figure is much like Feodore's but rather less stout. **She rides very well**, which she proved to my great alarm the other day, by keeping her seat though a horse of mine ran away with her full speed for at least half a mile. **What she does particularly well is dancing.** Music unfortunately she is not very fond of, though she plays on **the harp; I believe there is some idleness in the case**. There exists already great confidence and affection between us; she is desirous of doing everything that can contribute to my happiness, and I study whatever can make her happy and contented.

You will see by these descriptions that though my good little wife is not the tallest Queen, **she is a very great prize which I highly value and cherish**...

Now it is time I should finish my letter. Say everything that is kind to good Lehzen***, and believe me ever, **my dearest Love**, your faithful Friend and Uncle,

LEOPOLD R.

Upper class women were educated in European languages in the 19th century.

Upper class women were considered to be accomplished by their ability in things like riding, dancing, playing music and speaking languages.

Women were often seen as belonging to their husbands.

Superlatives (e.g. 'kindest', 'most gracious') are common in 19th-century writing.

Glossary

* Feodore — Victoria's half-sister, Princess Feodora

** Bourbon — the Bourbons were the French royal family

*** Lehzen — Princess Victoria's governess, Louise Lehzen

You will definitely have to analyse a 19th-century text...

It's important to make sure you're comfortable reading and understanding 19th-century texts. These pages might look more like History than English, but they'll help you to improve some of your answers.

Worked Exam-Style Question

Here's a sample question with a worked answer for you to have a look at. Read and learn...

Q1 Read the following extracts. Source A is an extract from a diary written in the 19th century, and Source B is from a speech written in the 21st century.

Source A

Dear Diary —

I've had quite a day today! Daddy and I took a trip to see the new steam train, which was being exhibited in James Square. It was fascinating — a clanking, grinding steel colossus, shiny as a new penny, with a great puff of steam that emerged from its funnel and curled into the summer sky. I've never seen the like — and to think, Daddy says one day they may be able to carry people from one end of the country to the other! I for one cannot wait.

Source B

Residents of Station Crescent! I know that you, like me, are plagued day-in, day-out with the sounds, smells and sights of the railway. Like me, many of you moved here at a time when three or four trains a day passed by, barely disturbing us at all. And like me, you've seen our area systematically invaded by a non-stop army of trains, impacting our quality of life — not to mention the price of our homes. The time has come to take a stand against the relentless growth of the railways.

Compare how these writers convey their different attitudes towards rail transport.

In your answer, you should:
- compare their different attitudes
- compare the methods they use to convey their attitudes.

Plan:

figurative language — "shiny as a new penny" in A, army metaphor in B

rhetorical devices in B — aims to persuade. A is more descriptive e.g. "curled" bit.

exclamation mark for excitement in A but for emotive effect in B

A wants more trains, B wants fewer trains

*You **don't** need to make a **detailed plan** for this type of question, but **quickly** jotting down your **ideas** (like this) can be helpful.*

*This is a great opening sentence. It makes a **clear point** that is focused on the **question**.*

*Use **linking words and phrases** to show that you're making a **comparison**.*

The writers of both sources use figurative language to convey their attitudes to rail transport. In Source A, the train is "shiny as a new penny". This simile suggests that the writer feels the train is exciting because it's so new. In contrast, the figurative language in Source B shows the writer's frustration with trains. He uses a metaphor to compare them to a "non-stop army", which makes them seem like a relentless and aggressive nuisance.

*This answer **identifies** a language technique and then explains its **effect**.*

*To make this paragraph better, you could mention **why** they might have these different attitudes by referring to the **contexts** of the sources.*

Worked Exam-Style Question

It's good to think about how the writer has conveyed their attitude through structure, as well as through language.

The attitudes in Source B are conveyed using rhetorical devices. The writer repeats the phrase "like me" to get the audience on side. The writer also uses direct address, such as "Residents of Station Crescent", to suggest that the audience are a united team, who are able to work together to change things. In Source A the attitudes are conveyed using descriptive language, such as "a great puff of steam that emerged from its funnel and curled into the summer sky". This shows how impressed the writer is by the new trains, feeling they are almost magical.

Phrases like this keep your answer focused on the second bullet point in the question — how attitudes are conveyed...

This quote does support the point, but it would be better to make it much shorter and then explain its effect more specifically.

Both of the writers use exclamation marks to make their attitudes clear. In Source A, they are used by the writer to emphasise their excited attitude to the steam train. On the other hand, in Source B, the writer uses an exclamation mark to show his dedication to the cause and to persuade the audience to agree that the trains are a problem.

... and phrases like these focus on the first bullet point (what the attitudes are and how they're different).

The writer in Source A hopes that there will be more trains. They "cannot wait" for the trains to be able to carry people from one end of the country to the other, and the phrase "I for one" implies that the author believes other people will feel the same. In Source B, the attitude is very different. This writer wants there to be fewer trains, because there used to be "three or four" and they use the phrase "relentless growth" to suggest to the audience that further expansion poses a real danger to the community.

Each paragraph in this answer makes a new comparison between the writers' attitudes. This shows a clear understanding of the differences.

The examiner will want to see that you can analyse the effect of individual words and phrases.

- This is a good answer. It clearly compares the writers' attitudes and it also discusses the writers' methods.
- To get better marks, this answer could be improved by:
  - using the different contexts of the sources to comment on why the attitudes might be different.
  - pointing out more subtle differences in the attitudes, e.g. the writer in Source A is writing about seeing one train on one particular day, whereas the writer in Source B is writing about living alongside multiple trains every day.
  - making sure that all the quotations are really precise.

Exam-Style Questions

Now that you've seen an example answer, have a go at these exam-style questions for yourself.

Q1   Read the following extracts. Source A is from a letter written in the 19th century, and Source B is from a newspaper article written in the 20th century.

Source A

Dear Mr Tinsham,
I read with concern your recent article on the new wave of art reaching British shores. With all due respect, I see it as nothing short of an abomination. It is created with a flagrant disregard for the conventions and traditions of classical art. These 'artists' seem not to have learnt from their predecessors, but instead insist on violating their canvasses with an assault of colour, which to view, in perfect honesty, is simply excruciating.

Source B

The London art scene has rarely been so exciting. We are seeing a real influx of artists who aren't afraid to throw off the iron shackles of 'traditional art' and champion self-expression. They're rule breakers, not intimidated by the giants of the past. They're revolutionaries, constantly looking forward, never back. Only by pushing the boundaries of modern art are we going to see any progression in the medium. When art conforms, it stagnates, and these new experimenters understand that.

These extracts are both about art.
Compare the writers' attitudes towards art and how they present their views.

Q2   Read the following extract from a novel.

> Annie went from room to room, shaking her head at the disarray. The house looked as if it had been burgled. In the living room, a bookcase had been thrown onto the floor, and paperbacks were scattered chaotically across the carpet. In the kitchen, the floor was a treacherous landscape of smashed crockery and broken glass.
> Annie frowned and headed cautiously up the stairs, following the crashing sounds into the master bedroom. Lucas stood with his back to her. His hair was a frantic mess, his movements manic as he pulled every item of clothing out of his wardrobe and launched them behind him. He was muttering frenetically under his breath.
> "Lucas," Annie said calmly. He spun around, surprised by her presence. His wide eyes were wild, beads of sweat had appeared on his forehead and his cheeks were red.
> "I can't find it," he said. "I've looked everywhere. It's lost. They'll kill me."
> "Don't be ridiculous. They're not going to kick you out just because you've lost your key to the clubhouse," said Annie, her arms folded.
> "What would you know about it?" said Lucas, his eyes flashing in annoyance.
> "They're obsessed with not letting any outsiders in. If they find out I've lost it... I'm doomed. Finished. Condemned."

"The writer is successful in bringing Annie and Lucas alive for the reader. You feel as if you can identify with both characters."

To what extent do you agree with this statement?
In your response, you could:

- write about your own impressions of Annie and Lucas
- evaluate how the writer has created these impressions.

Revision Summary

It's time for another Revision Summary. If you know your stuff, these questions will be very quick to answer. If you're not sure about any of them, go back to the relevant bits of this section and read them again.

1) What is the difference between explicit and implicit information?

2) Write down three examples of words or phrases you could use to show that you're making a comparison in an exam answer.

3) Name three things you can look at to work out who a text's audience is.

4) What audience is this Complete Revision and Practice book aimed at?

5) What is the difference between the writer's viewpoint and the writer's purpose?

6) Read these play reviews. Write down whether each writer's viewpoint is positive or negative.
   a) *This playwright's recent offerings on the London stage had established high expectations, but his latest "masterpiece" falls far short of that hype.*
   b) *I have never left a matinee performance and rushed straight to the box office to buy a ticket for that evening. Until now.*

7) List four common purposes of a piece of writing.

8) Give two examples of an informative text.

9) Can an informative text be biased? How?

10) Which of these techniques might a writer use to make a text entertaining?
    a) an engaging opening
    b) descriptive language
    c) lots of facts
    d) different sentence lengths

11) Write down three rhetorical techniques that might be used to argue or persuade.

12) How is the tone of writing that advises usually different from writing that argues or persuades?

13) True or false? *Texts that advise are always written in a formal register.*

14) What is the main purpose of literary fiction?

15) What is literary non-fiction?

16) Write down whether the following texts are literary fiction or literary non-fiction.
    a) the autobiography of a retired professional cricketer
    b) a short story about a trip to the seaside
    c) a piece of travel writing about Rome
    d) an opinion piece in a broadsheet newspaper

17) Is the register of a 19th-century text likely to be formal or informal?

18) Write down whether the following statements are true or false.
    a) Christianity had a big influence on people's lives in the 19th century.
    b) After they got married, most 19th-century women were expected to go out to work.
    c) Poor children were often sent away to boarding schools in the 19th century.
    d) Early 19th-century society was divided into the upper classes and working classes.
    e) Women didn't have as many rights as men in the 19th century.

Tone and Style

Tone and style can sometimes be difficult to describe, but they come through in the text's language.

Tone is the general Feeling created by the text

1) A writer's tone is the <u>feeling</u> the words are written with, which creates a particular <u>mood</u> and shows what the writer's <u>attitude</u> is. For example, the tone of a text might be:

- happy or sad
- serious or funny
- sombre or light-hearted
- emotional and passionate or cool and logical

Think of a writer's tone as being like someone's tone of voice when they're talking.

2) The main way to identify a text's tone is by looking at the <u>language</u>. For example, if a writer has used <u>informal</u> language, the tone might be quite <u>personal</u> or <u>familiar</u>, but <u>formal</u> language would suggest a more <u>serious</u> or <u>distant</u> tone.

3) <u>Punctuation</u> can also give you a clue about tone. For example, if there are lots of exclamation marks, that might suggest that the tone is very <u>emotional</u> or <u>passionate</u>.

4) Tone can reflect the <u>purpose</u> of a text (e.g. informative texts often have a serious tone) or the <u>audience</u> (e.g. a playful tone might suggest a younger audience).

Phillipa stood on the cold, dark street, peering up at the abandoned hotel. Despite her misgivings, she pushed tentatively on the front door, and it opened with an arthritic creak.

This passage has a <u>sinister</u> tone, which grips the reader. Adjectives ("cold, dark", "abandoned") and an adverb ("tentatively") help create the sense of <u>foreboding</u>.

Style is how the text is Written

1) A text's <u>style</u> is the overall way in which it's written, which includes <u>language choices</u>, <u>sentence forms</u> and <u>structure</u>.

2) There are lots of <u>different styles</u> you might encounter. E.g. <u>cinematic</u>, where the text is written as if the reader is watching a film, or <u>journalistic</u> which is a balanced way of writing reported news.

3) <u>Register</u> is the specific language (choice of words) used to match the writing to the <u>social situation</u> that it's for. Different situations require <u>different</u> registers, for example:

Register can be thought of as a part of style.

If you wrote a letter to your <u>local MP</u> to ask them to stop the closure of a local leisure centre, you might use a <u>formal register</u> (e.g. 'the closure will have a detrimental effect'). This is because the audience is an <u>authority figure</u> that you <u>don't know</u>.

If you wrote a letter to your <u>friend</u> to tell them about the leisure centre closure, you might use an <u>informal register</u> (e.g. 'it'll be rubbish when it shuts'). This is because the audience is someone you're <u>familiar</u> and <u>friendly</u> with.

4) Look out for how writers <u>adapt</u> their style and register to suit a text's intended <u>purpose</u> and <u>audience</u>.

Look out for sarcastic or ironic texts...

Sometimes the tone of a text will jump right out at you. But watch out for texts that have an ironic or sarcastic tone — they can be trickier to spot. Have a look at page 34 for more about these techniques.

Words and Phrases

Writers choose their words very carefully to produce a desired effect. This is something that you'll definitely need to write about in your exams. Have a look at these two pages to find out more...

Words and Phrases can be used to achieve Different Effects

1) For reading questions, you need to pay close attention to the reasons <u>why</u> a writer has used particular <u>words</u> or <u>phrases</u>.

2) Words can have subtle <u>implications</u> beyond their obvious meaning — these are called '<u>connotations</u>'. For example:

Analysing the connotations of words is a way of 'reading with insight'. There's more on this on p.5.

Pedro <u>shut</u> the door. *Pedro <u>slammed</u> the door.*	When the verb 'shut' is used, it <u>doesn't</u> imply anything about Pedro's <u>emotions</u>. The verb 'slammed' has a similar meaning to 'shut', but it gives the impression that Pedro is <u>angry</u> or <u>tense</u>.

I <u>sniggered</u> when I saw Peter's costume. *I <u>chuckled</u> when I saw Peter's costume.*	The verbs 'sniggered' and 'chuckled' both mean the writer <u>laughed</u>, but 'sniggered' has a slightly <u>nastier</u> connotation — as if the writer is making fun of Peter.

3) Words are often chosen to make the reader feel <u>emotionally involved</u> in a text. For example:

<u>*my*</u> *dear reader* <u>*your*</u> *beloved pet*	Phrases that use the <u>possessive determiners</u> 'my', 'your' and 'our' help to establish <u>familiarity</u> between the writer and the reader.

Determiners are words that help to identify nouns — in this case, they show who the noun belongs to.

a <u>fundamentally</u> flawed proposition *a <u>totally</u> unbelievable situation*	Some phrases use <u>intensifiers</u> to make the text seem more <u>emotive</u> and <u>powerful</u>. Intensifiers are adverbs like 'very', 'really' or 'extremely' that are used <u>alongside</u> strong adjectives to provide <u>emphasis</u>.

4) Writers might choose words that help to bring the text <u>alive</u> for the reader. For example:

it was <u>bigger than</u> a football pitch *it was <u>sunnier than</u> usual that day* 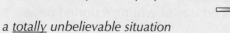	<u>Comparatives</u> are used to describe something in a way that <u>compares</u> it with something else. This can help the reader to <u>understand</u> or <u>visualise</u> something in the text.

the <u>worst</u> day of my entire life *the <u>largest</u> animal on the planet*	<u>Superlatives</u> are used to refer to the <u>most</u> or <u>least</u> of something. They can be used to <u>emphasise</u> or <u>exaggerate</u> something.

Words and Phrases

Words **Work Together** to create **Cumulative Effects**

1) Writers can use the words from a specific <u>semantic field</u> (the words associated with a particular <u>theme</u> or <u>topic</u>) to convey an idea to the reader. For example:

> *Dessert was simply <u>divine</u>; a <u>cloud-like</u> puff of pastry that was lighter than an <u>angel's wing</u>.*

> Here, the <u>semantic field</u> of <u>heaven</u> is used to make something sound <u>appealing</u>.

2) Keep an eye out for situations where particular <u>types</u> of words are <u>repeated</u>, e.g. sentences with lots of <u>adjectives</u> or paragraphs with lots of <u>verbs</u>.

3) You could comment on the <u>cumulative effect</u> of particular types of words — show you've thought about how the words in the text <u>work together</u> to create <u>tone</u> or <u>affect</u> the reader in some way, e.g.

> *Adjectives like 'electrifying', 'thrilling', 'tense' and 'intriguing' create a cumulative effect of <u>excitement</u>.*

> *The adverbs 'jovially', 'readily' and 'pleasantly' combine to create an impression of <u>enjoyment</u>.*

Try to pick out **Significant Words** and **Phrases**

Have a look at this text, which has been written to <u>persuade</u> its audience:

Adjectives like 'magical', 'beautiful', 'balmy', 'glistening' and 'sumptuous' have an alluring cumulative effect — they create a calming atmosphere.

Watch out for repeated grammatical constructions — they give the text emphasis.

A PICTURE-PERFECT PICNIC

Bijoux Birthdays invite you to celebrate **your special day** in style. Join us for a **magical** evening of entertainment on the **beautiful** banks of the River Fairer. Let us help you to **relax** in the **balmy** atmosphere of a warm summer's evening, **recline** next to the **glistening** waters and **indulge** in the most **sumptuous** of picnics.

We can tailor your evening to suit you. **We can** provide a refreshing feast for your senses. **We can** transport you to another place and time. Just **sit back** and **let us** do all the work. All you need to do is relax.

We have a large selection of menus for you to choose from, as well as a whole host of different entertainment acts — **maybe** you'd like a string quartet, or **perhaps** you'd be more interested in a circus act? Whatever your tastes, rest assured that we will be able to accommodate you.

If you're planning a celebration, Bijoux Birthdays really is the only choice.

Phrases that use possessive determiners establish familiarity with the reader and make the text more persuasive.

The list of three verbs — 'relax', 'recline' and 'indulge' — gives the text a convincing tone and makes the offer sound inviting.

Imperatives like 'sit back' and 'let us' give the text an authoritative tone, whilst the words 'perhaps' and 'maybe' give the impression that the reader has a choice.

Comments like "this is an intensifier" aren't quite good enough...

The technical grammar of words and phrases is important, but don't just point it out — you need to analyse its effects. Think about why certain words and phrases have been used and what impression they create.

Warm-Up Questions

The questions on this page are all about the things you've learnt in this section so far.
Before you answer the exam-style questions on the right, give these ones a go as a handy warm-up.

Warm-Up Questions

1) Is the tone of each of the following sentences sentimental, detached or upbeat?
   a) Investigators have recently confirmed that DNA found at the scene
      of the burglary matches that of suspect Fergus Maybach.
   b) I had a riot helping out at the birthday party — who would've guessed
      that kids were the perfect audience for my magic tricks?
   c) As he stared across the bay where they had first met, he remembered
      vividly the tinkle of her laughter and the floral scent of her hair.

2) Which of the sentences in question 1 is written in a journalistic style?

3) What is the tone of the following text? Explain your answer.

> At this point I was starting to get a tad — how shall I put it? — cheesed off. It's one thing being
> patient, accepting the fact that things don't always go to plan and that now and then delays
> just happen. It's quite another to be told, after paying good money for a ticket to Town A, that
> for no good reason you're taking a little detour through Village B, River C and Swamp D. I was
> finding it more and more difficult to follow what I had figured was the local way of dealing with
> difficulties — smiling and pretending to find the grim industrial scenery interesting. It wasn't.

4) Rewrite each of the following sentences so that they are in a formal register.
   a) Sorry, we don't take credit cards!
   b) Check you've got the proper kit to hand before you go any further.

5) Explain the different connotations of the underlined words in the sentences below.
   "Just go," she <u>whispered</u>.
   "Just go," she <u>spat</u>.

6) a) Is the semantic field of the passage below i) Shakespeare, ii) money or iii) shellfish?
   b) What impression does this create of the narrator?

> I wasn't interested in seeing my sister's school Shakespeare play, but I couldn't afford
> to miss being at the theatre that night. The owner of DigTech was going to be there
> watching his daughter, and I was desperate to sell him my latest design idea. I decided
> to buy myself some extra time by locking him inside the gents toilets with me during
> the interval. A bit drastic, perhaps, but you have to cash in on this sort of opportunity.

7) What is the cumulative effect of the verbs in this sentence?
   *The wind barged across the barren, open moorland and threw itself against the
   stoic stone walls of the cottage, wrenching the window shutters from their frames.*

Exam-Style Questions

Here are a couple of exam-style questions for you to have a go at. Keep in mind the theory you've just been reading about in this section — the writer's use of tone, style, register, and words and phrases.

Q1   Read the following extract from an adventure holiday brochure.

> If you're up to your neck in revision, the promise of a long summer holiday might be the only thing keeping you going. For most students, the dream will be of lazy days spent with mates, maybe playing video games, or getting a bit of a tan down the park. There's nothing wrong with wanting a break. You've earned it. But here at Adventure Action, we can give you the chance to do something unforgettable with your summer.
>
> If you're aged 15 to 18, you could spend four weeks on one of our incredible adventure and conservation programmes at breathtaking locations around the world. You could trek through dense rainforest in Peru, to help build primary schools in isolated villages. You could take a flight over ancient glaciers to volunteer at a remote bear sanctuary in Alaska. Or you could earn a scuba-diving certificate whilst working in a marine biology lab in The Bahamas. Our programmes are tailored to give you a fantastic experience, where you can bag loads of new skills and be a part of something important.
>
> **Adventure beyond the usual this summer. Apply to Adventure Action today.**

How does the writer use language to appeal to the reader?

Q2   Read the following extract from a piece of fiction.

> She raised an eyebrow at him icily. Her mouth was a stern, straight line. It did not twitch.
> "Please," he pleaded, "it was a mistake. It won't happen again."
> Her silence was stone cold. He began to wring his hands fretfully. He could feel the sweat prickling like needles on the back of his neck. The seconds crawled by excruciatingly as he waited for her to say something, anything. He briefly considered speaking, but was too fearful of aggravating her further.
> "Evidently," she said at last, "you can no longer be trusted." The only emotion in her voice was disdain.
> His breath caught painfully in his chest; he knew the worst was coming.
> "I have no use for people I cannot trust," she continued. "You are dismissed. Leave now. Resign your post. Never let me see your face again. Understood?"
> Trembling, he managed a clumsy nod.
> "Good. Now get out."
> He turned and, dragging his feet like a condemned man, left the room.

How does the writer use language to present the two characters in this extract?

You could mention the writer's choice of:

*   words and phrases
*   tone, style and register
*   sentence forms.

Imagery

Imagery is when a writer uses language to create a vivid picture in the reader's mind. It's most commonly used in literature and literary non-fiction (see pages 17-18 for more about these types of text).

Metaphors and Similes are Comparisons

1) Metaphors and similes describe one thing by <u>comparing</u> it to something else.

> <u>Metaphors</u> describe something by saying that it <u>is</u> something else. *His gaze <u>was</u> a laser beam, shooting straight through me.*

> <u>Similes</u> describe something by saying that it's <u>like</u> something else. They usually use the words <u>as</u> or <u>like</u>. *Walking through the bog was <u>like</u> wading through treacle.*

2) They help writers to make their <u>descriptions</u> more creative and interesting.

> *Her jumper was <u>as fluorescent orange as a traffic cone</u>.* This simile is more <u>vivid</u> and <u>interesting</u> than just saying "Her jumper was fluorescent orange."

3) Metaphors usually create a <u>more powerful image</u> than similes, because they describe something as if it <u>actually were</u> something else.

Personification is describing a Thing as a Person

1) Personification describes something as if it's a <u>person</u>. This could be in the way something <u>looks</u>, <u>moves</u> or <u>sounds</u>, or some other aspect of it. For example:

> **Describing an object as if it were alive**
> *The desk groaned under the weight of the books.*

> **Describing an abstract idea as if it were alive**
> *Fear stalked the children with every step they took.*

> **Describing an animal as if it were a person**
> *The cunning fox smiled with a self-satisfied grin.*

2) Personification makes a description more vivid (so it '<u>comes to life</u>' for the reader).

3) It can also help to give a sense of the <u>viewpoint</u> or <u>attitude</u> of the <u>writer</u> or <u>character</u>:

> *Military helicopters prowled the city, their menacing mechanical voices threatening to stamp out the smallest sign of activity.* This shows that the writer feels that the helicopters are an <u>intimidating</u> presence.

These are language features that are definitely worth learning...

Being able to pick out metaphors, similes and personification is a really useful skill — they're common in lots of literary texts. Just remember to closely analyse the effects of any language features that you spot.

Analogies

Analogies are often used when a writer is trying to argue or persuade their audience.

Analogies are really fancy **Comparisons**

Analogies are like extended similes (see p.30) — they also often use the word 'like'.

1) An analogy <u>compares</u> one idea to another to make it easier to <u>understand</u>.

2) Analogies provide <u>powerful</u> and <u>memorable</u> images. They can be more <u>familiar</u> or more <u>shocking</u> than the original idea, which makes it easier for the reader to <u>grasp the point</u>. For example:

Deforestation is happening at an incredible speed. An area of rainforest equal to twenty football pitches is lost every minute.	⟶	By <u>comparing</u> the area to football pitches, the writer makes it easier to <u>visualise</u> the scale of the problem.

Hoping your exams will go OK without opening your books is like hoping to win the lottery without buying a ticket.	⟶	By <u>comparing</u> the chances of success to an impossible situation, the writer <u>emphasises</u> how unlikely it is.

3) Analogies are common in <u>non-fiction</u> texts that are trying to <u>argue</u> a point or <u>persuade</u>, as they can help to get the writer's viewpoint across <u>clearly</u> and <u>forcefully</u>.

Think about **Why** the writer has used an analogy

This analogy helps the reader to visualise the volume of gas being produced.

This analogy is being used to scare the reader and to persuade them to act on climate change.

It's easy to throw facts and figures around, but very few people realise just how much greenhouse gas we are releasing into the Earth's atmosphere every year. Current figures suggest that it's almost 30 billion tonnes per annum — that's **equivalent** in weight to around **150 million blue whales**.

By pumping these gases into the air, we are steadily choking our planet to death. This is **like** starting a fire in your bedroom, then watching passively **as the room slowly fills with thick, black smoke until you can no longer breathe**.

If this sounds like madness to you, then you're not alone. The good news? We can fix it. If the whole world works together with enough determination, we can avert the climate change catastrophe that threatens us all.

The word 'equivalent' shows that this is a comparison.

Uses 'like', so this is another analogy.

Don't worry if you haven't heard of analogies before...

Writers use analogies to make their points clearer and easier to understand. They can also make a piece of writing more interesting — think about how you could use them in the writing section of your exams.

Language Features

Writers use lots of techniques to engage their readers and emphasise their points — here are four more...

Alliteration is when **Sounds** are **Repeated**

1) Alliteration is when words that are close together begin with the same sound:

> PM's panic!   Mum's magic medicine   Fairytale finish for Phoebe   Close call for kids

2) Writers might repeat hard sounds to give a harsh or scary feeling to their writing:

> *The crooked castle creaked ominously.*

3) Or they might use soft sounds to make a text sound gentle and appealing:

> *The jovial giant joked joyfully.*

4) Alliteration can help a writer to grab a reader's attention. It's often used for emphasis and to make key points more memorable.

> *Visit us to find the coolest Christmas decorations around — and we'll throw in a free festive floral arrangement if you spend over ten pounds!*

> Alliteration is used to emphasise the main reasons a customer should visit this shop.

Onomatopoeia **Mimics Sounds**

1) Onomatopoeic words sound like the noises they describe:

> whistle   squish   boom   gulp
>
> hiss   thud   smash   crackle

2) Onomatopoeia makes descriptions more powerful — it appeals to the reader's sense of hearing, which helps them imagine what the writer is describing.

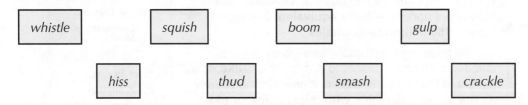

> *Just add our Milkshake Magic to a glass of milk, and listen to the powder fizz and crackle into a tasty drink that you'll be slurping up in no time!*

> These words create a strong impression of how the drink sounds to make the product seem exciting.

> *At night, I was kept awake by constant creaks and rustles; at times it almost sounded like someone was living in the rafters of the old house.*

> These words help to create a detailed scene that the reader can imagine clearly.

Language Features

Oxymorons are phrases that appear to Contradict themselves

1) An oxymoron is a phrase or sentence that <u>makes sense</u> but seems to <u>contradict itself</u>, because the words have <u>meanings</u> that don't seem to <u>fit together</u>.

2) Writers will sometimes use an oxymoron to <u>draw attention</u> to a particular <u>idea</u>.

> *a <u>deafening silence</u>* ⟶ Using an oxymoron to describe the silence <u>draws attention</u> to it — the silence has the same effect as a 'deafening noise' would.

3) They can also be used to add <u>humour</u> to a text:

> <u>*Nobody goes*</u> *to that ice rink — it's always <u>too crowded</u>.* ⟶ Oxymorons can sometimes be used to make something sound <u>ridiculous</u> — if nobody went to the ice rink, it wouldn't be crowded.

> *As you can imagine, that joke went down like a <u>lead balloon</u>.* ⟶ Balloons <u>can't</u> be made of lead — this <u>contradiction</u> adds <u>humour</u> to the text.

Hyperbole is intentional Exaggeration

Hyperbole is an example of a rhetorical device — see p.35.

1) <u>Hyperbole</u> is where a writer <u>deliberately exaggerates</u> something.

2) It can be a very <u>powerful</u> way of making a point:

> *The food took <u>forever</u> to arrive.* ⟶ This is obviously <u>not true</u> — the writer has used hyperbole to <u>highlight</u> that the food took a long time to arrive.

> *I've got a <u>million</u> things to do this evening.* ⟶ The writer doesn't <u>actually</u> have a million things to do — they've used hyperbole to <u>emphasise</u> how busy they are.

3) Look out for writers using hyperbole to try to <u>persuade</u> you of their <u>viewpoint</u>:

> *This car will <u>completely transform</u> your life.* ⟶ Here the writer is using hyperbole in order to <u>persuade</u> the reader to <u>buy</u> a certain car.

Remember that writers choose their language carefully...

Any language feature you see in a text will almost definitely have been put there deliberately by the writer. Think really carefully about the effect it's having on the reader, and why the writer has chosen to include it.

Irony and Sarcasm

Irony and sarcasm are two more techniques to watch out for. They're similar, but irony has a friendlier tone.

Irony is saying the Opposite of what you mean

1) Irony is when the <u>literal meaning</u> of a piece of writing is the exact <u>opposite</u> of its <u>intended meaning</u>.

2) The reader can tell the writer is being ironic from the <u>context</u> of the writing.

3) Writers often use irony to express their viewpoint, but it helps to make what they're saying more <u>humorous</u> or <u>light-hearted</u>.

It was pouring down with rain — perfect weather for a barbecue. The <u>context</u> (the rainy weather) shows that the writer actually means that it was <u>terrible</u> weather for a barbecue.

Yet again I was off to see my favourite person — the dentist. The phrase "<u>Yet again</u>" hints that this isn't something the writer wants to do. The dentist <u>isn't</u> actually the writer's favourite person — they're being <u>ironic</u>.

Sarcasm is Nastier than irony

1) <u>Sarcasm</u> is language that has a <u>mocking</u> or <u>scornful</u> tone. It's often intended to <u>insult someone</u> or <u>make fun</u> of them, or to show that the writer is <u>angry</u> or <u>annoyed</u> about something.

2) Sarcastic writing usually uses <u>irony</u> — but the tone is more <u>aggressive</u> and <u>unpleasant</u>.

The food took 90 minutes to arrive, which was just brilliant. I can think of no better way to spend a Saturday evening than waiting around for a plate of mediocre mush. The writer uses <u>irony</u> and a <u>sarcastic</u> tone to show his <u>frustration</u> and <u>anger</u> — it's meant to <u>insult</u> the restaurant that kept him waiting.

Satire is used to Mock people or society

1) <u>Satire</u> is a kind of writing that uses irony and sarcasm to <u>make fun</u> of a particular person or thing. It makes a <u>comment</u> on the <u>shortcomings</u> or <u>stupidity</u> of that person or aspect of society.

2) It's used particularly in <u>journalism</u> or <u>reviews</u>, and is often directed at politicians or topical issues.

Travelling by train has become a test of how well you can imitate a tinned sardine. If cramming people into a carriage was an Olympic sport, us Brits would be guaranteed a gold medal. The writer uses <u>satire</u> to criticise the experience of travelling by train. Satirical writers usually hope that <u>pointing out</u> a <u>fault</u> in society may lead to the fault being <u>corrected</u> or <u>improved</u>.

Use context to work out if a writer is using irony or sarcasm...

If the writer is being surprisingly positive or negative about something, then that's a good clue that irony or sarcasm might be at work. It should be fairly clear when they're being used — otherwise they'd be pointless.

Rhetoric

Rhetorical techniques make language more persuasive — they try to influence the reader in a certain way.

There are lots of **Rhetorical Techniques**

1) <u>Rhetorical questions</u> require no answer — they make readers <u>engage</u> with the text and realise the answer <u>for themselves</u>. This makes the reader feel like they're making up their <u>own mind</u>, when actually the writer is trying to make them think a certain way.

> *Is it right that footballers are paid such vast sums of money?*

2) Writers can use a <u>list of three</u> words or phrases to <u>emphasise</u> the point they're making. They often repeat three adjectives.

> *The cross-country run is <u>painful</u>, <u>pointless</u> and altogether <u>absurd</u>.*

Think about how other techniques (e.g. alliteration, sarcasm and hyperbole) could also be used as rhetorical devices.

3) Sometimes they might even repeat the <u>same</u> words or phrase to really <u>emphasise</u> their point.

> *The <u>cross-country run</u> is painful. The <u>cross-country run</u> is pointless. The <u>cross-country run</u> is altogether absurd.*

4) <u>Antithesis</u> is a technique where <u>opposing</u> words or ideas are presented <u>together</u> to show a <u>contrast</u>.

> *Just a <u>small</u> donation from you could have <u>huge</u> consequences for others.*

5) <u>Parenthesis</u> is when an <u>extra</u> clause or phrase is inserted into a complete sentence. Parenthesis can be used in many ways, such as to add <u>extra information</u> or to <u>directly address</u> the reader.

> *This issue, <u>as I'm sure you all agree</u>, is of the highest importance.*

Rhetorical devices **Add Impact** to an **Argument**

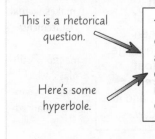

This is a rhetorical question.

Here's some hyperbole.

> This plan to give students across the country more homework is disgusting. **Can it really be fair to set us even more ridiculous and unnecessary assignments?** It's as if they don't think **we** work **every hour God sends** already! We cannot stand for this. **Join me** if you're interested in a better work/life balance. **Join me** to make our voices heard. **Join me** in my campaign for less homework!

The writer uses 'we' and 'us' to include the reader.

The writer repeats 'join me' three times.

Lots of political speech writers use rhetoric...

Remember, there are lots of different types of rhetorical techniques — this page just tells you about some of the most common ones. Make sure you analyse the effect of a rhetorical technique if you spot one.

Bias

If a text is biased, it doesn't give balanced view — the writer's opinion affects the writing and its message.

Biased writing is affected by the writer's **Opinions**

1) Biased writers don't usually lie, but they don't give the <u>full picture</u>.

2) Sometimes the writer <u>won't mention</u> something that opposes their viewpoint, or they'll <u>exaggerate</u> something that supports it.

3) Biased writing also often uses <u>generalisations</u> — sweeping statements that don't apply in all situations.

> *There's simply no doubt about it — everybody loves fish and chips.* This <u>isn't true</u> — the writer is making a <u>generalisation</u>.

4) Bias isn't always <u>obvious</u>, or even <u>deliberate</u>. Biased writers often <u>seem</u> to be talking in a neutral, factual way — while actually only presenting one point of view.

5) You need to be able to <u>recognise</u> bias, so that you don't mistake opinion for fact.

6) Look out for bias in non-fiction texts like <u>newspaper articles</u>, <u>autobiographies</u> and <u>reviews</u>.

> *Aigburth United were desperately unlucky not to win on Saturday night. They defended like heroes throughout the match, and only a shocking refereeing decision prevented a glorious victory.* → Watch out for <u>emotive language</u>, e.g. "heroes", and statements that could be <u>opinions</u>, e.g. "desperately unlucky" and "shocking refereeing decision". They will help you work out if a text is <u>biased</u> or not.

Texts can have **Different** amounts of **Bias**

These two texts are both arguing that Romeo and Juliet is an <u>important play</u>.
Source A is <u>biased</u>, but Source B is written in a more <u>balanced</u> way.

Biased writers may use hyperbole if they are trying to convince you about something.

They often make opinions sound like facts.

Source A — 19th-century review

Romeo and Juliet, **without the slightest shadow of a doubt**, is the very greatest work of literature ever to have been penned in the English language. It is truly the pinnacle of Shakespeare's momentous talent and **will never be matched by any playwright to come**.

Source B — 20th-century biography

Romeo and Juliet is **one of the most well-known** and widely studied works of literature to have ever been penned in the English language. It was **among the most popular of Shakespeare's plays** during his lifetime, and it is still performed to this day.

This text is less biased — it makes factual statements.

It mentions other plays, which makes it seem more balanced.

Always ask yourself whether a text is biased...

A good way to spot bias is when the writer presents their opinion as fact (by saying something confidently), but gives no evidence for it. This weakens their argument, as you can claim all sorts of absurd things this way.

Descriptive Language

You'll find descriptive language in both literary fiction and literary non-fiction texts.

Imagery makes text Interesting

1) Writers use descriptive <u>techniques</u> and <u>vocabulary</u> so that the reader gets a really clear <u>image</u> in their mind of what the writer's describing. It makes the text more <u>interesting</u>, <u>dramatic</u> and <u>convincing</u>.

2) <u>Descriptive techniques</u> include <u>imagery</u> such as metaphors, similes and personification (see p.30).

3) Writers often give <u>descriptions</u> based on their five <u>senses</u> (what they can <u>see</u>, <u>smell</u>, <u>hear</u>, <u>touch</u> or <u>taste</u>):

> *The docks had an overwhelming, fishy stench that made Steve's stomach lurch unpleasantly.* This appeals to the reader's sense of <u>smell</u> to give a sense of what the docks are like.

Descriptive language uses Interesting Words

1) Another sign of descriptive language is when the writer uses lots of <u>adjectives</u> — describing words such as 'huge' or 'fiery' that give a specific <u>impression</u> of something.

2) Writers might also use interesting <u>verbs</u>, such as 'saunter' instead of 'walk', to make their descriptions really <u>specific</u>.

> *The sun was setting over the sea. The view from the beach was incredible.* This example relies on the reader to picture <u>for themselves</u> what a nice sunset might look like.
>
> *The salty sea air whooshed around me as the dark-orange sun melted into the horizon, dyeing the cobalt sky a deep crimson.* This one uses interesting <u>adjectives</u> and <u>verbs</u> to help the reader to picture and even 'feel' what's going on.

3) Writers can also <u>build up</u> the description of something <u>throughout</u> their work. For example, by writing sentences with <u>contrasting</u> descriptions or descriptions that <u>agree</u> with each other.

Talk about the Effects of Specific Words

Uses lots of interesting verbs and adjectives.

The building is personified to emphasise how intimidating it is.

Henry **crept** slowly towards the **tall**, **dark**, **brooding** building, coming to a standstill in its looming shadow. Smoke billowed from its many chimneys, **stinging** his eyes and filling his nostrils with an **overpowering, acrid smell**. He watched the other workers scuttling in through the iron gates. With the colossal building **glowering down at him**, he shuddered, forced his right foot out in front of his left, and began to traipse towards the doors.

Describes the smell to add to the description.

Think about how a description makes you feel...

Lots of descriptive language is designed to have a strong effect on the reader. Writers will often try to create a really vivid picture of a scene, so that the reader can clearly imagine what it would be like to be there.

Warm-Up Questions

Use these warm-up questions to test your knowledge of language techniques, then have a go at some of the exam-style questions on the next two pages. Ready, set, write...

Warm-Up Questions

1) What impression is created by this metaphor?
   The glassy eye of the lake watched us in silent judgement.

2) Read the texts below. How does the use of an analogy in the second text make it more effective?

   > A running tap wastes around 6 litres of water for every minute it's left running.

   > A running tap wastes the equivalent of seventeen cups of tea for every minute it's left running.

3) Write down whether each of the sentences below uses personification, alliteration or onomatopoeia. Then explain the effect that the technique creates.
   a) The computer grumbled into life, before smugly telling me that it required six hours of updates.
   b) The buzz and chatter of the students ruined the tranquillity of the scene.
   c) Bag a Bargain at Brigson's — Portsmouth's Premier Pig Farm!

4) Briefly explain the difference between irony and sarcasm.

5) Is the following text sarcastic? Explain your answer using an example from the text.

   > Oh yeah, Ivan is a brilliant secretary — I especially appreciate the way he keeps forgetting to bring a pen and steals mine instead. And he's reorganised our files into a brand new system, which only he can understand — that's really made our lives easier.

6) For each sentence below, name the rhetorical technique and then explain its effect.
   a) Far from the sandwich heaven I'd been hoping for, I found myself in sandwich hell.
   b) I urge you, dear readers, to avoid this new restaurant at all costs.
   c) There's nothing worse than rain during an outdoor theatre performance.

7) Explain why the following text is biased. Use evidence from the text to support your answer.

   > By far the best hobby for young people is the card game "cribbage". All young people from the ages of eight to eighteen adore playing cribbage.

8) Write a paragraph about the effect of some of the descriptive language in the text below.

   > The air smelt of scorched grass. I could feel the blistering sun burning into my skin as I trudged slowly through the prickly, dry vegetation, my heavy load cutting cruel lines into my drooping shoulders. In the distance, the air shimmered in waves with the heat. I felt as if I were underwater, constantly being pulled back by the tidal drag of the temperature, every step an effort, every breath a trial.

Exam-Style Questions

To answer these exam-style questions, you need to draw on all of your knowledge about language techniques — have a quick glance back at pages 30-37 to refresh your memory, then get stuck into this lot.

Q1 Read the following extract from a piece of fiction.

> The landscape was dull steel. The sea was grey, the sky was grey and the mountains in the distance were grey. And we were grey too. Our meagre rations of bread and nameless slop had left us sallow-faced, with dark rings under our eyes. We huddled together nervously, like mice in a cage. A thin layer of snow carpeted the tundra already. It was only September; there would be plenty more snow to come. The wind whipped at our cheeks and we shivered.
>
> The soldiers were smoking by the hut, casting sideways glances at us once in a while, to make sure that we weren't doing anything foolish, like trying to escape. Eventually they trampled on their cigarettes and marched over to us — wolves in military uniform, coming to snarl at lambs.
>
> "There's work to do!" the officer in charge barked, clapping his gloved hands and then gesturing to the crates we'd unloaded. "Come on! Get a move on!" He fired his orders like cannon balls, and we dispersed frantically to do as he said. "If they're not all unpacked by nightfall, no one eats."

How does the writer use language to present the characters?
You could include the writer's choice of:

- words and phrases
- language features and techniques
- sentence forms.

Q2 Read the following extract from a piece of travel writing.

> The streets of Kuala Lumpur are a labyrinth of lost lanes, back-streets, dead-ends and alleys, which twist and turn and double back on themselves, constantly trying to bewilder the unaccustomed traveller. An apparently infinite series of haphazard side streets break out from the main street of the Chinatown area, like snakes winding across the desert. On every corner hang the pungent but irresistible smells of food stalls offering a cornucopia of exotic cuisines. Heavy trucks rumble past impatiently, whilst thousands of scooters whine and buzz like a swarm of bees, honking horns and hurling out exhaust fumes that stubbornly stagnate in the desperately hot air. The heat is relentless. Even standing still in the shade I can feel the sweat gathering on my forehead.
>
> In search of a bit of peace from the incessant heat and choking fumes, I make my way to the city centre park. Here, neat pathways wind their way leisurely through immaculate green lawns. On every side of the park, glimmering steel skyscrapers tower into the sky, peering down at the people walking below. It's like being surrounded by a giant metal rainforest, thronging with life.

How does the writer convey their feelings about Kuala Lumpur?
Refer to the language used in the text to support your answer.

Exam-Style Questions

Q3   Read the following extracts. Source A is from a letter written in the 19th century, and Source B is from a review posted on a travel website in the 21st century.

Source A
Dear Jane,

   I have arrived at my lodgings in Ware. They are satisfactory, if not impressive — the room must once have been decorated in good taste, but alas, it is the good taste of a bygone age. Nevertheless, the room is clean, tidy and of a good size. As I had expected, the mattress was not of the standard I am accustomed to (nor, for that matter, was the limited refreshment offered by the kitchens), but for a short stay, it will suffice.

Source B
The room smelt like its window hadn't been opened for about a century. The wallpaper was peeling. The carpet was a battlefield between all sorts of suspicious stains. Given the state of the rest of the room, I doubted that the 'fresh' bedding was clean, but it was the mattress that really drew my attention — it was like something from a Victorian prison cell, barely a few inches thick.

Compare how the writers show their different attitudes to their rooms.

In your answer, you should:

- compare the two writers' attitudes
- compare the techniques they use to convey their attitudes.

Q4   Read the following extract from a short story.

   "Howard, you made it!" Percy beamed, ushering me through the doors of his mansion. "Come in, come in — you don't want to miss a minute of this party; I promise you, it's my best yet!"

   He hastened me through the marble hallway towards the ballroom. I could already hear the thumping of music and the hum of voices. As the golden doors were opened, the noise hit me like a wave. The room was thronged with hundreds of guests, and they were all joking, laughing, making introductions. Their voices wove together into a single, undulating buzz of talk. Beyond their voices was the exuberant playing of the live band; drums and saxophones adding bass and melody to the already throbbing noise. There were other sounds too — the clinking of glasses, the occasional popping of champagne corks followed by cheers.

   And the colours! The men were all in tuxedos, cutting sharp lines of white and black, while the women were shimmering in silks of every colour — emerald and scarlet, gold and violet, cobalt and cerise. Lights glittered from the chandeliers, sparkling on the women's jewellery and the martini glasses and the silverware. The ballroom had become a never-ending kaleidoscope of wealth.

"The writer of this extract uses descriptive language very successfully. The reader really feels like they're at the party with Howard."

To what extent do you agree with this statement?

In your response, you could write about:

- your own impressions of the scene
- the techniques the writer has used to create these impressions.

Narrative Viewpoint

Literary texts will always have a narrator — a voice that is telling the story.

The **Narrative Viewpoint** is usually quite **Easy** to spot

1) A <u>first-person narrator</u> tells the story using words like 'I', 'we' and 'me'. A first-person narrator is often one of the <u>characters</u>, telling the reader <u>directly</u> about their feelings and experiences.

> *I stood on the fringes of the stage, waiting my turn, fear coursing through my veins.* A first-person narrator establishes a <u>stronger</u>, more <u>personal</u> connection with the reader.

2) A <u>second-person narrator</u> tells the story using words like 'you'. A second-person narrator talks as if the reader ('you') <u>is</u> one of the characters.

> *You turn your head to see her walking towards you. Your heart begins to race.* A second-person narrator makes the reader '<u>feel</u>' what the character is feeling.

3) A <u>third-person narrator</u> is not one of the characters. They tell the story using words like 'he' and 'she' to talk <u>about</u> the characters.

Some third-person narrators are omniscient — they know what all the characters are thinking. Others are limited — they only know what one character is thinking.

> *Ian's elated expression could mean only one thing: he had got a place at medical school.* A third-person narrator has a more <u>detached</u> viewpoint.

Narrators aren't always **Reliable**

1) When writing about a narrator, think about how <u>reliable</u> they are.

Narrators that can't be trusted are known as 'unreliable narrators'. There's more about these on p.102.

2) You might not be able to <u>trust</u> them fully if:

- they <u>don't know something</u>
- they're trying to <u>affect</u> the reader in some way, e.g. to make them <u>dislike</u> a particular character.

Think about how the **Narrator Presents** the **Characters**

Uses 'she' and is separate to the characters, so it's a third-person narrator.

> Polly was walking down the corridor when **she** noticed Alice walking towards her. Polly rolled her eyes and braced herself. "Hi Polly!" chirped Alice, with her **typically exhausting** optimism, "I hope I'll see you at the party later!"
> Polly's face contorted into an obviously forced smile as she nodded sharply in response.

Subjective phrases like 'typically exhausting' suggest that this narrator is biased and possibly unreliable.

Get to know these different narrative viewpoints...

It can be quite easy to forget about the narrator, because they're often not one of the characters directly involved in the story. But try to think about how they talk, and whether you can trust what they tell you.

Structure

Structure is all about the order in which writers present events and ideas to the reader.

Structure is important for **Fiction** and **Non-Fiction**

1) <u>Structure</u> is the way a writer <u>organises</u> their <u>ideas</u> within a text.

2) In <u>non-fiction</u> texts, writers will use structure to help them achieve their <u>purpose</u>. This might be to:

> - Build their <u>argument</u> to a powerful conclusion.
> - Reinforce the <u>persuasive</u> elements of their text through repetition.
> - Set out an <u>informative</u> text in a clear and balanced way.
> - Order their <u>advice</u> in a logical and easy-to-follow way.

3) In <u>fiction</u> texts, writers will structure their work in a way they think will <u>entertain</u> the reader. For example, story writing could have a <u>linear</u> or <u>non-linear</u> structure:

> Texts with a <u>linear</u> structure are arranged <u>chronologically</u> — events are described in the order in which they happened and the text <u>flows</u> naturally from <u>beginning</u> to <u>middle</u> to <u>end</u>.

> Texts with a <u>non-linear</u> structure are ordered in a way that makes the text <u>interesting</u>, rather than in chronological order. They might include things like <u>flashbacks</u>, changes in <u>perspective</u> or <u>time shifts</u>.

4) Linear texts tend to <u>build</u> towards some form of <u>climax</u>, whilst non-linear texts might <u>begin</u> with a <u>dramatic moment</u> and work <u>backwards</u> from there.

5) Whenever you write about <u>structure</u>, you need to show <u>how</u> the writer has used structure to produce a particular <u>effect</u> on the reader.

Writers use structure to **Focus** the reader's **Attention**

1) One of the easiest ways to write about <u>structure</u> is to think about how the writer is <u>directing</u> your <u>attention</u> as you read. There are lots of ways a writer can do this, for example:

> - The writer might draw the reader in by <u>describing</u> something <u>general</u>, then <u>narrow</u> their <u>focus</u> down to something more <u>specific</u>.
> - The writer could <u>describe</u> things along a <u>journey</u> and make you feel as if you are travelling with them. This might involve moving from the <u>outside</u> to the <u>inside</u> or just from one place to another.
> - A text might start with <u>description</u> and then move on to <u>dialogue</u>. This would shift your focus from <u>setting</u> to <u>characters</u>.
> - Often, a writer will use a <u>new paragraph</u> to start a <u>new topic</u>. This could be a <u>smooth</u> transition or it could have a <u>jarring</u> effect that draws the reader's attention to a particular part of the text.
> - In <u>non-fiction</u> texts, the writer will usually use paragraphs to <u>lead</u> you from their <u>introduction</u>, through their <u>main points</u> and on to their <u>conclusion</u>.

2) Often, <u>descriptive</u> writing will <u>show</u> rather than <u>tell</u> the reader what to <u>focus</u> on. For example, it might move the reader's attention from one place to another, acting like a camera shot does in a film. This type of writing is often called <u>cinematic writing</u>.

Structure

The **Narrative Viewpoint** will **Affect** the **Structure**

1) The narrator controls what the reader sees and what information they receive.

2) The narrator might withhold some information to create tension, or they could skip over certain parts of a story because they are biased.

3) Different narrators will have different effects on the structure of a text:

   - A third-person narrator (see page 41) will often have an overall view of the story, and so the structure might skip around to cover lots of different events.

   - For texts with a first-person narrator, the structure will probably follow that character's experiences quite closely.

4) Look out for texts that have more than one narrator. This might mean that the structure jumps around or alternates between the different perspectives.

5) Some texts use a frame narrative — this is when one story is presented within another. For example, the writer might use one character to narrate a story to another character. This allows the writer to move between multiple settings and sets of characters.

Think about **Different Elements** of structure

Think about the overall structure of the text as you read. Try to identify any perspective shifts or other obvious structural features.

The mountain looked mysterious in the half-light of the dusky evening. Its snow-capped peak stood alert, bathing in the embers of the setting sun. From there, my eye was drawn to the narrow path that wound its way past the dark woods and craggy outcrops. I traced the weaving path all the way down, until it vanished behind a magnificent church that loomed over the town nestled at the foot of the mountain.

This was the town of my youth.

This was the town where I had taken my first steps. **This was the town** where I had been to school, where I had battled through those tough teenage years and, finally, where I had first fallen in love.

I crossed the road and entered the alley that would take me into the warren of streets that wound their way around the foot of the church. When I finally emerged into the square, I was assaulted by a barrage of sights and smells that instantly took me back to my youth.

Immediately, I was back under the oak tree, crouching silently next to my best friend Sally. We were playing hide and seek with a boy named James Cotton, with whom we were both entirely fascinated. Obviously, at that age, this fascination manifested itself as bitter hatred, but later that would change — especially for Sally. Tomorrow morning I was to attend the wedding at which she would become Mrs Cotton.

As well as looking at the structure of the whole text, you'll need to look out for structural features at sentence and paragraph level. (There's more on sentence-level structure on pages 44-45.)

This text contains time shifts — it has a non-linear structure.

Structure is used to have an effect on the reader, just like language...

You need to think about how the writer is using structure to direct your attention to certain things. Look out for things like cinematic techniques, perspective shifts, single sentence paragraphs and recurring ideas.

Sentence Forms

You can write about the effects of different sentence forms in questions about both structure and language.

Sentences are made up of **Clauses**

1) A <u>clause</u> is a part of a sentence that has a <u>subject</u> and a <u>verb</u>. A clause usually <u>makes sense</u> on its own.

2) A <u>single clause</u> on its own is called a <u>simple sentence</u>.　　The <u>subject</u> is the person or thing <u>doing</u> the verb.

The sky was grey and sombre.	This is a single clause that is also a simple sentence. It has a <u>subject</u> ('The sky') and a <u>verb</u> ('was').

3) Simple sentences can be used to <u>explain</u> something <u>clearly</u> and <u>simply</u>. They are also often used to create a <u>sharp</u> or <u>abrupt</u> tone that keeps the reader <u>engaged</u> or creates <u>tension</u>.

4) A <u>compound sentence</u> has <u>two</u> main clauses, linked by a <u>conjunction</u> like 'or', 'but' or 'and'. <u>Both</u> clauses have to be able to make sense on their own. For example:

The sky was grey and sombre, and the rain lashed at our faces.	Writers can use compound sentences to do things like <u>expand</u> on their initial statement, creating more <u>detailed</u> and <u>interesting</u> descriptions.

5) <u>Complex sentences</u> have <u>two</u> or more clauses, but only <u>one</u> of them needs to make sense on its own.

Above the sleepy town, the sky was grey and sombre.	This is a complex sentence — 'Above the sleepy town' wouldn't work as a sentence on its <u>own</u>. This clause could go either <u>before</u> or <u>after</u> the main clause. Writers often <u>create interest</u> by using complex sentences to break up the <u>rhythm</u> of a text.

6) Writers use a variety of <u>sentence forms</u> to achieve different <u>effects</u> and keep the reader <u>interested</u>.

There are **Four Main Types** of sentence

1) Different <u>types</u> of sentences have different <u>purposes</u>:

- <u>Statements</u> deliver <u>information</u>, e.g. 'The referee made the decision.' They can be found in all texts, but they are particularly common in <u>informative</u> texts like newspaper articles, reports and reviews.

- <u>Questions</u> ask the reader something, e.g. 'What would you do in my situation?' They don't always require an <u>answer</u> — sometimes they are just there to <u>encourage</u> us to <u>think</u> about something.

- <u>Orders</u>, or <u>commands</u>, tell us to <u>do</u> something, e.g. 'Consider the effects of this in the long term.' They often use <u>imperative</u> verbs (verbs that give an instruction, like 'remember', 'think about' or 'go').

- <u>Exclamations</u> convey <u>strong emotions</u>, e.g. 'This is outrageous!' or 'This cannot be allowed to continue!' They usually end with an <u>exclamation mark</u>, and they're common in <u>persuasive</u> texts.

2) For the <u>reading questions</u>, it's a good idea to think about <u>how</u> and <u>why</u> writers have used particular <u>types</u> of sentence — bear in mind that different sentence types are suited to different <u>purposes</u>.

Sentence Forms

Writers use **Different Sentence Forms** to **Interest** the reader

1) Varying the <u>length</u> of sentences can create different <u>effects</u>. Here are a couple of <u>examples</u>:

These are just examples — the effects of different sentence lengths will vary from text to text.

> *The sky was growing darker. I couldn't see where I was going. I stumbled.*

Short simple sentences can be used to <u>build tension</u> or to create a <u>worried</u> and <u>confused</u> tone.

> *I waited excitedly at the foot of the stairs, listening to the footsteps above, thinking about the afternoon ahead, pacing the hall and counting down the minutes until we could set off.*

A longer, complex sentence could be used to give the impression of <u>time dragging</u>.

2) The <u>order</u> of words within sentences can also be chosen to create an <u>effect</u>. For example:

> *I had <u>never</u> seen such chaos <u>before</u>.*
>
> *<u>Never before</u> had I seen such chaos.*

Writers sometimes use <u>inversion</u> (<u>altering</u> the normal <u>word order</u>) to change the <u>emphasis</u> in a text. Here, inversion helps to emphasise the phrase '<u>Never before</u>'.

3) If you notice something about the way a writer has used sentences, don't just identify it — you need to <u>analyse</u> the <u>effects</u> to show how they <u>influence</u> the reader.

Comment on the **Effects** of different **Sentence Forms**

This is a long sentence that leaves the reader breathless by the end. It emphasises the feeling of weariness that the narrator is describing.

Short, simple sentences are used to reinforce the narrator's feelings of dread.

It was late evening by the time I returned home from the shops, tired and weary from barging my way past all the desperate Christmas Eve shoppers. It had been a long day, and I was ready for a relaxing bath and a long sleep. It wasn't until I was halfway up the path that I noticed the front door was ajar. **My heart began** beating wildly inside my chest as I hesitantly advanced. **My hands began** to shake. **My mind began** conjuring apparitions of the unspeakable horrors that could be lurking inside. Reaching the door, I took a deep breath and stepped across the threshold.

Everything was quiet and still. I crossed the hall and put down my shopping. **Everything looked normal. Nothing was out of place. Suddenly I heard a noise above me. Someone was upstairs. I gasped.** But then a change came over me: my fear **had turned to resolute anger. Seldom had I** experienced such intense fury in all my life. There was an intruder in my house, and they had no right to be there. I made for the stairs.

The repetition in the sentence beginnings 'My heart began', 'My hands began' and 'My mind began' gives emphasis to the physical effects of the narrator's fear.

The use of a colon shows that there is going to be some form of explanation. This highlights the move away from unexplained short simple sentences.

This inversion disrupts the usual word order and focuses the reader's attention on the narrator's anger.

This longer sentence marks a change in tone from fear to anger.

Make sure you can write confidently about sentences...

It'll really help you in questions about language and structures if you can talk about the effects of different sentence forms. Spend some time learning the technical terms for different forms and types of sentences.

Worked Exam-Style Question

Right, it's time for another worked answer...

Q1 Read the following extract. It is from the ending of a short story.

> The shot rang out. Jane powered off the blocks. The sound of the stadium had faded now, and only one thing mattered: putting one foot in front of the other, faster than she had ever done before. This was her race. She was born for this! Her blood pounded in her ears as she sprinted round the track.
>
> In the distance, the finish line was approaching. There were still two runners ahead of her. Faster! Jane urged herself on. Her legs burned. Her lungs screamed. But she was gaining on them. She overtook one. Still faster! At the last second, she overtook the final competitor and her foot came down first, landing triumphantly over the white line.
>
> Jane slowed to a halt, and doubled over with her hands on her knees as she gasped for breath. Wiping the sweat from her eyes, she looked up again at the stadium, and nearly cried with joy. Thousands and thousands of people were on their feet, cheering; they were waving flags and calling her name, smiles reaching from ear to ear. She could hardly believe it. All the months of hard training had paid off and she had achieved her lifelong dream: she had won a gold medal at the Olympics.

How is this text structured to engage the reader?

You could write about:

- where the writer focuses your attention at the beginning of the story
- how the writer changes the focus as the story continues
- any other structural features that you notice.

<u>Plan</u>

focus zoomed in on Jane, then further onto body parts, then to the runners/finish line — feel like you're experiencing it with Jane; short sentences = pace

focus moves to crowd after the race — use of longer sentences as Jane has now slowed down too

You <u>don't</u> need to make a <u>detailed plan</u> for this type of question, but <u>quickly</u> jotting down your <u>ideas</u> (like this) can be helpful.

The extract is structured to take the reader from the tension of the starting blocks to the joy of Jane's post-race celebrations. The extract begins with <u>a short, punchy sentence, which engages the reader's interest</u>. The writer then focuses in on the figure of Jane with another short sentence. This gives the reader an impression of dynamic movement and excitement. As the first paragraph progresses, the writer <u>focuses in further</u>, to describe Jane's body parts (her feet and her ears), <u>so it's like the reader is inside Jane's body</u>.

<u>Sentence forms</u> are an important structural feature, so it's great to comment on their <u>effect</u> like this.

The second bullet point asks you to write about <u>changes</u> in <u>focus</u>.

This is a good explanation, but to be even better, it could be <u>developed</u> by linking back to the question — putting the reader in Jane's position is a way of <u>engaging</u> the reader.

Worked Exam-Style Question

This question type is all about the <u>effect</u> on the <u>reader</u>.

In the second paragraph of the extract, the writer's focus changes to describe what Jane can see ahead of her. <u>This makes the reader feel like they're experiencing the race as well.</u> The single-word sentence "<u>Faster!</u>" is written as if from Jane's perspective, which <u>helps the reader to empathise with her determination and physical effort</u>.

<u>Support</u> your points with short quotations or references to the text.

The writer then uses <u>repetition</u> to describe Jane's exhaustion — "Her legs burned. Her lungs screamed." This emphasises that Jane's whole body is in pain. <u>As in the first paragraph</u>, describing individual body parts really helps to put the reader in Jane's position, and to show how <u>her exhaustion has progressed from earlier in the extract</u>. The short sentences in this paragraph also increase the <u>pace</u> of the text to mirror Jane's acceleration, which engages the reader's emotions as <u>the extract builds towards a climax</u>.

One way to <u>develop</u> a point is to <u>link</u> back to a point you made earlier.

You need to use <u>technical terminology</u> (like repetition) when you're analysing structural techniques.

Structural features are often used to change the <u>pace</u> of a text — look out for this.

You need to show an awareness of how the text is structured as a <u>whole</u>, as well as at a sentence level.

In the final paragraph, the writer uses longer sentences to slow the pace of the text, because Jane has crossed the finish line. The focus moves to the crowd, who are all "<u>on their feet, cheering; they were waving flags and calling her name, smiles reaching from ear to ear.</u>" This helps the reader to imagine the powerful reaction from the crowd, as if they are in the stadium celebrating themselves. The <u>change in viewpoint from inside Jane's head to a pan round the stadium</u> shows the change in Jane's focus too.

This example is fine, but it could be much <u>shorter</u>.

This is called <u>cinematic writing</u> — you could use the technical term here.

- This answer has explored a variety of structural features — sentence length, repetition and perspective shifts — and explained their effects on the reader. It also backs up these points with suitable examples, and uses technical terminology accurately.

- To get the very top marks, this answer could be improved by:

  - keeping quotations precise.

  - using a few more technical terms, e.g. simple sentence, narrative viewpoint, cinematic writing.

  - making sure all points are fully developed by including a bit more detail.

Exam-Style Questions

You know the drill by now — use these exam-style questions to help you practise for the real thing.

Q1 This is the ending to a short story. Joan is eighty-six years old, and one of the nurses from her care home has volunteered to take her to the beach.

> They arrived shortly before lunchtime. The seagulls squawked noisily overhead, swooping and circling, bright as doves against the blue sky. The nurse pushed the wheelchair down the boardwalk. Looking out over the sand and the grey-green sea, Joan was transfixed.
>
> The first time she had been to the beach was as a little girl, shortly before the war broke out. It had been a hot day. The beach was full of people sprawled on multicoloured deck chairs and picnic blankets, lending the scene a carnival feel. She remembered the smell of the water as she raced into the sea for the first time. She remembered the feeling of damp sand between her fingers and toes, and how the sea salt had dried into tiny crystals on her skin. Her mother had packed a picnic of hard-boiled eggs and potato salad. It had been the best day of her life so far, and as her father had bundled her into a towel, tired and sun-soaked, ready to go home, she had already been looking forward to the next visit.
>
> Now Joan watched the children race delightedly across the sand like she had done. Her nurse bought her fish and chips for lunch. Joan bought sticks of rock for her great-grandchildren. As the sun was going down, and they headed back to the car, Joan looked back over her shoulder. She knew there wouldn't be a next visit — but she didn't mind. She had seen the sea again.

How has the writer structured the text to add interest to the ending of the story?
You could write about:

- where the writer focuses your attention at the beginning of the story
- how and why the writer changes the focus as the story continues
- any other structural features that interest you.

Q2 Read the following extract. It is from the opening to a short story.

> The theatre hummed with expectant conversation as the spectators began to fill the stalls. The red velvet seats and gentle golden lighting gave the impression of being caught in the centre of a giant ruby. There was a magical feeling, as if everyone knew they were going to witness something spectacular that night, and eyes kept flickering over to the theatre drapes, wondering when the show would begin.
>
> Backstage, biting his fingernails down to the nail-bed, was the one they were all waiting for. Mikhail had been told by everyone he met that he was the greatest tenor of all time. Conductors had shed a tear when he sang, audiences had wept openly. But that never stopped him from feeling sick with nerves before a performance. What if his voice faltered? What if he forgot the words? What if he disappointed them all?
>
> "Sixty seconds to curtain," the stage manager called to him. Mikhail took a deep breath. His palms were damp with sweat. His legs felt like jelly. He didn't know if he was ready for this.

How does the structure of this text work to engage the reader?
You could write about:

- where the writer focuses your attention at the beginning of the story
- how and why the writer changes the focus as the story continues
- any other structural features that interest you.

Revision Summary

If you've got to grips with this section, these questions will be a breeze. If there are any you can't do or get wrong, you need to pop back to the relevant page and study up. Don't move on until you can do them all.

1) Are the following definitions for tone or style?
   a) This is the overall way in which the text is written.
   b) This is the feeling the words are written with.

2) Would you expect the register of the following types of writing to be formal or informal?
   a) a job advert for the role of bank manager
   b) a newspaper article reporting on changes to the tax system
   c) an article about mountain biking on a website aimed at teenagers

3) Write a sentence that uses a superlative.

4) What is the difference between a metaphor and a simile?

5) Which of the following are metaphors and which are similes?
   a) He was as hairy as a dog.
   b) On the racetrack my sister was a whippet.
   c) You look like something the cat dragged in.

6) Matt says "the writer uses personification — he describes the young girl as if she were an animal." Why is Matt wrong?

7) Why might a writer give the weight of a cruise ship in elephants rather than in tonnes?

8) Choose an alliterative adjective to go with 'badger' to make the badger sound:
   a) attractive
   b) dangerous

9) Write out three examples of onomatopoeic words.

10) Which of the following is an oxymoron?
   a) *It was a bittersweet victory.*
   b) *I love apples, but I hate pears.*

11) Write a sentence that uses hyperbole.

12) What is irony?

13) What is the main thing you can look at to work out if a writer is being sarcastic?

14) Name three rhetorical techniques.

15) True or false? *It'll always be obvious if a text is biased.*

16) Which word fills in the blank? *Writers often give descriptions based on the five _____.*

17) What are the three types of narrative viewpoint? Write down a brief definition for each one.

18) What is a linear structure?

19) Are the following sentences simple, compound or complex?
   a) Gazing longingly out to sea, the sailor dreamed of adventure.
   b) I waited for an hour, but he never arrived.
   c) She listened in shock to the news on the radio.
   d) The sun rose reluctantly, casting sombre shadows across the fields.

20) What are the four main types of sentence?

Writing with Purpose

All writing has a purpose, so you need to make it clear in both your fiction and non-fiction writing.

Work out the **Purpose** of your writing

See pages 10-14 for more about writer's purpose.

1) The purpose of your writing might be to <u>inform</u>, <u>advise</u>, <u>argue</u> or <u>persuade</u>, or <u>entertain</u>. It could even be <u>more than one</u> of these.

2) Sometimes it will be <u>obvious</u> what the <u>purpose</u> of your writing needs to be:

> Write a speech in which you **persuade** a group of parents that families should spend more quality time together.

This question directly tells you that your purpose is to persuade the reader.

3) It can be <u>less obvious</u> though, so sometimes you'll need to <u>work it out</u>:

> You are going to enter a writing competition at your school. Write a **story** using one of the following titles:
>
> a)   The Wrong Choice
>
> b)   The Yellow Box
>
> c)   A Shadow in the Courtyard

The purpose isn't explicitly stated in this question, but you're writing a story, so you can assume that the main purpose is to entertain.

Structure your writing to **Suit** your **Purpose**

1) Different purposes will need different <u>structures</u>, so you'll need to think about a <u>structure</u> that will help you achieve your purpose most effectively.

2) You can lay out your structure by writing a <u>plan</u>, so that it stays <u>consistent</u> throughout your answer:

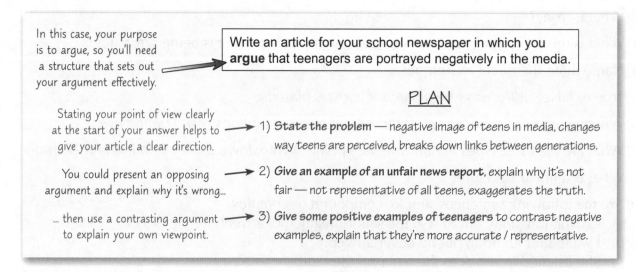

In this case, your purpose is to argue, so you'll need a structure that sets out your argument effectively.

> Write an article for your school newspaper in which you **argue** that teenagers are portrayed negatively in the media.

PLAN

Stating your point of view clearly at the start of your answer helps to give your article a clear direction.

→ 1) **State the problem** — negative image of teens in media, changes way teens are perceived, breaks down links between generations.

You could present an opposing argument and explain why it's wrong...

→ 2) **Give an example of an unfair news report**, explain why it's not fair — not representative of all teens, exaggerates the truth.

... then use a contrasting argument to explain your own viewpoint.

→ 3) **Give some positive examples of teenagers** to contrast negative examples, explain that they're more accurate / representative.

Writing with Purpose

Choose your **Tone**, **Style** and **Register** to match your purpose

1) You need to show that you can <u>adjust</u> your <u>tone</u>, <u>style</u> and <u>register</u> (see p.25) to suit your purpose.

2) For example, an <u>informative</u> text might have a <u>serious</u>, <u>reserved</u> style, with a <u>formal</u> register:

> *The UK's younger generation show signs of frustration at the way they are perceived. Studies show that up to 95% of 18-24 year-olds feel that their stance on environmentalism is being ignored.*

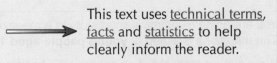

This text uses <u>technical terms</u>, <u>facts</u> and <u>statistics</u> to help clearly inform the reader.

3) A <u>persuasive</u> text needs to be more <u>subjective</u> (based on personal feelings). It might try to create a <u>personal</u> tone that involves the reader in a text:

See p.35 for some rhetorical techniques that help to achieve this.

> *Like me, you must be weary of the incessant criticism. We're intelligent young citizens who understand the issues threatening our planet. Why are we being ignored?*

This text uses a <u>rhetorical question</u> and the pronouns 'you' and 'we' to <u>involve</u> and <u>persuade</u> its audience.

4) Texts that <u>entertain</u> need to choose a tone, style and register that will keep the reader <u>interested</u>, so that they <u>enjoy</u> reading the text:

> *I'd never in my life needed a break so badly. My airless writing room had begun to feel suffocating; so had the frustration of my unending writer's block. I gave up, threw down my pen, and went out for a walk.*

Fiction texts might use a <u>dramatic</u> tone and <u>interesting language</u> to entertain the reader.

> *After a sell-out solo tour, lead singer Yuri returns to his roots with relish. He leads a pitch-perfect performance, supported by a band who still love to employ the crash and thud of heavy percussion.*

This non-fiction text uses <u>alliteration</u> and <u>onomatopoeia</u> to entertain the reader.

5) A text written to <u>advise</u> might use a <u>friendly</u> tone and an <u>informal</u> register:

> *Use a pencil to sketch out a rough outline of your landscape. Don't worry about getting it completely accurate for now, as you can fix any small mistakes once you begin painting.*

This text uses the phrase "Don't worry" and the pronoun "you" to create a <u>reassuring</u>, <u>friendly</u> tone.

6) When you adjust your <u>writing</u> to suit your purpose, make sure you still use <u>sophisticated vocabulary</u> — to do well in your exams, you'll need to show that you're able to use <u>complex language</u> in your writing.

There are marks available for adapting your writing to fit a purpose...

Don't forget that writing can often have more than one purpose (see p.10) — make sure you think about all the reasons that you're writing, so that you can adapt your style and produce a really impressive answer.

Writing for an Audience

For each writing task, you need to bear in mind your audience — that means anyone who's going to hear or read your writing. You then need to adapt your tone, style and register so that it's right for your audience.

Work out **Who** your **Audience** is

1) Usually the question will specify a <u>particular audience</u>:

> You are going to submit a short story to a magazine. The magazine is aimed at **young people aged 14-18**.
>
> Write a short story about somebody who has travelled a long way.

Here's the audience — 'young people aged 14-18'.

2) Sometimes you might need to work out from the <u>question</u> who your audience is. The <u>form</u> and <u>content</u> will give you some clues:

> 'Students should attend classes virtually. In today's digital society, it's illogical that students still have to leave the house to go to **school**.'
>
> Write a **broadsheet newspaper article** in which you explain your point of view on this statement.

This statement is about schools, so the audience will be people interested in education, such as parents or teachers.

You're writing a broadsheet newspaper article, so your audience will mostly be well-educated adults.

Choose a **Tone, Style** and **Register** that fit your **Audience's Age**

1) You'll need to <u>adapt</u> your <u>tone</u>, <u>style</u> and <u>register</u> so that it <u>suits</u> the <u>age</u> of your audience.

See p.25 for more on tone, style and register.

2) If you're addressing a <u>younger</u> audience, you might use a more <u>light-hearted</u> tone and an <u>informal</u> register, with a <u>colloquial</u> or <u>chatty</u> style.

> *Dogs can make brilliant pets, but you've got to be careful — they're a big responsibility. They need feeding, walking and, above all, lots of love and attention!*

<u>Informal punctuation</u> (such as the exclamation mark) and relatively <u>simple</u> language make this text accessible for a younger audience.

3) A <u>formal</u>, <u>serious</u> register that doesn't use any <u>slang</u> might work better for <u>older</u> audiences. You might also use a more <u>complex</u> style than you would for a younger audience.

> *The Prime Minister has today announced several changes in the way that students will be assessed throughout their school careers. The proposed changes have been met with strong criticism by many, including the Shadow Minister for Education.*

This uses a <u>formal</u> register, with <u>long sentences</u> and fairly <u>complex vocabulary</u>.

Writing for an Audience

Think about how well you **Know** your audience

1) You could be asked to write for a <u>familiar</u> audience, e.g. a letter to a friend. To do this, you might write in an <u>informal</u> register, and use a <u>friendly</u> tone:

> *You really should stop eating sweets and drinking sugary drinks — they're very unhealthy, and I'm a bit worried about the damage you could be doing to your teeth.*

This text uses the <u>first person</u> ('I') and <u>informal phrases</u> like 'a bit' to appeal to the reader.

2) If you're writing to an <u>unknown</u> audience instead, it would be better to use an <u>impersonal</u> tone and a <u>formal</u> register:

> *Dear Sir,*
> *I read your article, dated 12th October, with some concern. As a student and a teenager myself, I feel compelled to point out that you have not fully considered the issue at hand.*

This text is quite <u>formal</u> — it addresses the reader as "Sir" and uses <u>complex sentences</u> to create an <u>authoritative</u> tone.

Consider your **Audience's Expertise**

1) Different audiences will have different levels of <u>expertise</u> in the subject you're writing about.

2) You might be writing for an audience who <u>don't know much</u> about the topic you're writing about, e.g. if you're asked to <u>advise</u> them about something. That means you need to use a <u>clear</u>, <u>direct</u> tone and style:

> *There are many different ways to deal with online bullying. The first thing you need to do is report it. You can usually do this on the social media site itself. If you don't feel comfortable doing this, you could talk to a parent or guardian instead.*

This text mostly uses <u>simple sentences</u> to make the advice <u>easy</u> to <u>understand</u> for an audience without much expertise.

3) If you're writing for an audience with <u>more expertise</u>, such as a report for a panel of experts, your register should be more <u>formal</u>, with a style that uses more <u>specialised</u> language than if you were writing for a <u>general</u> audience:

> *Having fully evaluated their cost-effectiveness and potential benefit, this committee recommends that the measures outlined herein be implemented immediately, in order to grow profit in line with expectations from the Board.*

This uses <u>specialised language</u> and a <u>complex sentence structure</u> to create a <u>formal</u> register.

You always need to show that you can write well...

You should always aim to show your writing skills to the examiner — even if you're writing informally or for a young audience, you still need to make sure you include a range of vocabulary and sentence types.

Writing Stories

Story-writing is a task that might pop up in your exams. You could be asked to write a short story, or focus on writing a particular bit, like the opening or the ending. Read these pages carefully for some tips.

Grab your reader's **Attention** from the start

1) It's good to <u>start</u> your stories with an <u>opening sentence</u> that'll make your <u>reader</u> want to <u>carry on</u> reading.

   You could start with a <u>direct address</u> to the reader:

   > *Everybody has a bad day now and again, don't they? Well, I'm going to tell you about a day that was much, much worse than your worst day ever.*

   Or you could try a description of a particularly <u>unusual character</u>:

   > *Humphrey Ward was, without a shadow of a doubt, the most brilliant (and most cantankerous) banana thief in the country.*

   Try to avoid clichéd openings like 'Once upon a time'.

2) If you start your story in the <u>middle of the action</u>, it'll create a <u>fast-paced</u> atmosphere that makes the reader want to find out <u>what happens next</u>:

   > *I couldn't believe it. He was gone. "He must be here," I thought to myself as I went through the shed, desperately throwing aside box after box. It was no use. Peter had run away, and it was all my fault.*

3) This example <u>explains</u> some of what's happening after a few sentences, which keeps up the <u>fast pace</u> of the narrative — so the story stays <u>interesting</u>.

4) You could also try <u>prolonging</u> the mystery to create <u>tension</u> in your narrative. Just make sure you <u>reveal</u> what's going on before it gets too <u>confusing</u> for your audience.

5) However you start your writing, you need to make sure it's <u>engaging</u> and <u>entertaining</u> for the reader — so whatever you do, don't <u>waffle</u>.

Try to build the **Tension** from the **Start**

> Your school is making a creative writing anthology that will be sold to other pupils. You have decided to submit a piece of writing.
> Write the opening part of a story about a trip to the beach.

This story starts in the middle of the action — we don't know who the narrator is or why they're shouting.

Use key words to show as clearly as possible that you're answering the question.

The waves drowned out my shouts as they crashed against the rocks with thundering force. **I had only closed my eyes for a minute, and now I had awoken to find that Amy was nowhere to be seen.** I scanned the deserted **beach**, searching for any sign of my beautiful daughter.
   Amy had been wearing a blue pinafore dress that made her look like Alice in Wonderland. I remembered joking with her about how funny it would be if the Queen of Hearts had suddenly appeared to chase her along the sands. She had merely giggled and returned to the digging project that was taking up all her attention. **But where was she now?**

This text solves the mystery of what's going on fairly quickly to maintain the pace.

Try to keep the tension building as you move on from your opening paragraphs.

Writing Stories

Make your **Language** and **Narrative Viewpoint** fit the task

1) Different <u>word choices</u> will have different <u>effects</u>, so you'll need to pick vocabulary that creates the right <u>tone</u> for your story. For example:

> *The door screeched open and I carefully entered the dingy cellar. Shadows cast by my torch leapt up at me through the gloom.*

Words like '<u>screeched</u>', '<u>dingy</u>' and '<u>gloom</u>' make this writing sound <u>spooky</u>.

> *I burst noisily through the thicket of trees and sprinted towards the shore. The men were still chasing me, bellowing threats.*

Words like '<u>burst</u>', '<u>sprinted</u>' and '<u>chasing</u>' make this writing sound <u>exciting</u> and <u>dramatic</u>.

2) You also need to think about what <u>narrative viewpoint</u> you're going to use (see p.10).

3) A <u>first-person narrator</u> uses the pronouns 'I' and 'we', as they're usually one of the <u>characters</u> in the story.

> *I quickly scanned the book for anything that might help. My heart was racing; I knew I needed to work fast.*

The first-person narrative makes things more <u>dramatic</u> by helping the reader to <u>imagine</u> the story is happening to them.

4) A <u>third-person narrator</u> uses words like 'he' and 'she' to talk <u>about</u> the characters from a <u>separate</u> viewpoint.

> *Shamil lit the bonfire carefully, then retreated back a few metres as the feeble fire began to crackle and spit.*

The narrator isn't part of the story. This creates <u>distance</u>, as the narrative voice and the characters are <u>separate</u> from each other.

Use **Descriptive Techniques** to make your text **Engaging**

Write the opening part of a story suggested by this picture:

Make clear references to the prompt you're given in the question.

Use techniques like alliteration and repeating patterns to add rhythm to your text.

Combine visual imagery with other senses to help the reader imagine they are there with the narrator.

Using figurative language, like similes and personification, will help to make your text more engaging.

This description uses a third-person narrator, so the narrative isn't limited by the rider's perspective.

The sun dipped low beneath the looming, dusky sky. Its daytime glory was reduced to the **fading flicker** of a tiny ember that only just protruded above the dark horizon.

Down in the valley, the camp hummed with activity: **people milled about like ants, erecting tents, cooking meals and lighting fires**, the smoke from which **crept stealthily** up the side of the mound, eventually reaching **the rider's** nostrils and filling him with **the warming aromas of home.**

A glance beyond the confines of the camp revealed the open plains beyond, as they bathed in the warmth of the dying light. Come nightfall, these plains would transform from places of refuge into discordant wastelands, answerable only to the laws of nature.

Writing Stories

It's important to write a **Good Ending**

1) Whether you're asked to write the <u>end</u> of a story, or a <u>different part</u>, it's still important that you <u>finish well</u> — you want to leave the examiner with a <u>great impression</u> of your writing abilities.

2) Here are some <u>examples</u> of different ways that you could <u>end</u> a story:

> • You could finish with an unexpected <u>plot twist</u> that will <u>shock</u> the reader.
>
> • You could show the <u>main character</u> coming to some kind of <u>realisation</u>.
>
> • You could create a <u>cliffhanger</u> ending by finishing with a <u>question</u>. This will leave the reader thinking about what will happen <u>next</u>.
>
> • You could have a <u>neat</u>, <u>happy ending</u> that will <u>satisfy</u> the reader.

3) If you find you're running out of time, think up a <u>quick ending</u> — make sure you show how the story ends, and finish with a short, <u>punchy</u> line.

4) Under absolutely no circumstances use the ending, "And it was all a <u>dream</u>."

Try to make your **Ending** as **Powerful** as possible

> Write the ending of a story about somebody who made a bad decision.

The narrator has had a realisation, which hints to the reader that the story is about to come to an end.

I knew I should never have stolen the vase. It had been a moment of madness. I had just seen it sitting there, and it looked so beautiful and elegant. All of my problems stemmed from that decision, that single flash of foolishness.

Your final paragraphs should build the tension towards a climax that will resolve the action.

I spent a long time wondering what to do with the vase. I studied it intently. It was too beautiful to discard, too dazzling to keep concealed any longer. Eventually, I made a decision. I took it to the cliff and threw it over, watching it smash on the rocks below. It was an awful sight, but at least **my guilty secret was gone forever.**

After you've given a satisfying ending, you could go on to add an unexpected twist that leaves the reader with doubt in their mind.

Late that night, the wind was howling around my tent, and the rain was pelting down on the canvas. Suddenly, there was a huge crash of thunder and a blinding flash of lightning. Terrified, I ran out of the tent, only to be greeted by a strange apparition: **there, sitting on top of a tree stump, was the missing vase. It was completely whole.** Not a single crack was visible on its smooth, shiny exterior. I whirled around and scoured the field for any sign of an intruder. **That was when I saw the old, hunched man walking slowly away.**

However you end your text, make sure it's exciting and powerful.

Your ending needs to be original and engaging...

You really shouldn't use clichéd endings like "it was all a dream" or "they all lived happily ever after" — all they do is prove to the examiner that you haven't thought very carefully or creatively about your answer.

Writing Descriptions

You could be asked to write a description of a character or scene. The aim is to give your audience a detailed idea of what you're describing, so you'll need to use words to paint a vivid picture in their mind.

Descriptions are Detailed

1) Descriptions use strong <u>visual</u> language to create an <u>impression</u> of a person or place for the reader.

2) You <u>don't</u> need to include as much <u>plot</u> or <u>action</u> — focus mostly on <u>describing</u> the subject.

3) Even though there's no <u>plot</u>, you still need to have some <u>structure</u> to your writing — e.g. you could start with a <u>general</u> description, then go on to describe some more <u>specific</u> details.

4) The purpose of a description is normally to <u>entertain</u> the reader, so you need to adapt your writing <u>style</u> accordingly, and keep your <u>language</u> interesting.

5) Descriptions need <u>detail</u>. For example, a <u>character</u> description might include:

- A character's <u>physical features</u>, e.g. hair colour, clothing.
- A character's <u>personality</u>, e.g. they could be funny, serious, reserved, extroverted.
- Any other particular <u>features</u> that reveal <u>more</u> about them, e.g. any nervous habits.
- Your <u>personal opinion</u>, e.g. what you like or dislike about them.

Use Language to describe a Character or Scene

Write a character description about someone who is intimidating.

You can use the character's habits to create an impression of their personality.

The woman's fingernails tapped impatiently against the wood of the mantelpiece. She was standing still, but the motion of her perfectly-manicured fingernails, and the impatient huffs of air that were regularly expelled from between her thin lips, made her seem restless and agitated. Somehow she gave off the impression that she never really stopped moving.

One way to structure your writing is to start with a tiny detail, then expand outwards.

Use figurative language to show off your descriptive skills.

She was an angular exclamation mark of a woman, and she stuck out like a sore thumb against our familiar, homely surroundings. She wore her dark hair short; it had been meticulously combed into an unforgiving style that cut into her sharp cheekbones. Her suit was an inky black colour, which only served to emphasise her militantly slender form. When she spoke, **her voice was low and commanding**, and her expression was set into a permanent frown that was half-angry, half-distracted, and **wholly intimidating.**

You can write from any narrative viewpoint, as long as it's appropriate to your purpose and audience.

Use the five senses to create a really detailed description.

Don't lose your focus — remember that your answer needs to be about somebody intimidating.

She was the most terrifying person I had ever met.

Try to use a good variety of descriptive language...

There are plenty of techniques to choose from here: metaphors, similes, alliteration, personification, the five senses, adjectives, repetition, onomatopoeia, hyperbole — the important thing is to use them engagingly.

Warm-Up Questions

Feeling chilly? No fear — these questions will get you feeling toasty in no time (when it comes to your English Language skills, that is). Use them as an introduction to the longer writing tasks on the next page.

Warm-Up Questions

1) Which of the following techniques are common in persuasive writing?
   a) an impersonal tone   b) rhetorical questions
   c) technical terms   d) emotive language

2) Rewrite the informative text below so that it persuades the reader to visit the church.

   > ### Lyttlewich Church
   >
   > Situated in the rural village of Lyttlewich, Howtonshire, Lyttlewich Church is one of the oldest churches in the country: some parts of the church were built in 984 AD. The church receives thousands of visitors a year, and is particularly renowned for its artwork, which has recently been restored.

3) Rewrite each sentence below so that it's appropriate for an audience who have no expertise on the subject.
   a) Fertilisers provide phosphorus and potassium, which are essential for plant growth.
   b) The ossicle bones in the ear (the malleus, incus and stapes) are some of the smallest in the human skeleton.
   c) Roman legionaries used javelins and throwing-darts to defeat their enemies.

4) Write down a good opening sentence for each of the texts below.
   Make sure it's suitable for the audience given in the question.
   a) An article for a teenage magazine, in which you say that schools should spend more time teaching students how to manage their money.
   b) Instructions for a primary school student to teach them how to bake a cake.

5) Write the closing sentences for each of the stories below.
   a) A story about a spaceship that crashes on an alien planet.
   b) A story set on a desert island.

6) Imagine you are going to write a short story about somebody who's lost in a forest.
   a) What narrative viewpoint would you use? Give a reason for your answer.
   b) Write down two descriptive adjectives you could use, and explain their effect.
   c) Write down a simile you could use.

7) Write a descriptive sentence about a busy leisure centre based on each of the following senses.
   a) sight   b) sound   c) touch   d) smell and/or taste

8) You have been asked to write a description of a family member. Draw a spider diagram showing your ideas for things you might include.

Exam-Style Questions

These exam-style questions are about fiction writing, which you could be asked to do in your exam.
It's a good idea to make a quick plan for your answers, to make sure your writing is well-organised.

Q1

You have been asked to write a piece for a storytelling event at your local library.
Your writing will be read aloud to an audience of adult library users.

Write the beginning of a story about somebody who goes camping.

Q2

You want to submit a piece of creative writing to be published in your local newspaper.
The paper's editor will decide which submissions to publish.

Write a short story that is set in your local area.

Q3

You are going to enter a writing competition run by your school newspaper.
The competition is being judged by your head teacher.

Write a description suggested by this picture:

Writing Newspaper Articles

You might be asked to write a newspaper article in your exams — here are some pointers on how to do it.

Newspaper articles **Report Events** and **Offer Opinions**

1) A newspaper's main purpose is to <u>inform</u> people about <u>current affairs</u> and <u>other topics</u> of interest.

2) Some newspaper articles <u>directly report</u> news. They convey <u>facts</u> about a <u>story</u> or <u>theme</u>, often using an <u>unemotional</u> tone and a <u>sophisticated</u> style to make the information seem <u>accurate</u> and <u>reliable</u>.

3) Other newspaper articles offer the <u>viewpoint</u> of the <u>writer</u> on a news story or theme. These are sometimes called <u>commentaries</u>, <u>columns</u>, <u>editorials</u> or <u>opinion pieces</u>.

4) As well as <u>informing</u> the reader, <u>commentaries</u> try to <u>entertain</u> their audience by making readers engage with the <u>personality</u> of the writer.

Commentaries need to **Engage** their **Audience**

1) To grab the audience's <u>interest</u>, a commentary might use a <u>personal</u> tone and a <u>conversational</u> style to help convey the writer's opinions and personality.

> *It seems to me that this lot all need to take a deep breath and stop whinging. Nobody's going to bulldoze our green spaces any time soon — they'll have to spend 25 years making a planning application first.*

This uses <u>colloquial</u> words to create a conversational tone and <u>sarcasm</u> to convey the viewpoint of the writer.

2) <u>Rhetorical techniques</u> (see p.35) are commonly used in commentaries to help get the writer's opinions across forcefully and to encourage readers to <u>agree</u> with the writer.

> *What happened to the good old days, when the presence of a heap of spuds on the table at dinnertime brought delight all round? Has all this 'health food' nonsense made us forget our faithful starchy friend?*

This uses <u>rhetorical questions</u> to engage and persuade the reader.

The **Layout** of an article is **Important**

Newspaper articles often use <u>layout features</u> to engage the reader's attention and convey information clearly.

Headlines tell you, very briefly, what an article is about. Headlines need to capture the audience's interest so that they carry on reading the article.

Straplines are short statements that expand on the headline. They try to hook the reader, after the headline has got their initial interest.

SECRET WEDDING FOR DUTTON DUO

Private ceremony for TV's cutest couple

By our showbiz reporter, Joe Snooping

Actors Simon Tremble and Katie Davies, stars of the TV series *Dutton Manor*, married yesterday at a secret ceremony in the Lake District.

LOVE AT FIRST SIGHT
According to insiders, the pair got together just three months ago and their engagement was only announced publicly last week. Thirty close friends and family, including several co-stars, joined them to celebrate, and pop sensation Al Blue performed at the reception.

DIRECTOR IS 'DELIGHTED'
Director of the series, Julian Parker, told The Daily Gossip that he was 'absolutely delighted' for the couple and added that they are 'perfect for each other'. However, he refused to comment on rumours that Simon's character in the show may be killed off when the new series begins in April.

COUPLE TO HONEYMOON IN CARIBBEAN
After their wedding, the couple jetted off on honeymoon to the beautiful island of Antigua. They will stay at a luxury beach resort for two weeks before returning to London to set up their new home.

Articles often start with a short paragraph that gives an overview of the story or theme.

Subheadings are used to split an article up. Each subheading briefly tells you what the next section of text is about, often in an interesting or humorous way.

Writing Newspaper Articles

Newspapers have **Varying Audiences**

1) Newspapers are broadly split into two types — tabloids and broadsheets.

2) Tabloids (such as *The Sun* and *The Mirror*) tend to focus on more sensational stories, making their news stories accessible and with a wide appeal.

3) Broadsheets (such as *The Telegraph* and *The Guardian*) are thought of as more formal, 'high-brow' journalism — focusing on what are thought to be more sophisticated topics.

4) In the exam, you might be told which form to write in, e.g. 'a broadsheet newspaper article' — make sure you adapt your tone, style and register to the right audience.

5) Most newspapers also publish articles on the internet. If you're asked to write a news article for an online audience, think about how your audience might be different (e.g. younger or with a different level of understanding about the subject), and adapt your writing to suit.

Make your article **Interesting** for the reader

A well-known travel writer has published an article in which she claims that guided tours are 'uncultured', and that the only way to see the 'true heart of a country' is by going 'off the beaten track'.

You have been asked to write an article for a broadsheet newspaper in which you explain your opinion on the travel writer's comments.

Use a strapline to summarise the article in an interesting way.

You're giving an opinion, so your tone should be quite personal.

Make sure you link your answer to the prompt you're given in the question.

Opinion articles often combine a conversational style with complex sentences and vocabulary.

FORGET THE ROAD LESS TRAVELLED

Pay no attention to those who tell you otherwise: guided tours are the best way to experience somewhere new.

At some point or other, we've all been faced with a travel snob: that particular breed of rough-and-tumble traveller who knows all about where to go, what to see and, most importantly, how to see it. The travel snob thinks that guided tours are for the uncultured bores of this planet. The travel snob believes in travel without a destination. And yet, the travel snob will always find time to tell you about a 'hidden gem' that only they can take you to.

You would think someone so educated in the ways of the world would have realised the irony by now — travel snobs are themselves tour guides. The places that they think are 'off the beaten track' are transported, by their own recommendation, right onto 'the beaten track'. They are the one beating the track; they are leading the tourists away from their well-populated honeypot attractions into 'the heart of things'.

In the meantime, guided tours are often run by local people, who will frequently have a real treasure trove of local knowledge. How can a throwaway recommendation from an outsider possibly surpass that? Anybody who wants to see the true heart of a country must be guided by the people who live in it.

Your headline needs to be short and punchy to engage the reader.

Use rhetorical devices like repetition to make your writing entertaining and persuasive.

You can use a sarcastic tone to give your writing a sense of personality.

You need to get the style right in a newspaper article...

It's worth having a look at some real newspaper articles as part of your revision. You'll soon start to spot some patterns in the vocabulary and structure that they use, which will help you write better articles yourself.

Writing Leaflets

Leaflets need to give the reader lots of information in a clear, organised way.

Leaflets can have Varied Audiences and Purposes

1) Leaflets can have <u>any</u> purpose, but they're often used to <u>advise</u> (e.g. a leaflet advising the reader to open a savings account) or <u>persuade</u> an audience (e.g. to vote for a particular political party).

2) They can have a <u>general audience</u> (e.g. a leaflet about the importance of healthy eating) or a more <u>specific audience</u> (e.g. a leaflet advertising a particular museum or exhibition).

3) Leaflets need a <u>clear structure</u> to <u>break up</u> information. This could include:

- a clear title
- subheadings
- bullet points
- boxes around extra bits of information

It's important to break up the information in a leaflet, but don't waste time in the exam trying to make it look pretty or drawing pictures.

4) Leaflets also need to <u>grab the reader's attention</u>, so that they <u>remember</u> all the information they're given. You can use <u>language techniques</u>, such as <u>lists of three</u> or <u>direct address</u>, to achieve this.

Organise your Leaflet in a Clear and Interesting way

The government wants to encourage teenagers to exercise more.
Write the text for a leaflet in which you advise students about how to keep fit.

KEEPING FIT THE EASY WAY

Exercise is important for your health, but as a student **your time and budget may be limited**. Fortunately, there are many cheap, simple, fun ways to keep fit.

Use a title to catch the reader's attention.

You're writing for students, but you should still use a formal register and Standard English.

<u>Walk the walk</u>

Walking costs you nothing, and it doesn't require too much spare time. You could try:

- **Walking to a friend's house instead of asking your parents for a lift.**
- **Planning a longer route to a destination you already walk to.**
- **Getting off the bus or train a few stops early and walking the rest of the way.**

Use interesting subheadings to organise your answer and hold the reader's interest.

Use bullet points to break information up for the reader.

<u>Pedal power</u>

If you own a bike, cycling is an excellent way to keep fit. Look at your council's website to see if there are cycle routes nearby, or **plan a safe route on your local roads**.

<u>Dance the night away</u>

Dancing can help to maintain your fitness and improve your coordination, regardless of your skill level. Try looking for tutorial videos on the internet to help you learn.

Imperatives and direct address create a clear, confident tone.

<u>Your turn...</u>

These are just a few ideas; there are many more options available. Whether it's **skipping, skating or salsa**, there will certainly be something for you.

Alliteration and a list of three emphasise the variety of activities on offer.

Short paragraphs can help to break up the information in a text.

You need to match your writing to the audience in the question...

Leaflets can be written for a wide variety of different audiences. Make sure your leaflet is adapted to the audience you're given in the question — choose a suitable writing style that uses appropriate language.

Travel Writing

Travel writing needs to effectively convey your feelings about the place you're writing about.

Travel Writing is Personal and Descriptive

1) Travel writing is an <u>account</u> of a writer's travels to a specific <u>place</u>.

2) If you're asked to produce some travel writing, you'll need to convey your <u>thoughts</u> and <u>opinions</u> about the place you're writing about, as well as give some <u>information</u> about it.

3) A piece of travel writing can <u>entertain</u> the reader (e.g. if it's in a book or magazine), <u>inform</u> them (e.g. if it's in a travel guide), or <u>persuade</u> them to visit a destination.

4) However, it's usually written for a <u>combination</u> of these purposes, e.g. <u>travel guides</u> are often written to both <u>inform</u> and <u>entertain</u> the reader.

5) Travel writing usually has a <u>personal</u> tone, and it's almost always written in the <u>first person</u>. Try to write in a <u>conversational</u> style, but don't forget to use lots of <u>descriptive techniques</u> too.

Use Interesting Language to Convey your Opinions

> Imagine you have just visited New York.
>
> Write an article about your trip for a travel magazine. Your article should include descriptions of the city and your own opinions.

This question asks you to write a magazine article. It needs to be entertaining and informative, and could also persuade the reader to agree with your point of view.

An interesting, punchy title can help to grab your audience's attention.

Dismayed in Manhattan

Lucy Farthing says "no thanks" to New York.

I've travelled to many cities during my career as a travel writer, and it's fair to say that there are a few I'd rather have avoided. **None, however, have quite matched up to the levels of discomfort, disappointment and sheer frustration I experienced in the city of New York.**

Use personal pronouns like 'I' to make the tone of your writing more personal.

I suspect my high expectations didn't help. Before embarking on my trip, I'd been regaled with stories from friends and family of gleaming, soaring skyscrapers and the vibrant, bustling streets of downtown Manhattan. "It's the best city in the world!" I was told.

What I realised instead, somewhere between my fifth cup of overpriced coffee and my fourteenth hour-long queue, was that **New York is the city of nightmares**. Not only did it feel like the world's busiest city, it felt like the **noisiest**, too; by the end of my week there I found myself longing for the joys of silence and solitude. Maybe for some, New York is a city where dreams come true, but it was certainly far from the **inspiring haven** I had hoped to find.

Make your opinion on the city very clear.

Try to use all five senses to create a sense of the atmosphere of the place.

Use interesting language to make your text more entertaining.

You're allowed to be negative in your writing...

You don't necessarily have to write positively about the place you're describing. It's fine to have a negative opinion, as long as you're clear and you use the appropriate language, tone and style for your audience.

Writing Reports and Essays

Reports and essays use a similar tone and style, but they do have one difference — their typical audience.

Reports and Essays are Similar

1) Reports and essays should be <u>impersonal</u> and <u>objective</u> in tone — you'll need to go through the arguments <u>for</u> and <u>against</u> something, then come to a conclusion that demonstrates your <u>own point of view</u>.

2) Reports and essays should follow a <u>logical structure</u>. They need to have:

- An <u>introduction</u> that sets up the <u>main theme</u>.
- Well-structured <u>paragraphs</u> covering the <u>strengths</u> and <u>weaknesses</u> of the arguments.
- A <u>conclusion</u> that ties things together and offers <u>your own</u> point of view.

3) The purpose of reports and essays is almost always to <u>inform</u>, but they often <u>advise</u> their audience too.

4) You need to make sure you write for the correct <u>audience</u> — <u>essays</u> usually have quite a <u>general</u> audience, but <u>reports</u> are normally written for a <u>particular</u> person or group of people.

Reports should Analyse and Advise

Your school has a certain budget for extra-curricular activities. This year, they have a small amount of money left over, and they are deciding whether to award it to the rock-climbing club or the film society.

Write a report for the board of governors in which you discuss the options and make a recommendation of what you think they should do.

<u>A Report Into The Possible Uses Of The Extra-Curricular Budget</u>

By: John Coughton

Prepared For: Board of Governors

Date: 21st April 2015

This report has been commissioned by the board of governors to identify the best use of the funds available for extra-curricular activities at St. Swithins Park Secondary School. Two options have been investigated: the rock-climbing club and the film society. After careful consideration of the evidence collected from various interviews and data analysis, **the conclusion has been reached that the film club is the most logical recipient of the excess funds.**

On the one hand, the rock-climbing club appears to be the most obvious choice as it is the most costly to run: the club organises frequent expeditions involving expensive equipment and high travel costs. Having said that, the club does charge a members' fee, which helps to alleviate some of this financial burden.

At the start, show that you are clearly aware of who your audience is.

You don't need to create any suspense — give your opinion in the introduction.

Phrases like 'on the one hand' show that you have thought about both sides of the argument.

Your language should be very formal and impersonal, but you still need to convey a viewpoint.

In the real answer, you would go on to include several more paragraphs and finish with a conclusion that gives advice.

Give an opinion in your report or essay...

Reports and essays are quite simple to write — just make sure that you're being as objective, analytical and formal as possible. But you must make sure that you still show a viewpoint by coming to a conclusion.

Writing Reviews

People read reviews to find out the writer's opinion about something, so you need to express yours clearly.

Reviews should Entertain as well as Inform

1) A <u>review</u> is a piece of writing that gives an <u>opinion</u> about how <u>good</u> something is
   — it might be a book, a piece of music or even an exhibition.

2) <u>Reviews</u> can appear in lots of <u>different</u> publications. If you have to write a review
   in the exam, the question will usually tell you <u>where</u> it's going to appear.

3) The <u>publication</u> where your review appears will affect what kind of <u>audience</u> you're writing for
   and <u>how</u> you write. For example, a film review for a teen magazine could be <u>funny</u> and <u>chatty</u>,
   but a review of a Shakespeare play for a broadsheet newspaper should be <u>serious</u> and <u>informative</u>.

4) You should also pay attention to <u>purpose</u>. Your review could have <u>several</u> different purposes:

   - Your review needs to <u>entertain</u> the reader.

   - You also need to <u>inform</u> the reader about the thing you're reviewing, based on your <u>own opinion</u>.

   - You might also need to <u>advise</u> the reader whether or not to see or do the thing you're reviewing.

5) <u>Don't</u> get too hung up on <u>describing</u> everything in minute detail — it's much
   more important that you give your <u>opinion</u>. Just keep your review <u>engaging</u>
   by focusing on the <u>interesting bits</u> and using <u>sophisticated language</u>.

Your review needs to Give an Evaluation

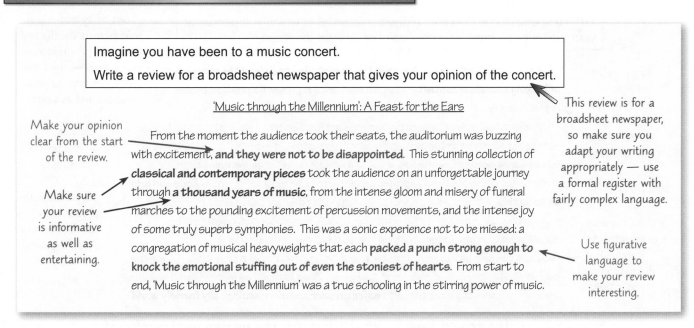

Imagine you have been to a music concert.

Write a review for a broadsheet newspaper that gives your opinion of the concert.

'Music through the Millennium': A Feast for the Ears

Make your opinion clear from the start of the review.

Make sure your review is informative as well as entertaining.

From the moment the audience took their seats, the auditorium was buzzing with excitement, **and they were not to be disappointed**. This stunning collection of **classical and contemporary pieces** took the audience on an unforgettable journey through **a thousand years of music**, from the intense gloom and misery of funeral marches to the pounding excitement of percussion movements, and the intense joy of some truly superb symphonies. This was a sonic experience not to be missed: a congregation of musical heavyweights that each **packed a punch strong enough to knock the emotional stuffing out of even the stoniest of hearts**. From start to end, 'Music through the Millennium' was a true schooling in the stirring power of music.

This review is for a broadsheet newspaper, so make sure you adapt your writing appropriately — use a formal register with fairly complex language.

Use figurative language to make your review interesting.

Your opinion needs to be very clear in a review...

Reviews are quite a nice thing to write — they're all about your opinions, which means you can say exactly what you think. You should try to express your thoughts clearly, and in a way that entertains the reader.

Writing Speeches

A speech needs to be powerful and moving. You should aim to have an emotional effect on your audience.

Speeches need to be Dramatic and Engaging

1) <u>Speeches</u> are often written to <u>argue</u> or <u>persuade</u>, so they need to have a <u>dramatic</u>, <u>emotional impact</u> on their audience.

2) One way to make a speech persuasive is to give it an effective <u>structure</u> — arrange your points so that they build <u>tension</u> throughout your answer, then end with an <u>emotive</u> or <u>exciting</u> climax.

3) You can use lots of <u>language techniques</u> to make your writing <u>engaging</u> and <u>persuasive</u>:

These accusations are hateful, hurtful and humiliating. →	<u>Alliteration</u> and the use of a <u>list</u> of three adjectives make this <u>sound</u> strong and angry.

Persuasive language techniques like these are known as rhetorical devices — see page 35.

Do we really have no other option? The current situation is a disgrace! →	<u>Rhetorical questions</u> and <u>exclamations</u> engage the reader and make your writing sound more like <u>spoken language</u>.

4) Remember that speeches are <u>spoken</u>, not read. Try to use techniques that are effective when they're spoken <u>out loud</u>.

Your speech should Make People Think

> You have been asked to attend an animal welfare conference which is all about the practice of keeping animals in zoos.
>
> Write a speech to be delivered at the conference, in which you persuade your audience to agree with your point of view on the issue.

Start off by addressing your listeners directly and announcing the reason for your speech — show that you've understood your purpose and audience.

Try to use lots of personal pronouns like 'I', 'you' and 'we' to engage your audience.

Ladies and gentlemen, I have called you here today to defend the practice of keeping animals in captivity. I believe that zoos represent a positive presence in this country.

The vast majority of modern British zoos are focused on conservation and education. To my mind, these important values are worth preserving. It is essential that we give our youngsters a sense of awareness about the world around them. **We must** impress upon the youth of today the need to protect endangered species and habitats. **Zoos can help us to do this.** Modern zoos offer extensive opportunities for these kinds of educational experiences: there are interactive exhibitions, talks from conservationists and live question-and-answer forums that will help to educate our young people.

You could use repetition to increase the dramatic impact of your speech. →

Zoos can help us inspire a generation with the importance of conservation. **Zoos can help us** raise awareness of environmental issues. **Zoos can help us** by providing a space in which we can work together to build a **safer, greener and more ecologically friendly world**.

The word 'must' creates a confident tone.

Vary the lengths of your sentences to show pauses and emphasis.

Use rhetorical devices like lists of three to make your argument sound more forceful.

Practise using some rhetorical devices in your writing...

There are plenty of famous speeches throughout history — you could try looking at some of the techniques they use. Your speech doesn't have to impress a crowd of people, but it does have to impress the examiner.

Writing Letters

Letters are always addressed to a particular person or group of people. This means that they have very specific audiences, so it's very important that you tailor your letter to suit that audience.

Letters can be **Formal** or **Informal**

1) If you're asked to write a <u>letter</u>, look at the <u>audience</u> to decide how formal your register should be.

2) If the letter is to someone you <u>don't</u> know well, or to someone in a position of <u>authority</u>, keep it <u>formal</u> with a <u>serious</u> tone. This means you should:

- Use <u>formal greetings</u> (e.g. 'Dear Sir/Madam') and <u>sign-offs</u> (e.g. 'Yours sincerely' if you've used their name, 'Yours faithfully' if you haven't).
- Use <u>Standard English</u> and <u>formal vocabulary</u>, e.g. you could use phrases like 'In my opinion...' or 'I find this state of affairs...'.

Letters often start with the address of the sender, the address of the recipient and the date.

3) If the letter is to someone you <u>know</u>, or someone who <u>isn't</u> in a position of authority, you might use a more <u>informal</u> register and <u>personal</u> tone. This means you should:

- Start with your reader's <u>name</u>, e.g. 'Dear Jenny', and <u>sign off</u> with 'best wishes' or 'warm regards'.
- Make sure you still write in <u>Standard English</u> (so no <u>text speak</u> or <u>slang</u>) and show the examiner that you can use interesting <u>vocabulary</u> and <u>sentence structures</u>.

State your Viewpoint clearly

> You have read a newspaper article which states:
> 'International travel is not worth the cost.'
> Write a letter to the newspaper in which you argue for or against this statement.

Bristol, 22nd February

Dear Sir or Madam,

    I read with dismay your recent article regarding international travel. As a regular traveller myself, **I strongly disagree with your assertion that international travel is not worth the cost**. The benefits of international travel far outweigh the expenses incurred: it broadens the mind, adds to your wealth of experience and heightens your awareness of the world around you.

    The article claims that **UK holidays are cheaper and provide similar benefits**. If you are not deterred by the threat of drizzle, perhaps that is true. To me, however, **it is worth spending a fraction more to avoid wasting your holidays sheltering from the British rain**.

Yours faithfully,
Ms Karen Samuels

This letter is for somebody in a position of authority, so it uses a formal greeting and sign-off.

Formal language like this helps to set the right tone for your letter and shows that you've understood your audience.

You need to make your viewpoint on the statement clear.

Introducing a counter-argument, then contradicting it, can help to build up your argument.

Your answer would need to be longer than this in the exam, with a few more paragraphs that support your argument.

You need to write for your audience, but keep your writing high level...

You will need to pay attention to purpose and audience — make sure your letter completes the task in the question and is written in an appropriate style. Even if the letter is to a friend, you still need to write well.

Warm-Up Questions

Here's another page of warm-up questions for you to have a go at — they're a brilliant way to consolidate everything you've learnt in this section. When you've done these, have a look at the worked exam-style question on the next two pages, then try some for yourself on page 71.

Warm-Up Questions

1) Read the extract below. Write down its purpose and the audience you think it's aimed at.

> I know it's difficult for car-lovers like us, but the facts speak for themselves — we must drive less and walk more if we are to have any hope of rescuing our beleaguered environment.

2) Read the extract below, which is from a short story.

> The clown pretended to slip on a banana skin, cartwheeling his arms and legs in a manner so ridiculous that we couldn't help but laugh.

   a) What narrative viewpoint does this story use?
   b) Rewrite this extract using a different narrative viewpoint.

3) Write the opening paragraph of a newspaper commentary about the opening of a new hospital in your area.

4) Read the extract below. Do you think it is from a leaflet or an essay?
   Write a few sentences explaining your answer.

> Come to Caleb's Kitchen today, for:
> • Delicious, freshly made food.
> • A warm and welcoming environment.
> • And on top of all that, unbelievably low prices!

5) The extract below is from a travel brochure. Rewrite it so that it's suitable for a teenage audience.

> You'll need to invest in a comprehensive travel insurance package, so that you can be sure that medical and legal help will be there should you need it.

6) Write a short review of a book, film or television programme you have read or watched recently.

7) You have been asked to give a speech to the parents of a Year Six class at a local primary school, to persuade them to send their child to your secondary school.
   Write a brief plan to show how you would structure your speech.

8) Read the extract from a letter below. Is this letter for a familiar or unfamiliar audience?
   Explain your answer.

> Dear Horace,
> How absolutely delightful to hear from you! We haven't spoken in yonks, have we?

Worked Exam-Style Question

Cast your eyes over this worked exam-style answer, which is for a writing question.

Q1

"In order to prepare young adults for the challenges of raising a family, it should be made compulsory for them to spend time volunteering with young children."

Write an article for a broadsheet newspaper in which you argue for or against this statement.

When you're planning, it might help to jot down all your <u>ideas</u> first, and then <u>organise</u> them afterwards.

PLAN

own experience at nursery in Y10 — negative — put off having children. Cover some counter-arguments. My arguments = time pressure on young people; not all want to become parents; natural anyway? Where do you find all the children/parental permission etc.

- Para 1: own experience at nursery in Y10

- Para 2: Counter-arguments: skills (selflessness, communication, imagination), responsibility, prep for parenthood

- Para 3: not all want to become parents (figure?); those who do will be fine (natural process)

- Para 4: time pressure on young people as it is — studying, home life, part-time job already perhaps, already pressured enough into thinking of future

- Para 5: logistical problems (finding the children; those children's parents' views on it; how/who/what)

- Para 6: conclusion — well done to those doing it, sure it's rewarding, but shouldn't be compulsory

Make sure you know what your overall <u>opinion</u> is <u>before</u> you start writing.

It's great to use interesting language techniques, like <u>similes</u>, to help your reader to <u>empathise</u> with you.

Your <u>opinion</u> on the statement needs to be <u>clear</u> — even if you don't state it explicitly like this.

DON'T PUSH TEENS INTO PARENTING PRACTICE

When I was fifteen, my school Careers Advisor decided that the best way to teach her Year Tens about the wonderful ways of life was to dump them into the world of work. And so, <u>like a bemused traveller without a map</u>, I found myself, dazed and confused, in my local preschool. I have nothing against this preschool in particular, but the week I spent there was one of the most unpleasant of my life. After the fourth day of being smeared with paint, wet sand and the bodily fluids of various toddlers, I swore I would never work with children again. <u>Which is why I find it remarkable that there are proposals to make this experience compulsory.</u>

It is true that there are several strong arguments in favour of making volunteering with young children compulsory for young adults. It would teach them the patience, selflessness and imaginative thinking necessary for raising a child — important lessons for future parenthood. Furthermore, after first-hand exposure to young

Using an <u>anecdote</u> provides an <u>engaging</u> opening.

The <u>descriptive language</u> in this sentence helps the reader to imagine the scene at the preschool.

Show that you're responding to the <u>prompt</u> in the question.

Worked Exam-Style Question

The second paragraph is <u>slightly inappropriate</u> for the <u>form</u> — it's become a bit like an essay. It would be better if the <u>style</u> was <u>less formal</u>...

children, other young adults may decide that parenthood would not suit them at all, and be able to make more informed choices later in life.

However, I struggle to comprehend how any young adult could actually finish their compulsory volunteering thinking "yes please". The lessons I was taught at the preschool included "there is no such thing as a clean child" and "home time is the only time worth treasuring". <u>It's also worth remembering</u> that some young people already have no intention of becoming parents. In a recent survey, <u>10%</u> of them said they had no desire to have children. I would like to see how many of the other 90% flock to join them after an <u>enforced week of torture</u> such as mine.

...like this. This kind of <u>informal phrase</u> is better suited to a broadsheet newspaper article.

<u>Facts and figures</u> are <u>appropriate</u> for a broadsheet newspaper article.

<u>Hyperbole</u> can be used to add <u>humour</u>, making your answer <u>entertaining</u>.

This is before we even consider that many young people simply wouldn't have the time for volunteering. My own week of work experience meant losing a week of lessons while studying for my GCSEs. Plenty of young people are already ground to the bone, juggling <u>home life, academics and extra-curricular activities</u> in the hope of getting that important first job. <u>Surely this should take priority over spending stressful time with children?</u>

Rhetorical techniques (like <u>rhetorical questions</u> and <u>lists of three</u>) make your answer more <u>persuasive</u>.

Broadsheet newspaper articles should have a <u>personal tone</u>.

Where these children would come from is another mystery. <u>Personally</u>, I can't imagine my own parents willingly donating me for an unknown teenager to take care of. I also feel sorry for whichever local schools, preschools or councils would become responsible for dealing with the <u>mountains of paperwork</u> involved.

This <u>metaphor</u> adds <u>emphasis</u> to the point about logistical problems.

This conclusion refers back to the <u>statement</u> in the question, which links the answer together nicely, and shows good <u>organisation</u>.

In theory, bringing young people and young children together for voluntary work seems like a lovely idea. I'm sure there are plenty of young people who already volunteer with young children, and I'm sure they benefit from it. This does not mean that we should start forcing all of their peers into it too — a few hours with a messy, crying child isn't going to prepare you <u>for the challenges of raising a family</u>, because you're never going to want to have a family at all.

- This answer is mostly well-matched to its form (a broadsheet newspaper article), and shows a good awareness of purpose (to persuade and entertain) and audience (readers of a broadsheet newspaper).

- It also uses a variety of language techniques effectively (e.g. similes, hyperbole and rhetorical questions).

- The structure is good too. It's written in clear paragraphs, with an engaging introduction and conclusion.

- To get the very top marks, this answer could use some more ambitious vocabulary and punctuation. The second paragraph would also need to be better-matched to the form in the question.

Exam-Style Questions

These questions will help you to prepare for any non-fiction writing questions that come up in your exams. Make sure you spend a few minutes making a brief plan for each of your answers — in the real exam, there will be marks for writing a well-organised, well-structured response.

Q1

Write an article for a broadsheet newspaper arguing that the rise in the use of tablet computers and smartphones is bad for the nation's health.

Q2

One of your classmates has said: "I think going to bed early is a waste of time. All the good television programmes are on late at night."

Write a speech in which you try to persuade your class that it's important to get a full night's sleep.

Q3

"Young people should widen their horizons. It's important that they travel and experience new cultures before they start their adult life."

Write a piece of travel writing in which you explain your point of view on this statement.

Q4

A proposal has been made to build multiple new houses in a rural area near you.

You have decided to write a letter to your local newspaper editor explaining your point of view on this proposal. You could write in favour of or against the proposal.

Write a letter to the newspaper giving your views.

Revision Summary

Have a go at these questions to test your knowledge of Section Four.
And no peeking at the section while you do them. That's cheating.

1) What would be the purpose of an answer to this question?
   Write the opening of a short story about a lost pet.

2) True or false? *You never have to work out the audience in a writing question — it will be stated for you explicitly every time.*

3) What three things do you always need to match to your purpose and audience?

4) Give two ways in which you could start a story so that it's engaging for the reader.

5) Rewrite this sentence so that it has a first-person narrative viewpoint.
   Frances skulked down the hallway, delaying her arrival at her Maths classroom.

6) Give one effect of using a third-person narrative viewpoint.

7) Which of these would not be a good way to end a story?
   a) A question that creates a cliffhanger.
   b) An unexpected plot twist to shock the reader.
   c) And they all lived happily ever after.

8) True or false? *You don't need to include as much plot or action when writing a description.*

9) If you're asked to write a description of a character, you might describe their physical features.
   a) What's another thing you could describe about them?
   b) Write a brief description of a famous person.

10) Give two layout features that you could include in a newspaper article.

11) What is a broadsheet newspaper?

12) Name two structural features that you could use to break up information in a leaflet.

13) What would be the form and purpose, and who would be the audience, in an answer to this exam question?
    "Holidays to Europe are overrated — today's European cities are busy, expensive and dull."
    Imagine you have just visited a city in Europe. Write an article for a travel magazine in which you explain your point of view on this statement.

14) Briefly describe the logical structure you should use when writing a report or an essay.

15) What is the main difference between a report and an essay?

16) How should your style of writing be different in a game review for a teen magazine, and an album review for a broadsheet newspaper?

17) What is usually your main purpose when you're writing a speech?

18) Write down an example opening and ending for:
    a) a letter to a local councillor, arguing in favour of building a new shopping centre near where you live
    b) a letter to a named teacher, asking for an extension on your homework deadline.

Introduction to English Literature

It's time to get to grips with English Literature. You'll probably have to sit two exams — here's what to expect...

You'll study a Range of Texts for GCSE English Literature

1) If you're taking English Literature, you'll study a wide range of poetry, prose and drama. The texts you'll have to study, and answer questions on, are:

- a Shakespeare play — e.g. 'Macbeth', 'The Merchant of Venice'.
- a novel from the 19th century — e.g. 'A Christmas Carol', 'Jane Eyre'.
- a modern (post-1914) play or novel — e.g. 'Blood Brothers', 'Animal Farm'.
- an anthology of poetry written between 1789 and now.

Sections Five, Six and Seven are full of advice on writing about prose and drama. Sections Eight and Nine will help you with poetry questions.

2) In the exam, you'll also have to write about unseen poems — poems you haven't studied in class.

- For most exam boards there will be two unseen poems — you'll have to analyse and compare them.
- For other exam boards there might be a question on an unseen poem that you have to compare with a poem you have studied.

Section Ten is all about preparing for the unseen poetry part of your course.

3) Some exam boards will give you an extract from a novel or play you haven't studied, which you'll have to compare with a text you have studied. Ask your teacher exactly what you'll have to do in the exam.

Assessment Objectives are the Skills you need for the Exam

1) The assessment objectives cover all the things you need to do to get a good grade in the exams. They are:

AO1
- Give your own thoughts and opinions on the text.
- Back up your interpretations using evidence from the text (e.g. quotes).

AO2
- Explain how writers use language, structure and form, and what effect this has on the reader.
- Use technical terms to support your analysis.

AO3
- Show that you understand how the text relates to the context in which it was written or set.

AO3 and AO4 aren't assessed on every question — check with your teacher if you want to know where they're assessed.

AO4
- Use a range of sentence structures and vocabulary, so that your writing is clear and effective.
- Write accurately, paying particular attention to spelling, punctuation and grammar.
- AO4 counts for 5% of your overall mark — flick to Section Eleven for advice on writing well.

You don't need to remember the assessment objectives word for word...

There's no need to memorise these assessment objectives — they're just here to give you an idea of the things you need to think about when you're revising, and when you're writing your answers in the exam.

Writing About Prose and Drama

Prose and drama are similar in lots of ways, so this section covers some of the common features found in the two types of text. Sections Six (drama) and Seven (prose) deal with issues specific to each type of writing.

Questions could be about **Themes**, **Characters** or **Settings**

1) Read the question <u>carefully</u> to make sure you're clear on <u>what</u> it is asking you to focus on. This could be:

- the <u>personality</u> of a <u>character</u>
- a specific <u>mood</u> or <u>atmosphere</u>
- a specific <u>theme</u> or <u>message</u>
- <u>attitudes</u> towards a theme or issue
- <u>relationships</u> between <u>characters</u>

2) Most questions will ask you to <u>comment</u> on <u>how</u> the writer <u>presents</u> something to the reader. This means that you need to focus on <u>language</u>, <u>structure</u> and <u>form</u>. Here are some <u>examples</u> of the <u>types</u> of question that might come up in the exam:

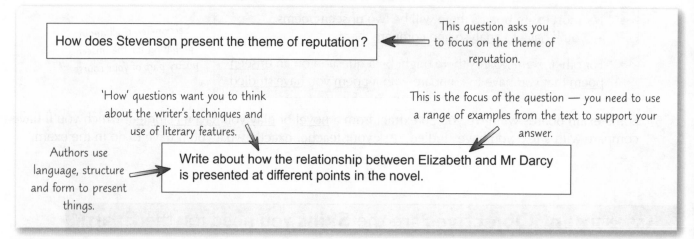

> How does Stevenson present the theme of reputation?

This question asks you to focus on the theme of reputation.

'How' questions want you to think about the writer's techniques and use of literary features.

This is the focus of the question — you need to use a range of examples from the text to support your answer.

Authors use language, structure and form to present things.

> Write about how the relationship between Elizabeth and Mr Darcy is presented at different points in the novel.

Some questions ask about an **Extract** from the **Text**

1) The exam question might ask you to focus on the <u>whole text</u>, an <u>extract</u> from the text, or <u>both</u>.

2) If you're asked to write about an extract, it's <u>doubly important</u> to focus on things like <u>language</u>, <u>structure</u> and <u>form</u>. The examiner knows that you've got the text in front of you, so they're expecting you to <u>pick out</u> and <u>explain</u> some of the features in it.

You could get a question asking you to compare an extract from the text you've studied with an extract from a different text. Make sure you read the instructions carefully.

3) Here is an <u>example</u> of the <u>type</u> of question that might come up:

It's clear that you need to focus only on the extract. Don't make any points about the rest of the text.

> Write about the presentation of childhood in this extract.
>
> Focus only on the extract below rather than the rest of the text you've studied.

This means that you need to explore how the theme is presented in the extract <u>and</u> in the rest of the text.

> Using the extract below as a starting point, write about how Dickens presents the theme of justice in 'Great Expectations'.

Writing About Prose and Drama

Make sure you **Answer** the **Question** you're given

1) It's important to focus on the <u>question</u> — read it <u>carefully</u> a couple of times <u>before</u> planning your answer.

2) Some questions might give you <u>bullet points</u> of things to consider when writing your essay.
   If there <u>aren't</u> any bullet points, then it might be useful to <u>write</u> some of your <u>own</u>, for example:

> Explore how Brontë presents the character of Mrs Reed in 'Jane Eyre'.
>
> • What does Mrs Reed say and do in the novel?   • How does she treat other characters?
> • How does Brontë want the reader to feel about Mrs Reed? How does she achieve this?

3) Make sure <u>everything</u> you write in your essay <u>answers the question</u>
   — irrelevant points <u>won't</u> get you any <u>marks</u>.

Mrs Reed is Jane's aunt. She lives at Gateshead Hall with her children: John, Eliza and Georgiana.	This is <u>too general</u> — it doesn't tell you anything about <u>how</u> Brontë presents the character of Mrs Reed.
Brontë presents Mrs Reed as a stern, bitter character, who treats the young Jane with "miserable cruelty". →	This is much better — it <u>comments</u> on the <u>presentation</u> of Mrs Reed's character and includes a <u>quote</u> from the text to support the point.

Make sure you **Know** the text in **Detail**

1) You need to show the examiner that you know the text <u>really well</u>,
   and that you understand <u>what happens</u> and the <u>order</u> it happens in.

2) Make sure you're familiar with <u>all</u> the <u>characters</u> in the text — the examiner will be
   impressed if you make references to the <u>minor characters</u> as well as the major ones.

See pages 76-77 for more on writing about characters.

3) Learn some key <u>quotes</u> from the text that you can use in your essay to <u>support</u> your points.

Introduce some of your **Own Ideas**

1) Write about your <u>personal response</u> to the text. Think about what <u>emotions</u>
   it evokes and whether you <u>like</u> or <u>empathise</u> with certain characters.

The reader feels sympathetic towards Pip as he reads the names of his dead parents on the gravestone.	Don't use "I" when you're talking about your personal response — use "<u>the reader</u>" when you're writing about a novel and "<u>the audience</u>" for plays.

2) To get a <u>top grade</u>, you need to find something <u>original</u> to say about the text.
   You can make whatever point you like, as long as you can <u>back it up</u> with <u>evidence</u> from the text.

The best way to keep focused on the question is to write a plan...

Take a couple of minutes at the start of each question to plan how you're going to write your answer.
It will help you get all of your ideas down before you begin and keep you focused on the question.

Writing About Characters

You need to know about something called 'characterisation' — this means the methods that an author uses to convey information about, or make the reader feel a certain way about, a character in the text.

Characters are always there for a **Reason**

1) When you're answering a question about a character, bear in mind that characters always have a purpose.

2) This means that you can't talk about them as if they're real people — make it clear that the author has created them to help get a message across.

3) A character's appearance, actions and language all help to get this message across.

Find bits where the writer **Describes** the characters

Find descriptions of how the characters look, and then think about what this might say about them.

> In 'Lord of the Flies,' Golding's description of Jack's face as "crumpled" and "ugly without silliness" implies that he might have a sinister and unpleasant personality.

Look at the way characters **Act** and **Speak**

1) Look at what characters do, and then consider what that says about them.

2) Try to work out why a character does something. Most characters are motivated by a variety of things, but there's usually one main driving force behind what they do.

> In 'Romeo and Juliet', Tybalt's confrontational and violent actions (e.g. stabbing Mercutio) are ultimately driven by his fierce loyalty to the Capulets.

3) The way characters, including the narrator, speak tells you a lot about them.

4) Remember to think about why the author is making their characters speak the way they do. Think about how the author wants you, the reader, to perceive the character.

> In 'An Inspector Calls', Birling repeatedly shouts "Rubbish!" to dismiss what other people have said. But he finishes his own sentences with "of course", to make his own claims seem obvious and matter-of-fact. This means that the audience perceives him to be arrogant and opinionated.

Look at how the characters treat **Other People**

The writer can tell you a lot about their characters by showing you how they get on with others. It can reveal sides to their character that they keep hidden from the other main characters.

> My rage was without bounds; I sprang on him, impelled by all the feelings which can arm one being against the existence of another.

$\implies$ In 'Frankenstein', Victor is kind and polite to most of the characters in the novel, but his attack on the monster reveals his concealed anger and violence.

Writing About Characters

Make sure you're **Prepared** for **Character Questions**

Characters are <u>key elements</u> of any text, so it's not really a surprise that examiners <u>enjoy</u> asking about them in exams. Here are some <u>important questions</u> to think about when you're <u>studying</u> or <u>revising</u> characters:

Why is the character important?

- How do they affect the <u>plot</u>?
- Do they represent a particular <u>point of view</u>?
- What would <u>happen</u> if they <u>weren't there</u>?

Madame is a key character in 'Never Let Me Go' — she provides a link with the world outside Hailsham, and her apparent disgust with the children hints at the wider world's perception of them.

Does the character change over the course of the story?

- Does the character <u>learn anything</u>?
- Does their <u>personality</u> or <u>behaviour</u> change?
- Are the changes <u>positive</u> or <u>negative</u>?
- How do these changes <u>affect</u> the character?

Over the course of 'A Christmas Carol', Ebenezer Scrooge becomes more charitable, generous and empathetic thanks to his experiences with the ghosts. This contrasts with the miserly and selfish character the reader meets at the start of the book.

How does the writer reveal the character's personality?

- <u>How</u> are the character's actions and experiences <u>presented</u> to the reader?
- Is the <u>reader's view</u> of the character the <u>same</u> as other <u>characters' view</u> of them?

The cold-hearted nature of Estella in 'Great Expectations' is revealed by her frequent attempts to "deceive and entrap" men. The reader is able to see her true nature more clearly than Pip, who is blinded by his love for her.

How is the character similar or different to other characters?

- How does the character <u>relate</u> to <u>other characters</u>?
- Do <u>differences</u> between characters <u>impact</u> on the <u>plot</u>?
- What is the writer <u>showing</u> us through these differences?

In some ways, Linda turns into Mrs Johnstone in 'Blood Brothers', becoming a housewife at a young age whilst also having to provide for the family.

Does the reader like or sympathise with the character?

- <u>Why</u> does the reader <u>feel</u> that way about the character?
- <u>How</u> does the writer <u>shape</u> the reader's feelings about the character?
- How does the reader's <u>opinion</u> of the character <u>affect</u> their opinion of the <u>text</u> as a whole?

The reader sympathises with Meena in 'Anita and Me' because her loyalty and trust is betrayed by Anita. Having the narrative in Meena's voice helps create empathy, as it means that Meena's viewpoint is heard throughout.

Always use examples from the text to back up your answer...

You may have lots of great ideas about a character, but the examiner will only take you seriously if you support your ideas with evidence. Learning quotes about a character is a good way to prepare for this.

The Writer's Techniques

There are lots of marks available in English Literature for commenting on the way writers use language.

Analysing the writer's use of **Language** is key

1) Writers <u>select</u> the <u>language</u> they use carefully — it's up to you to work out <u>why</u> they've chosen a particular <u>word</u> or <u>phrase</u>, and to explain the <u>effect</u> that it has.

2) Look out for any <u>interesting</u>, <u>unusual</u> or <u>specialist vocabulary</u> — think about why it's been used. Take note of any <u>repeated</u> words and phrases too — they will have been repeated for a <u>reason</u>.

> *Anita Rutter laughs "in reverberated echo as the heavens slowly crumbled and fell".* → In 'Anita and Me', Syal uses <u>mythological</u> language to show how <u>powerful</u> Anita is in relation to Meena — she is described as if she were a <u>god</u>.

3) Examining the language used by <u>characters</u> is really important — think about the <u>way</u> characters speak, <u>why</u> they speak in that way and whether the way they speak is <u>different</u> to other characters.

> *"D' they call y' Eddie?"*
>
> *"Gis a sweet"* → In 'Blood Brothers', Russell uses <u>informal</u>, <u>colloquial</u> language for the Johnstone family — they <u>omit letters</u> off the end of words and use <u>non-standard pronouns</u>. This language is used to reflect their <u>social class</u>.

> *Hyde speaks "with a flush of anger" and makes inhuman noises, e.g. he screams in "animal terror".* → In 'Dr Jekyll and Mr Hyde', Stevenson uses language to reinforce Hyde's <u>incivility</u> — Hyde does not speak as gentlemen were expected to, suggesting to other characters that something is <u>not right</u>.

Look out for **Imagery**

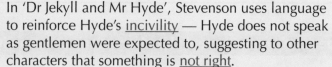

Imagery is particularly common in prose texts, but it does crop up in plays too — Shakespeare uses lots of it.

1) <u>Imagery</u> is when an author uses <u>language</u> to create a <u>picture</u> in the reader's mind, or to describe something more <u>vividly</u>. It can add to the reader's or the audience's <u>understanding</u> of the story.

2) <u>Similes</u> describe something by saying that it's <u>like</u> something else:

> *No one can conceive the variety of feelings which bore me onwards, <u>like a hurricane</u>, in the first enthusiasm of success.* → In 'Frankenstein', Shelley uses the simile "like a hurricane" to <u>emphasise</u> the <u>power</u> of Victor's <u>feelings</u>.

3) <u>Metaphors</u> describe something by saying it <u>is</u> something else:

> *The <u>instruments of darkness</u> tell us truths.* → In 'Macbeth', Banquo's <u>suspicion</u> of the three Witches is shown by his use of the metaphor "instruments of darkness" to describe them.

4) <u>Personification</u> describes something (e.g. an animal, object or aspect of nature) as if it were <u>human</u>:

> *It was a wild, cold, seasonable night of March, with a pale moon, <u>lying on her back</u>...* → In 'Dr Jekyll and Mr Hyde', the <u>personification</u> of the moon makes it seem that the whole world has been <u>turned upside down</u> by Jekyll's secret.

The Writer's Techniques

Comment on **Sentence Structure**

1) It's not just particular words and phrases that you can comment on — you should also look at how writers use <u>sentences</u> and <u>paragraphs</u> to reinforce their points.

And among us animals let there be perfect unity, perfect comradeship in the struggle. All men are enemies.	In 'Animal Farm', Old Major uses a mix of <u>long</u> and <u>short sentences</u>, as well as <u>rhetoric</u>, to make his speech <u>persuasive</u>.

2) Different <u>sentence lengths</u> create different <u>effects</u>, e.g. a succession of <u>short</u> sentences could build <u>tension</u> or <u>excitement</u>, whereas <u>long</u> sentences might show a character getting <u>carried away</u> with their <u>emotions</u>.

"Seen him?" repeated Mr Utterson. "Well?" *"That's it!" said Poole. "It was this way."*	At the climax of 'Dr Jekyll and Mr Hyde', the characters talk in <u>short bursts</u>. This creates <u>suspense</u> by suggesting that events are happening at a <u>fast pace</u>.

There were great round, pot-bellied baskets of chestnuts, shaped like the waistcoats of jolly old gentlemen, lolling at the doors, and tumbling out into the street in their apoplectic opulence.	In 'A Christmas Carol', Dickens uses <u>long sentences</u> to describe the activity on the streets when Scrooge walks through London. This gives the Christmas scenes a sense of <u>endless</u> cheer, emphasising the joy Scrooge has excluded himself from.

Pay attention to **Descriptions** and **Settings**

1) Writers use <u>settings</u> to influence the way you <u>feel</u> about what's happening.

2) In the exam, you could get a passage that <u>describes</u> one of the settings from the text and be asked to talk about how the author has used it to create <u>atmosphere</u>.

3) You need to look at the writer's <u>descriptions</u> and think about <u>why</u> they have been included and <u>what effect</u> they have.

Alleys and archways, like so many cesspools, disgorged their offences of smell, and dirt, and life, upon the straggling streets.	In 'A Christmas Carol', Dickens uses descriptive language to present his reader with a <u>realistic</u>, <u>harsh</u> vision of <u>poverty</u> in London.

I did not dare return to the apartment which I inhabited, but felt impelled to hurry on, although drenched by the rain which poured from a black and comfortless sky.	In 'Frankenstein', this <u>bleak</u> and <u>dismal</u> setting reflects Victor's <u>hopeless and gloomy mood</u>.

When shall we three meet again? *In thunder, lightning, or in rain?* *Hover through the fog and filthy air.*	In 'Macbeth', the Witches repeatedly describe the <u>bad weather</u>. This reflects the <u>sinister atmosphere</u> created by the Witches' arrival.

The Writer's Techniques

Writers can present their ideas using **Symbolism**

1) Symbols can be used to reinforce the <u>themes</u> that run through a text. Look out for things that could be a <u>symbol</u> for something else, e.g. a <u>thunderstorm</u> could be a symbol for <u>destruction</u>.

> *In 'An Inspector Calls', Priestley uses Eva Smith as a symbol. Her first name sounds like 'Eve', the first woman (in the Biblical account of creation), which suggests she symbolises all women. Her surname is very common and it's also the word for a tradesman, which implies that she represents all ordinary, working-class women.*

> *In 'Great Expectations', the size and splendour of Satis House symbolises the wealth and grandeur of the upper classes. However, it is crumbling and run-down, which could symbolise their decay.*

2) Symbols are often used to create <u>additional meanings</u>. If the literal meaning of a sentence sounds strange, try to work out whether there's another layer of meaning.

> *This boy is Ignorance. This girl is Want. Beware them both...* In 'A Christmas Carol', Dickens uses the characters of Ignorance and Want to <u>symbolise</u> the <u>problems</u> caused by society's neglect of the <u>poor</u>.

Structure is always important

1) <u>Structure</u> is the <u>order</u> that events happen in. Make sure you think about how a writer has put a text together, and what the <u>effect</u> of this is.

2) Structural devices can be used to make a text more <u>interesting</u>. For example:

There's more information about the structure of plays on p.90 and prose texts on p.100.

- <u>foreshadowing</u> gives <u>hints</u> about what will happen <u>later on</u> in the story.

> *In 'Never Let Me Go', Kathy frequently hints at how significant the character of Madame is to the students' lives, but her exact role in the system is not revealed until near the end of the novel. This creates suspense, as the reader waits for the mystery of the students' existence and Madame's role in their lives to be resolved.*

- <u>flashbacks</u> temporarily <u>shift</u> the story back in time, often showing something from the <u>past</u> that is significant in the <u>present</u>.

> *The opening of 'The History Boys' shows Irwin in a wheelchair, before Bennett moves time backwards twenty years and Irwin is able to walk. The audience is therefore left wondering what happens to Irwin and expects that something is going to occur during the course of the play to explain his disability.*

Remember to write about the effect on the reader...

It's important to refer to the techniques that the writer uses, but if you want the top marks you'll also need to mention how those techniques affect the reader (or the audience if it's a play).

Context

Texts are influenced by the time and place they're written and set in, as well as by the person who wrote them. You need to consider these influences for each text you study.

Texts are shaped by the **Context** they were written in

1) Think about the <u>setting</u> of the <u>text</u> and <u>what was happening</u> when it was written.

2) Here are a few <u>questions</u> you should ask yourself when thinking about <u>context</u>:

Where is the text set?
Did the writer base the <u>setting</u> on their own experiences?

When was the text written?
- <u>What was happening</u> at the time the text was written?
- What was <u>society</u> like?

When does the story take place?
Did the writer base the story in the <u>time</u> in which they lived or a different time?

What do you know about the writer?
- Where is the writer <u>from</u>?
- What is their <u>background</u>?

What genre is the text part of?
- Is the text part of a <u>literary movement</u>?
- Was the writer <u>influenced</u> by other texts?

Show you're aware of the **Issues** the text raises

1) You need to show the examiner that you're aware of the <u>wider issues</u> raised by the text, and <u>comment</u> on how these issues are <u>portrayed</u> in the text.

2) Here are some of the <u>issues</u> that you should look out for:

Social or cultural issues
Authors often <u>comment</u> on the <u>society</u> they're living in, particularly the <u>faults</u> they associate with it. → *'Blood Brothers' examines social class, and how it can determine the course of people's lives.*

Historical or political issues
Writers may focus on a particular <u>historical situation</u> or <u>political issue</u>. → *George Orwell wrote 'Animal Farm' in 1945 as an allegory for events which took place around that time in Communist Russia.*

Moral issues
Sometimes a text aims to challenge the reader with a <u>moral message</u>. → *'Frankenstein' raises the question of whether advances in science are beneficial or dangerous for mankind.*

Philosophical issues
Some writers explore a <u>philosophical question</u> through their texts. → *In 'Romeo and Juliet', Shakespeare questions what romantic love actually is.*

A little research can go a long way...
Whatever text you're studying, you'll need to think about the writer, the period in which it was written and set, and the issues it raises. Taking some time to research a few key facts will help improve your grades.

Themes and the Writer's Message

Texts don't just tell a story — they explore significant issues and questions.

Think about the **Themes** of the text

1) Texts usually have something to say about the <u>society</u> in which they were <u>written</u> or <u>set</u>.

2) Think carefully about the <u>themes</u> of the text, and what the writer might have been <u>saying</u> about them.

Fate

- Do we control our own lives or are they controlled by fate? *Characters in 'Romeo and Juliet' blame fate for their problems. This makes the audience question whether what is happening is indeed down to fate or whether the characters should take responsibility for their actions.*

Gender

- How do the lives of men and women differ?
- What is the impact of gender inequality? *In 'Pride and Prejudice', the Bennet sisters cannot inherit their father's estate because they are female. Their best chance of independence and financial security is to marry well.*

Social Class

- What is the impact of social class on characters' lives?
- Is it right that social class is so important? *In 'An Inspector Calls', Priestley contrasts the actions and qualities of the working-class characters with those of the middle classes to highlight the unfairness of the class system.*

Ambition

- Is ambition healthy or destructive?
- How can we control our ambition? *By showing Macbeth's downfall, Shakespeare gives the audience a warning about the destructive nature of ambition.*

Love

- What is the true nature of love?
- How far will we go to pursue love? *In 'Much Ado About Nothing', Shakespeare contrasts Claudio's shallow, fickle feelings for Hero with the deep love that develops between Beatrice and Benedick.*

Work out the writer's **Overall Message**

1) Think about <u>why</u> the writer might have <u>written</u> the book or play.

2) Look at the <u>issues</u> and <u>questions</u> the text raises.

Dickens' message in 'A Christmas Carol' is that the rich have a duty to help those less fortunate than themselves.

The central message of 'Lord of the Flies' is that all humans have evil inside them and are capable of committing terrible deeds.

You need to study the text carefully to work out the message...

It might take a while to work out the writer's overall message, so make sure you read the text carefully. The fates of characters, significant passages of speech and the ending of the text are all worth examining.

Using Quotations

You're not allowed to take any of your texts into the exam, so you're going to need to learn some quotations...

Learn **Key Quotations** that are relevant to **Characters** and **Themes**

1) When you're reading a text, make a <u>note</u> of some <u>good quotes</u> to learn. Examiners aren't expecting you to memorise big chunks of text, so the quotes you pick out should be <u>short</u> and <u>snappy</u>.

2) You need to use the quotes to <u>back up</u> the <u>points</u> in your essay, so make sure the quotes you choose are <u>relevant</u> to things you're likely to write about in the exam, e.g. a <u>key character</u>, <u>theme</u> or <u>technique</u>.

3) When you're <u>revising</u>, it's a good idea to make <u>lists</u> of <u>key quotes</u> for each theme or character.

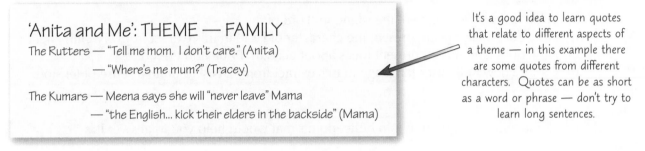

'Anita and Me': THEME — FAMILY

The Rutters — "Tell me mom. I don't care." (Anita)
— "Where's me mum?" (Tracey)

The Kumars — Meena says she will "never leave" Mama
— "the English... kick their elders in the backside" (Mama)

It's a good idea to learn quotes that relate to different aspects of a theme — in this example there are some quotes from different characters. Quotes can be as short as a word or phrase — don't try to learn long sentences.

Embed **Short Quotations** into your sentences

Quoting from Shakespeare is covered on page 92.

1) The <u>best</u> way to use quotes is to <u>embed</u> (insert) them into your <u>sentences</u>. This just means that they should be a <u>natural part</u> of a sentence, allowing you to go on to <u>explain</u> how the quote <u>supports</u> your <u>point</u>.

In 'An Inspector Calls', the Inspector describes Eva positively, calling her "<u>pretty</u>" and "<u>lively</u>", which makes the audience feel more sympathetic towards her.

2) Using shorter quotations allows you to explain the <u>same point</u> in <u>fewer words</u>.

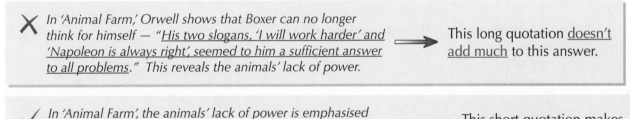

✗ *In 'Animal Farm', Orwell shows that Boxer can no longer think for himself — "<u>His two slogans, 'I will work harder' and 'Napoleon is always right', seemed to him a sufficient answer to all problems</u>." This reveals the animals' lack of power.*

This long quotation <u>doesn't add much</u> to this answer.

✓ *In 'Animal Farm', the animals' lack of power is emphasised by Boxer's repetition of "<u>Napoleon is always right</u>", which shows that he can no longer think for himself.*

This short quotation makes this answer much <u>snappier</u>.

3) If you get an <u>extract question</u> (see page 74) make sure you quote <u>accurately</u> from the text you're given. But <u>don't be tempted</u> to quote huge chunks of text — always be <u>selective</u> with the quotes you use and make sure you explain their <u>significance</u> or <u>effect</u>.

When it comes to quotations, try to keep them short...

When you're revising quotations, there's no point learning long chunks of text — short phrases or single words are easier to learn. They'll also help keep your answers concise, which will please the examiners.

Warm-Up Questions

You'll need your set texts to hand when you're answering these questions, but don't worry — you don't need to write any long answers (yet). If you don't know what texts you're studying, now would be a good time to find out from your teacher.

Warm-Up Questions

1) Look at the different types of question in the box and read the sample questions below. For each sample question, write down what type of question you think it is.

   - **theme**   • **setting**   • **characterisation**   • **writer's techniques**

   a) What is the significance of the island in 'Lord of the Flies'?
   b) How does Shakespeare present the character of Feste in this extract from 'Twelfth Night'?
   c) How does Jane Austen present ideas about class in 'Pride and Prejudice'?
   d) Explore how Kelly uses language in this extract from 'DNA' to build a sense of tension.

2) Break the following question into bullet points that would help you to answer it:

   Does Shakespeare present fate as a stronger force than free will?

3) Choose a character from one of the texts you have studied.
   Find five key quotations which illustrate something about their personality.
   Write a sentence explaining what each quotation tells you about them.

4) For the character you chose in question 3, explain how you feel about that character and how the author has made you feel that way.
   Use evidence from the text to back up your argument.

5) Using one of your set texts, find one example of:
   a) simile
   b) metaphor
   c) personification

6) Choose an extract from a text you have studied in class, in which the writer builds a particular atmosphere (e.g. frightening, gloomy, joyful).
   Explain how the writer creates that atmosphere, and what effect it has on the reader.
   Remember to use evidence from the text to back up your argument.

7) Using a text you have studied in class, identify an unusual structural feature (e.g. an instance of foreshadowing, a flashback or a jump in time).
   Write a short paragraph describing the feature and explaining its effect.

Warm-Up Questions

8) Read the passages below. For each one, write a sentence or two stating what you think each object or action in bold is a symbol for, and explaining your view.

   a) *In 'Lord of the Flies', the boys use the* **conch shell** *to bring order to their meetings — whoever is holding it is allowed to speak, while everyone else has to keep quiet and listen.*

   b) *In 'Jane Eyre', Mr Rochester proposes to Jane underneath the old* **chestnut tree** *in the grounds of Thornfield. That night, the tree is struck by lightning and split down the middle. Later, Jane discovers that Mr Rochester is already married, so she refuses to marry him and runs away.*

   c) *In 'Never Let Me Go', the students are forced into a particular way of life over which they have very little control. When they discuss their futures, many of them claim that they would like to have jobs that involve* **driving***.*

9) Choose a text you have studied in class and answer the following questions about it.
   a) When was the text written? Is it set at this time or in a different period?
   b) How does the writer portray the time in which the text is set?
   c) Do the characters encounter any problems related to the text's context, e.g. based on class, race or gender?

10) Choose a text you have studied in class. Write down three of the text's key themes (e.g. social class, gender, power). For each theme, write down an example from the text and explain how it relates to the theme. ←

Your examples for this question could be events in the story, characters' reactions to events, or quotes from the text.

11) Think about two of your set texts. What do you think the message of each one is?

12) Which of the following paragraphs shows a better use of quotations? Explain your answer.

   a) *In 'Anita and Me', Meena has unrealistic, childish dreams of what her future holds. She describes winning a talent show and becoming a "major personality" as her "most realistic escape route" from her current life.*

   b) *In 'Anita and Me', Meena has unrealistic, childish dreams of what her future holds. She watches a talent show and says "I knew that this could be my most realistic escape route from Tollington, from ordinary girl to major personality in one easy step."*

Exam-Style Questions

Writing about texts is an acquired skill — you can only get better at it by practising. The next two sections go into more detail about drama and prose, and you'll find some practice exam questions at the end of each section. To get you into the swing of it, have a go at answering these. You should be able to answer all of them, no matter which exam board you're doing.

Q1 Choose a character from a Shakespeare play you have studied. Focusing on one scene in the play, explain how Shakespeare uses language to show the character's personality.

Q2 Choose a passage from a prose text you have read which you find particularly tense or exciting. Write about the methods the author has used to create tension or excitement in the passage.

Q3 Choose a drama text that you have studied. Explore how the author presents **either** power **or** love **or** social class.

Q4 Choose a 19th-century text that you have studied. How are ideas about society important to the text? You must refer to the context of the text in your answer.

Revision Summary

There's just one page left till this section is over. Keep going — these questions are a great measure of what you've taken in. If you get stuck on any of the questions, have another read of the relevant page, then try again. You should be able to answer questions like these in your sleep...

1) What is the most important thing to do when making a point in an answer?
   a) Make sure it answers the question.
   b) Make sure it refers to context.
   c) Only have one point per paragraph.

2) You've decided which exam question you are going to answer. What should you do before you start planning your answer?

3) Which of the following sentences is better to include in an essay?
   a) *The foreshadowing in 'Never Let Me Go' meant I was intrigued about the story —*
      I wanted to keep reading.
   b) *The use of foreshadowing in 'Never Let Me Go' creates intrigue, and makes the reader*
      want to find out more.

4) What is characterisation?

5) Give three examples of things you could write about when answering a question about a particular character.

6) What is the difference between a simile and a metaphor?

7) What is the word given to the type of imagery where something (like an animal or object) is described as if it were human?

8) Why might a writer choose to use a shorter sentence instead of a longer sentence?

9) Write a brief explanation of what authors can use settings for.

10) Explain what symbolism is. Give an example of a symbol from a text you have studied.

11) What is foreshadowing?

12) What are flashbacks?
    a) Times when a character's vision goes blank for a couple of seconds and then returns.
    b) Moments when the writer describes something as if it were a human.
    c) Parts where the scene shifts to an earlier time.

13) Give three questions to ask yourself when thinking about the context of a text.

14) Give three examples of themes that are often addressed in texts.

15) Message questions can be hard to spot — but what is the one thing they'll all essentially be asking you?

16) When quoting a text, why should you try to include short quotations rather than long quotations?

17) Give two examples of things you need to be especially careful of when quoting from the text to answer an extract question.

Reading Plays

Writers use stage directions to show what's happening on stage. Different types of speech give clues about a character's personality, their relationships with other characters and their innermost thoughts.

Stage Directions describe the action on stage

Stage directions are usually written in italics or put in brackets to distinguish them from things that are said.

1) When you're reading a play, look out for the <u>stage directions</u>.
    These are <u>instructions</u> from the <u>playwright</u> to the director and the actors
    — they can tell you a lot about <u>how</u> the playwright wants the play to be <u>performed</u>.

2) There are lots of things to look out for in the stage directions. For example, <u>music</u> and <u>sound effects</u> might be used to create a specific <u>mood</u>, or the <u>set</u> may be designed to create a certain <u>atmosphere</u>.

A bass note, repeated as a heartbeat.	In 'Blood Brothers', Russell uses <u>music</u> to build <u>tension</u>. This stage direction emphasises the significance of the moment, and highlights Mrs Johnstone's <u>fear</u>.

3) Stage directions can also describe the characters' <u>actions</u> and the use of <u>props</u>.

Christopher puts his hands over his ears. He closes his eyes... He starts groaning.	In 'The Curious Incident of the Dog in the Night-Time', Stephens uses stage directions to <u>tell</u> the actor playing Christopher <u>how to act</u>, and to give the audience an insight into the character's <u>personality</u>.

Stage directions reveal what the writer **Wants**

You should write about how the stage directions reveal the playwright's <u>intentions</u>.

Action

We see Mickey comb the town, breaking through groups of people, looking, searching, desperate... *('Blood Brothers' — Willy Russell)*	These stage directions <u>describe</u> what's happening on stage — Mickey's desperate search makes this scene <u>dramatic</u>.

Staging

The dining-room of a fairly large suburban house... It has good solid furniture... *('An Inspector Calls' — J. B. Priestley)*	In these opening stage directions, Priestley establishes <u>how</u> he would like the <u>set</u> to <u>look</u>. The set reflects the <u>class</u> and <u>status</u> of the Birlings.

Characterisation

Jo dances on dreamily. *('A Taste of Honey' — Shelagh Delaney)*	This stage direction occurs after Jo has agreed to <u>marry</u> her boyfriend. It hints at her <u>longing to escape</u> and her <u>dreams</u> of a better life.

Dialogue

Irwin *(thoughtfully) That's very true.* *('The History Boys' — Alan Bennett)*	The stage direction here tells the actor playing Irwin <u>how</u> he should <u>deliver</u> his line.

Reading Plays

Plays contain **Different** types of **Speech**

1) <u>Dialogue</u> is when two or more characters are speaking.
   It shows how characters <u>interact</u> with each other.

> **Eric** *If you think that's the best she can do —*
> **Sheila** *Don't be an ass, Eric.*
> **Mrs Birling** *Now stop it, you two.*
>
> *('An Inspector Calls' — J.B. Priestley)*

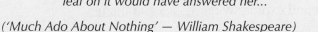

This dialogue hints at the <u>tensions</u> that exist between the characters.

2) A <u>monologue</u> is when <u>one character</u> speaks for a long time and the other characters on stage <u>listen</u> to them.

> **Benedick** *O, she misused me past the endurance of a block! An oak but with one green leaf on it would have answered her...*
>
> *('Much Ado About Nothing' — William Shakespeare)*

After Beatrice offends him, Benedick gives a <u>monologue</u> in which he conveys his <u>frustration</u> to Don Pedro. His <u>exaggerated</u> complaints emphasise the <u>strength</u> of his emotions.

3) In a <u>soliloquy</u>, a <u>single character</u> speaks their <u>thoughts out loud</u> — other characters can't hear them. This reveals to the audience something of the character's <u>inner thoughts</u> and <u>feelings</u>.

> **Mrs Johnstone** *Only mine until*
> *The time comes round*
> *To pay the bill*
>
> *('Blood Brothers' — Willy Russell)*

Mrs Johnstone's song 'Easy Terms' acts as a <u>soliloquy</u> about how she can't keep the things she has bought. Her sorrow is made more <u>poignant</u> by the fact that Mrs Lyons has pressured her into giving up one of her children.

4) An <u>aside</u> is like a soliloquy, but it is usually a <u>shorter comment</u> which is only heard by the <u>audience</u> — other characters don't hear it.

> **Macbeth** *(aside)   Glamis, and Thane of Cawdor:*
> *The greatest is behind. (To Rosse and Angus)*
> *Thanks for your pains.*
>
> *('Macbeth' — William Shakespeare)*

Macbeth's first remarks are heard only by the <u>audience</u>, then he returns to addressing <u>other characters</u>. This allows the audience to see what he is <u>thinking</u>, and emphasises that he is <u>hiding</u> things from the other characters.

Some playwrights use stage directions more than others...

Different writers use different methods. Shakespeare didn't use many stage directions — he relied instead on characters' speech to tell the story. Modern writers tend to use more stage directions than Shakespeare.

Writing About Drama

When you're writing about a play, keep in mind the fact that it's intended to be watched by an audience.

Write about the **Language** of the play

1) You need to write in <u>detail</u> about the <u>language</u> used in the play.

2) Writers often use <u>imagery</u>, like <u>similes</u>, <u>metaphors</u> and <u>personification</u>.

> *My bounty is as boundless as the sea,*
> *My love as deep; the more I give to thee*
> *The more I have, for both are infinite.*
>
> *(Romeo and Juliet, William Shakespeare)*

Juliet uses a <u>simile</u> to compare her love for Romeo to the sea, saying that it is both as endless and as deep.

> *Life's but a walking shadow, a poor player*
> *That struts and frets his hour upon the stage*
> *And then is heard no more.*
>
> *(Macbeth, William Shakespeare)*

Macbeth <u>personifies</u> life, comparing it to an <u>actor</u> whose influence is limited to his time on stage. This shows that Macbeth thinks life is brief and pointless.

3) You also need to write about how playwrights use <u>dialogue</u>, for example how particular scenes are used to develop <u>characters</u>, reveal the <u>plot</u> and explore wider <u>issues</u> and <u>themes</u>.

> **Mrs Lyons** *When are you due?*
> **Mrs Johnstone** *Erm, well, about... Oh, but Mrs...*
> **Mrs Lyons** *Quickly, quickly, tell me...*
>
> *(Blood Brothers, Willy Russell)*

This <u>dialogue</u> shows that Mrs Lyons is more <u>powerful</u> than Mrs Johnstone — her interruption and use of <u>imperatives</u> like "tell me" show that she controls the conversation.

4) Think about the <u>effects</u> the language and dialogue have on the <u>audience</u>.

> *In the opening scene of 'DNA' by Dennis Kelly, Jan and Mark constantly speak over and interrupt one another. This increases the pace of the scene and makes it more difficult for the audience to follow, which helps to convey a sense of the stress and confusion that Jan and Mark are experiencing.*

A play's **Structure** is important too

You need to think about how the play is <u>structured</u>. For example:

1) How does the playwright use <u>act</u> and <u>scene breaks</u>?

> *Each act of 'An Inspector Calls' ends on a cliffhanger, and at the beginning of the next act, the "scene and situation are exactly as they were" at the end of the previous act. This builds the tension and sense of pressure that the Birlings are under.*

2) How does the playwright show <u>changes</u> in <u>time</u>?

> *In 'Blood Brothers', Russell uses a montage (a series of short scenes) to move time forwards four years. The speed at which time passes on stage symbolises the fleetingness of youth, and gives the audience the sense that the play is moving rapidly towards its tragic ending.*

Writing About Drama

Show you know that plays are intended to be **Watched** not **Read**

Plays are written to be <u>acted on stage</u>, not read silently from a book. This means that you shouldn't refer to the '<u>reader</u>' — talk about the '<u>audience</u>' instead.

> *Siobhan acts as a kind of narrator in 'The Curious Incident of the Dog in the Night-Time' — she reads segments of Christopher's work, which helps the audience make sense of what's happening, and gives them an insight into Christopher's mind.*

→ You should comment on how the play works on <u>stage</u> and how this <u>impacts</u> on the <u>audience</u>.

Show you appreciate **Stagecraft**

1) You also need to show that you appreciate the writer's <u>stagecraft</u> — their <u>skill</u> at writing for the <u>stage</u>. Playwrights use features like <u>silences</u>, <u>actions</u> and <u>sound effects</u> to create a mood, reveal something in a certain way or add drama to a situation — these things are usually mentioned in <u>stage directions</u> (see p.88).

2) Appreciating the stagecraft means asking yourself a few <u>key questions</u>:

- How would this scene <u>look on stage</u>?

- How would the <u>audience react</u>?

- Is it <u>effective</u>?

3) Writers might use stagecraft to vary the <u>pace</u> of the play to keep it interesting for the audience. For example, in Act Two of 'Blood Brothers', Russell uses <u>simultaneous conversations</u> to create a fast-paced scene:

> *Mickey and Sammy are speaking on one side of the stage whilst Edward and Linda are speaking on the other side. Both conversations have life-changing consequences, and the combination of the two dialogues emphasises the fact that both twins are at a crossroads in their lives.*

4) Writers can also use stagecraft to increase the <u>tension</u>, particularly at a <u>climactic moment</u> in the play. In the final act of 'Romeo and Juliet', Shakespeare uses <u>dramatic irony</u> to build up the suspense:

> *Romeo fights Paris in the tomb while the audience, knowing that Friar Lawrence is on his way, hope he'll arrive and avert the tragedy. He arrives too late: Romeo has already killed Paris and committed suicide. These events happen in a very short space of time, and the tension is incredible. Even though the audience knows from the start of the play that Romeo and Juliet will both die, we still hope that they won't.*

Dramatic irony is where the audience knows something that a character on stage doesn't know.

Reading the play aloud will help you understand it...

Remember — plays are meant to be watched, not read. Some plays have a particular rhythm to them that is more noticeable when you read them aloud. Reading aloud can also help you to remember key quotes.

Writing About Shakespeare

You'll need to know a bit about Shakespeare for your exam. The next few pages will give you a hand.

Shakespeare's plays can be **Serious** or **Funny**

Make sure you're clear on the <u>genre</u> of the play you're studying:

Tragedy

- <u>Tragedies</u> often focus on <u>big topics</u> — e.g. love, death, war, religion. They are usually about the <u>sad</u> or <u>terrible downfall</u> of the main character.

- Tragedies can be <u>moving</u> and often have a <u>moral message</u>.

- Some of Shakespeare's tragedies are set in an <u>imaginary</u> or <u>historical</u> world. The characters are often <u>kings</u>, <u>queens</u> or other <u>rulers</u>.

- Examples include 'Macbeth' and 'Romeo and Juliet'.

Shakespeare also wrote history plays (e.g. 'Henry V'). These plays are based on real historical events.

Comedy

- <u>Comedies</u> are written to make the audience <u>laugh</u>.

- Events and characters are often <u>silly</u> and <u>exaggerated</u>.

- Comedies can still have a <u>moral message</u> though.

- Examples include 'Much Ado About Nothing' and 'Twelfth Night'.

Make sure you know how to **Quote** from **Shakespeare's Plays**

1) The way you quote something from <u>Shakespeare</u> differs slightly depending on whether the lines are in <u>prose</u> or <u>verse</u> (poetry). If each <u>new line</u> of the text starts with a <u>capital letter</u>, it's <u>verse</u>, but if a new line just <u>carries on</u> from the previous line <u>without</u> a capital letter, it's <u>prose</u>.

2) If it's <u>prose</u>, then just quote as you would do from a <u>novel</u>.

3) If it's <u>verse</u>, then you need to be careful about <u>line breaks</u>. If you quote something that goes over <u>more than one line</u> in the <u>original text</u>, you need to show this using a <u>slash</u> — '/'.

In 'Macbeth', the Witches speak in rhyming couplets, for example, "<u>When the hurly-burly's done, / When the battle's lost and won.</u>" This makes their speech sound unnatural and mysterious.

This answer uses a quote that's in <u>verse</u> and goes over <u>two lines</u>, so it uses a '/' to show where the <u>line break</u> is in the original text.

In 'The Tempest', Trinculo uses exclamation and rhetorical questions, for example, "<u>Out o' your wits and hearing too? A pox o' your bottle!</u>" This highlights his anger at Stephano.

Trinculo speaks in <u>prose</u> in this scene, so there's no need to mark any line breaks in the quote.

Writing About Shakespeare

Show you're aware that Shakespeare was writing **400 Years Ago**

1) Shakespeare (1564-1616) wrote his plays about 400 years ago, so it's not surprising that some of the language, themes and ideas can seem a bit strange to us.

2) He lived at the end of a period of European history known as the Renaissance — a time when there were lots of developments in the arts, politics, religion and science. The theatre was very popular at this time.

3) Shakespeare was aware of his audience when writing his plays. A wide range of people went to watch his plays, from the very rich to servants and labourers. Shakespeare tended to include complex imagery and puns for the educated nobles, and slapstick for the uneducated poor.

4) Many people in Shakespeare's Britain believed in the supernatural — people were executed for witchcraft, and superstitious behaviour was common. Several of Shakespeare's plays have supernatural elements, e.g. the Witches in 'Macbeth' and the spirits in 'The Tempest'. The audience would usually have taken these supernatural characters seriously.

5) Shakespeare was keen to keep the British king or queen of the day happy. His plays often had a royal audience — both Elizabeth I and James I enjoyed performances of his plays.

> *There are many features in 'Macbeth' which could have been included to please King James I. For example, the events following Duncan's murder show the negative consequences for those who try to seize power from the reigning king. James was also obsessed with stamping out witchcraft — Shakespeare's portrayal of the Witches as wholly evil would have pleased the king.*

Learn about **Theatrical Performances** in Shakespeare's time

Knowing a bit about theatrical performances in Shakespeare's time will help you to write top answers about his plays. Here are some of the key features:

1) Only men were allowed to act on stage — all the female roles were played by boys. Shakespeare's comedies include lots of jokes about girls dressing up as boys.

2) Most of the actors wore elaborate costumes that were based on the fashions of when the play was written, and that reflected the status of the character. Plays set overseas, e.g. in ancient Rome or Greece, used costumes appropriate to the location.

3) Musicians helped to create atmosphere in the theatre. They also made sound effects, such as the thunder at the beginning of 'Macbeth'.

4) Plays didn't use much scenery — sets were simple so that they could show different locations in a play, and could be adapted easily to be used for several different plays.

Think about how Shakespeare kept his audience entertained...

When you write about one of Shakespeare's plays, remember that he intended it to be performed on stage. Mentioning how a particular method would have affected the audience is a great way to pick up marks.

Shakespeare's Language

When you're writing about a Shakespeare play, you need to take a close look at the language, and think about the effect it would have on someone watching the play.

Shakespeare uses lots of **Imagery**

Shakespeare's <u>imagery</u> includes similes, metaphors and personification.

> *Now does he feel his title*
> *Hang loose about him, like a giant's robe*
> *Upon a dwarfish thief.*
>
> *'Macbeth' Act 5, Scene 2*

Angus uses a <u>simile</u> to suggest that Macbeth's duties as King are too much for him, like clothes that are too big.

> *With as little a web as this will I*
> *ensnare as great a fly as Cassio.*
>
> *'Othello' Act 2, Scene 1*

Iago uses a <u>metaphor</u> to compare himself to a spider and Cassio to a fly. This shows how easily he believes he will be able to trap Cassio.

Look out for **Striking Words** and **Phrases**

When you read through the text, make a note of any words that <u>jump out at you</u>. Think about why they're important, and what effect they have.

> *If you tickle us, do we not laugh? If you poison us, do*
> *we not die? And if you wrong us, shall we not revenge?*
>
> *'The Merchant of Venice' Act 3, Scene 1*

Shylock's <u>emotive speech</u> uses <u>rhetorical questions</u> to show that as a Jew he's no different to Christians. The mention of <u>revenge</u> hints at his <u>anger</u>.

> *When the battle's lost and won.*
>
> *'Macbeth' Act 1, Scene 1*

The Witches use <u>paradox</u> — this hides their motives from the other characters and the audience, and emphasises that <u>nothing is as it seems</u>.

Humour is also important in Shakespeare's plays

Shakespeare uses lots of <u>puns</u> and <u>jokes</u>. They can help to <u>relieve tension</u>, <u>lighten the mood</u> and highlight <u>key themes</u>.

> *Ask for me tomorrow, and you shall*
> *find me a grave man.*
>
> *'Romeo and Juliet' Act 3, Scene 1*

Mercutio makes a joke about his own <u>death</u>, playing on the <u>double meaning</u> of "grave" ('serious', and 'a place to put dead bodies').

> **Viola** *Save thee, friend, and thy music.*
> *Dost though live by thy tabor?*
> **Feste** *No, sir, I live by the church.*
>
> *'Twelfth Night' Act 3, Scene 1*

Feste plays on the meaning of the phrase "live by" — Viola asks if he <u>makes a living</u> by playing his tabor (drum), and he deliberately <u>misinterprets</u> her, replying that he <u>lives near</u> the church.

Shakespeare's Language

Look at Shakespeare's **Verse Forms**

1) Shakespeare wrote his plays in a mixture of <u>poetry</u> and <u>prose</u>.
You can tell a lot about a <u>character</u> by looking at the <u>way</u> they <u>speak</u>.

2) The majority of Shakespeare's lines are written in <u>blank verse</u> (unrhymed iambic pentameter). Blank verse sounds <u>grander</u> than prose and can be used by almost any characters, but <u>lower-class</u>, <u>comic</u> and <u>mad</u> characters generally <u>don't</u> use it.

> A line written using iambic pentameter usually has 10 syllables (five unstressed and five stressed).

If music be the food of love, play on;
Give me excess of it, that, surfeiting,
The appetite may sicken, and so die.

'Twelfth Night' Act 1, Scene 1

Orsino is a <u>powerful duke</u>, so it is appropriate that he speaks in <u>blank verse</u>. It also makes his speech sound <u>formal</u> and lacking in real <u>passion</u>, which suggests that he's really only in love with the <u>idea</u> of being in love.

3) Sometimes Shakespeare uses <u>rhymed iambic pentameter</u> to make speech sound <u>dramatic</u> and <u>impressive</u>, e.g. at the beginning and end of a scene, or when a posh character is speaking.

From forth the fatal loins of these two foes
A pair of star-cross'd lovers take their life,
Whose misadventur'd piteous overthrows
Doth with their death bury their parents' strife.

'Romeo and Juliet' Prologue

The Prologue acts as an introduction to the play, when the audience are told that Romeo and Juliet are doomed to die. The <u>importance</u> of this message is emphasised by the fact that it is in <u>rhymed iambic pentameter</u>.

4) The rest of Shakespeare's writing is in <u>normal prose</u>. <u>Funny bits</u> and dialogue between more minor or lower-class characters are usually written in prose.

Come hither, neighbour Seacole. God hath blest you
with a good name: to be a well-favoured man is the
gift of fortune, but to write and read comes by nature.

'Much Ado About Nothing' Act 3, Scene 3

Dogberry is a <u>lower-class</u> and <u>comical</u> character. He therefore speaks in <u>prose</u> rather than verse. This makes his speech sound <u>natural</u> and <u>informal</u>.

Look out for switches between **Verse** and **Prose**

1) If a character <u>changes</u> their speech pattern from poetry to prose, or vice versa.

2) This can give you important clues about their <u>state of mind</u>.

The thane of Fife had a wife. Where is she now? —
What, will these hands ne'er be clean? — No more
o' that, my lord, no more o' that.

'Macbeth' Act 5, Scene 1

Lady Macbeth generally speaks in <u>verse</u>, but when she is sleep-walking she speaks in <u>prose</u>, which shows her <u>loss of control</u>.

Get to grips with the Shakespeare play you're studying...

It's important that you know your Shakespeare text really well. If there are any bits of the play that you don't understand, take the time to reread them carefully and work out what they mean before the exam.

Warm-Up Questions

Plays come in different shapes and sizes, but the way you study them should be pretty much the same — pay close attention to the play's language, structure and stagecraft and you'll be scoring marks all over the place. These questions should get you in the mood for the exam. Take a look at the suggested answers on page 187 when you're done.

Warm-Up Questions

1) In one of the plays you have studied, find an example of how the writer uses stage directions to create a specific mood or atmosphere.

2) Write a brief definition of each of the terms below.
   Then, using a set play you have studied, find an example of each term.

   | Monologue | Aside | Soliloquy |

3) Find one example of each of the following dramatic techniques in a play you have studied:
   a) imagery
   b) repetition
   c) the rhythm of a character's words having a powerful effect.

4) Find an example of humour in a Shakespeare play you have studied.
   What effect does it have on the scene?

5) Choose a Shakespeare play you have studied in class. Pick a passage you find particularly effective (e.g. frightening, funny or tense) and write two or three paragraphs explaining how Shakespeare makes it so effective. Hint: think about form, structure and language.

6) Read the following extracts, and then complete the tasks below.

   > Don Pedro: My love is thine to teach. Teach it but how,
   > And thou shalt see how apt it is to learn
   > Any hard lesson that may do thee good.
   >
   > *Much Ado About Nothing* Act 1, Scene 1

   > Feste: Those wits that think
   > they have thee do
   > very oft prove fools,
   > and I that am sure
   > I lack thee may pass
   > for a wise man. For
   > what says Quinapalus?
   > 'Better a witty fool
   > than a foolish wit.'
   >
   > *Twelfth Night* Act 1, Scene 5

   > Prince: A glooming peace this morning with it brings,
   > The sun, for sorrow, will not show his head.
   > Go hence, to have more talk of these sad things;
   > Some shall be pardoned, and some punishèd.
   >
   > *Romeo and Juliet* Act 5, Scene 3

   a) For each extract, write down whether it is in verse, blank verse or prose.
      Write a sentence explaining how you can tell.
   b) What effect does the metre and rhyme scheme of the Prince's speech have?

Worked Exam-Style Question

Here's an example of how to write a top-notch essay about a play. Give it a read through, even if you aren't studying 'Macbeth' — it shows you the kind of thing you'll need to include in any exam answer.

Q1 Discuss whether the character of Macbeth is a tragic hero or a cruel tyrant.

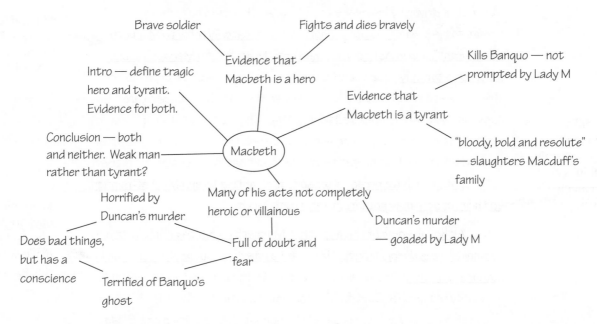

A tragic hero could be defined as someone who fights bravely for what he believes in, but who is ultimately the cause of his own downfall. A cruel tyrant is someone who uses his power for his own ends, rather than for the good of the people he governs. <u>In 'Macbeth', there is evidence for the central character being both a hero and a tyrant. In essence, however, he is neither; he is instead a character who is easily controlled by others.</u>

Outline your argument in the <u>introduction</u>.

Remember to include <u>quotes</u>, and <u>explain</u> how they support your points.

At the outset of the play, the Captain calls Macbeth "brave", and says that when he was outnumbered by Norwegian troops, he <u>"Doubly redoubled strokes upon the foe". This gives the impression that Macbeth is unafraid of physical combat, and is loyal to the king, even in the face of overwhelming odds.</u> Duncan calls him "valiant cousin! worthy gentleman!", which shows the high regard that he holds Macbeth in. Macbeth shows the same courage at the end of the play when, knowing that he has been tricked by the witches and that Macduff will kill him, he "will not yield". At this point, Macbeth could be described as a hero, because he fights bravely for his cause, and as tragic, because he is undone by his own ambition and thirst for power.

Having a paragraph discussing <u>each point of view</u> gives a clear <u>structure</u>.

Try to pick out the <u>example</u> that illustrates your point <u>best</u>, rather than just listing the events of the play.

However, between the beginning and end of the play, Macbeth is defined less by his bravery than by his cruel, and sometimes cowardly, actions. <u>The most clear-cut example</u> of this is when Macbeth hires two murderers to ensure that Macduff's wife and children are "Savagely slaughtered", because the witches' apparition warns him to

Worked Exam-Style Question

"beware Macduff". These cruel and unnecessary murders show how far Macbeth is driven by his desire to be king, and his need to destroy any threat to his power. The other characters repeatedly refer to Macbeth as a "tyrant", and in Act Four, Scene Three, Malcolm and Macduff discuss Macbeth's tyranny: "Each new morn, / New widows howl, new orphans cry". This suggests that Macbeth is ruling by terror and that murders are common. Macbeth is prepared to go to any lengths to maintain his power, and at this point in the play he seems to be behaving as a tyrant. However, since Malcolm has lost his father and Macduff has fled Scotland in fear of his life, both men have personal reasons for wanting to end Macbeth's reign, so their reports may not be entirely trustworthy.

It's good to look at how other characters react to Macbeth.

This looks beyond the obvious meaning and thinks about the characters' motives.

Although some of the acts that Macbeth commits are undoubtedly tyrannical, he is deeply troubled by what he has done, suggesting that he is not simply a tyrant. He is reluctant to murder Duncan, and is only driven to it by Lady Macbeth's taunts. After committing the murder, it is clear that Macbeth feels very guilty. He says "Methought I heard a voice cry, 'Sleep no more! / Macbeth does murder sleep,' the innocent sleep". His rambling speech, with its repetition of "sleep", shows that he is confused, upset and plagued by guilt. The theme of hallucination and imagination, shown here in the voice Macbeth hears, recurs throughout the play, usually as a sign of his troubled conscience. For example, after having Banquo murdered, Macbeth sees his ghost at the banquet, showing that he is horrified at what he has done.

Keep referring back to the question to make sure you stay focused.

Good analysis of how the writer uses language to achieve an effect.

It's great to show that you've thought about the broader themes of the play.

As a brave man, unused to physical fear, Macbeth is frightened of being thought weak, cowardly or unmanly. It is this fear, at least in part, that drives him to acts of tyranny. At first, this is because Lady Macbeth questions his bravery and manliness, and later because he questions it himself, and feels the need to prove himself. When Macbeth is killed, the audience feels a mixture of relief, pity and regret. If he was purely a tyrant, his death would come as a relief, so the audience's reaction at this point demonstrates that his character is more complex than this.

Think carefully about why characters act they way they do.

This is a good personal response to the play.

In summary, at various points in the play Macbeth is a hero, and at others he is a tyrant. However, his guilt about his acts of tyranny and the fact that he is driven to some of these acts by others shows that he is not a straightforward tyrant, but is instead a complicated character, driven by his own ambition and easily manipulated by other people. Ultimately, he is neither hero nor tyrant; he is human.

Write a strong, memorable conclusion to sum up your argument.

Exam-Style Questions

Now that you've revised drama, have a go at these practice exam questions. You don't have to answer them all, but you'll find it useful to at least write a plan for any that are relevant to your set plays.

Q1 Explain what the events of **either** 'Romeo and Juliet' **or** 'Macbeth' **or** 'Julius Caesar' say about the importance of fate versus free will.

Q2 With reference to **either** Act 3 Scene 4 of 'Twelfth Night' **or** Act 3 Scene 5 of 'The Merchant of Venice' **or** Act 2 Scene 1 of 'Much Ado About Nothing', discuss Shakespeare's use of comedy.

Q3 For a play you have studied, discuss the importance of a central character to the play as a whole.

Q4 With reference to **either** 'The Tempest' **or** 'Macbeth', explore how Shakespeare presents the supernatural.

Q5 With reference to a post-1914 play you have studied, discuss how the relationship between two central characters is presented at different points in the play.

Writing About Prose

Structure and language are key to prose. One's the arrangement of the words, and the other's the style.

Structure is how the writer puts the text together

1) Writers work hard to present and communicate their ideas effectively. Your challenge is to work out why they've structured their novel in a certain way and what the effect of their decisions is.

2) The novel might be split into chapters or sections. This may be in order to create cliffhangers or switch the focus of the plot.

> 'Jane Eyre' is divided into three separate volumes — original readers of the book had to buy each volume separately. Brontë used cliffhangers at the end of the first two volumes, which would have encouraged readers to buy the next volume.

3) Think about how the novel starts and ends, and what the impact of this may be on the reader.

> 'Animal Farm' has a cyclical structure — elements at the start of the book repeat themselves at the end, but under Napoleon's rule rather than Farmer Jones'. For example, by the end of the book Napoleon has become a drunk, just like Jones. This shows that the new regime is mirroring the old one.

4) Some plots move forwards chronologically (in time order). Others are non-chronological.

> 'A Christmas Carol' includes three episodes set in different time periods, each of which jumps between different times and places. This gives them a dreamlike quality.

5) The novel may have one main plot, or several plots that link together.

> 'Pride and Prejudice' has several different stories which interlink. The revelations about Wickham, the romance between Bingley and Jane, and Mr Collins' search for a wife all make the novel more interesting. They also allow Austen to further explore themes such as social class and gender.

Writers sometimes use Structural Devices

For more on flashbacks and foreshadowing, see page 80.

1) The author may use specific structural devices such as flashbacks, foreshadowing and different narrative structures.

2) A frame narrative is where the main story is told within the frame of another story.

> 'Frankenstein' uses a frame narrative — Walton's letters frame Victor's story, which in turn acts as a frame for the monster's account. This frame narrative prompts the reader to question their judgement of events — Walton presents Frankenstein as a "wonderful man", but this is undermined by events in Frankenstein's own narrative.

3) An embedded narrative is where several different stories are told within the main story.

> In 'Dr Jekyll and Mr Hyde', Stevenson uses several embedded narratives, in the form of written documents (Lanyon's letter, Jekyll's statement) and testimonies from characters such as Mr Enfield. These make the story appear more authentic and make the reader curious — each narrative adds another piece of evidence as the reader slowly starts to form a full picture of who Mr Hyde is.

Writing About Prose

Comment on the writer's choice of **Language**

1) Authors love using <u>descriptive language</u>, including <u>similes</u>, <u>metaphors</u> and <u>personification</u>, so look out for this and comment on <u>why</u> it's been used.

> *"bloodthirsty snarling"*
>
> *"the tearing of teeth and claws"*
>
> In 'Lord of the Flies', Golding uses animal imagery to describe the boys, showing that they are becoming more savage.

2) Particularly keep an eye out for any language or imagery that's <u>repeated</u> — there's usually a reason for this.

> *he locked the note into his safe*
>
> *Utterson locked the door of his business room*
>
> *he turned to examine the door in the by-street. It was locked*
>
> In 'Dr Jekyll and Mr Hyde', there are numerous images of <u>locked doors</u>. These are used to symbolise <u>secrecy</u>, and the way that humans try to <u>hide</u> their <u>dual nature</u>.

3) The language used by <u>characters</u> is also really important. For example:

> *"Yow can come with uz, right, but don't say nothin'"*
>
> In 'Anita and Me', Meena uses <u>Midlands dialect words</u>, <u>slang</u> and <u>non-standard grammar</u> to try to fit in and impress Anita.

> *"Be calm! I entreat you to hear me, before you give vent to your hatred on my devoted head. Have I not suffered enough that you seek to increase my misery?"*
>
> The monster in 'Frankenstein' uses <u>eloquent language</u>. This makes him sound more <u>human</u>, so the reader <u>empathises</u> with him.

Characters' Thoughts are often described

You can find more information about analysing characters on pages 76-77.

1) Novels and short stories give <u>descriptions</u> of characters' thoughts and behaviour — the narrator often informs you about what <u>characters</u> are <u>thinking</u>.

2) <u>Look out</u> for those bits, <u>quote</u> them, and comment on how they help answer the question.

> *The head, he thought, appeared to agree with him. Run away, said the head silently...*
>
> The narrator of 'Lord of the Flies' describes Simon's <u>thoughts</u> and <u>imagined conversation</u> with the pig's head. This allows the reader to experience Simon's <u>hallucinations</u>.

> *She grew absolutely ashamed of herself. Of neither Darcy nor Wickham could she think without feeling she had been blind, partial, prejudiced, absurd.*
>
> The narrator of 'Pride and Prejudice' gives a detailed description of how Elizabeth <u>feels</u> after she reads Darcy's account of Wickham. This allows the reader to fully <u>understand</u> Elizabeth's emotions and subsequent actions.

Don't be afraid to be original...

When it comes to language and structure, there are no wrong points (as long as you have evidence to back them up). If you think of something original about a text, remember it in case you can use it in the exam.

Analysing Narrators

The narrator is the person telling the story — they are the link between the reader and the plot.

There are **Different Types** of **Narrator**

1) All <u>prose</u> texts have a <u>narrator</u> — a <u>voice</u> that's telling the story.

2) A <u>first-person</u> narrator is a character who tells the story from their <u>perspective</u>, e.g. Pip narrates 'Great Expectations' and Kathy narrates 'Never Let Me Go'. You get a first-hand description of exactly what the character <u>sees</u>, <u>does</u> and <u>thinks</u> all the way through the story.

> *In what ecstasy of unhappiness I got these broken words out of myself, I don't know. The rhapsody welled up within me, like blood from an inward wound, and gushed out.*

In 'Great Expectations', Pip's narration is very <u>personal</u> and appeals to the reader's <u>emotions</u>. This helps the reader to <u>empathise</u> with him.

3) A <u>third-person</u> narrator is a separate voice, created by the author to tell the story — this type of narrator is used in 'A Christmas Carol' and 'Pride and Prejudice'. They usually describe the thoughts and feelings of several <u>different characters</u>, making them more of a <u>storyteller</u> than a <u>character</u>.

4) Third-person narrators can be <u>omniscient</u> (all-knowing) or <u>limited</u> (only aware of the thoughts and feelings of one character). They may also describe only what can be <u>seen</u> or <u>heard</u> — for example, in 'Animal Farm', the narrator usually just presents the reader with <u>factual information</u>.

> *To Catherine and Lydia, neither the letter nor its writer were in any degree interesting.*

The <u>omniscient</u>, <u>third-person</u> narrator of 'Pride and Prejudice' gives the reader an insight into the <u>thoughts</u> of many of the characters, even though the story follows Elizabeth most closely.

Not all narrators are **Reliable**

1) Don't automatically <u>trust</u> what a narrator says — they may be <u>unreliable</u>. This is particularly common with first-person narrators, who see things from their <u>own point of view</u>.

> *I have recorded in detail the events of my insignificant existence...*

The first-person narrator of 'Jane Eyre' calls herself "<u>insignificant</u>", but the fact that she's the <u>main character</u> in the book suggests this <u>isn't true</u>.

2) The narrator is <u>not</u> the <u>same</u> person as the author, but watch out for examples of the writer's <u>viewpoint</u> being <u>revealed</u> through the narrator. For example:

> *Scrooge! a squeezing, wrenching, grasping, scraping, clutching, covetous old sinner!*

The third-person narrator of 'A Christmas Carol' has <u>strong opinions</u> on Scrooge, which seem to be <u>Dickens's views</u>.

The narrator and the writer are not the same person...

Always remember that what the narrator thinks is not necessarily the same as what the writer thinks. In the exam, refer to how the writer uses the narrator, rather than taking what the narrator says at face value.

19th-Century Fiction

You have to study a 19th-century novel, so the next three pages contain some useful background information on life in the period. This will help you understand the texts better, and to write more informed essays.

There was a **Big Gap** between the **Upper** and **Lower Classes**

1) <u>Class</u> was <u>important</u> in the 19th century — your class <u>determined</u> what <u>kind</u> of life you had.

2) Early 19th-century society was divided between the <u>rich upper classes</u> (who <u>owned</u> the <u>land</u>, didn't need to <u>work</u> and so <u>socialised</u> a lot) and the <u>poorer working classes</u> (who <u>relied</u> on the upper classes for work, and were often <u>looked down on</u> because of it).

3) The <u>Industrial Revolution</u> created opportunities for more people to <u>make money</u>, meaning that the <u>middle classes</u> grew in <u>size</u> and <u>influence</u> throughout the century.

4) However, the fact that the <u>middle classes</u> relied on a <u>profession</u> or <u>trade</u> for their wealth meant that they were <u>looked down on</u> by the <u>upper classes</u>.

In the Industrial Revolution, technological advances meant that goods could be produced by machines in factories, rather than by hand in people's homes. This resulted in many people moving from working in farming (and living in the countryside) to working in manufacturing (and living in cities).

'Pride and Prejudice' examines and criticises judgements based on social status. Austen mocks 19th-century class prejudices by showing that characters' behaviour is down to personality, not class.

Many cities were **Overcrowded** and had **Terrible Living Conditions**

1) In the 19th century, millions of people moved from the countryside to the <u>cities</u> in search of <u>work</u> in the new factories. As a result, the <u>population</u> of cities grew rapidly and uncontrollably.

2) Most of these people ended up living in <u>slums</u> of cheap, overcrowded housing. There was often no proper drainage or <u>sewage</u> system, and many families had to share one tap and toilet. Overcrowding led to <u>hunger</u>, <u>disease</u> and <u>crime</u>.

Dickens uses 'A Christmas Carol' to highlight the problems and poverty of working-class London. He contrasts the wealth of Scrooge with the poverty of the Cratchit family.

Women were often **Dependent** on men

1) During the 19th century, <u>women</u> were normally <u>dependent</u> on the <u>men</u> in their family, especially in the <u>upper classes</u>. It was usually men who <u>earned a living</u> or <u>owned land</u> which generated income from rent.

2) A woman's best chance of a <u>stable future</u> was a good <u>marriage</u> — there were very few <u>job</u> options available for upper and middle-class women, and women often weren't allowed to <u>inherit</u> land or money.

3) Women didn't have the <u>vote</u>, and generally had to do what their <u>husband</u> <u>told them</u> — they were expected to stay at home and look after children.

'Jane Eyre' was unusual at the time of publication not only because it was written by a woman, but also because its main character is a determined and sometimes outspoken woman. By the end of the novel, Jane is both emotionally and financially independent.

19th-Century Fiction

Education was Not Compulsory until the late 19th century

1) Education was a <u>privilege</u> — only <u>wealthy</u> families could afford to send children away to school, or to hire a <u>governess</u> to live with them and teach the children.

2) Boys' education was more of a <u>priority</u>, and many girls weren't educated at all. An academic education was seen as <u>unnecessary</u> for women — girls from <u>rich</u> families were taught <u>art</u>, <u>music</u> and <u>dance</u> as this would help them to get a <u>husband</u>, and girls from <u>poorer</u> families were expected to go straight into a <u>job</u> that didn't require an <u>education</u>.

3) Many schools were run by the <u>Church</u> and supported by <u>charity donations</u>. The <u>government</u> began funding schools in <u>1833</u>, but the funding was very limited.

4) School <u>wasn't compulsory</u> until <u>1880</u>, when an Education Act finally made it compulsory for children between the ages of <u>five</u> and <u>ten</u> to attend school.

> *In 'Great Expectations', Pip receives hardly any formal education as a child. He is desperate to gain an education, believing this is key to becoming a gentleman, and attempts to improve his education throughout the novel.*

Reputation was important

1) In middle and upper-class society, it was important to be <u>respectable</u>.

2) The middle and upper classes were expected to have <u>strong morals</u> and to help others. They were also expected to keep their emotions under <u>strict control</u> and to <u>hide</u> their desire for things like sex and alcohol.

3) If someone was seen doing anything which <u>wasn't</u> considered respectable, their <u>reputation</u> could be <u>ruined</u>. To <u>protect</u> their reputation, people often kept their <u>sinful behaviour</u> and desires <u>secret</u>.

> *The gentlemen in 'Jekyll and Hyde' are concerned with their reputations. Jekyll creates Hyde in order to hide his sins and preserve his reputation, and Utterson consistently tries to protect Jekyll's reputation. The book explores how this obsession with reputation can actually be destructive.*

Many texts were influenced by Romanticism and the Gothic genre

1) 'Romanticism' had a big impact on <u>literature</u> and <u>art</u> in the late 18th century and the early 19th century.

2) The 'Romantics' tried to capture <u>intense emotions</u> and <u>experiences</u> in their work, and were especially influenced by <u>nature</u>. They saw nature as a <u>powerful force</u> that could <u>inspire</u> and <u>restore</u> people.

3) Many 19th-century writers were influenced by the <u>Gothic</u> genre — this generally involved a <u>mysterious location</u>, <u>supernatural elements</u>, <u>troubling secrets</u> and elements of <u>madness</u>.

4) The <u>double</u> (or <u>doppelgänger</u>) is another key feature of Gothic novels — it's where two characters are presented as if they are each a <u>version</u> of the other.

> *'Frankenstein' includes aspects of the 'Romantic' and the Gothic. Frankenstein travels to the Alps in the hope that the "magnificence" of nature will help him to forget his "sorrows", but it is there that he meets the monster, who is presented as the other side of him.*

19th-Century Fiction

Victorian society was very **Religious**

1) <u>Christianity</u> had a strong influence on life in Victorian Britain. To be good Christians, many people believed they should live by a strict <u>moral code</u> — attending church regularly, avoiding alcohol and exercising sexual restraint.

2) However, others believed that being a good Christian meant being <u>charitable</u> and <u>forgiving</u>.

> *At the end of 'A Christmas Carol', Scrooge resolves to "honour Christmas" and to continue his generosity and goodwill "all the year". This appears to be Dickens's view of being a good Christian.*

Darwin's theory of **Evolution** was **Controversial**

1) In the early 1800s, Christianity taught that <u>God</u> created every species to be <u>perfectly adapted</u> to its environment. The Book of Genesis also taught that humans were made in <u>God's image</u>, different from all <u>other animals</u> and ruling over them.

2) In contrast, some scientists, including Charles Darwin, claimed that all creatures <u>evolved</u> from common ancestors through a process called '<u>natural selection</u>'.

3) Darwin also claimed that humans shared a <u>common ancestor</u> with <u>apes</u>. This went against the Christian idea that man's nature was <u>different</u> from that of other animals. People found this <u>unsettling</u> because it means there may be an <u>animalistic</u> side to everyone, capable of <u>uncivilised</u> acts and <u>violent</u> crimes.

> *In 'Dr Jekyll and Mr Hyde', Hyde is described as the "animal within" Jekyll. Utterson describes him as "hardly human", and Poole says he is "like a monkey". Stevenson may be hinting that Hyde is a less evolved version of Jekyll.*

Scientists were **Investigating** where **Life** comes from

1) Many 19th-century scientists were fascinated with the <u>origins of life</u>. Some believed that studying <u>electricity</u> might reveal what gives life to people and animals.

2) Scientists experimented with passing <u>electric currents</u> through animal and human bodies. The current made the bodies <u>move</u>, which led some to conclude there was a type of 'animal electricity' (later called '<u>galvanism</u>') within <u>living things</u>.

> *In 'Frankenstein', Shelley implies that Victor uses electricity to animate the monster — he infuses a "spark of being" into a "lifeless thing". This suggests Shelley was influenced by contemporary science.*

Make sure that the context you use is relevant...

Make sure the facts you include in your essay are relevant to the question you're answering or the text you're writing about. Context is a great way to pick up marks though, so be sure to learn these pages.

Warm-Up Questions

When you're writing an exam answer about prose texts, always think about the language, the structure and the issues raised in the texts. You also need to remember to focus on the detail and to choose your quotes wisely. Start with the questions on this page, and the exam questions on p.109 should be no problem at all.

Warm-Up Questions

1) Choose a prose text that you have studied. Open it at the first page and read the opening paragraph. Write down three things that you notice about the author's style.

2) Using a prose text you have studied in class, find a passage that uses descriptive language to set the scene. Write a short paragraph explaining how the writer makes this description vivid. (Hint: think about their use of imagery, interesting vocabulary and appeals to the senses.)

3) Think about a central character in one of the prose texts you have studied, and write a short paragraph for each of the following questions.
   a) Why is this character important to the novel?
   b) Do you sympathise with this character? Why or why not?
   c) How does this character change over the course of the text?

4) Choose a prose text you have studied. Does the text have a first-person or third-person narrator? Write a short paragraph about the effect this narrator has on the text.

5) Read the passage below.
   a) Make a list of all of the words and phrases that are about reputation.
   b) Using your list from part a), write a short paragraph about the importance of reputation for women in nineteenth-century Britain.

> "This is a most unfortunate affair, and will probably be much talked of. But we must stem the tide of malice, and pour into the wounded bosoms of each other the balm of sisterly consolation."
>
> Then, perceiving in Elizabeth no inclination of replying, she added, "Unhappy as the event must be for Lydia, we may draw from it this useful lesson: that loss of virtue in a female is irretrievable; that one false step involves her in endless ruin; that her reputation is no less brittle than it is beautiful; and that she cannot be too much guarded in her behaviour towards the undeserving of the other sex."

Worked Exam-Style Question

It can be tricky to fit language, structure, form and context into one answer.
Here's an example of a great answer which includes all these things.

Q1 Discuss how Golding uses symbolism to show the conflict between civilisation and savagery in 'Lord of the Flies'.

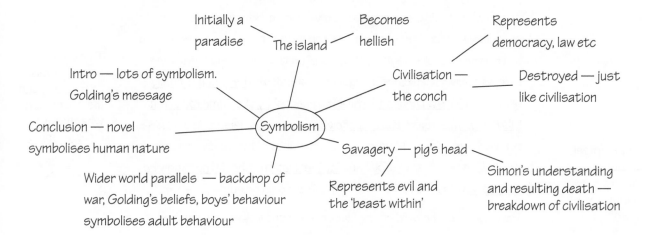

It's good to think about how the question relates to the novel's <u>message</u>.

'Lord of the Flies' is an allegorical novel that explores the battle between good and evil, civilisation and savagery. One of the major ways that Golding portrays this battle is through the use of symbolism. <u>Many of the characters, settings, objects and events in the novel are symbolic, and help to convey the author's message — that evil lives inside every human being and will come to the surface given the right conditions.</u>

<u>The setting of the island itself is symbolic.</u> At the beginning of the novel it is a paradise, an "imagined but never fully realized place", with plenty of fresh water, fruit and fire wood, where the boys can "have fun" until they are rescued. By the end of the novel, the island is "burning wreckage", with more in common with hell than paradise. This symbolises the boys' loss of innocence and their descent into chaos and savagery. <u>The loss of innocence is particularly evident in Ralph</u> who, at the beginning of the novel, is excited at the prospect of living without adults and "savoured the right of domination", but by the end of the novel has become aware of "the darkness of man's heart" — the evil that exists inside everyone.

This paragraph gives a good introduction to the subject, by discussing <u>large-scale</u> symbols before the essay goes into more <u>detail</u>.

This makes it <u>obvious</u> what the paragraph will be about and gives the answer a <u>clear structure</u>.

<u>The clearest symbol of civilisation is the conch.</u> It is one of the major reasons for the boys voting for Ralph as leader: "The being that had blown that... was set apart". <u>The description of Ralph's "stillness" and calling him a "being" rather than a boy give him an almost God-like quality, meaning that the conch becomes a powerful symbol of authority.</u> It is used to summon the boys to meetings, and because only the boy holding it is allowed to speak, it comes to represent democracy and the rules of society. As civilisation is

You need to think about the <u>language</u> the writer uses and the <u>effect</u> it has.

Worked Exam-Style Question

eroded and replaced by savagery, so too the conch begins to lose its power for all of the boys except Piggy and Ralph, who continue to use it even when their group consists only of them, Sam and Eric. The other boys do have respect for the conch, but it is easily overwhelmed by their newfound savagery: "Piggy held up the conch and the booing sagged a little, then came up again to strength." The conch is finally shattered "into a thousand white fragments" by the same rock that kills Piggy. This marks the end of civilisation on the island. From this point forward, Jack's tribe lose any semblance of humanity and even Ralph acts like an animal, obeying "an instinct that he did not know he possessed" to escape, running and hiding from the hunt.

Think about how symbols change through the novel, and what these changes mean.

Don't forget to put in quotes to support your points.

The pig's head, the Lord of the Flies, is the opposite of the conch — it is a symbol of chaos, savagery and the evil inside each human being. Originally intended as an offering to "the Beast", the pig's head is most powerfully symbolic when it 'talks' to Simon, telling him that the beast is inside them: "You knew, didn't you? I'm part of you?". Its words foreshadow Simon's death because, when he tries to explain what he has learned to the others, they fear that he is the beast, which drives them to kill him with "teeth and claws". This marks a major turning point in the boys' descent from civilisation to savagery. At the end of the novel, the conch is destroyed in Jack's camp, and Ralph uses the stick from the Lord of the Flies as a weapon. This shows that civilisation has been completely overcome by savagery, and that even Ralph has become corrupted by the power of evil.

Details like this show that you know the text really well and have given it a lot of thought.

The naval officer who rescues the boys symbolises both civilisation and savagery. Despite his smart uniform and politeness, he is a symbol of war, and shows the reader that the boys' savagery reflects the savagery of the adult world. This is in keeping with Golding's beliefs about society. His experiences during World War II led him to realise that even 'civilised' people are capable of committing evil acts.

Shows that you know about the writer's background and beliefs.

Although 'Lord of the Flies' contains many other symbols of civilisation and savagery, the conch and the pig's head convey most powerfully the author's message that evil exists in everyone, and that if the rules of civilisation are removed, anybody can become savage and commit evil acts. In this way, Golding draws parallels with historical events and questions the assumption that people can be fully 'good' or that society can be completely 'civilised'.

Remember to write a brief conclusion to sum up your answer.

Exam-Style Questions

Answering the questions on this page should give you a good chance to practise what you've learned ready for the exam. Whatever text you've studied, there's at least one question for you.

Q1 Discuss how the theme of prejudice is presented in **either** 'Anita and Me' **or** 'Frankenstein' **or** 'Pride and Prejudice'.

Q2 Choose one of the following themes, and explore how it is presented in a prose text you have studied.
a) marriage and relationships
b) power
c) reputation
d) social class

Q3 What methods does the writer use to create a sense of fear in a prose text you have studied?

Q4 How does the writer present ideas about the nature of evil in **either** 'Lord of the Flies' **or** 'Dr Jekyll and Mr Hyde'?

Q5 Analyse the extent to which the main character is shown to change or stay the same during the course of a prose text you have studied.

Poetry — What You Have To Do

Poetry is an important part of your English Literature GCSE. The next three sections will get you up to speed with what you need to do to write cracking poetry essays.

You'll write about poetry in **At Least One** of your Literature exams

The poetry aspect of your GCSE English Literature course is divided into two main sections:

1) <u>Poetry anthology</u> (see Section Nine) — you'll study a group (or 'cluster') of poems in class. The poems will share common themes.

2) <u>Unseen</u> poetry (see Section Ten) — in the exam, you have to write about one or more poems that you've never seen before. You'll get a copy of them in your exam paper and have to <u>analyse</u> them on the spot.

You could be asked about any poem from the group you've studied, so you need to know them all well.

Think about **Language**, **Structure** and **Form**

For writing about language, see pages 112-115. For more on form and structure, see page 111.

You should always write about <u>language</u>, <u>structure</u> and <u>form</u> in your answers on poetry.

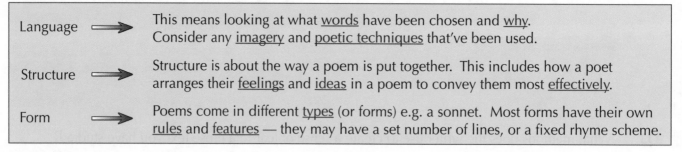

Language ⟶	This means looking at what <u>words</u> have been chosen and <u>why</u>. Consider any <u>imagery</u> and <u>poetic techniques</u> that've been used.
Structure ⟶	Structure is about the way a poem is put together. This includes how a poet arranges their <u>feelings</u> and <u>ideas</u> in a poem to convey them most <u>effectively</u>.
Form ⟶	Poems come in different <u>types</u> (or forms) e.g. a sonnet. Most forms have their own <u>rules</u> and <u>features</u> — they may have a set number of lines, or a fixed rhyme scheme.

You must show you **Appreciate** what the **Poet** is doing

1) Once you've identified points about language, structure and form, think about the <u>effects</u> that these features create.

2) To get the top marks, you need to consider what these effects <u>suggest</u> about the <u>speaker</u>, or how they <u>make</u> the <u>reader</u> feel.

3) You're the reader, so you should include your <u>personal opinion</u> — you can be as creative as you like, as long as you <u>back up</u> your idea with a <u>relevant quote</u> from the poem.

Back up your point with some evidence from the poem.

Think about how it makes the reader feel.

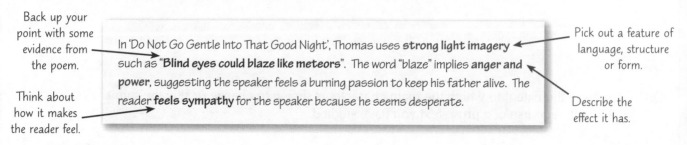

In 'Do Not Go Gentle Into That Good Night', Thomas uses **strong light imagery** such as "**Blind eyes could blaze like meteors**". The word "blaze" implies **anger and power**, suggesting the speaker feels a burning passion to keep his father alive. The reader **feels sympathy** for the speaker because he seems desperate.

Pick out a feature of language, structure or form.

Describe the effect it has.

Go over the poem several times to properly understand it...

When you read a poem, don't be put off if you don't understand it right away. Go over it a couple of times and start to look at language, structure and form — they often give you a clue about the poem's meaning.

Form and Structure

Form and structure are all about the way a poem is put together. Have a look at this page to find out more.

Poetry comes in **Different Forms**

Sometimes poets use a certain form but break some of its rules for effect.

Different forms (or <u>types</u>) of poems follow different rules — that's how you can tell them apart. You need to be able to <u>recognise</u> different forms of poetry for your exam.

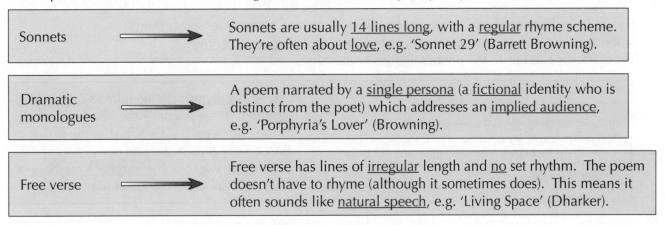

Sonnets	→	Sonnets are usually <u>14 lines long</u>, with a <u>regular</u> rhyme scheme. They're often about <u>love</u>, e.g. 'Sonnet 29' (Barrett Browning).
Dramatic monologues	→	A poem narrated by a <u>single persona</u> (a <u>fictional</u> identity who is distinct from the poet) which addresses an <u>implied audience</u>, e.g. 'Porphyria's Lover' (Browning).
Free verse	→	Free verse has lines of <u>irregular</u> length and <u>no</u> set rhythm. The poem doesn't have to rhyme (although it sometimes does). This means it often sounds like <u>natural speech</u>, e.g. 'Living Space' (Dharker).

Learn the correct **Terms** to describe **Form**

To discuss form properly in the exam, you need to <u>know</u> and <u>use</u> the correct <u>technical terms</u>:

- A <u>stanza</u> (or verse) is a group of lines.

- A <u>tercet</u> is a three-line stanza.

- A <u>quatrain</u> is a four-line stanza.

- A <u>couplet</u> is a <u>pair of lines</u>, usually with the same <u>metre</u> (see p.113).

- A rhyming <u>couplet</u> is a couplet where the <u>final words</u> of each line <u>rhyme</u>.

- A <u>rhyming triplet</u> is where the <u>final words</u> of <u>three</u> successive lines <u>rhyme</u> with each other.

Structure is how a poem is arranged

Structure is how the poet <u>arranges</u> their <u>feelings</u> or <u>ideas</u> in a poem to convey them most effectively. Two poems with the <u>same form</u> can be structured very differently.

Think about:

1) How a poem <u>begins</u> and <u>ends</u>. See if the poet <u>goes back</u> to the same ideas, or if the poem <u>progresses</u>.

2) Any <u>pauses</u> or <u>interruptions</u> in ideas in the poem.

3) Changes in <u>mood</u>, <u>voice</u>, <u>tense</u>, <u>rhyme scheme</u>, <u>rhythm</u> or <u>pace</u>.

Once you've <u>identified</u> a structural feature, you must always explain <u>why</u> you think the poet has used it.

Don't ignore form and structure...

It can be easy to concentrate on language, but you need to write about structure and form as well to get top marks. You can write about any poem's form, even if it's to say that it doesn't have a regular one.

Poetic Techniques

Poets use lots of techniques to get their message across. Here are the ones you need to know.

Rhyme can add Power to the poet's message

1) Rhyme helps a poem develop its beat or <u>rhythm</u>. Poets can also use it to reinforce the poem's <u>message</u>.

2) Rhyme can be <u>regular</u> (occurring in a set pattern), <u>irregular</u> (with no pattern) or <u>absent</u> from a poem.

3) This creates different <u>effects</u> — regular rhyme schemes can create a sense of <u>control</u>, whereas an irregular rhyme scheme might show <u>chaos</u> or <u>unpredictability</u>. These effects can link to the poem's <u>themes</u> or message.

> *"We stood by a pond that winter day,*
> *And the sun was white, as though chidden of God,*
> *And a few leaves lay on the starving sod;*
> * – They had fallen from an ash, and were grey."*
>
> *('Neutral Tones' — Thomas Hardy)*

The <u>ABBA rhyme scheme</u> mirrors the <u>cyclical structure</u> of the poem — the 'A' rhyme returns at the end of each stanza, just as the image of the pond returns at the end of the poem. This reflects the way that the <u>narrator's memory</u> of the break-up returns to affect him.

4) Sometimes rhymes occur within lines, too. These are called <u>internal rhymes</u>.

> *"With your straight, <u>strong</u>, <u>long</u>*
> *Brown hair..."*
>
> *('Catrin' — Gillian Clarke)*

Clarke uses <u>internal rhymes</u> to <u>emphasise</u> prominent aspects of Catrin's <u>appearance</u>, <u>personality</u> and <u>mannerisms</u>.

Rhythm alters the Pace and Mood of a poem

1) Rhythm is the <u>arrangement</u> of beats within a line. It's easier to <u>feel</u> a rhythm than to see it on the page.

2) Like rhyme, rhythm can be <u>regular</u> or <u>irregular</u>. A <u>strong</u> rhyme scheme often creates a <u>regular</u> rhythm.

3) Rhythm can affect the <u>pace</u> (speed) and <u>mood</u> of a poem — a fast rhythm can make a poem seem <u>rushed</u> and <u>frantic</u>, whereas a slow and regular rhythm can make a poem seem <u>calm</u>.

4) Sometimes poets use rhythm to <u>imitate</u> sounds related to the poem, e.g. a heartbeat or beating drums.

> *"Half a league, half a league,*
> * Half a league onward"*
>
> *('The Charge of the Light Brigade'*
> *— Alfred Tennyson)*

Tennyson uses a <u>regular</u>, <u>relentless rhythm</u> in these lines to create a <u>fast pace</u>. This imitates the sound of the <u>galloping horses</u>.

5) The rhythm often reflects the poem's <u>themes</u>, how the narrator is <u>feeling</u> or the overall <u>message</u>.

> *"Oh! my God! the down,*
> *The soft young down of her"*
>
> *('The Farmer's Bride' — Charlotte Mew)*

Mew uses <u>monosyllabic</u> words to <u>break down</u> the poem's <u>rhythm</u>. This draws attention to the narrator's loss of <u>self-control</u>.

Poetic Techniques

Metre is the Pattern of Syllables in a line

1) In poetry, the rhythm of a line is created by <u>patterns</u> of <u>syllables</u>. If the patterns are <u>consistent</u>, then the poem's rhythm is <u>regular</u>.

A syllable is a single unit of sound, for example, 'beat' has one syllable and 'sonnet' has two syllables.

2) <u>Metre</u> is the technical term for these patterns. There are different types of metre, depending on which syllables are <u>stressed</u> (emphasised) and which are <u>unstressed</u>.

> <u>Iambic pentameter</u> is a metre that's commonly used in poetry. It has 10 syllables in a line — an <u>unstressed</u> syllable followed by a <u>stressed</u> syllable, repeated five times over.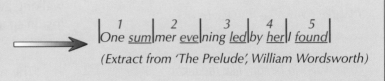
>
> | 1 | 2 | 3 | 4 | 5 |
> | *One <u>sum</u>* | *mer <u>eve</u>* | *ning <u>led</u>* | *by <u>her</u>* | *I <u>found</u>* |
>
> *(Extract from 'The Prelude', William Wordsworth)*

Punctuation affects how a poem Flows

Punctuation can affect the <u>pace</u> of a poem, emphasise <u>specific words</u>, or <u>interrupt</u> a poem's <u>rhythm</u>.

1) When punctuation creates a <u>pause</u> during a line of poetry, this is called a <u>caesura</u>.

> *"Happy and proud; at last I knew*
> *Porphyria worshipped me; surprise"*
>
> *('Porphyria's Lover' — Robert Browning)*
>
> The semicolons create <u>caesurae</u> which make the poem sound <u>fragmented</u>, reflecting the narrator's <u>unstable mind</u>.

2) <u>Enjambment</u> is when a <u>sentence</u> or <u>phrase</u> runs over from <u>one line</u> of poetry into the <u>next one</u>. Often enjambment puts emphasis on the <u>last word</u> of the first line or on the <u>first word</u> of the next line.

> *"All I ever did was <u>follow</u>*
> *In his broad shadow"*
>
> *('Follower' — Seamus Heaney)*
>
> 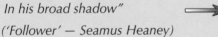 The <u>enjambment</u> puts stress on the <u>final word</u> of the first line, emphasising the way the narrator trails behind his father.

> *"I'm all*
> *alone. You ring, quickdraw"*
>
> *('Quickdraw' — Carol Ann Duffy)*
>
> Duffy uses <u>enjambment</u> to <u>separate</u> the last word from the rest of the sentence, <u>emphasising</u> how <u>alone</u> the narrator feels.

3) An <u>end-stopped line</u> is a line of poetry that ends in a <u>definite pause</u>, usually created by <u>punctuation</u>. End-stopped lines can help to maintain a <u>regular rhythm</u> and can also affect the <u>pace</u> of a poem.

> *"Who told my mother of my shame,*
> *Who told my father of my dear?*
> *Oh who but Maude, my sister Maude,*
> *Who lurked to spy and peer,"*
>
> *('Sister Maude' — Christina Rossetti)*
>
> Rossetti uses <u>repeated end-stopped lines</u>, which help to give the poem a strong <u>rhythm</u>. This emphasises the narrator's anger.

Poetic Techniques

Similes and Metaphors add power to Descriptions

1) Similes <u>compare</u> one thing to another — they often contain the words '<u>like</u>' or '<u>as</u>'.

2) Similes are frequently used to <u>exaggerate</u> — the poet usually wants to <u>emphasise</u> something.

> *"like a satellite*
> *Wrenched from its orbit, go drifting away"*
> *('Walking Away' — C. Day Lewis)*

The narrator uses the simile of a "<u>satellite</u>" that is "<u>Wrenched from its orbit</u>" to describe his son walking away. This creates the image of an object <u>lost</u> in space, emphasising the father's <u>anxiety</u>.

> *"She walks in beauty, <u>like the night</u>*
> *Of cloudless climes and starry skies"*
> *('She Walks in Beauty' — Lord Byron)*

The narrator uses a simile that <u>emphasises</u> how beautiful the woman is by comparing her to the <u>night sky</u>.

3) Metaphors describe something as though it <u>is</u> something else.

4) They take an object or person and give it the <u>qualities</u> of something else. This means that the poet can put a lot of <u>meaning</u> into a few words.

> *"the <u>foetus of metal</u> beneath his chest"*
> *('The Manhunt' — Simon Armitage)*

The narrator uses the metaphor "<u>the foetus of metal</u>" to describe the bullet in her partner's chest — this makes the bullet seem like an active part of the man, suggesting that he is <u>still living</u> with its effects.

> *"the blown*
> *and broken <u>bird's egg of a skull</u>"*
> *('Mametz Wood' — Owen Sheers)*

This metaphor compares the soldier's skull to a <u>bird's egg</u>, which emphasises its <u>fragility</u>.

Personification gives an object Human Qualities

1) Personification means describing an <u>object</u> as if it feels or behaves in a <u>human way</u>.

2) It can add <u>emotion</u> or alter the <u>mood</u> of a poem — this can really help the poet convey their <u>message</u>.

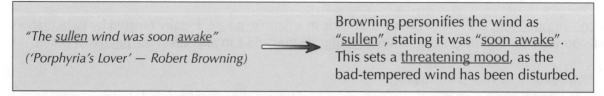

> *"The <u>sullen</u> wind was soon <u>awake</u>"*
> *('Porphyria's Lover' — Robert Browning)*

Browning personifies the wind as "<u>sullen</u>", stating it was "<u>soon awake</u>". This sets a <u>threatening mood</u>, as the bad-tempered wind has been disturbed.

> *"That <u>regiment</u> of <u>spite</u> behind the shed"*
> *('Nettles' — Vernon Scannell)*

Scannell personifies the nettles as an <u>army</u>, suggesting that they are a <u>dangerous enemy</u>, intent on hurting people.

Poetic Techniques

Imagery isn't just visual

1) Poets often appeal to all the senses (touch, sight, sound, smell and taste) — this is called <u>sensory imagery</u>.

2) Sensory imagery helps to create a <u>vivid image</u> in the reader's mind.

"the skin of his finger is <u>smooth</u> and <u>thick</u> like <u>warm ice</u>." *('Climbing My Grandfather' — Andrew Waterhouse)*	Waterhouse uses sensory imagery such as "smooth", "thick" and "like warm ice" to show the <u>close bond</u> between the narrator and their grandfather.
"<u>Our brains ache</u>, in the merciless iced east winds that knive us… Wearied we keep awake because <u>the night is silent</u>… <u>Low, drooping flares</u> confuse our memory of the salient…" *('Exposure' — Wilfred Owen)*	The poem uses three senses (<u>touch</u>, <u>sound</u> and <u>sight</u>) to describe how the soldiers feel. The use of so many senses emphasises their pain and confusion.

Poets use the Sounds of words for effect

The sounds words create can alter the <u>mood</u>, <u>pace</u> and <u>tone</u> of a poem. Here are some of the most common <u>techniques</u> that use sound for effect:

 Mood is the atmosphere of a poem, and tone is the feeling the words are spoken with.

1) <u>Alliteration</u> is where words that are close together <u>start</u> with the <u>same sound</u>.

"me with my <u>h</u>eartful of <u>h</u>eadlines" *('Letters from Yorkshire' — Maura Dooley)*	The repeated 'h' sound creates a sense of <u>heaviness</u>, which reflects the narrator's <u>discontent</u> with her life.

2) <u>Assonance</u> is when <u>vowel</u> sounds are <u>repeated</u>.

"How should I gr<u>ee</u>t th<u>ee</u>?" *('When We Two Parted' — Lord Byron)*	The <u>assonant long</u> 'ee' sounds <u>draw out</u> each word — this reflects the <u>long-lasting</u> nature of the narrator's <u>pain</u>.

3) <u>Sibilance</u> is when sounds create a '<u>hissing</u>' or '<u>shushing</u>' effect.

"My mother <u>sh</u>ade<u>s</u> her eye<u>s</u> and look<u>s</u> my way" *('Eden Rock' — Charles Causley)*	The '<u>s</u>' and '<u>sh</u>' sounds create a <u>hushed tone</u>, reflecting the <u>tranquillity</u> of the scene.

4) <u>Onomatopoeia</u> is when a word <u>mimics</u> the sound it's describing.

"To get out of that blue <u>crackling</u> air" *('Bayonet Charge' — Ted Hughes)*	The word "crackling" makes the air sound <u>electric</u>, emphasising the <u>danger</u> of the battlefield.

Knowing the technical terms can earn you more marks...

Analysing the poem, giving evidence for your points and discussing the effect on the reader are your main priorities, but being able to name the techniques a poet uses is a great way to pick up some extra marks.

Comparing Poems

In the exam you'll have to compare two poems — they could be seen or unseen. Here are some general tips.

Compare both poems in Every Paragraph

1) When you're asked to compare poems, you need to find <u>similarities</u> and <u>differences</u> between them.

2) This means you need to discuss <u>both poems</u> in <u>every paragraph</u>. There's a lot to squeeze in, so it's important to <u>structure</u> your paragraphs well.

3) <u>Comparative words</u> help you to do this. They clearly show the examiner if the point you're making is a <u>similarity</u> or <u>difference</u> between the two poems. Here are a few examples:

similarly	equally	in contrast	however	conversely

Compare Language, Structure and Form

When you plan your answer, make sure you consider <u>language</u>, <u>structure</u> and <u>form</u> — that way you won't forget to write about them in your essay.

Language

- Think about the <u>language techniques</u> the poets have used, e.g. <u>rhyme</u>, <u>imagery</u>, <u>sound</u>.
- Comment on how the language used in each poem is <u>similar</u> or <u>different</u>, and explain <u>why</u>.

Both 'Before You Were Mine' and 'Sonnet 29' use <u>onomatopoeia</u> to emphasise <u>strong emotions</u>. Duffy's verb "stamping" reflects the mother's <u>frustration</u> about her loss of freedom. Similarly, Barrett Browning's use of "burst" and "shattered" emphasise the narrator's <u>passion</u>.

Structure

- Compare the <u>beginnings</u> and <u>endings</u> of the poems, and how the ideas and feelings presented are developed.
- Comment on changes in <u>mood</u>, <u>voice</u>, <u>tense</u> and <u>tone</u> — think about <u>the effect</u> this has.

In 'London', the narrative <u>begins</u> and <u>ends</u> on the dismal streets of London, suggesting that its inhabitants are <u>unable to escape</u> the suffering found there. In contrast, 'War Photographer' <u>ends</u> in a different place to where it <u>begins</u>. However, the fact that the photographer is starting another assignment highlights the <u>unending cycle</u> of war and violence.

Form

- See if the poems have a specific <u>form</u> and explain <u>why</u> you think the poet has made that choice.
- Compare the <u>effects</u> of form in each poem. Think about how they relate to the <u>themes</u>.
- Check if any rules are broken for <u>effect</u>, e.g. a sonnet with 15 lines instead of 14.

'Sonnet 43' is a <u>sonnet</u>. By choosing a form traditionally used for love poems, Barrett Browning stresses <u>the strength of the love</u> between the narrator and her beloved. On the other hand, 'Living Space' is written in <u>free verse</u> — the <u>irregular line lengths</u> defy constraint, which echoes the <u>uncontrollable force of poverty</u>.

Compare the poems in every paragraph...

The examiner wants to see you're comparing the poems. Make it easy for them — use linking words and phrases like 'in contrast' or 'whereas' to clearly show that you're making comparisons between the poems.

Warm-Up Questions

When it comes to poetry, you need to look at the overall message of the poem — but don't forget to focus on smaller things too, such as line endings, punctuation and even the vowel sounds in the middle of words. They all have a part to play. To see if you've got to grips with this section, have a go at these questions.

Warm-Up Questions

1) Write a brief definition of each of the following poetic techniques:
   a) Onomatopoeia   b) Caesura   c) Enjambment

2) Write out the sentences below. For each sentence, underline the letters or words that are used to create the effect in brackets.
   Write a sentence for each example explaining the effect of the technique used.

   "the fizzy, movie tomorrows / the right walk home could bring." (**onomatopoeia**)
   (Before You Were Mine, Carol Ann Duffy)

   "They accuse me of absence, they circle me." (**sibilance**)
   (The Emigrée, Carol Rumens)

   "a blockade of yellow bias binding around your blazer." (**alliteration**)
   (Poppies, Jane Weir)

   "All the alleyways and side streets blocked with stops" (**assonance**)
   (Belfast Confetti, Ciaran Carson)

3) The extract below personifies dawn on a battlefield. Write two paragraphs describing the impression you get of the speaker's feelings and how this impression is created.

   > Dawn massing in the east her melancholy army
   > Attacks once more
   >
   > Exposure, Wilfred Owen

4) Read the extract below. Write a sentence explaining the effect of each of the following features of the extract:
   a) The rhyme scheme.
   b) The use of direct address.
   c) Enjambment.

   > That's my last Duchess painted on the wall,
   > Looking as if she were alive. I call
   > That piece a wonder, now: Frà Pandolf's hands
   > Worked busily a day, and there she stands.
   > Will't please you sit and look at her? I said
   > 'Frà Pandolf' by design, for never read
   > Strangers like you that pictured countenance,
   > The depth and passion of its earnest glance,
   > But to myself they turned (since none puts by
   > The curtain I have drawn for you, but I)
   >
   > My Last Duchess, Robert Browning

Revision Summary

This is the first of three sections on poetry, so there's more to get to grips with before you're ready for the poetry part of your exam. This section should give you a good basic knowledge of the things you need to cover when you write about poems. So, if you can answer the questions on this page you should be well on the way to getting some great marks in your exam. If not, look back over the section until you get them right.

1) There are three main elements of a poem that you have to write about in the exam. One is the language of the poem. What are the other two?

2) What should you include to back up each of your ideas about the poem?

3) What is the difference between form and structure?

4) Write a sentence describing each of these forms of poem:
   a) Dramatic monologue
   b) Sonnet
   c) Free verse

5) What is:
   a) a stanza?
   b) a couplet?
   c) a quatrain?

6) Write a brief explanation of what an irregular rhyme scheme is.

7) What two aspects of a poem does the rhythm alter?

8) Below are two lines from a poem. What is the metre? How can you tell?

   Shall I compare thee to a summer's day?
   Thou art more lovely and more temperate.
   (Sonnet 18 — William Shakespeare)

9) What is the difference between enjambment and end-stopping?

10) Find two examples of sensory imagery from the poems you have studied. Explain their effect on the reader.

11) Explain the difference between a simile and a metaphor. Give an example of each from the poems you have studied.

12) Write a sentence explaining what each of these technical terms means:
   a) alliteration
   b) sibilance
   c) assonance

13) What are "boom", "splash" and "crunch" all examples of?

14) Give two examples for each of the following:
   a) comparative words you could use when explaining the similarity between two poems.
   b) comparative words you could use when explaining the difference between two poems.

15) Is the following statement true or false?
   "It's best to compare two poems by writing several paragraphs about one and then several paragraphs about the other."

The Poetry Anthology

If you're doing English Literature, you'll study a collection of poems in class and write about them in the exam.

This is what you'll have to do in the **Exam**

1) You'll probably be given a copy of <u>one poem</u> from your anthology, and asked to compare it with <u>another</u> poem of your <u>choice</u>. You need to choose a poem that has <u>similar themes</u> to the one you're given.

2) You <u>won't</u> have a copy of the anthology in the exam, so make sure you know <u>all</u> the poems really well.

For some exam boards, you might be asked to compare a poem from your anthology with a poem you haven't seen before — see Section Ten for more on how to tackle unseen poetry. Ask your teacher exactly what to expect in the exam.

Read the **Question** carefully and **Underline** key words

1) If your exam board offers <u>more than one</u> poetry cluster, make sure you're looking at the <u>right one</u>. Read the question carefully. Underline the <u>theme</u> and any other <u>key words</u>.

2) Here are a couple of examples of the kind of <u>question</u> you might get in the exam:

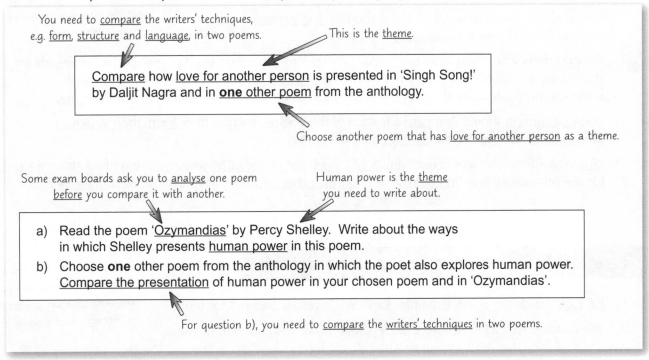

You need to <u>compare</u> the writers' techniques, e.g. <u>form</u>, <u>structure</u> and <u>language</u>, in two poems.

This is the <u>theme</u>.

<u>Compare</u> how <u>love for another person</u> is presented in 'Singh Song!' by Daljit Nagra and in **one** <u>other poem</u> from the anthology.

Choose another poem that has <u>love for another person</u> as a theme.

Some exam boards ask you to <u>analyse</u> one poem <u>before</u> you compare it with another.

Human power is the <u>theme</u> you need to write about.

a) Read the poem '<u>Ozymandias</u>' by Percy Shelley. Write about the ways in which Shelley presents <u>human power</u> in this poem.

b) Choose **one** other poem from the anthology in which the poet also explores human power. <u>Compare the presentation</u> of human power in your chosen poem and in 'Ozymandias'.

For question b), you need to <u>compare</u> the <u>writers' techniques</u> in two poems.

There are **Three Main Ways** to get marks

There are <u>three main things</u> to keep in mind when you're <u>planning</u> and <u>writing</u> your answer:

- Give your own <u>thoughts</u> and <u>opinions</u> on the poems and support them with <u>quotes</u> from the text.
- <u>Explain</u> features like <u>form</u>, <u>structure</u> and <u>language</u>.
- Describe the <u>similarities</u> and <u>differences</u> between poems and their <u>contexts</u>.

The key to success is having a good knowledge of the poems...

At the risk of sounding like a broken record, it's crucial that you know the poems really well for the exam — learn some key quotes from each one that you can include in your answer to back up your points.

How to Structure Your Answer

A solid structure is essential — it lets the examiner follow your argument nice and easily.

Start with an **Introduction** and end with a **Conclusion**

1) Your introduction should begin by giving a clear answer to the question in a sentence or two. Use the rest of the introduction to briefly develop this idea — try to include some of the main ideas from your plan.

2) The main body of your essay should be three to five paragraphs of analysis.

3) Finish your essay with a conclusion — this should summarise your answer to the question. It's also your last chance to impress the examiner, so try to make your final sentence memorable.

You'll probably have to **Compare** two poems

Remember to start a new paragraph every time you start comparing a new feature of the poems.

1) You might be asked to write an essay about a single poem, but you'll usually have to compare two poems.

2) For questions where you have to compare two poems, structure each paragraph by writing about one poem and then explaining whether the other poem is similar or different. Don't just write several paragraphs about one poem, followed by several paragraphs about the other.

3) Every paragraph should compare a feature of the poems, such as their form, their structure, the language they use or the feelings they put across.

4) Link your ideas with words like 'similarly', 'likewise' or 'equally' when you're writing about a similarity. Or use phrases such as 'in contrast' and 'on the other hand' if you're explaining a difference.

Use **P.E.E.D.** to structure each paragraph

This extract shows how to use P.E.E.D. in a comparison essay, but the same structure applies if you're writing about a single poem.

1) P.E.E.D. stands for: Point, Example, Explain, Develop. See p.3 for more.

2) You can use P.E.E.D to structure each paragraph of your answer, like this:

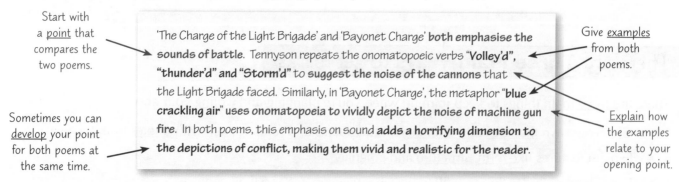

Start with a point that compares the two poems.

Give examples from both poems.

Sometimes you can develop your point for both poems at the same time.

Explain how the examples relate to your opening point.

'The Charge of the Light Brigade' and 'Bayonet Charge' **both emphasise the sounds of battle.** Tennyson repeats the onomatopoeic verbs "Volley'd", "thunder'd" and "Storm'd" **to suggest the noise of the cannons** that the Light Brigade faced. Similarly, in 'Bayonet Charge', the metaphor "**blue crackling air" uses onomatopoeia to vividly depict the noise of machine gun fire.** In both poems, this emphasis on sound **adds a horrifying dimension to the depictions of conflict, making them vivid and realistic for the reader.**

P.E.E.D. is a good way to structure an essay, but it's not essential...

P.E.E.D. is a framework you can use to make sure your paragraphs have all the features they need to pick up marks — it's a useful structure to bear in mind, but you don't have to follow it rigidly in every paragraph.

How to Answer the Question

Now you're up to speed with how to structure your answer, there are a few other things you should keep in mind when answering an exam question on your anthology poems.

Look closely at Language, Form and Structure

1) To get <u>top marks</u>, you need to pay <u>close attention</u> to the <u>techniques</u> the poets use.

2) <u>Analyse</u> the <u>form</u> and <u>structure</u> of the poems, which includes their <u>rhyme scheme</u> and <u>rhythm</u>.

3) Explore <u>language</u> — think about <u>why</u> the poets have used certain <u>words</u> and <u>language techniques</u>.

4) You also need to <u>comment</u> on the <u>effect</u> that these techniques have on the <u>reader</u>. The examiner wants to hear what <u>you think</u> of a poem and how it makes <u>you feel</u>.

5) This is the kind of thing you could write about <u>language</u>:

> 'Poppies' makes frequent references to the injury and bereavement caused by conflict. The poem opens with a reference to the poppies placed "on individual war graves". **By emphasising the personal, individual loss that conflict can cause, Weir highlights the narrator's fear that her own son will be killed in battle.** The narrator's anxiety about the violence of conflict is further suggested by the depiction of poppy petals as "spasms of paper red". This metaphor evokes a vivid image of the physical injury that the narrator fears her son may suffer as a soldier, which **helps the reader to understand the narrator's fears and to empathise with her.**

Analyse the effects of key quotes.

Always develop your ideas.

Always Support Your Ideas with Details from the Text

1) You need to <u>back up your ideas</u> with <u>quotes</u> from or <u>references</u> to the text.

2) <u>Choose</u> your quotes <u>carefully</u> — they have to be <u>relevant</u> to the point you're making.

3) <u>Don't</u> quote <u>large chunks</u> of text — instead, use <u>short</u> quotes and <u>embed</u> them in your sentences.

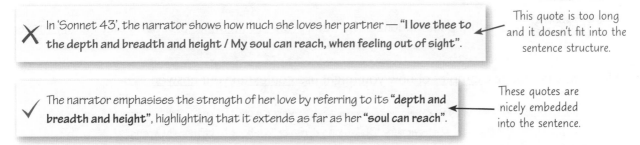

✗ In 'Sonnet 43', the narrator shows how much she loves her partner — **"I love thee to the depth and breadth and height / My soul can reach, when feeling out of sight".**

This quote is too long and it doesn't fit into the sentence structure.

✓ The narrator emphasises the strength of her love by referring to its **"depth and breadth and height"**, highlighting that it extends as far as her **"soul can reach"**.

These quotes are nicely embedded into the sentence.

4) <u>Don't</u> forget to <u>explain</u> your quotes — you need to use them as <u>evidence</u> to support your <u>argument</u>.

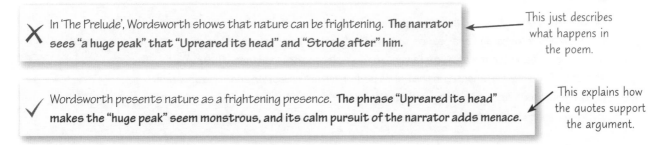

✗ In 'The Prelude', Wordsworth shows that nature can be frightening. **The narrator sees "a huge peak" that "Upreared its head" and "Strode after" him.**

This just describes what happens in the poem.

✓ Wordsworth presents nature as a frightening presence. **The phrase "Upreared its head" makes the "huge peak" seem monstrous, and its calm pursuit of the narrator adds menace.**

This explains how the quotes support the argument.

How to Answer the Question

Give Alternative Interpretations

1) You need to show you're aware that poems can be <u>interpreted</u> in <u>more than one</u> way.

2) If a poem is a bit <u>ambiguous</u>, or you think that a particular line or phrase could have several <u>different meanings</u>, then <u>say so</u>.

> In 'Ozymandias', Shelley refers to the sculptor as the "hand that mocked" the statue. On the surface, the word **"mocked"** shows only that the sculptor created the artwork. However, Shelley may also be playing on the second meaning of the word "mocked" (to make fun of); the **"wrinkled lip and sneer"** of the statue suggest that the sculptor disliked Ozymandias, hinting that he may have intended to ridicule the leader by his unflattering depiction.

Remember to support your interpretations with evidence from the poem.

3) Be <u>original</u> with your ideas — just make sure you can back them up with an <u>example</u> from the text.

Show some Wider Knowledge

1) To get a top grade, you need to <u>explain</u> how the <u>ideas</u> in the poems relate to their <u>context</u>.

2) When you're thinking about a particular poem, consider these aspects of <u>context</u>:

Historical — Do the ideas in the poem relate to the <u>time</u> in which it's <u>written</u> or <u>set</u>?

Geographical — How is the poem shaped and influenced by the <u>place</u> in which it's set?

Social — Is the poet <u>criticising</u> or <u>praising</u> the <u>society</u> or <u>community</u> they're writing about?

Cultural — Does the poet draw on a particular aspect of their <u>background</u> or <u>culture</u>?

Literary — Was the poet influenced by other <u>works of literature</u> or a particular <u>literary movement</u>?

3) Here are a couple of <u>examples</u> of how you might use <u>context</u> in your <u>answer</u>:

> In 'London', Blake's reference to the "chimney-sweeper's cry" creates a vivid picture of child labour, which was common in the late 18th century. Blake considered child labour to be morally wrong, and he may have included this emotive image in order to boost public sympathy for his views.

> Browning is thought to have based the speaker in 'My Last Duchess' on the Duke of Ferrara, an important nobleman in Renaissance Italy. The Italian Renaissance was a time of great artistic innovation, but it was also infamous for its violence and bloodshed. These dual aspects of society are reflected in the Duke's pride in his art collection and in his apparent lack of guilt about seemingly having had his wife killed.

How to Answer the Question

Use **Sophisticated Language**

1) Your writing has to sound <u>sophisticated</u> and <u>precise</u>.

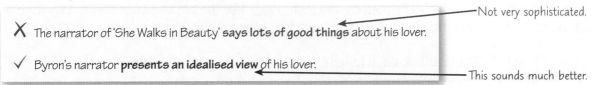

Not very sophisticated.

✗ The narrator of 'She Walks in Beauty' **says lots of good things** about his lover.

✓ Byron's narrator **presents an idealised view** of his lover.

This sounds much better.

2) It should be <u>concise</u> and <u>accurate</u>, with no <u>vague words</u> or <u>waffle</u>.

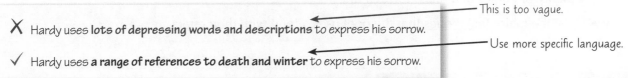

This is too vague.

✗ Hardy uses **lots of depressing words and descriptions** to express his sorrow.

✓ Hardy uses **a range of references to death and winter** to express his sorrow.

Use more specific language.

3) Your writing should also show an <u>impressive range</u> of <u>vocabulary</u>.

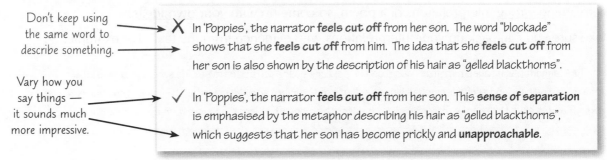

Don't keep using the same word to describe something.

✗ In 'Poppies', the narrator **feels cut off** from her son. The word "blockade" shows that she **feels cut off** from him. The idea that she **feels cut off** from her son is also shown by the description of his hair as "gelled blackthorns".

Vary how you say things — it sounds much more impressive.

✓ In 'Poppies', the narrator **feels cut off** from her son. This **sense of separation** is emphasised by the metaphor describing his hair as "gelled blackthorns", which suggests that her son has become prickly and **unapproachable**.

4) However, make sure you <u>only</u> use words that you know the <u>meaning</u> of. For example, don't say that a poem has a '<u>volta</u>' if you don't know what it <u>really means</u> — it will be <u>obvious</u> to the examiner.

Use **Technical Terms** where possible

1) To get top marks, you need to use the <u>correct technical terms</u> when you're writing about poetry.

2) Flick back to Section Eight for more on these terms, or have a look at the <u>glossary</u> at the back of the book.

Don't write	**Write**
✗ Simon Armitage uses <u>good images</u>.	✓ Simon Armitage uses <u>effective metaphors</u>.
✗ The poet uses <u>words that are also sounds</u>.	✓ The poet uses <u>onomatopoeia</u>.
✗ The <u>sentences run on from line to line</u>.	✓ The poet uses <u>enjambment</u>.

Exam practice makes perfect...

The best way to make sure you've understood all of this is to get lots of practice — have a go at some of the exam-style questions on p.128, and make sure you cover the main points on these last three pages.

How to Write a Top Grade Answer

If you're aiming for a grade 9, you're going to have to do a little bit extra. Here are a few tips...

Know the Poems inside out

You have to know the poems, their key themes and techniques like the back of your hand. Everyone has their own ways of understanding poetry, but here are a few ideas of how to get to grips with them:

- Read the poems again and again, highlight bits, jot down notes — whatever works for you.
- Make a list of the key themes, and note down plenty of quotes that relate to each one.
- List the major techniques that the poet uses, along with their effect.

Memorise your lists in time for the exam.

Be as Original as you can

1) There are no wrong interpretations of a poem, so come up with your own ideas.

2) Make sure you can back up your interpretations with evidence from the text. For example:

> In 'The Manhunt', Armitage's narrator describes the soldier's scar as a "frozen river". This creates a vivid image of a river eroding a land surface, emphasising the depth of the injury and the power of the object that harmed him. The fact that the scar is "frozen" implies that, for the moment at least, no more damage is being done.

Write about the poems Critically

1) Being critical means giving your own opinions about the poems — e.g. how effective you think the poet's techniques are, and why you think this.

2) You need to phrase your opinions in a sophisticated way. For example:

> In 'Neutral Tones', the phrase "God-curst sun" compels the reader to experience the scene as Hardy's narrator does: a bleak, lifeless landscape, devoid of hope and forsaken by God.

Get to grips with Context

It's not enough just to mention a link to context — you need to really explore the effect it has on the poem, or on your understanding of it. For example:

> In common with other Romantic poets, Wordsworth viewed nature as a powerful force that could inspire and transform people. This is evident in the extract from his autobiographical poem 'The Prelude'; the encounter with the "huge peak" leaves him in a "grave / And serious mood", seemingly forcing him to contemplate his own mortality and place in the Universe.

For a top grade, think originally and critically...

When it comes to grade 9, the examiner wants your interpretation and your opinion of the poems. Have a look at the sample answer on pages 126-127 for some ideas of how to write a great poetry essay.

Warm-Up Questions

For a poetry essay, you need to know what to write about and how to write it. When you answer the questions on this page, practise using sophisticated language so it becomes second nature by the time the exam comes round. Remember to use technical terms whenever possible as well.

Warm-Up Questions

1) In your anthology, find a poem that rhymes.
   What effect does the use of rhyme have in this poem?

2) Choose a poem from your anthology that is written in the first person and one that is written in the third person. Do you find it easier to empathise with the first-person narrator or the characters described by the third-person narration? Write a paragraph explaining your answer.

3) For each of the following aspects of form and structure, find an example from any of the poems in your anthology. Write a sentence explaining the effect each example has on the reader.
   a) End-stopping.
   b) Caesurae.
   c) Dramatic monologue.
   d) Enjambment.

4) Using two of your answers to question 3, write a paragraph comparing the form and structure of two of the poems, and explaining how the poets use form and structure to help convey their messages.

5) For each of the following language techniques, find an example from any of the poems in your anthology. Write a sentence explaining the effect each example has on the reader.
   a) Repetition.
   b) Onomatopoeia.
   c) Alliteration.
   d) Assonance.

6) Using two of your answers to question 5, write a paragraph comparing the language of two of the poems, and explaining how the poets use language to help convey their messages.

7) Pick one more poem from your anthology. How does the poet use imagery in the poem? Write a paragraph about your favourite image, explaining what effect it has on you.

Worked Exam-Style Question

Comparison questions can be particularly tricky, so here's an example of how you might answer one.

Q1 Read 'Bayonet Charge' by Ted Hughes. Choose one other poem from the anthology and compare how the reality of conflict is presented in the two poems.

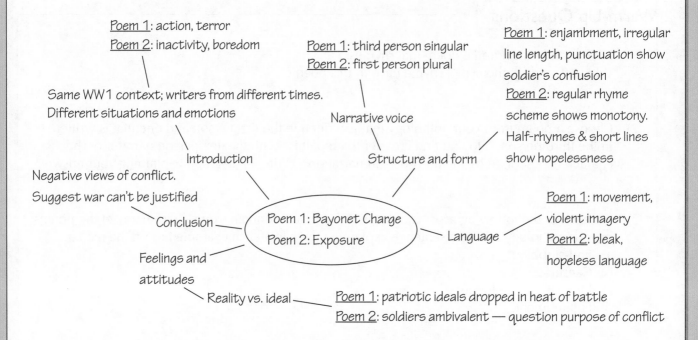

Poem 1: action, terror
Poem 2: inactivity, boredom

Poem 1: third person singular
Poem 2: first person plural

Poem 1: enjambment, irregular line length, punctuation show soldier's confusion
Poem 2: regular rhyme scheme shows monotony. Half-rhymes & short lines show hopelessness

Same WW1 context; writers from different times. Different situations and emotions

Narrative voice

Introduction

Structure and form

Negative views of conflict. Suggest war can't be justified

Conclusion

Poem 1: Bayonet Charge
Poem 2: Exposure

Language

Poem 1: movement, violent imagery
Poem 2: bleak, hopeless language

Feelings and attitudes

Reality vs. ideal

Poem 1: patriotic ideals dropped in heat of battle
Poem 2: soldiers ambivalent — question purpose of conflict

Compare the poems in your opening sentence.

Although the action of both 'Bayonet Charge' and 'Exposure' occurs on the battlefields of World War One, the poems offer two very different portrayals of the reality of conflict. While 'Bayonet Charge' depicts the violent action and overwhelming terror experienced by a soldier going into battle, 'Exposure' focuses on the boredom and inactivity of men waiting in the freezing trenches of the Western Front while "nothing happens" on the battlefield. Both poets present war as a profoundly negative experience, in which hope, faith and sense of self are overpowered by pain and fear.

Sum up the main argument of your essay.

The poems use different narrative voices. 'Bayonet Charge' is written in the third person. The anonymity of the subject, "he", and the fact that he is the only human mentioned in the poem make him seem isolated and alone, even though it is clear that he must be surrounded by other soldiers. This sense of isolation heightens the feeling of terror in the poem by reflecting the soldier's acute focus on his own survival. In contrast, 'Exposure' is written in the first person plural ("our memory", "we hear"), which creates a sense of the shared suffering experienced by the millions of soldiers who fought and died in the First World War. This emphasises the vast scale of misery and loss of life in the war.

Try to develop your ideas.

Compare the poems' form and structure.

The poets also use other aspects of form and structure to present the reality of conflict. In 'Bayonet Charge', Hughes uses enjambment and uneven line lengths to create an irregular rhythm, echoing the confusion experienced by the soldier. The irregular rhythm is heightened by caesurae in lines 11 and 15. These help to turn

Use the correct technical terms.

Worked Exam-Style Question

the second stanza into a pause in the action, which reflects the soldier's experience of time apparently standing still as he struggles to understand "the reason / Of his still running". In contrast, Owen uses a regular rhyme scheme (ABBAC) to emphasise the monotony experienced by the soldiers. Despite this regularity, half-rhymes such as "wire" / "war" create a sense of jarring discomfort that mirrors the soldiers' suffering.

The different experiences of conflict presented in 'Exposure' and 'Bayonet Charge' are conveyed through <u>the contrasting language the poets use</u>. Owen's language is bleak and hopeless — dawn is personified as a "melancholy army" "massing in the east", a metaphor which has a powerful effect on the reader by subverting their expectations — dawn is usually a symbol of hope, but here it only brings more "poignant misery". The soldiers' sense of hopelessness is also evident in the phrase "love of God seems dying", <u>which suggests that the horrific reality of conflict is causing them to lose their faith in God, or perhaps to believe that a God who can subject them to such suffering has lost faith in them</u>. In contrast to this bleak imagery, 'Bayonet Charge' is filled with frantic movement. Active verbs such as "running" and "stumbling" help to create a vivid image of the soldier's desperate actions as he races into battle. The sense of movement in the poem is also conveyed by the opening phrase, "<u>Suddenly he awoke</u>", which places the reader in the middle of the action from the start. <u>This gives the poem a nightmarish quality, highlighting the feelings of confusion and terror that are driving the soldier.</u>

Compare the <u>language</u> used in the two poems.

Suggest <u>more than one interpretation</u> of the poem.

Use <u>quotes</u> to support your argument.

Explain the <u>effect</u> of the examples you give.

Both poems suggest that the reality of conflict does not match up to the ideal. In 'Bayonet Charge', Hughes questions the patriotic ideals of "King, honour, human dignity, etcetera", arguing that in the heat of battle they are "Dropped like luxuries" as terror takes over. <u>Information about the horrors of World War One was readily available in the 1950s when Hughes wrote this poem, and there is a sense of pity for the soldiers who fought.</u> Similarly, in 'Exposure', the narrator questions whether anything is achieved by the soldiers' sacrifice. On the surface, the phrase "Since we believe not otherwise can kind fires burn" suggests the soldiers believe their sacrifice is necessary to protect the "kind fires" of home, but the complex, broken syntax reflects their lack of conviction that this is true. <u>This reveals the alienation many soldiers felt: they believed no-one at home appreciated their sacrifice.</u>

Bring in some <u>contextual</u> details to your answer.

'Bayonet Charge' and 'Exposure' both present vividly negative views of the reality of conflict for soldiers on the front line. The experience of the soldiers in the two poems is very different: Hughes focuses on the raw terror and active suffering of a soldier going into battle, whereas Owen concentrates on the hopelessness and passive suffering of men dying from exposure. However, both poets use structure, form and vivid imagery to powerfully convey the soldiers' suffering. <u>Both narrators question the patriotic ideals used to justify war, suggesting instead that there can be no justification for the bleak and dehumanising reality of conflict.</u>

Your last sentence should <u>sum up your argument</u>, and it needs to be <u>memorable</u>.

Exam-Style Questions

Now it's time to put all you've learned about how to write a great answer into practice. Not all of these questions will be relevant to your anthology, but there should be at least one question you can answer.

Q1 Compare how feelings towards another person are presented in one poem by Elizabeth Barrett Browning and one other poem from your poetry anthology.

Q2 Compare the ways in which time is presented in two poems from your anthology.

Q3 Explore the ways in which the effects of conflict are presented in one poem by Wilfred Owen and one other poem from your poetry anthology.

Q4 Compare the way that a sense of place is created in two poems you have studied.

Q5 "Striving for power is ultimately pointless."

Using this statement as a starting point, compare the presentation of human power in two poems from your anthology.

Remember to comment on how the poems are written.

Five Steps to Analysing a Poem

You'll have to analyse unseen poetry at some point in your English Literature exams — here's how to do it.

The examiner is looking for **Four Main Things**

You'll usually be asked to answer a question on an <u>unseen poem</u>, and then <u>compare</u> it with another poem. To impress the examiner, you need to:

1) Show that you <u>understand</u> what the poems are <u>about</u>.

2) Write about the <u>techniques</u> used in the poems.

3) Use the <u>correct technical terms</u> to describe the techniques in the poems.

4) <u>Support</u> every point you make with <u>quotes</u> or <u>examples</u> from the poems.

Five Steps to analysing an unseen poem

Pick out the important bits of the poem as you read it — underline them or make notes.

1) Work out what the poem's about

• Work out the <u>subject</u> of the poem, e.g. the poem is about the narrator's relationship with his parents.

• Think about <u>who</u> is <u>speaking</u>, and <u>who</u> the poem is <u>addressing</u> — e.g. the narrator's lover, the reader...

2) Identify the purpose, theme or message

• Think about <u>what</u> the poet is saying, <u>why</u> they've written the poem, or what <u>ideas</u> they're using.

• The poem could be an <u>emotional response</u> to something. It might aim to <u>get a response</u> from the <u>reader</u>, or put across a message or an opinion about something.

3) Explore the emotions, moods or feelings

• Consider the <u>different emotions or feelings</u> in the poem and identify its <u>mood</u>.

• Look at how the poet <u>shows</u> these emotions (see step 4).

4) Identify the techniques used in the poem

• Find the <u>different techniques</u> the poet has used and how they create <u>emotions</u>, <u>moods</u> or <u>feelings</u>. Think about <u>why</u> the poet has used them, and what <u>effect</u> they create.

• Techniques can be related to <u>language</u> (<u>alliteration</u>, <u>onomatopoeia</u>, <u>imagery</u> etc.), <u>structure</u> (the order of <u>ideas</u> and any changes in <u>mood</u> or <u>tone</u>) and <u>form</u> (<u>line</u> and <u>stanza</u> length, <u>rhyme schemes</u> etc.).

5) Include your thoughts and feelings about the poem

• Examiners love to hear what <u>you think</u> of a poem and how it makes <u>you feel</u>. Think about how well the poem gets its <u>message</u> across and what <u>impact</u> it has on you.

• Try <u>not</u> to use "<u>I</u>" though — don't say "I felt sad that the narrator's brother died", it's much <u>better</u> to say "It makes the reader feel the narrator's sense of sadness at the death of his brother."

• Think about any <u>other ways</u> that the poem could be <u>interpreted</u>.

Always read the poem with the question in mind...

The first thing to do when you're analysing a poem is to read the question carefully and underline the key words. That'll help you to identify aspects of the poem that are directly relevant to the question.

Worked Exam-Style Question

On the next three pages is a step-by-step guide to answering an unseen poetry question in the exam.
The first stage is to read the question carefully and annotate the relevant parts of the poem.

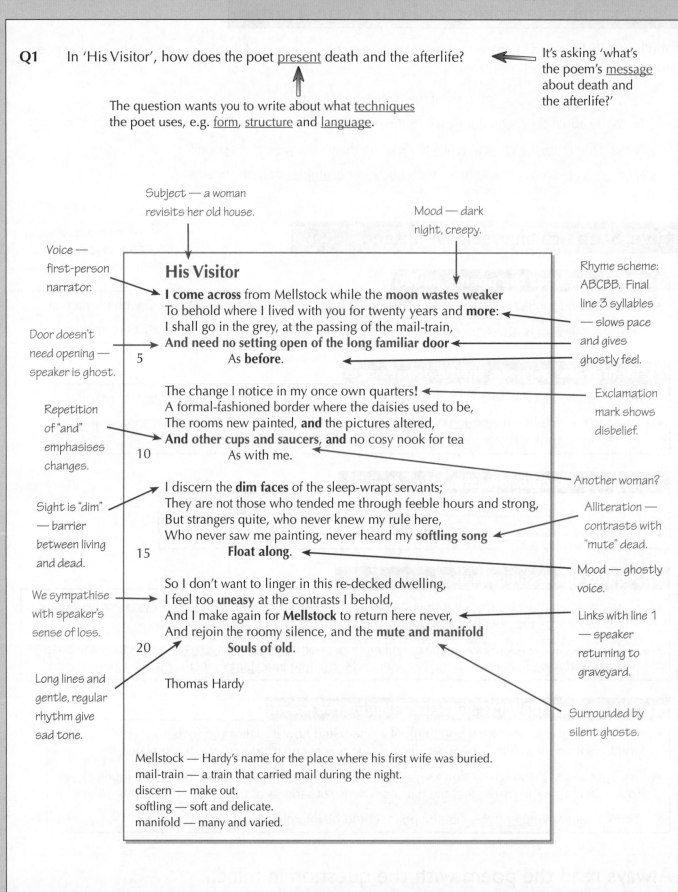

Q1 In 'His Visitor', how does the poet <u>present</u> death and the afterlife?

It's asking 'what's the poem's <u>message</u> about death and the afterlife?'

The question wants you to write about what <u>techniques</u> the poet uses, e.g. <u>form</u>, <u>structure</u> and <u>language</u>.

Voice — first-person narrator.

Subject — a woman revisits her old house.

Mood — dark night, creepy.

Rhyme scheme: ABCBB. Final line 3 syllables — slows pace and gives ghostly feel.

Door doesn't need opening — speaker is ghost.

Repetition of "and" emphasises changes.

Sight is "dim" — barrier between living and dead.

We sympathise with speaker's sense of loss.

Long lines and gentle, regular rhythm give sad tone.

Exclamation mark shows disbelief.

Another woman?

Alliteration — contrasts with "mute" dead.

Mood — ghostly voice.

Links with line 1 — speaker returning to graveyard.

Surrounded by silent ghosts.

His Visitor

I come across from Mellstock while the **moon wastes weaker**
To behold where I lived with you for twenty years and **more:**
I shall go in the grey, at the passing of the mail-train,
And need no setting open of the long familiar door
5   As **before.**

The change I notice in my once own quarters!
A formal-fashioned border where the daisies used to be,
The rooms new painted, **and** the pictures altered,
And other cups and saucers, **and** no cosy nook for tea
10   As with me.

I discern the **dim faces** of the sleep-wrapt servants;
They are not those who tended me through feeble hours and strong,
But strangers quite, who never knew my rule here,
Who never saw me painting, never heard my **softling song**
15   **Float along.**

So I don't want to linger in this re-decked dwelling,
I feel too **uneasy** at the contrasts I behold,
And I make again for **Mellstock** to return here never,
And rejoin the roomy silence, and the **mute and manifold**
20   **Souls of old.**

Thomas Hardy

Mellstock — Hardy's name for the place where his first wife was buried.
mail-train — a train that carried mail during the night.
discern — make out.
softling — soft and delicate.
manifold — many and varied.

Worked Exam-Style Question

Once you've got to grips with the poem, spend five minutes planning your answer.
Then get writing your answer — just make sure you refer back to your plan as you write.

Plan:

1. Intro
- Subject — a ghost visits her former home.
- Sorrow of dead.

2. Death isn't the end
- Ghost narrator.
- Ghost is sad, not scary — reader sympathises with her.

3. The dead are powerless
- She is "uneasy" at the changes, but can't do anything about them.
- Her only choice is to "rejoin the roomy silence".
- Sad tone (reinforced by gentle, regular rhythm) — living move on, dead don't.

4. Separation between dead and living
- She doesn't need the door opened — she's formless.
- Living are unaware of her.
- Living are "dim faces" — indistinct.
- Living are vocal — "softling song". Dead are "mute".

5. Effect of death on the living
- Poet vs. narrator. He imagines her response.
- Guilt at the changes/new wife?

6. Conclusion
- Dead always with us.
- Living and dead are separate but impact on each other.

Don't spend too long on your plan. It's only rough work, so you don't need to write in full sentences.

Focus on three or four key points about the poem.

Remember to write about what the poet says and how they say it.

The poem 'His Visitor' describes the return of a ghost to the home she shared with her partner for "twenty years and more". In it, the poet imagines her resentment of the changes that have occurred since her death, indirectly revealing his own guilt at allowing these changes to take place. The poem suggests that although the living can affect the dead, and vice versa, ultimately they are separate states with no point of contact.

Clear start, showing that you've understood the poem.

Write about the poem's main messages early on in your essay.

The most obvious point the poet makes about death is that it is not the end. Although the narrator of the poem never explicitly states that she is a ghost, it is made clear when she says, for instance, that she arrives by night and needs "no setting open" of the door. The use of the first person makes the reader empathise with the sadness of the narrator, breaking down the stereotype of ghosts being frightening.

Always use quotes to back up points.

Give a personal response to the poem.

Worked Exam-Style Question

Write about feelings and mood, and use quotes to back up your points.

The feeling of sorrow is emphasised by the powerlessness of the narrator. Although she is "uneasy" at the changes that have been made to her former home, the only way she can ease her discomfort is to leave and "return here never". Death therefore involves giving up a loved home and all that is familiar, and instead accepting the loneliness that comes with joining the "roomy silence". The gentle rhythm of the poem reinforces the narrator's loneliness. The three-syllable lines that end each stanza are separated from the rest of the stanza by the change in rhythm, but they are linked to it by rhyme. They have the effect of making each stanza seem to tail off wistfully, reinforcing the narrator's sorrow, while their content shows her fixation on "before". This suggests that, while the living are able to move forward, the dead are trapped in the past.

Comment on form and the effect it has.

The poet also suggests that death divides the narrator from the living world. The colours of the poem are muted: the "grey" of night and the moon that "wastes weaker" create a feeling of unreality that contrasts with the "cosy nook" of the past. The "dim faces" of the sleeping servants may be shadowy because it is night, or because the narrator exists in the spiritual world, so to her, the material world is vague and unclear. Although the narrator is aware of her surroundings, she cannot interact with them, instead passing through the "long familiar door". The silence of the dead is emphasised by the alliteration of "mute and manifold", which contrasts with the "softling song" of the narrator when she was alive.

Write about any imagery in the poem.

Think about different interpretations to help you get top marks.

Mention and explain any poetic devices that you spot.

The poem also gives clues about the impact of death on the living. By imagining how "uneasy" the narrator feels at the "contrasts" she sees, Hardy gives the reader a hint of the guilt he feels at moving on while she cannot. The changes described are not large, but the use of an exclamation mark and the repetition of "and" in the second stanza shows how significant the poet believes they would have been to the narrator. The mention of "other cups and saucers", traditionally chosen by women, hint that the dead woman's place may have been taken by another woman. This may explain the poet's guilt. However, the fact that he is so concerned with what the ghost would feel suggests, ironically, that he has not really moved on.

Think about any hidden meanings the poem might contain.

Give a good personal response wherever you can.

Mention specific language features and explain why the poet used them.

The central message of the poem is that the living and the dead inhabit two separate worlds. Hardy explores this through his use of a ghostly first-person narrator, a gentle regular rhythm which reflects her sad drifting around the house and her eventual return to "roomy silence".

Sum up the what and how in your final paragraph.

Comparing Two Poems

As well as analysing an unseen poem, you might have to compare it with another poem. Here are a few tips.

You might have to **Compare Two** unseen poems

For more on how to structure an answer where you're comparing two poems, see page 116.

1) In the exam, you'll probably have to compare <u>two unseen poems</u>, or you might have to compare <u>one unseen poem</u> with a poem from your <u>poetry anthology</u>.

2) This means that you need to write about the <u>similarities</u> and <u>differences</u> between them.

3) You'll need to discuss the <u>techniques</u> the poets use and their <u>effect on the reader</u>, so focus on the <u>structure</u>, <u>form</u> and <u>language</u> used in the two poems.

Four Steps to answering a comparison question

Don't start writing <u>without thinking</u> about what you're going to say — follow these <u>four steps</u> to organise your ideas:

1) **Read the question**

- <u>Read</u> the question carefully and <u>underline</u> the key words.

- Check whether the question asks you to write about a specific <u>theme</u>, e.g. 'conflict' or 'family'.

2) **Annotate the poems**

- Go through and <u>annotate</u> the poems, focusing on the <u>techniques</u> used and the <u>effect</u> they have on the reader.

- As you're annotating the second poem, look for <u>similarities</u> and <u>differences</u> with the <u>techniques</u> you picked out in the first poem.

<u>Read</u>, <u>Annotate</u>, <u>Plan</u>, <u>Write</u>. To help you remember these four steps, try: <u>Really</u> <u>Angry</u> <u>Penguins</u> <u>Wobble</u>.

3) **Plan your answer**

- Identify <u>three or four</u> key <u>similarities and/or differences</u> that you're going to write about.

- Write a <u>short plan</u> that outlines the <u>structure</u> of your answer.

4) **Write your answer**

- <u>Use</u> your plan to make sure that <u>every paragraph</u> you write discusses <u>one similarity or difference</u> between the two poems. This could be in their <u>themes</u> and <u>ideas</u>, or their <u>form</u>, <u>structure</u> and <u>language</u>.

- Use <u>linking words and phrases</u>, e.g. 'in contrast' or 'similarly', to make it really clear that you're <u>comparing</u> the two poems.

You're comparing two poems, so make sure you write about both...

In comparison questions, the examiner wants you to discuss the similarities and differences between the two poems. Make this easy for them by including at least one clear comparison in every paragraph.

Worked Exam-Style Question

Here's another worked example. Use it to get some ideas about how to approach a comparison question.

Q1 'His Visitor' and 'Ghosts' both explore <u>people's feelings on visiting a former home</u>. Compare the ways these feelings are <u>presented</u> in the two poems.

You need to compare the poets' <u>techniques</u>, e.g. <u>form</u>, <u>structure</u> and <u>language</u>, in the two poems.

This is the <u>theme</u> you'll be looking at.

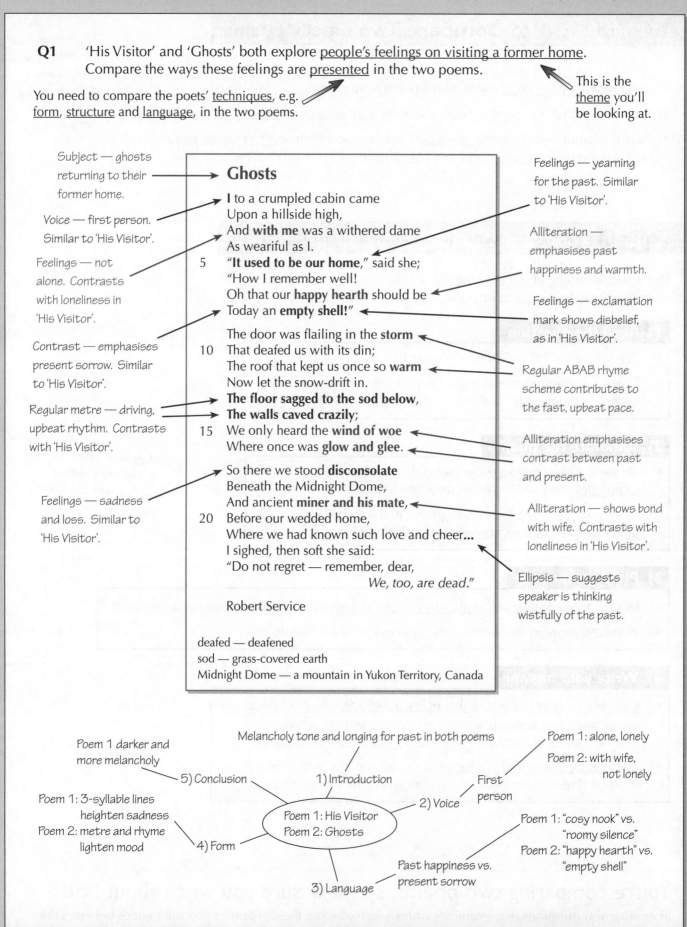

Subject — ghosts returning to their former home.

Voice — first person. Similar to 'His Visitor'.

Feelings — not alone. Contrasts with loneliness in 'His Visitor'.

Contrast — emphasises present sorrow. Similar to 'His Visitor'.

Regular metre — driving, upbeat rhythm. Contrasts with 'His Visitor'.

Feelings — sadness and loss. Similar to 'His Visitor'.

Ghosts

I to a crumpled cabin came
Upon a hillside high,
And **with me** was a withered dame
As weariful as I.
5 "**It used to be our home**," said she;
"How I remember well!
Oh that our **happy hearth** should be
Today an **empty shell!**"

The door was flailing in the **storm**
10 That deafed us with its din;
The roof that kept us once so **warm**
Now let the snow-drift in.
The floor sagged to the sod below,
The walls caved crazily;
15 We only heard the **wind of woe**
Where once was **glow and glee.**

So there we stood **disconsolate**
Beneath the Midnight Dome,
And ancient **miner and his mate**,
20 Before our wedded home,
Where we had known such love and cheer**...**
I sighed, then soft she said:
"Do not regret — remember, dear,
        We, too, are dead."

Robert Service

deafed — deafened
sod — grass-covered earth
Midnight Dome — a mountain in Yukon Territory, Canada

Feelings — yearning for the past. Similar to 'His Visitor'.

Alliteration — emphasises past happiness and warmth.

Feelings — exclamation mark shows disbelief, as in 'His Visitor'.

Regular ABAB rhyme scheme contributes to the fast, upbeat pace.

Alliteration emphasises contrast between past and present.

Alliteration — shows bond with wife. Contrasts with loneliness in 'His Visitor'.

Ellipsis — suggests speaker is thinking wistfully of the past.

Poem 1 darker and more melancholy

Melancholy tone and longing for past in both poems

Poem 1: alone, lonely

Poem 2: with wife, not lonely

5) Conclusion

1) Introduction

First person

Poem 1: His Visitor
Poem 2: Ghosts

2) Voice

Poem 1: 3-syllable lines heighten sadness
Poem 2: metre and rhyme lighten mood

4) Form

3) Language

Past happiness vs. present sorrow

Poem 1: "cosy nook" vs. "roomy silence"
Poem 2: "happy hearth" vs. "empty shell"

Worked Exam-Style Question

Show that you've <u>understood</u> the <u>question</u>.

'His Visitor' and 'Ghosts' are both melancholy poems in which a ghostly narrator returns to their former home and is distressed to find that it has changed dramatically. Although the poems convey similar feelings about visiting a former home, the poets <u>use narrative voice, language and form in different ways to put these feelings across</u>.

Explain how the <u>techniques</u> in the poems affect the <u>reader</u>.

Embed <u>short</u> <u>quotes</u> into your writing.

Both poems use a first-person narrator, and in both cases this makes the narrator's feelings about their former home seem real and immediate, <u>encouraging the reader to empathise with them</u>. The narrator of 'His Visitor' returns home alone, and her isolation is conveyed by her repeated use of the first-person singular pronoun "I". This isolation emphasises the narrator's loneliness as she revisits the once-familiar house, now filled with "<u>strangers</u>". In 'Ghosts', however, the narrator is accompanied by his wife. Their close connection is highlighted by the use of the collective pronouns "we" and "us", and by the alliterative description of them as a "miner and his mate". In contrast to 'His Visitor', loneliness is not a prominent emotion in 'Ghosts', and instead Service focuses on the narrator's sadness at the destruction of his former home.

Show that you understand the <u>imagery</u> in the poems.

Introduce your paragraphs with a <u>comparison</u>.

<u>Both poets use language to emphasise the contrast</u> between past happiness and present sorrow. In 'His Visitor', <u>the "cosy nook" symbolises the warmth and comfort that the house once offered the narrator</u>, and contrasts with the "roomy silence" of the afterlife. Similarly, in 'Ghosts' the "happy hearth" represents the joy and warmth of the past, and contrasts starkly with the "empty shell" that the house has become. In both poems, such contrasts highlight the narrators' yearning for the past. This sense of longing is further emphasised by repeated use of phrases associated with the past, <u>such as "As before" and "used to be"</u>, suggesting that both narrators are fixated on the way things were.

Use <u>quotes</u> to support your <u>argument</u>.

The form of 'His Visitor' plays an important role in conveying the narrator's feelings. The three-syllable lines that end each stanza slow the poem's pace and give it an irregular rhythm, with each stanza trailing off wistfully. <u>This creates a powerful sense of sadness and melancholy, which reinforces the feelings of loss and longing that are conveyed through the poem's language.</u> In contrast, the regular metre and simple ABAB rhyme scheme of 'Ghosts' give the poem a faster pace and a driving, upbeat rhythm. The rhythm lightens the mood, making the poem seem <u>less bleak and melancholy than 'His Visitor'</u>.

Write about how <u>form</u> conveys meaning.

Remember to <u>compare</u> the two poems.

<u>Summarise</u> the <u>similarities</u> and <u>differences</u> in your conclusion.

'His Visitor' and 'Ghosts' both use language to convey similar feelings of sadness, loss and longing for the past, and regret at the changes to their former homes. However, differences in the poets' use of narrative voice and form mean that, overall, the tone of 'His Visitor' is darker and more melancholy than that of 'Ghosts'.

Warm-Up Questions

Before you answer the questions at the bottom of the page, read the poem all the way through and annotate anything you think is important. Once you've got an idea of what the poem's about, the techniques the poet uses and why she uses them, you'll be ready to answer the questions.

Warm-Up Questions

Spring in War-Time

Now the sprinkled blackthorn snow
Lies along the lovers' lane
Where last year we used to go—
Where we shall not go again.

5   In the hedge the buds are new,
By our wood the violets peer—
Just like last year's violets, too,
But they have no scent this year.

Every bird has heart to sing
10   Of its nest, warmed by its breast;
We had heart to sing last spring,
But we never built our nest.

Presently red roses blown
Will make all the garden gay...
15   Not yet have the daisies grown
On your clay.

Edith Nesbit

blackthorn — a bush with white flowers in spring

1) Write down what you think the poem is about, in just one sentence.

2) What do you think the narrator means by "we never built our nest" in the 3rd stanza?

3) How does the poet create a contrast between the signs of spring and the narrator's feelings in the poem?

4) What is the rhyme scheme of this poem and why do you think that the poet chose it?

5) The last line of the poem has a different rhythm. Why do you think that the poet has done this?

Exam-Style Questions

On the next two pages are questions about two poems that you probably won't have read before. The questions you have to answer in the exam might be a bit different to these, but they'll always test your ability to analyse and compare poems.

Q1   Read the poem below. What do you think the poet is saying about what it can feel like to be left alone? How does the poet present her ideas?

At Sea

With nothing to do now he's gone,
she dusts the house,
sweeps the bleached verandah clear of sand.
The broom leaves a trail of grit on the step,
5   a sprinkling under the hook where it hangs.

A coat for a pillow,
she sleeps downstairs,
dreams the loathed ocean is coming for her,
climbing the cliffs,
10   creeping in through the door.

She wakes to the screaming gulls,
his shirts on the line
and the high tide's breakers'
chill in her arms.

Jennifer Copley

Exam-Style Questions

Q2 'At Sea' and 'The Sands of Dee' both describe the power of the sea.
Compare the way the poets present the sea in these two poems.

The Sands of Dee

'O Mary, go and call the cattle home,
And call the cattle home,
And call the cattle home
Across the sands of Dee;'
5   The western wind was wild and dank with foam,
And all alone went she.

The western tide crept up along the sand,
And o'er and o'er the sand,
And round and round the sand,
10   As far as eye could see.
The rolling mist came down and hid the land:
And never home came she.

'Oh! is it weed, or fish, or floating hair—
A tress of golden hair,
15   A drowned maiden's hair
Above the nets at sea?
Was never salmon yet that shone so fair
Among the stakes on Dee.'

They rowed her in across the rolling foam,
20   The cruel, crawling foam,
The cruel, hungry foam,
To her grave beside the sea:
But still the boatmen hear her call the cattle home,
Across the sands of Dee.

Charles Kingsley

Sands of Dee — a sandy bay in North Wales
dank — damp and unpleasant
o'er — over
tress — a piece of hair or a plait

Writing Well

Being able to use good spelling, punctuation and grammar is important for both Language and Literature.

Writing Well will get you a Better Grade

Some of your English marks are for <u>how</u> you write, not <u>what</u> you write. Here's what you'll be marked on:

1) <u>Standard English</u>
   Examiners will expect you to use standard (or <u>formal</u>) English (unless you're writing in the voice of a character). Don't slip into <u>slang</u> or <u>local dialect</u> — that'll make your writing harder to understand.

2) <u>Punctuation (see p.140)</u>
   Punctuation is brilliant for making your writing smooth, clear and punchy — but only if you get it <u>right</u>. Make sure you know how to use sophisticated punctuation to impress the examiner.

3) <u>Spelling (see p.144)</u>
   Accurate spelling will get you extra marks. Learn to avoid <u>common spelling mistakes</u> and make sure you can spell <u>technical</u> words correctly, e.g. onomatopoeia, rhetorical.

4) <u>Tenses (see p.145)</u>
   Tenses tell your readers <u>when</u> things happened (i.e. in the past, present or future). Make sure you're using the right tense and be <u>consistent</u> — don't change tense without a good reason.

5) <u>Sentences (see p.146)</u>
   Sentences come in all shapes and sizes — from short and simple to long and complex. Use a <u>mixture</u> of correct sentence types to get the <u>effect</u> you want.

6) <u>Vocabulary (see p.147)</u>
   You'll need to use some <u>flashy words</u> in the exam, including <u>technical terms</u> and <u>connectives</u>. Avoid <u>clichés</u> (corny phrases used all the time), e.g. 'at the end of the day', and <u>informal words</u> like 'O.K.'

7) <u>Paragraphs (see p.148)</u>
   Using paragraphs lets you organise your writing into <u>manageable sections</u>. They can also be used to create different effects, e.g. a one-sentence paragraph can make an important point stand out.

Avoid these Common Mistakes

Follow these <u>rules</u> in the exam — otherwise it could really affect your grade.

Don't put the word '<u>them</u>' in front of names of objects — always use '<u>those</u>'.	✗ *Do you really want <u>them</u> problems?* ✓ *Do you really want <u>those</u> problems?*
Don't write '<u>like</u>' when you mean '<u>as</u>'.	✗ *Macbeth did <u>like</u> Lady Macbeth told him.* ✓ *Macbeth did <u>as</u> Lady Macbeth told him.*
'<u>Who</u>' is used to talk about people. '<u>That</u>' or '<u>which</u>' is used for everything else.	✓ *I stared at the man, <u>who</u> turned away.* ✓ *It was his expression <u>that</u> made me curious.*

Check your work to avoid common mistakes...

Make sure you leave plenty of extra time to check through your answers and correct any mistakes that you notice. This section will help you to understand what kind of errors you need to be looking for.

Punctuation

You need to punctuate your writing correctly — the more accurate you are, the clearer your answers will be.

Start and Finish your sentences Correctly

Always <u>start</u> sentences with a <u>capital letter</u>. Sentences always <u>end</u> with either:

- a <u>full stop</u> — use these for most sentences, especially in formal writing.
- a <u>question mark</u> — use these if the sentence is asking a question.
- an <u>exclamation mark</u> — use these if you want your sentence to have a strong impact.

All these ways of ending a sentence mark a definite <u>pause</u> before the next sentence starts.

Use Commas to put Pauses in sentences

Commas are a great way to improve the way your writing flows.

1) Commas are used to <u>separate</u> the parts of long sentences so that the meaning is clear. For example:

In the valley below, the villages seemed very small.   Without the comma, the sentence would begin 'In the valley below the villages'.

2) Commas are also used to <u>break up</u> items in a <u>list</u>:

The waves reared, twisted, leapt and raged around the stricken boat.   The commas separate the different <u>verbs</u> listed in the sentence.

In a list, the last two items are always separated by a connective instead of a comma.

3) <u>Pairs of commas</u> work like brackets to add <u>extra information</u> to the <u>middle</u> of sentences:

The novel, despite its melancholy start, finishes on an optimistic note.   The sentence would <u>still work</u> without the bit in the middle.

Colons and Semicolons Link parts of a sentence

1) Colons are used to <u>link</u> parts of a sentence if the second part <u>explains</u> the first part:

The mood of the poem changes towards the end: it becomes much more solemn.   You should only use a colon if the first part <u>leads on to</u> the second part.

2) Semicolons are used to turn <u>two related sentences</u> into one. Both sentences must be about the <u>same thing</u> and must make sense <u>on their own</u>. A semicolon marks a stronger pause than a comma:

Immigration was a source of tension in the 1950s; the novel's language reflects this.   The parts on either side of the semicolon are <u>connected</u> and <u>equally important</u>.

Imagine reading your sentences out loud...

As you're reading through your work, it can be helpful to imagine reading each sentence out loud. If you think you'd run out of breath before the end of the sentence, you probably need some more punctuation.

Apostrophes

Loads of people get apostrophes wrong, but they're actually not that hard. You just need to learn a few rules.

Add an **Apostrophe** to show who **Owns** Something

1) Apostrophes show when something <u>belongs</u> to someone or something.

> *The <u>writer's</u> tone is aggressive.* ⟹ The tone <u>belonging</u> to the writer is aggressive.

2) There's one exception to this rule: '<u>it's</u>' <u>with</u> an apostrophe is short for 'it is' or 'it has' — '<u>its</u>' <u>never</u> has an apostrophe to show belonging.

> *The elephant lifted <u>its gnarled trunk</u> and lumbered slowly away.* ⟹ The trunk belongs to the elephant, so 'its' <u>doesn't</u> have an apostrophe.

It gets a bit tricky with **Groups** of people or things

If you're writing a plural word, just add the correct letters to the end — <u>never</u> use an apostrophe to show something is plural.

There are two golden rules here:

1) If a plural already ends in <u>s</u>, you need to put an apostrophe on the <u>end</u> to show possession.

> *The <u>boys'</u> heart rates quickened as they heard the car approaching.* ⟹ There is more than one boy, so the apostrophe needs to go <u>after</u> the 's'.

2) If the plural doesn't end in <u>s</u> (for example mice, men, women, sheep), just follow the <u>normal rule</u>.

> *The <u>men's</u> authority is undermined in the play.* ⟹ The word 'men' is already plural, so just add an apostrophe and 's' <u>to the end</u>.

Apostrophes can show where there's a **Missing Letter**

You can <u>shorten</u> some pairs of words by sticking them together and cutting out letters — as long as you <u>replace</u> those letters with an apostrophe.

> *I am → I'm* ⟹ The letter 'a' has been removed, so an apostrophe goes <u>in its place</u>.

Here are some common examples of words that need an <u>apostrophe</u>:

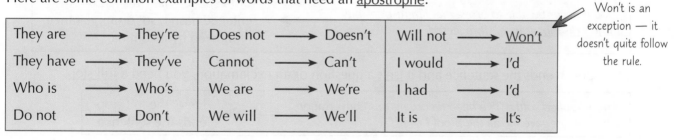

They are	→	They're	Does not	→	Doesn't	Will not	→	<u>Won't</u>
They have	→	They've	Cannot	→	Can't	I would	→	I'd
Who is	→	Who's	We are	→	We're	I had	→	I'd
Do not	→	Don't	We will	→	We'll	It is	→	It's

Won't is an exception — it doesn't quite follow the rule.

Be careful when you're writing formally...

It's generally best to avoid shortening words in your exam answers, as it's often seen as an informal way of writing. The only exception to this is if you're writing in an informal register for a writing question.

Speech Marks

Speech marks are a really important piece of punctuation. Make sure you know how to use them properly.

Speech Marks show that someone's Speaking

To see how to use quotation marks to quote from texts, flick to page 83.

1) Speech marks (or <u>quotation</u> marks) mark the <u>start</u> and <u>end</u> of what someone has said.

> *"You're going to regret that," growled Tom.* $\Longrightarrow$ Tom's speech begins on 'You're' and ends on 'that'.

2) You need to start a new <u>paragraph</u> every time a new person speaks.

> *"What makes you think I'll regret it?" asked Arthur.*
> *"I could make your life very difficult," replied Tom.* $\Longrightarrow$ When Tom replies to Arthur, the writer starts a new paragraph.

Always start speech with a Capital Letter

1) <u>Speech</u> always starts with a capital letter — even if it doesn't begin the sentence.

> *Arthur muttered, "<u>You</u> think you're untouchable. I'm not afraid of you."* $\Longrightarrow$ 'You' starts with a capital letter, even though it's in the middle of the sentence.

2) If speech is split into two sections, you <u>don't</u> need a capital letter at the start of the second section.

> *"You should be afraid of me," Tom sneered, "<u>because</u> everybody else is."* $\Longrightarrow$ Tom's speech is interrupted by the narration, so 'because' doesn't need a capital letter.

End speech with a Punctuation Mark

When you put punctuation at the end of your speech, it should go <u>before</u> the speech mark.

1) Spoken questions end with a <u>question mark</u>, and exclamations with an <u>exclamation mark</u>.

> *"Why do you think that <u>is?</u>" asked Arthur.*
> *"You know full <u>well!</u>" shouted Tom.* $\Longrightarrow$ The punctuation goes at the end of the speech, but before the speech marks.

2) If the speech has finished but the sentence hasn't, use a <u>comma</u>.

> *"You'll never be able to prove that I'm responsible for Jo's <u>disappearance</u>," Tom jeered.* $\Longrightarrow$ Tom's speech has finished but the sentence hasn't, so 'disappearance' is followed by a comma.

3) If the speech ends the sentence and it <u>isn't</u> a question or an exclamation, you need a <u>full stop</u>.

> *Arthur replied softly, "I've been recording this conversation, and you just gave me all the proof I <u>need</u>."* $\Longrightarrow$ Here, the full stop ends the sentence.

Be careful of your punctuation...

Actually remembering to use speech marks is easy enough — it's working out where all the punctuation goes that's the problem. Practise before the exam so that you get into good habits before it really counts.

Negatives

You may hear double negatives in everyday speech, but it's important not to use them in your exams.

'No' isn't the Only negative word

1) The easiest way to make a phrase negative is to add '<u>no</u>' or '<u>not</u>'.

> *There <u>is</u> a logical solution to the situation.* ⟹ *There <u>is no</u> logical solution to the situation.*
>
> *The poem <u>is</u> written in free verse.* ⟹ *The poem <u>is not</u> written in free verse.*

2) Words ending in <u>-n't</u> are also negative.

> *This argument <u>has</u> got a lot of credibility.* ⟹ *This argument <u>hasn't</u> got a lot of credibility.*

Don't use a Double Negative

Words ending in '<u>-n't</u>' are <u>negative</u>, so you <u>don't</u> need to add '<u>no</u>' or '<u>not</u>'.

> *I <u>don't</u> agree with <u>no</u> politicians.* ⟶ This really means 'I <u>do</u> agree with politicians'. <u>Two negative words</u> in the same phrase make it <u>positive</u>. You should only use <u>one negative</u> at a time.

The word 'None' has Different Meanings

1) '<u>None</u>' is a word that can cause problems. As a <u>pronoun</u> it means '<u>not one</u>' or '<u>not any</u>':

> *<u>None</u> of my friends came to see me off.* ⟹ Here, 'None' means '<u>not one</u>'.

> *There are <u>none</u> of these techniques in the poem.* ⟹ Here, 'none' means '<u>not any</u>'.

2) 'None' can also mean '<u>not at all</u>':

> *The house was <u>none</u> the worse for its faded paint and weather-beaten feel; it only added to the building's charm.* ⟶ This means that the appearance of the house doesn't make it worse <u>at all</u>.

3) 'None' should <u>not</u> be used with other negative words:

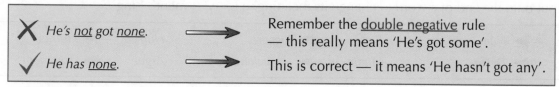

> ✗ *He's <u>not</u> got <u>none</u>.* ⟶ Remember the <u>double negative</u> rule — this really means 'He's got some'.
>
> ✓ *He has <u>none</u>.* ⟶ This is correct — it means 'He hasn't got any'.

Keep an eye out for double negatives when you check your work...

If you're in a rush to finish, it's easy to slip up and make a mistake like using a double negative. That's why it's so important to leave enough time to give each of your exam answers a good, thorough read-through.

Spelling

Here are some common spelling traps to try to avoid when you're writing your answers...

Don't confuse **Different Words** that **Sound** the **Same**

Words that <u>sound</u> similar can mean completely different things. Here are some common examples:

effect/affect

1) <u>Effect</u> is a <u>noun</u> — it is the result of an action. ⟹ *The emotive language has a powerful <u>effect</u> on the reader.*

2) <u>Affect</u> is a <u>verb</u> meaning to act on or influence something. ⟹ *Dim lighting <u>affects</u> the mood of the scene.*

practise/practice

1) <u>Practise</u> is a <u>verb</u>. ⟹ *He <u>practised</u> his lines until his head swam.*

2) <u>Practice</u> is a <u>noun</u>. ⟹ *The <u>practice</u> of fox hunting is cruel and unnecessary.*

where/were/wear

1) <u>Where</u> is used to talk about <u>place</u> and position. ⟹ *<u>Where</u> had she seen that symbol before?*

2) <u>Were</u> is a past tense form of the verb '<u>to be</u>'. ⟹ *The boys <u>were</u> hiding behind a statue.*

3) <u>Wear</u> is a <u>verb</u> used with clothes, hair, jewellery etc. ⟹ *He <u>wears</u> armour of burnished gold.*

there/their/they're

1) <u>There</u> is used for <u>place</u> and position. ⟹ *Jo dived behind the sofa and waited <u>there</u>, listening hard.*

2) <u>Their</u> shows <u>possession</u>. ⟹ *Both poets use metaphors to emphasise <u>their</u> message.*

3) <u>They're</u> is the short form of '<u>they are</u>'. ⟹ *<u>They're</u> the most dramatic lines in the play.*

Watch out for these **Common Spelling Mistakes**

1) Words can have <u>silent</u> letters. Some silent letters are commonly found at the <u>start</u> of words (e.g. '<u>kn</u>' and '<u>wr</u>') and others are often found at the <u>end</u> of words (e.g. '<u>bt</u>' and '<u>mn</u>').

know, knock, write, wrong, doubt, debt, solemn, autumn. ⟹ You don't say these letters, but you must write them.

2) Some words <u>change</u> their spelling when you add a <u>suffix</u>. A suffix is a letter or group of letters put onto the end of a word to change its meaning, e.g. '-y', '-ment', '-ing'.

Humour ⟹ *Humorous*		*Big* ⟹ *Biggest*		*Hurry* ⟹ *Hurried*
Die ⟹ *Dying*		*Mimic* ⟹ *Mimicking*		*Argue* ⟹ *Argument*

3) Make sure you know which words use '<u>ie</u>' (e.g. p<u>ie</u>ce, bel<u>ie</u>ve) and which use '<u>ei</u>' (e.g. th<u>ei</u>r, rec<u>ei</u>ve).

Learn to spell tricky subject-specific terms...

Watch out for tricky writers' names and technical terms, too — your essays will be much less convincing (and you'll miss out on some easy marks) if you've misspelled words like 'Shakespeare' or 'onomatopoeia'.

Types of Words

Saying "the poem is full of descriptive adverbs" will get you more marks than "there are lots of nice words".

Every Word in a sentence has its own Job

1) <u>Nouns</u> are naming words — they might refer to a <u>person</u>, <u>place</u> or <u>thing</u>. This includes groups of people or things (e.g. class, team) and words for ideas (e.g. truth, beauty, fear).

2) <u>Proper nouns</u> refer to a specific person, place or thing (e.g. Alice, London, Wednesday, July). Proper nouns <u>always</u> begin with a <u>capital letter</u>.

3) A <u>pronoun</u> is a word that replaces a noun, e.g. he, she, it, them.

4) <u>Possessive pronouns</u> are pronouns that show ownership, e.g. his, hers, ours, theirs.

5) <u>Verbs</u> are 'doing' or 'being' words. They describe the <u>action</u> in a sentence, e.g. I <u>write</u>, she <u>sleeps</u>. They also tell you how something <u>is</u>, <u>was</u> or <u>will be</u>.

Adjectives can liven up your writing — avoid boring ones like 'good' and swap them for more interesting ones like 'wonderful'.

6) <u>Adjectives</u> describe <u>things</u> and <u>people</u>, e.g. difficult, gentle, passive.

7) <u>Adverbs</u> describe <u>how</u> an action is done, e.g. slowly, viciously, passionately.

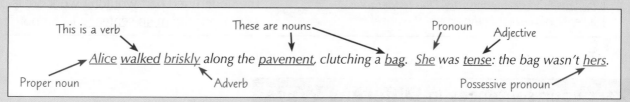

This is a verb   These are nouns   Pronoun   Adjective

Alice walked briskly along the pavement, clutching a bag. She was tense: the bag wasn't hers.

Proper noun   Adverb   Possessive pronoun

Verbs Change according to Who did the action and When

When you're writing, make sure your verbs are in the correct <u>form</u> and the correct <u>tense</u>.

A verb has to match its <u>subject</u> — the person or thing that's 'doing' or 'being' in the sentence. ✗ *The writer <u>use</u> imagery in the play.*
✓ *The writer <u>uses</u> imagery in the play.*

A verb's subject can be <u>singular</u> (only <u>one</u> person or thing) or <u>plural</u> (<u>more than one</u> person or thing). → *The poem <u>has</u> an upbeat tone.*
Both poems <u>have</u> an upbeat tone.

Verbs change according to whether the action is happening in the <u>past</u>, <u>present</u> or <u>future</u>. → *The sun <u>glared</u> down upon the pitiful figures.*
The sun <u>glares</u> down upon the pitiful figures.
The sun <u>will glare</u> down upon the pitiful figures.

<u>Don't</u> change verb tenses in your writing by mistake. ✗ *The writer <u>uses</u> rhetorical questions, which <u>made</u> the text persuasive.*
✓ *The article <u>uses</u> rhetorical questions, which <u>make</u> the text persuasive.*

Make sure you use the correct technical terms...

If you write about a word type in your exam, make sure you've identified it correctly. Be careful not to mix up similar-sounding terms by mistake, like adverbs and adjectives, or the different types of pronoun.

Sentences

If you're looking for top marks, you need to think about varying your sentences and ordering them logically.

Vary the **Style** of your sentences

Including the odd question or command in your writing can help the reader feel more involved.

The examiners will be impressed if you use a mixture of sentence types <u>effectively</u>.
There are <u>three main types</u> to choose from:

1) A <u>simple sentence</u> has a subject and <u>one</u> main verb.

> *The text focuses on life in India.* The <u>subject</u> here is 'the text' and the <u>verb</u> is 'focuses'.

2) A <u>compound sentence</u> usually has <u>two or more</u> parts, each containing a verb.
    The parts are linked together by words such as <u>and</u> or <u>but</u>.

> *<u>Byron</u> uses metaphors, but <u>Hardy</u> uses similes.* The <u>linking word</u> here is the word '<u>but</u>'.

3) A <u>complex sentence</u> contains a part that wouldn't make sense on its own.
    This part is joined to the main sentence by a word like <u>if</u>, <u>as</u>, <u>because</u> or <u>although</u>.

> *<u>Because the protagonist dies</u>, the reader feels
> a sense of despair at the end of the novel.* The underlined part <u>wouldn't work</u> on its own
> — it needs the <u>main sentence</u> to support it.

Start your sentences in **Different Ways**

<u>Varying</u> the <u>beginning</u> of your sentences makes your writing more <u>interesting</u> to read.

> *<u>There</u> was a chill in the air as Jo approached the house. <u>There</u>
> was nobody around. <u>There</u> was a door and Jo knocked on it.* This extract is <u>boring</u> — all the
> sentences begin in the same way.
>
> *<u>There</u> was a chill in the air as Jo approached the house.
> <u>Nobody</u> was around. <u>Jo</u> knocked on the door.* This extract is more <u>interesting</u> because
> the sentences start in different ways.

Chronological Order makes things **Easy** to **Follow**

Your sentences need to be in a sensible <u>order</u> — if the examiner can't follow them easily you'll miss out on
marks. <u>Chronological order</u> (the order in which things happened) is the most logical order to write in.

> *James flung himself sideways and rolled into a bush. He was running
> away because the man had started chasing him. As he had run around
> the corner he had seen the bush — it was the perfect hiding place.* The sentences <u>aren't</u> in
> chronological order, so it's
> <u>not clear</u> what's happening.
>
> *James flew around the corner, running hard. The man pursuing
> him was catching up — he'd never make it. Suddenly, he
> flung himself sideways and rolled, unnoticed, into a bush.* The sentences <u>are</u> in chronological
> order so this is <u>easy</u> to follow.

Use these tips to improve your writing...

This page has lots of ways to make your writing more sophisticated. Varying your sentence types and
the way you start your sentences will make your answers a whole lot more interesting for the examiner.

Writing Varied Sentences

You need to be able to write interesting sentences that aren't repetitive. Here are a few pointers...

Use **Descriptive Language** to make your writing interesting

Descriptive language creates interesting <u>visual images</u> for the reader.

1) You could <u>compare</u> two things using less than, more than, etc.

> *The lace was <u>more delicate</u>*
> *<u>than</u> a finely spun web.*
>
> *It was <u>colder than</u> an Arctic winter.*
>
> *She was the <u>most beautiful</u> woman in Millom.*

 These descriptions are <u>more</u> interesting than saying 'it was delicate', 'it was very cold' or 'she was beautiful'.

> *When you compare, either say "more than..." or "the most...", <u>or</u> use the form of the word that ends in "er" or "est". Don't do both.*

2) You could use a <u>simile</u> (saying one thing is <u>like</u> another).

> *Beth felt <u>as</u> happy <u>as</u> a hippo in a mud pool.*
>
> *I'd forgotten my gloves and my fingers were <u>like</u> blocks of ice.*

 Similes usually use the words 'like' or 'as' to <u>compare</u> one thing to another.

3) You could use a <u>metaphor</u> (describing one thing as if it <u>is</u> something else). There needs to be an <u>obvious link</u> between the thing you're talking about and the metaphor you're using to describe it.

> *John's face <u>was</u> a waxen mask that betrayed no emotion.*

John's face wasn't literally a mask, but the language creates a <u>strong visual image</u>.

Use **Different Words** for the **Same Thing**

1) Don't fall into the trap of using the same <u>adjectives</u> all the time — especially vague ones like "<u>nice</u>" or "<u>weird</u>".

> *I went to a <u>nice</u> Indian restaurant last night. The waiters were <u>nice</u> to us and the food was <u>nice</u>.*

This may be 'correctly' written, but it's not going to score you top marks because it's <u>boring</u>.

> *I went to a <u>fantastic</u> Indian restaurant last night. The waiters were <u>friendly</u> to us and the food was <u>delicious</u>.*

This is much better. Using different adjectives paints a more <u>interesting picture</u>.

2) Try not to repeat the same <u>verbs</u> either.

> *Rashid <u>looked</u> into the cave and <u>looked</u> around before going in. The cave <u>looked</u> deserted.*

This is <u>dull</u> and <u>repetitive</u>.

> *Rashid <u>peered</u> into the cave and <u>glanced</u> around before going in. The cave <u>appeared</u> deserted.*

By varying the verbs, the writing becomes more <u>interesting</u> and <u>informative</u>.

Using interesting words can improve your marks...

Including some interesting vocabulary from time to time will impress the examiner, especially if you can use and spell it correctly. Just don't go overboard — the examiner needs to be able to understand your answer.

Paragraphs

In the heat of the exam it's easy to forget to start new paragraphs, but they're key to getting a good grade.

Start a **New Paragraph** every time something **Changes**

You need to start a new paragraph every time <u>something new</u> is introduced. For example:

1) When you introduce a new <u>person</u>.

> *<u>Horrified, Liam</u> sank to the floor. His guitar was broken and he was due on stage in two minutes.*
> *<u>Then he saw Keith</u>, the skinny boy who always got picked on. He was carrying a guitar case.*

 The first paragraph is about Liam. When Keith is <u>introduced</u>, a new paragraph begins.

2) When you start writing about a new <u>place</u>.

> *The <u>playing fields</u> were peaceful. There was no one around except Pete.*
> *<u>Further down the valley</u>, a huge cloud of dust rose into the sky, racing towards the school.*

 The first paragraph is about the playing fields. The events of the second paragraph are happening <u>somewhere else</u>.

3) When you start writing about a different <u>time</u>.

> *At the start of 'Lord of the Flies', Ralph and Jack are friendly and treat each other with respect. When building the fire they work together "with triumphant pleasure".*
> *<u>By the end of the novel</u>, their relationship has deteriorated...*

 The new paragraph is about a <u>different time</u> in the novel.

You also begin a new paragraph each time a new person speaks — see p.142.

4) When you start writing about a new <u>topic</u>.

> *<u>Smoking is bad for your health</u>. It causes many serious problems, from gum disease to cancer.*
> *In addition, <u>smoking is expensive</u>. Cigarette prices rise all the time, but people are always prepared to pay more.*

These paragraphs talk about two <u>different aspects</u> of smoking. Each paragraph makes <u>one clear point</u>.

Paragraphs need to be **Linked** and **Varied**

You can order paragraphs however you like — as long as the order you've chosen makes sense to the reader.

1) You've got to <u>link</u> every paragraph with the one before and the one after.

- You could use <u>connectives</u> (linking words) — therefore, however, on the other hand etc.

- Or you could <u>refer back</u> to something you've said in the one above.

> *Terrorism plays a huge role in society today. We can't turn on the news without feeling threatened or <u>afraid</u>.*
> *Is a world where violence and <u>fear</u> are commonplace really one we want our children to grow up in?*

 The 'fear' in the second paragraph <u>refers back</u> to feeling 'afraid' in the first paragraph.

2) Don't make your paragraphs too repetitive — try starting with a <u>rhetorical question</u> like the example above, or create a <u>one-sentence paragraph</u> for effect.

Use paragraphs to make your answers clearer...

Paragraphs give structure to your answer and break it into separate points so it's easier to read. You can also use them creatively to make your work that bit more interesting — the trick is to vary their structure.

Warm-Up Questions

Have a go at these warm-up questions to see how much you've learnt from this chapter.

Warm-Up Questions

1) Write a few sentences to explain what standard English is.

2) Write out the following passage, adding in suitable punctuation:

> The purpose of punctuation is to make writing clearer written language lacks the pauses and changes of tone that help the listener hear the differences between words clauses and sentences without punctuation its possible for ambiguities and confusion to creep in who knows what you could accidentally say if you don't punctuate

3) Decide whether the following sentences need a colon or a semicolon:
   a) I'd like you to buy some groceries __ milk, bread, frankfurters and anything else you fancy.
   b) He was the bravest of men, the greatest of men __ they called him Keith.

4) Write out these sentences, adding apostrophes in the correct places:
   a) The lollipop ladys lollipop had been stolen.
   b) The girls faces fell as they saw what the homework was.
   c) Its a sale bonanza aboard the Shoe Ship this weekend — everythings half price in the worlds only floating shoe shop!

5) Write out the following sentences, adding in speech marks to show where people are speaking. Don't forget to capitalise the first word and start a new paragraph when someone starts speaking.

> I just don't believe you, said Mark. But I've never told a lie before, replied Jenny. There was a silence before Mark muttered not a lie I've found out about, at least. Jenny pretended not to hear him, and asked so what did you do last weekend, then?

6) In each of the following sentences, work out which of the words in bold is correct:
   a) Dave wasn't sure **where/wear** to park his car.
   b) Felicity spent two hours deciding what she should **wear/were** to the party.
   c) The chilli flakes had a horrible **affect/effect** on the cake's flavour.
   d) Nathan was determined to **practise/practice** his spelling every day.
   e) The twins celebrated **there/their** birthday together every year.

7) Rewrite the following simple sentences as a) a compound sentence, and b) a complex sentence. You can add or take away words if necessary.
   "It rained every day for two months. The continual rain made Martha grumpy."

8) Describe someone you know using at least four similes.

Revision Summary

There's quite a lot of stuff to take on board here. Browse back over the section, and when you feel confident, try these questions. Check for any you got wrong, then have another go. It may take a little while, but you need to be able to sail through the questions like a knife through butter...

1) True or false: *You should try to use dialect words, slang and clichés when writing in standard English.*

2) Write these sentences out, correcting the mistakes:
   a) Pass me them pliers, Florence.
   b) Ronnie did like he was asked.
   c) The cake who was on the table looked delicious.

3) Give three uses of commas.

4) What are colons used for?

5) Write these sentences out, correcting the mistakes:
   a) The hamster has looked very happy since I brushed it's coat.
   b) Its nice to see a smile on its little face.

6) Write these words out in full:
   a) Couldn't
   b) I'll
   c) Would've

7) Shorten these words by cutting out letters and replacing them with apostrophes.
   The first one has been done for you.
   a) I will not = I won't   b) can not   c) I had   d) it is   e) they are

8) True or false: *You should use apostrophes to show that something is plural.*

9) What should speech always start with when you're writing? And what should it end with?

10) "It's never a good idea to use no double negatives in your writing." Correct this sentence.

11) Which one of these statements is correct?
   a) We where going to a fancy party.
   b) I decided to wear my favourite dress.
   c) I don't know were that idea came from.

12) What do proper nouns always begin with?

13) What are verbs?

14) What do adjectives describe?

15) What do adverbs describe?

16) Name three things that change the way a verb is written.

17) When you are writing, why might you start your sentences in different ways?

18) What is chronological order?

19) Write down one example of a simile and one example of a metaphor.

20) True or false: *It's good to vary the adjectives and verbs that you use.*

21) Write down two examples of words or phrases you could use to link paragraphs together.

Spoken Language Assessment

The Spoken Language assessment is all about communicating effectively and clearly in front of an audience. It can seem quite daunting, but you'll feel a whole lot better if you're fully prepared for it.

You'll have to give a Presentation

1) You'll be given a task — this is usually delivering a presentation or a speech.

2) Your teacher might give you some guidelines, but normally you can choose your own topic:

- You could talk about a subject you're interested in, for example:

| a type of music you like | a sport you play | your favourite hobby |

- You might discuss something that concerns you, for example:

| addiction to social media | underage drinking |

You might be able to use visual prompts, for example pictures or slides — check with your teacher.

- You could give your opinion on a current topic, for example:

| a news story | a new rule proposed at your school |

- ... or you could talk about a personal experience, for example:

| a holiday you've been on | a childhood memory | an important event in your life |

3) Choose a topic that you care about. If you're not interested, there's no way your audience will be.

4) You need to answer questions on your presentation, so the more you know about the topic, the better.

You'll be assessed on Three Main Things

1) Unlike your English exams, your spoken language task will be assessed by your teacher.

2) You'll need to show that you can do three main things:

- Present your ideas and information clearly — this will usually be to your class and your teacher.

- Listen to any questions or feedback for your presentation and reply appropriately.

- Speak using standard English — you need to use correct grammar and avoid slang. There's more about this on p.153.

3) You also need to listen carefully when other people are giving their presentations, and ask any relevant questions you can think of.

Spoken Language Assessment

Match your **Presentation** to your **Purpose**

1) You'll need to work out what your <u>purpose</u> is and how to <u>achieve</u> it.

2) You should choose your vocabulary carefully so that it helps you to <u>achieve</u> your <u>purpose</u>.

Writing a speech is like writing a non-fiction text — Section Four gives you some tips on how to do this.

 <u>International media conglomerates</u> make the movie industry <u>monotonous</u>. The vocabulary is <u>too technical</u> and makes the sentence hard to follow.

 <u>Large film companies</u> make the movie industry <u>bland</u>. These words are <u>simpler</u>, so the sentence is easier to understand.

3) If you're trying to <u>persuade</u> your audience to agree with your point of view, you should use some <u>rhetorical devices</u>.

See p.35 for some more rhetorical devices you might use.

Why waste your money on frivolous meals, parties and holidays? Don't you think you should be saving it for something important instead? This uses <u>rhetorical questions</u> and the <u>pronoun</u> 'you' to <u>persuade</u> the reader by making them feel <u>involved</u>.

Do some **Research** about your topic

1) Think about what to include in your presentation — research any <u>facts</u> or <u>statistics</u> that you can use to <u>support</u> your argument or add <u>interest</u> to your speech.

 If you spend too much time watching TV or using the computer, your grades will suffer. This is quite <u>vague</u>, so it doesn't <u>support</u> the speaker's argument very well.

 <u>A recent study</u> has shown that GCSE pupils who spend more than one hour a night watching TV or using the computer, will, on average, do worse in their exams. This uses <u>evidence</u> to <u>strengthen</u> the argument the speaker is making.

2) Remember, you'll be asked <u>questions</u> at the end of your presentation. Make sure you do enough research to be really <u>confident</u> about your topic, so that you can answer <u>any question</u> you get asked.

Structure your presentation so that it's **Clear**

You'll need to <u>structure</u> your presentation clearly:

- Make sure you have a clear <u>introduction</u> stating the <u>topic</u> you've chosen. If you're putting across an argument, let the audience know your <u>point of view</u>.

- Plan what <u>order</u> to cover your points in. For example, if you're discussing a topic, you might give all your points <u>for</u> it, followed by all your points <u>against</u>.

- End your presentation with a <u>strong conclusion</u> — this could sum up the <u>key points</u> of your speech, or give your <u>own opinion</u> on the subject.

Spoken Language Assessment

Make sure you **Speak Clearly**

Speak up and look around the room when you're talking — that way everyone can hear you.

1) Your presentation needs to be easy for your audience to follow — make sure you <u>speak clearly</u> and <u>slowly</u>.

2) Don't repeat yourself unless you're doing it for <u>effect</u>. Keep your points <u>concise</u> — stating them again in different words wastes valuable time.

 We might succeed because we might be able to do what we need to, but we might also fail if we don't do what we need to. We'll only know once we succeed or fail. This is <u>waffly</u> and <u>repetitive</u>, which makes it sound <u>dull</u>.

✓ *Perhaps we'll succeed. Perhaps we'll fail. Only time will tell.* → Here, repetition is used for <u>effect</u> — it helps the speaker make a <u>strong, memorable point</u>.

3) Draw attention to the most important <u>facts</u>. Then the audience will remember them.

One and a half acres of forest is cut down every second — that's <u>the size of 66 football pitches</u>. → Linking a statistic to something the audience <u>can relate to</u> makes it more <u>memorable</u>.

Comparisons like these are called 'analogies' — there's more about them on p.31.

Use **Standard English**

Grammar mistakes are easy enough to avoid once you know how — see pages 139 and 143 for some common errors.

<u>Standard English</u> means <u>formal</u> English — the kind of language you'd use in an essay. You need to <u>speak</u> in standard English when you do your <u>speech</u> or <u>presentation</u>.

1) Don't speak in the <u>informal way</u> you might when talking to your friends.

✗ *Some people are, like, "P.E. is completely pointless".* → This is too <u>informal</u> and <u>familiar</u>.

✓ *Some people maintain that P.E. is completely pointless.* → This is much better.

2) Don't use <u>slang</u> or <u>local dialect</u> words that some people might not understand.

✗ *Local residents were <u>gutted</u> at the decision.* → "Gutted" is a <u>slang</u> term.

✓ *Local residents were <u>disappointed</u> with the decision.* → The <u>formal</u> wording is more appropriate.

3) Use <u>correct grammar</u>.

✗ *The issue <u>aren't</u> high on the political agenda.* → This sentence is <u>grammatically incorrect</u>.

✓ *The issue <u>isn't</u> high on the political agenda.* → The word 'isn't' is correct here.

Don't rush through your presentation...

You might find the idea of a spoken language assessment quite scary, but don't be tempted to rattle off your speech just to get it over with. Take your time, speak clearly and make eye contact with your audience.

Section Twelve — Spoken Language Assessment

Here are some <u>practice papers</u> to test how well-prepared you are for your GCSE English Language exams.

- There are <u>two</u> practice papers in this section:
  Paper 1: Fiction   (pages 154-157)
  Paper 2: Non-Fiction   (pages 158-162)

Your exams might be structured differently to these practice papers. Check with your teacher if you're not sure.

- Before you start each paper, read through all the <u>instructions</u>, <u>information</u> and <u>advice</u> on the front.

- You'll need some paper to write your answers on.

- When you've finished, have a look at the answers starting on page 197 — they'll give you some ideas of the kind of things you should have included in your answers.

- <u>Don't</u> try to do both of the papers in one sitting.

CGP Practice Exam Paper
GCSE English Language

General Certificate of Secondary Education

GCSE
English Language

Paper 1: Fiction

Time allowed: 1 hour 45 minutes

Centre name				
Centre number				
Candidate number				

Surname	
Other names	
Candidate signature	

Instructions to candidates
- Answer **all** the questions.
- Write your answers in **black** ink or ball-point pen.
- Write your name and other details in the boxes above.
- Cross out any rough work that you do not want to be marked.
- You should **not** use a dictionary.

Information for candidates
- The marks available are given in brackets at the end of each question.
- There are 80 marks available for this exam paper.
- You must use good English and clear presentation in your answers.

Advice for candidates
- You should spend about 15 minutes reading through the source and all five questions.

This extract is the opening of a short story set in New Zealand, written in 1922 by Katherine Mansfield.

At the Bay

Very early morning. The sun was not yet risen, and the whole of Crescent Bay was hidden under a white sea-mist. The big bush-covered hills at the back were smothered. You could not see where they ended and the paddocks and bungalows began. The sandy road was gone and the paddocks and bungalows the other side of it; there were no white dunes covered with reddish grass beyond them;
5 there was nothing to mark which was beach and where was the sea. A heavy dew had fallen. The grass was blue. Big drops hung on the bushes and just did not fall; the silvery, fluffy toi-toi* was limp on its long stalks, and all the marigolds and the pinks in the bungalow gardens were bowed to the earth with wetness. Drenched were the cold fuchsias, round pearls of dew lay on the flat nasturtium leaves. It looked as though the sea had beaten up softly in the darkness, as though one immense wave had come
10 rippling, rippling — how far? Perhaps if you had waked up in the middle of the night you might have seen a big fish flicking in at the window and gone again...

Ah-Aah! sounded the sleepy sea. And from the bush there came the sound of little streams flowing, quickly, lightly, slipping between the smooth stones, gushing into ferny basins and out again; and there was the splashing of big drops on large leaves, and something else — what was it? — a faint stirring and
15 shaking, the snapping of a twig and then such silence that it seemed some one was listening.

Round the corner of Crescent Bay, between the piled-up masses of broken rock, a flock of sheep came pattering. They were huddled together, a small, tossing, woolly mass, and their thin, stick-like legs trotted along quickly as if the cold and the quiet had frightened them. Behind them an old sheep-dog, his soaking paws covered with sand, ran along with his nose to the ground, but carelessly,
20 as if thinking of something else. And then in the rocky gateway the shepherd himself appeared. He was a lean, upright old man, in a frieze* coat that was covered with a web of tiny drops, velvet trousers tied under the knee, and a wide-awake* with a folded blue handkerchief round the brim.

One hand was crammed into his belt, the other grasped a beautifully smooth yellow stick. And as he walked, taking his time, he kept up a very soft light whistling, an airy, far-away fluting that sounded
25 mournful and tender. The old dog cut an ancient caper or two and then drew up sharp, ashamed of his levity, and walked a few dignified paces by his master's side. The sheep ran forward in little pattering rushes; they began to bleat, and ghostly flocks and herds answered them from under the sea. "Baa! Baaa!" For a time they seemed to be always on the same piece of ground. There ahead was stretched the sandy road with shallow puddles; the same soaking bushes showed on either side and the same
30 shadowy palings*. Then something immense came into view; an enormous shock-haired giant with his arms stretched out. It was the big gum-tree outside Mrs. Stubbs' shop, and as they passed by there was a strong whiff of eucalyptus. And now big spots of light gleamed in the mist. The shepherd stopped whistling; he rubbed his red nose and wet beard on his wet sleeve and, screwing up his eyes, glanced in the direction of the sea. The sun was rising. It was marvellous how quickly the mist thinned, sped
35 away, dissolved from the shallow plain, rolled up from the bush and was gone as if in a hurry to escape; big twists and curls jostled and shouldered each other as the silvery beams broadened. The far-away sky — a bright, pure blue — was reflected in the puddles, and the drops, swimming along the telegraph poles, flashed into points of light. Now the leaping, glittering sea was so bright it made one's eyes ache to look at it. The shepherd drew a pipe, the bowl as small as an acorn, out of his breast pocket,
40 fumbled for a chunk of speckled tobacco, pared off a few shavings and stuffed the bowl. He was a grave, fine-looking old man. As he lit up and the blue smoke wreathed his head, the dog, watching, looked proud of him.

Glossary
*toi-toi — a type of tall grass
*frieze — coarse woollen cloth
*wide-awake — a type of wide-brimmed hat
*palings — pointed fence-posts

Section A: Reading

*You should spend about 45 minutes answering **all** the questions in this section.*

1   Read **lines 1 to 11** of the source.

   Give **four** things from these lines that show what Crescent Bay looks like beneath the mist.

   (4 marks)

2   Read **lines 16 to 22** of the source.

   How does the writer use language in these lines to present the shepherd and his animals?

   You might want to refer to the writer's use of:
   *   specific words and phrases
   *   language techniques
   *   sentence structure.

   (8 marks)

3   Now think about the **whole source**.

   This extract is from the beginning of a short story.

   How has the writer structured the text to engage the reader?

   You might want to refer to:
   *   how the extract begins
   *   how and why the focus of the extract changes as it goes on
   *   any other elements of structure that you find interesting.

   (8 marks)

4   Read from **line 23** to **the end of the source**.

   "The writer is successful in creating a detailed and interesting scene for the reader. It is like watching a film of what is happening."

   How far do you agree with this statement?

   You should include:
   *   your perceptions of the scene
   *   the techniques the writer has used to influence your perceptions
   *   evidence from the text to support your ideas.

   (20 marks)

Section B: Writing

You should spend about 45 minutes answering the question in this section.

Only complete ONE of the tasks below.

There are 24 marks available for the content of your writing,
and for structuring your ideas in a clear and organised way.

There are a further 16 marks available for the technical accuracy of your writing,
including spelling, punctuation and grammar.

You are advised to plan your answer.

5   You have decided to enter a creative writing competition for school children.
    A panel of published authors will judge your writing.

Either:
Write a description inspired by this picture:

Or:
Write the beginning of a story that takes place in a misty setting.

Or:
Write a story that uses **one** of the following titles:

a)   The Lake

b)   Moving On

c)   The Broken Boat

(40 marks)

General Certificate of Secondary Education

GCSE
English Language
Paper 2: Non-Fiction

Time allowed: 1 hour 45 minutes

Centre name					
Centre number					
Candidate number					

Surname	
Other names	
Candidate signature	

Instructions to candidates
* Answer **all** the questions.
* Write your answers in **black** ink or ball-point pen.
* Write your name and other details in the boxes above.
* Cross out any rough work that you do not want to be marked.
* You should **not** use a dictionary.

Information for candidates
* The marks available are given in brackets at the end of each question.
* There are 80 marks available for this exam paper.
* You must use good English and clear presentation in your answers.

Advice for candidates
* You should spend about 15 minutes reading through the sources and all five questions.

Source A

The following text is an extract from an article written by a nanny, Monica Albelli.
It was published in a broadsheet newspaper in 2013.

Confessions of a Nanny

Being a nanny — whether you're a Mary Poppins, a Nanny McPhee or a Mrs Doubtfire — is a very tricky job. You have to be liked by two opposing "teams" to which a "perfect" nanny means completely different things. "You must be kind, you must be witty, very sweet and fairly pretty... If you don't scold and dominate us, we will never give you cause to hate us" — this is how the
5   children in Mary Poppins, Michael and Jane, want the newspaper ad for their nanny to read. Their father, Mr Banks, is keener on discipline. Mrs Banks seems to believe perfection lies somewhere in between that and the children's ideal.

I have always loved children and had a natural ability to connect with them with ease, no matter their gender, nationality or character. But when you're a nanny, kids come with parents.
10   And parents come with problems, opinions and expectations of their own, often in conflict between themselves.

Lesley, a successful publisher, and Brian, a dentist, were Scots in their mid-40s. They worked long hours but seemed to love Therese, seven, Tom, nine, and William, 11. Their approach when it came to the kids' upbringing though was completely different from each other. Confident
15   and motivated, Lesley believed her children's time should be spent doing homework, reading books or playing educational games. Brian, cheerful and laid back, wanted us to "just have fun". He asked me not to be strict with the kids, while Lesley kept pressuring me to turn them into responsible and hard-working individuals. I would arrive at their house to find a note from Brian, asking me to take them to the park, and then receive a text from Lesley with a to-do list.

20   Lesley would often come home late to find the kids already asleep. "I'm not a good mum," she once confessed. "I'm actually a bit jealous. I think they are starting to like you more than they like me."

I reassured her that this was not true and that she was doing her best.

The kids and I had bonded. Once, as I was getting ready to leave, Tom curled around my
25   leg, while Lesley tried to persuade him he had to let me go. They liked having me around so much that they started asking Brian if I could sleep over. Had we bonded too much?

Then things changed. Lesley seemed upset about something, and Brian was more and more absent. One day they told me they wouldn't be needing me any more as they had decided to get an au pair, who could also help with the house. I knew that wasn't the real reason. They had, I
30   realised, been asking me to become everything they weren't and, as soon as I started to achieve that, they felt threatened.

I tried to see it from their point of view. Being a nanny is difficult, but being a parent is even harder. Having a nanny is also hard.

I remembered what a friend used to say whenever I shared my frustrations with her: "You
35   care too much. It's just a job."

Should a nanny be indifferent, see herself as a doctor and treat all family members as her patients, being impartial and never getting emotionally involved? How can Mary Poppins be indifferent? She is cool and funny, strict at times, but always caring — the perfect nanny. But she is a fictional character, and so are Mr and Mrs Banks, and Michael and Jane.

40   Many dysfunctional families later, I have learned to care at the same time as keeping a distance, and that there is no such thing as the perfect family — or the perfect nanny.

Source B

The following text was written by Charlotte Brontë, a famous 19th-century author. Charlotte was working as a governess — a woman employed to teach and care for the children in a household. This is an extract from a letter written to her sister in 1839.

Dearest Lavinia,*

    I am most exceedingly obliged to you for the trouble you have taken in seeking up my things and sending them all right. The box and its contents were most acceptable.

    I have striven hard to be pleased with my new situation. The country, the house, and the
5   grounds are, as I have said, divine. But, alack-a-day! there is such a thing as seeing all beautiful around you — pleasant woods, winding white paths, green lawns, and blue sunshiny sky — and not having a free moment or a free thought left to enjoy them in. The children are constantly with me, and more riotous, perverse, unmanageable cubs never grew. As for correcting them, I soon quickly found that was entirely out of the question: they are to do as they like. A complaint to Mrs. Sidgwick
10 brings only black looks upon oneself, and unjust, partial excuses to screen the children. I have tried that plan once. It succeeded so notably that I shall try it no more. I said in my last letter that Mrs. Sidgwick did not know me. I now begin to find that she does not intend to know me, that she cares nothing in the world about me except to contrive how the greatest possible quantity of labour may be squeezed out of me, and to that end she overwhelms me with oceans of needlework, yards of cambric
15 to hem, muslin night-caps to make, and, above all things, dolls to dress. I do not think she likes me at all, because I can't help being shy in such an entirely novel scene, surrounded as I have hitherto been by strange and constantly changing faces. I see now more clearly than I have ever done before that a private governess has no existence, is not considered as a living and rational being except as connected with the wearisome duties she has to fulfil. While she is teaching the children, working for
20 them, amusing them, it is all right. If she steals a moment for herself she is a nuisance. Nevertheless, Mrs. Sidgwick is universally considered an amiable woman. Her manners are fussily affable. She talks a great deal, but as it seems to me not much to the purpose. Perhaps I may like her better after a while. At present I have no call to her. Mr. Sidgwick is in my opinion a hundred times better — less profession, less bustling condescension, but a far kinder heart.

25   As to Mrs. Collins' report that Mrs. Sidgwick intended to keep me permanently, I do not think that such was ever her design. Moreover, I would not stay without some alterations. For instance, this burden of sewing would have to be removed. It is too bad for anything. I never in my whole life had my time so fully taken up.

    Don't show this letter to papa or aunt, only to Branwell.* They will think I am never satisfied
30 wherever I am. I complain to you because it is a relief, and really I have had some unexpected mortifications to put up with. However, things may mend, but Mrs. Sidgwick expects me to do things that I cannot do — to love her children and be entirely devoted to them. I am really very well. I am so sleepy that I can write no more. I must leave off. Love to all. — Good-bye.

C. BRONTË.

Glossary
* A nickname for Charlotte's sister, Emily.
* Branwell — their brother.

Section A: Reading

*You should spend about 45 minutes answering **all** the questions in this section.*

1   Read **lines 1 to 19** of **source A**.

There are **four correct statements** in the list below.
Shade in the boxes of the statements that are **true**.

A   Monica Albelli thinks being a nanny is a difficult job. ☐

B   Parents and children usually look for the same things in a nanny. ☐

C   Parents almost always agree on the duties of a nanny. ☐

D   Lesley and Brian are both professionals of a similar age. ☐

E   Lesley and Brian are affectionate parents. ☐

F   Brian likes his children to play educational games. ☐

G   Both parents think discipline is important. ☐

H   Lesley and Brian sometimes gave Monica conflicting instructions. ☐

(4 marks)

2   Refer to **both sources** for this question.

Using evidence from **both** sources, summarise the differences
between Lesley and Mrs Sidgwick.

(8 marks)

3   Refer **only** to **source B** for this question.

Charlotte Brontë is trying to influence her sister. How does she do this?

You should write about:
*   what she says
*   her language and tone.

(12 marks)

4   Refer to **both sources** for this question.

Both texts are about looking after other people's children. Compare the writers' views on this subject.

You should write about:
*   the writers' attitudes to looking after other people's children
*   the methods they use to put across their attitudes.

(16 marks)

Section B: Writing

You should spend about 45 minutes answering the question in this section.

There are 24 marks available for the content of your answer,
and for structuring your ideas in a clear and organised way.

There are a further 16 marks available for the technical accuracy of your answer,
including spelling, punctuation and grammar.

You are advised to plan your answer.

5   "Parents are often too strict with their children. They expect them to work far too hard,
at school and at home. Young people should be allowed to have fun while they still can."

Write an article for a broadsheet newspaper in which you
argue for or against this statement.

(40 marks)

Here are some <u>practice papers</u> to test how well-prepared you are for your GCSE English Literature exams.

- There are <u>two</u> practice papers in this section:
  Paper 1: Modern Texts and Poetry   (pages 163-169)
  Paper 2: Shakespeare and 19th-Century Prose   (pages 170-180)

- Before you start each paper, read through all the <u>instructions</u>, <u>information</u> and <u>advice</u> on the front.

- You'll need some paper to write your answers on.

- When you've finished, have a look at the answers starting on page 199 — they'll give you some ideas of the kind of things you should have included in your answers.

- <u>Don't</u> try to do both of the papers in one sitting.

Your exams might be structured differently to these practice papers. Check with your teacher if you're not sure.

CGP Practice Exam Paper:
GCSE English Literature

General Certificate of Secondary Education

GCSE
English Literature

Surname
Other names
Candidate signature

Centre name
Centre number
Candidate number

Paper 1:
Modern Texts and Poetry

Time allowed: 2 hours 15 minutes

Instructions to candidates
- Write your answers in **black** ink or ball-point pen.
- Write your name and other details in the boxes above.
- Cross out any rough work that you do not want to be marked.
- You should **not** use a dictionary.

Information for candidates
- The marks available are given in brackets at the end of each question.
- There are 96 marks available for this exam paper.
- 4 marks are allocated for accuracy in spelling, punctuation and the use of vocabulary and sentence structures in Section A. These are given in brackets at the end of each question.
- You should spend about **45 minutes** on each section.

Section A: Modern Texts

Answer **one** question from this section.

You should spend about 45 minutes on this section.

JB Priestley: *An Inspector Calls*

1 Write about the character of Arthur Birling and the way he is presented in *An Inspector Calls*.
Write about:
- the techniques that Priestley uses to present Arthur Birling
- how Priestley uses the character to convey his own ideas.

(28 marks)
(+4 marks for spelling, punctuation and grammar)

Meera Syal: *Anita and Me*

2 How does Syal present the theme of friendship in *Anita and Me*?
Write about:
- ideas about friendship in the novel
- how these ideas are presented.

(28 marks)
(+4 marks for spelling, punctuation and grammar)

William Golding: *Lord of the Flies*

3 How does Golding present the theme of fear in *Lord of the Flies*?
Write about:
- ideas about fear in the novel
- how these ideas are presented.

(28 marks)
(+4 marks for spelling, punctuation and grammar)

Willy Russell: *Blood Brothers*

4   Write about the character of Mickey and the way he changes during the course of *Blood Brothers*.
Write about:
- how Mickey changes as the play develops
- the techniques that Russell uses to present Mickey.

(28 marks)
(+4 marks for spelling, punctuation and grammar)

George Orwell: *Animal Farm*

5   What does the theme of education and learning contribute to the meaning of *Animal Farm*?
Write about:
- ideas about education and learning in the novel
- how these ideas are presented.

(28 marks)
(+4 marks for spelling, punctuation and grammar)

Alan Bennett: *The History Boys*

6   Write about education and the way it is presented in *The History Boys*.
Write about:
- ideas about education in the play
- how these ideas are presented.

(28 marks)
(+4 marks for spelling, punctuation and grammar)

Section B: Poetry Anthology

Answer **one** question from this section.

You should spend about 45 minutes on this section.

EITHER

1 Compare how nature is presented in William Wordsworth's
'The Prelude: Stealing the Boat' and one other poem you have studied.

(32 marks)

OR

2 Compare how the narrator presents freedom and constraint in
William Blake's 'London' and one other poem you have studied.

(32 marks)

OR

3 Compare how the breakdown of a relationship is presented in Thomas Hardy's
'Neutral Tones' and one other poem you have studied.

(32 marks)

OR

4 Compare how power is presented in Robert Browning's 'My Last Duchess'
and one other poem you have studied.

(32 marks)

OR

5 Compare how attitudes to conflict are presented in Alfred Tennyson's 'The Charge
of the Light Brigade' and one other poem you have studied.

(32 marks)

OR

6 a) Write about the way love is presented in one poem by Elizabeth Barrett Browning.

(12 marks)

  b) Compare the presentation of love in your chosen poem and one other poem you have studied.

(20 marks)

OR

7 a) Write about the way feelings for another person are presented in 'She Walks in Beauty' by Lord Byron.

(12 marks)

  b) Compare the presentation of feelings for another person in 'She Walks in Beauty' and one other poem you have studied.

(20 marks)

OR

8 Choose a poem by Wilfred Owen that explores ideas about the reality of war. Compare how the reality of war is presented in your chosen poem and one other poem you have studied.

(32 marks)

OR

9 Choose a poem by Seamus Heaney that explores ideas about childhood. Compare how childhood is presented in your chosen poem and one other poem you have studied.

(32 marks)

Section C: Unseen Poetry

Read the following two poems.

If you are doing **AQA**, you should **only** answer questions 1 and 3.

If you are doing **Eduqas**, you should **only** answer questions 2 and 4.

If you are doing **any other exam board**, you should **only** answer question 4.

You should spend about 45 minutes on this section.

Read the poem below.

For a Five-Year-Old

A snail is climbing up the window-sill
into your room, after a night of rain.
You call me in to see, and I explain
that it would be unkind to leave it there:
5   it might crawl to the floor; we must take care
that no one squashes it. You understand,
and carry it outside, with careful hand,
to eat a daffodil.

I see, then, that a kind of faith prevails:
10   your gentleness is moulded still by words
from me, who have trapped mice and shot wild birds,
from me, who drowned your kittens, who betrayed
your closest relatives, and who purveyed
the harshest kind of truth to many another.
15   But that is how things are: I am your mother,
and we are kind to snails.

Fleur Adcock

1   In *For a Five-Year-Old*, how does the poet present the narrator's attitude to parenthood?

(24 marks)

2   Write about *For a Five-Year-Old* and how you respond to it.
You may wish to consider:
- what the poem is about and the way that it is structured
- the message that the poet is trying to convey
- the poet's choice of language and the effects it creates.

(12 marks)

Read the poem below. In both 'For a Five-Year-Old' and 'The Beautiful Lie', the poets write about relationships between adults and children.

The Beautiful Lie

He was about four, I think… it was so long ago.
In a garden; he'd done some damage
behind a bright screen of sweet-peas
– snapped a stalk, a stake, I don't recall,
5   but the grandmother came and saw, and asked him
"Did you do that?"

Now, if she'd said *why* did you do that,
he'd never have denied it. She showed him
he had a choice. I could see in his face
10   the new sense, the possible. That word and deed
need not match, that you could say the world
different, to suit you.

When he said "No", I swear it was as moving
as the first time a baby's fist clenches
15   on a finger, as momentous as the first
taste of fruit. I could feel his eyes looking
through a new window, at a world whose form
and colour weren't fixed

but fluid, that poured like a snake, trembled
20   around the edges like northern lights, shape-shifted
at the spell of a voice. I could sense him filling
like a glass, hear the unreal sea in his ears.
This is how to make songs, create men, paint pictures,
tell a story.

25   I think I made up the screen of sweet-peas.
Maybe they were beans, maybe there was no screen:
it just felt as if there should be, somehow.
And he was my – no, I don't need to tell that.
I know I made up the screen. And I recall very well
30   what he had done.

Sheenagh Pugh

3 What are the similarities and differences in the way these poems present relationships between adults and children?

(8 marks)

4 Compare *For a Five-Year-Old* by Fleur Adcock and *The Beautiful Lie* by Sheenagh Pugh.
You should write about:
- what the poems are about and the way that they are structured
- the messages that the poets are trying to convey
- each poet's choice of language and the effects it creates.

(Eduqas — 20 marks)
(All other boards — 32 marks)

General Certificate of Secondary Education

GCSE
English Literature

| Surname |
| Other names |
| Candidate signature |

Paper 2: Shakespeare and 19th-Century Prose

Centre name					
Centre number					
Candidate number					

Time allowed: 1 hour 50 minutes

Instructions to candidates
- Write your answers in **black** ink or ball-point pen.
- Write your name and other details in the boxes above.
- Cross out any rough work that you do not want to be marked.
- You should **not** use a dictionary.

Information for candidates
- The marks available are given in brackets at the end of each question.
- There are 80 marks available for this exam paper.
- Marks are allocated for accuracy in spelling, punctuation and the use of vocabulary and sentence structures in Section A. These are given in brackets at the end of each question.
- You should spend about **55 minutes** on each section.

Section A: Shakespeare

Answer **one** question from this section.

You should spend about 55 minutes on this section.

William Shakespeare: *Much Ado About Nothing*

1   Answer part *(a)* **and** part *(b)*.

(a) Read the extract below. Look carefully at the way Benedick and Beatrice speak and behave in this extract. What impression would the audience get of these characters?

(15 marks)

(b) How does Shakespeare present the relationship between Hero and Claudio at different points in the play?

(20 marks)
(+5 marks for spelling, punctuation and grammar)

From Act 1, Scene 1. *In this scene, Don Pedro, Benedick and Beatrice are talking.*

	DON PEDRO:	... Be happy, lady, for you are like an honourable father.
	BENEDICK:	If Signior Leonato be her father, she would not have his head on her shoulders for all Messina, as like him as she is. [*Don Pedro and Leonato talk aside*]
5	**BEATRICE:**	I wonder that you will still be talking, Signior Benedick: nobody marks you.
	BENEDICK:	What, my dear Lady Disdain! Are you yet living?
	BEATRICE:	Is it possible disdain should die, while she hath such meet food to feed it as Signior Benedick? Courtesy itself must convert to disdain, if you come in her presence.
10	**BENEDICK:**	Then is courtesy a turncoat. But it is certain I am loved of all ladies, only you excepted; and I would I could find in my heart that I had not a hard heart, for truly I love none.
	BEATRICE:	A dear happiness to women, they would else have been troubled with a pernicious suitor. I thank God and my cold blood, I am of your humour for that; I had rather hear my dog bark at a crow than a man swear he loves me.
15		
	BENEDICK:	God keep your ladyship still in that mind, so some gentleman or other shall scape a predestinate scratched face.
	BEATRICE:	Scratching could not make it worse, and 'twere such a face as yours were.
	BENEDICK:	Well, you are a rare parrot-teacher.
20	**BEATRICE:**	A bird of my tongue is better than a beast of yours.
	BENEDICK:	I would my horse had the speed of your tongue, and so good a continuer. But keep your way, a God's name, I have done.
	BEATRICE:	You always end with a jade's trick, I know you of old.

William Shakespeare: *Macbeth*

2   Read the extract below, then answer the question.

Using this extract as a starting point, write about how
Shakespeare explores masculinity in *Macbeth*.

(35 marks)
(+5 marks for spelling, punctuation and grammar)

From Act 1, Scene 7. *At this point in the play, Lady Macbeth is
chastising Macbeth for his unwillingness to kill Duncan.*

Lady Macbeth:	Art thou afeard
	To be the same in thine own act and valour
	As thou art in desire? Wouldst thou have that
	Which thou esteem'st the ornament of life,
5	And live a coward in thine own esteem,
	Letting 'I dare not' wait upon 'I would,'
	Like the poor cat i' the adage?
Macbeth:	Prithee, peace:
	I dare do all that may become a man;
10	Who dares do more is none.
Lady Macbeth:	What beast was't, then,
	That made you break this enterprise to me?
	When you durst do it, then you were a man;
	And, to be more than what you were, you would
15	Be so much more the man. Nor time nor place
	Did then adhere, and yet you would make both:
	They have made themselves, and that their fitness now
	Does unmake you. I have given suck, and know
	How tender 'tis to love the babe that milks me:
20	I would, while it was smiling in my face,
	Have pluck'd my nipple from his boneless gums,
	And dash'd the brains out, had I so sworn as you
	Have done to this.

William Shakespeare: *Romeo and Juliet*

3 Answer part *(a)* **and** part *(b)*.

(a) How does Shakespeare show Romeo's thoughts and feelings in the extract below?

(15 marks)

(b) Using evidence from the text, write about points in the play when the audience might feel sympathetic towards Juliet.

(20 marks)

(+5 marks for spelling, punctuation and grammar)

From Act 2, Scene 2

	[*enter Juliet above*]
Romeo:	But soft, what light through yonder window breaks?
	It is the east and Juliet is the sun!
	Arise fair sun and kill the envious moon
	Who is already sick and pale with grief
5	That thou her maid art far more fair than she.
	Be not her maid since she is envious,
	Her vestal livery is but sick and green
	And none but fools do wear it. Cast it off.
	It is my lady, O it is my love!
10	O that she knew she were!
	She speaks, yet she says nothing. What of that?
	Her eye discourses, I will answer it.
	I am too bold. 'Tis not to me she speaks.
	Two of the fairest stars in all the heaven,
15	Having some business, do entreat her eyes
	To twinkle in their spheres till they return.
	What if her eyes were there, they in her head?
	The brightness of her cheek would shame those stars
	As daylight doth a lamp. Her eyes in heaven
20	Would through the airy region stream so bright
	That birds would sing and think it were not night
	See how she leans her cheek upon her hand.
	O that I were a glove upon that hand,
	That I might touch that cheek.

William Shakespeare: *The Merchant of Venice*

4 Read the extract below, then answer the question.

Using this extract as a starting point, explore how Shakespeare presents ideas of justice and mercy in *The Merchant of Venice*.

(35 marks)
(+5 marks for spelling, punctuation and grammar)

From Act 4, Scene 1. *At this point in the play Portia, disguised as a lawyer, is presiding over Antonio's trial.*

Portia:		The quality of mercy is not strained;
		It droppeth as the gentle rain from heaven
		Upon the place beneath. It is twice blest;
		It blesseth him that gives and him that takes.
5		'Tis mightiest in the mightiest; it becomes
		The thronèd monarch better than his crown.
		His sceptre shows the force of temporal power,
		The attribute to awe and majesty,
		Wherein doth sit the dread and fear of kings;
10		But mercy is above this sceptred sway;
		It is enthronèd in the hearts of kings;
		It is an attribute to God himself,
		And earthly power doth then show likest God's
		When mercy seasons justice. Therefore, Jew,
15		Though justice be thy plea, consider this:
		That, in the course of justice, none of us
		Should see salvation: we do pray for mercy,
		And that same prayer doth teach us all to render
		The deeds of mercy. I have spoke thus much
20		To mitigate the justice of thy plea,
		Which if thou follow, this strict court of Venice
		Must needs give sentence 'gainst the merchant there.

Section B: 19th-Century Prose

Answer **one** question from this section.

You should spend about 55 minutes on this section.

Charles Dickens: *A Christmas Carol*

1 Read the extract below from Chapter 3, then answer the question.

With reference to the extract below and the novel as a whole, write about how poverty is presented in *A Christmas Carol*.

(40 marks)

In this extract, the Ghost of Christmas Present reveals Ignorance and Want to Scrooge.

From the foldings of its robe, it brought two children; wretched, abject, frightful, hideous, miserable. They knelt down at its feet, and clung upon the outside of its garment.
"Oh, Man! look here. Look, look, down here!" exclaimed the Ghost.
They were a boy and girl. Yellow, meagre, ragged, scowling, wolfish; but prostrate, too, in
5   their humility. Where graceful youth should have filled their features out, and touched them with its freshest tints, a stale and shrivelled hand, like that of age, had pinched, and twisted them, and pulled them into shreds. Where angels might have sat enthroned, devils lurked, and glared out menacing. No change, no degradation, no perversion of humanity, in any grade, through all the mysteries of wonderful creation, has monsters half so horrible and dread.
10   Scrooge started back, appalled. Having them shown to him in this way, he tried to say they were fine children, but the words choked themselves, rather than be parties to a lie of such enormous magnitude.
"Spirit! are they yours?" Scrooge could say no more.
"They are Man's," said the Spirit, looking down upon them. "And they cling to me, appealing
15   from their fathers. This boy is Ignorance. This girl is Want. Beware them both, and all of their degree, but most of all beware this boy, for on his brow I see that written which is Doom, unless the writing be erased. Deny it!" cried the Spirit, stretching out its hand towards the city. "Slander those who tell it ye! Admit it for your factious purposes, and make it worse. And bide the end!"
"Have they no refuge or resource?" cried Scrooge.
20   "Are there no prisons?" said the Spirit, turning on him for the last time with his own words. "Are there no workhouses?"
The bell struck twelve.

Robert Louis Stevenson: *The Strange Case of Dr Jekyll and Mr Hyde*

2 Read the extract below from 'Henry Jekyll's Full Statement of the Case', then answer the question.

Using this extract as a starting point, write about how Stevenson explores morality in the novel.

(40 marks)

_____

In this extract, Jekyll questions whether he is to blame for the crimes that Hyde has committed.

I was the first that could thus plod in the public eye with a load of genial respectability, and in a moment, like a schoolboy, strip off these lendings and spring headlong into the sea of liberty. But for me, in my impenetrable mantle, the safety was complete. Think of it — I did not even exist! Let me but escape into my laboratory door, give me but a second or two to mix

5   and swallow the draught that I had always standing ready; and whatever he had done, Edward Hyde would pass away like the stain of breath upon a mirror; and there in his stead, quietly at home, trimming the midnight lamp in his study, a man who could afford to laugh at suspicion, would be Henry Jekyll.

The pleasures which I made haste to seek in my disguise were, as I have said, undignified;

10   I would scarce use a harder term. But in the hands of Edward Hyde, they soon began to turn towards the monstrous. When I would come back from these excursions, I was often plunged into a kind of wonder at my vicarious depravity. This familiar that I called out of my own soul, and sent forth alone to do his good pleasure, was a being inherently malign and villainous; his every act and thought centred on self; drinking pleasure with bestial avidity from any degree of

15   torture to another; relentless like a man of stone. Henry Jekyll stood at times aghast before the acts of Edward Hyde; but the situation was apart from ordinary laws, and insidiously relaxed the grasp of conscience. It was Hyde, after all, and Hyde alone, that was guilty. Jekyll was no worse; he woke again to his good qualities seemingly unimpaired; he would even make haste, where it was possible, to undo the evil done by Hyde. And thus his conscience slumbered.

Jane Austen: *Pride and Prejudice*

3   Read the extract below from Chapter 1, then answer the question.

Using this extract as a starting point, explore how Austen portrays the relationship between Mr and Mrs Bennet.

(40 marks)

In this extract, Mrs Bennet is trying to persuade Mr Bennet to visit Mr Bingley, who has just moved in to nearby Netherfield Park.

"I see no occasion for that. You and the girls may go, or you may send them by themselves, which perhaps will be still better, for as you are as handsome as any of them, Mr. Bingley may like you the best of the party."

"My dear, you flatter me. I certainly have had my share of beauty, but I do not pretend to be
5   anything extraordinary now. When a woman has five grown-up daughters, she ought to give over thinking of her own beauty."

"In such cases, a woman has not often much beauty to think of."

"But, my dear, you must indeed go and see Mr. Bingley when he comes into the neighbourhood."

"It is more than I engage for, I assure you."
10   "But consider your daughters. Only think what an establishment it would be for one of them. Sir William and Lady Lucas are determined to go, merely on that account, for in general, you know, they visit no newcomers. Indeed you must go, for it will be impossible for us to visit him if you do not."

"You are over-scrupulous, surely. I dare say Mr. Bingley will be very glad to see you; and I will
15   send a few lines by you to assure him of my hearty consent to his marrying whichever he chooses of the girls; though I must throw in a good word for my little Lizzy."

"I desire you will do no such thing. Lizzy is not a bit better than the others; and I am sure she is not half so handsome as Jane, nor half so good-humoured as Lydia. But you are always giving her the preference."
20   "They have none of them much to recommend them," replied he; "they are all silly and ignorant like other girls; but Lizzy has something more of quickness than her sisters."

"Mr. Bennet, how can you abuse your own children in such a way? You take delight in vexing me. You have no compassion for my poor nerves."

"You mistake me, my dear. I have a high respect for your nerves. They are my old friends. I
25   have heard you mention them with consideration these last twenty years at least."

Charlotte Brontë: *Jane Eyre*

4 Read the extract below from Chapter 37 (Volume 3, Chapter 11), then answer the question.

Using this extract as a starting point, write about Mr Rochester and the way he changes throughout the novel.

(40 marks)

In this extract, Jane has returned to find Rochester at Ferndean.

"Jane! you think me, I daresay, an irreligious dog: but my heart swells with gratitude to the beneficent God of this earth just now. He sees not as man sees, but far clearer: judges not as man judges, but far more wisely. I did wrong: I would have sullied my innocent flower — breathed guilt on its purity: the Omnipotent snatched it from me. I, in my stiff-necked rebellion, almost
5   cursed the dispensation: instead of bending to the decree, I defied it. Divine justice pursued its course; disasters came thick on me: I was forced to pass through the valley of the shadow of death. His chastisements are mighty; and one smote me which has humbled me for ever. You know I was proud of my strength: but what is it now, when I must give it over to foreign guidance, as a child does its weakness? Of late, Jane — only — only of late — I began to see
10   and acknowledge the hand of God in my doom. I began to experience remorse, repentance, the wish for reconcilement to my Maker. I began sometimes to pray: very brief prayers they were, but very sincere.

"Some days since: nay, I can number them — four; it was last Monday night, a singular mood came over me: one in which grief replaced frenzy — sorrow, sullenness. I had long had the
15   impression that since I could nowhere find you, you must be dead. Late that night — perhaps it might be between eleven and twelve o'clock — ere I retired to my dreary rest, I supplicated God, that, if it seemed good to Him, I might soon be taken from this life, and admitted to that world to come, where there was still hope of rejoining Jane.

"I was in my own room, and sitting by the window, which was open: it soothed me to feel
20   the balmy night-air; though I could see no stars, and only by a vague, luminous haze, knew the presence of a moon. I longed for thee, Janet! Oh, I longed for thee both with soul and flesh! I asked of God, at once in anguish and humility, if I had not been long enough desolate, afflicted, tormented; and might not soon taste bliss and peace once more. That I merited all I endured, I acknowledged — that I could scarcely endure more, I pleaded; and the alpha and omega of my
25   heart's wishes broke involuntarily from my lips in the words, 'Jane! Jane! Jane!'"

Charles Dickens: *Great Expectations*

5   Read the extract below from Chapter 8, then answer the question.

Using this extract as a starting point, write about how Dickens presents Miss Havisham.

(40 marks)

_____

In this extract, Pip meets Miss Havisham for the first time.

She was dressed in rich materials — satins, and lace, and silks — all of white. Her shoes were white. And she had a long white veil dependent from her hair, and she had bridal flowers in her hair, but her hair was white. Some bright jewels sparkled on her neck and on her hands, and some other jewels lay sparkling on the table. Dresses, less splendid than the

5   dress she wore, and half-packed trunks, were scattered about. She had not quite finished dressing, for she had but one shoe on — the other was on the table near her hand — her veil was but half arranged, her watch and chain were not put on, and some lace for her bosom lay with those trinkets, and with her handkerchief, and gloves, and some flowers, and a prayer-book, all confusedly heaped about the looking-glass.

10   It was not in the first moments that I saw all these things, though I saw more of them in the first moments than might be supposed. But, I saw that everything within my view which ought to be white, had been white long ago, and had lost its lustre, and was faded and yellow. I saw that the bride within the bridal dress had withered like the dress, and like the flowers, and had no brightness left but the brightness of her sunken eyes. I saw that the dress had been

15   put upon the rounded figure of a young woman, and that the figure upon which it now hung loose, had shrunk to skin and bone. Once, I had been taken to see some ghastly waxwork at the Fair, representing I know not what impossible personage lying in state. Once, I had been taken to one of our old marsh churches to see a skeleton in the ashes of a rich dress, that had been dug out of a vault under the church pavement. Now, waxwork and skeleton seemed to

20   have dark eyes that moved and looked at me. I should have cried out, if I could.

Mary Shelley: *Frankenstein*

6   Read the extract below from Chapter 24 (Volume 3, Chapter 7), then answer the question.

Using this extract as a starting point, write about how Shelley explores revenge in *Frankenstein*.

(40 marks)

In this extract, Frankenstein describes his desire for revenge on the monster.

... How I have lived I hardly know; many times have I stretched my failing limbs upon the sandy plain and prayed for death. But revenge kept me alive; I dared not die and leave my adversary in being.

When I quitted Geneva my first labour was to gain some clue by which I might trace the
5   steps of my fiendish enemy. But my plan was unsettled; and I wandered many hours round the confines of the town, uncertain what path I should pursue. As night approached, I found myself at the entrance of the cemetery where William, Elizabeth, and my father reposed. I entered it and approached the tomb which marked their graves. Everything was silent, except the leaves of the trees, which were gently agitated by the wind; the night was nearly dark; and the scene would have
10   been solemn and affecting even to an uninterested observer. The spirits of the departed seemed to flit around and to cast a shadow, which was felt but not seen, around the head of the mourner.

The deep grief which this scene had at first excited quickly gave way to rage and despair. They were dead, and I lived; their murderer also lived, and to destroy him I must drag out my weary existence. I knelt on the grass and kissed the earth, and with quivering lips exclaimed, "By the
15   sacred earth on which I kneel, by the shades that wander near me, by the deep and eternal grief that I feel, I swear; and by thee, O Night, and the spirits that preside over thee, to pursue the daemon who caused this misery, until he or I shall perish in mortal conflict. For this purpose I will preserve my life: to execute this dear revenge will I again behold the sun and tread the green herbage of earth, which otherwise should vanish from my eyes for ever. And I call on you, spirits of the dead;
20   and on you, wandering ministers of vengeance, to aid and conduct me in my work. Let the cursed and hellish monster drink deep of agony; let him feel the despair that now torments me."

Answers

Section Two — English Language: Reading Texts

Page 15 — Warm-Up Questions

1) a) Rita
   b) Rita
   c) Samuel
   d) E.g. "bad enough that we have to go to this reunion at all"
      E.g. "Rita glared pointedly at her watch"
      E.g. "admiring his reflection"

2) a) adults
   b) novices

3) E.g. 'Writer A dislikes mixed schools, and believes that all schools should be single-sex. In contrast, Writer B believes that mixed schools are better. Writer B also differs from Writer A because Writer B thinks parents should have a choice in which type of school their children attend, whereas Writer A thinks that all students should attend single-sex schools, regardless of their own or their parents' preferences.'

4) a) To advise. E.g. 'because the writer uses simple language that the reader will understand to suggest what the reader should do'.
   b) To entertain. E.g. 'because the writer uses descriptive verbs such as "crawling" and "gallop" to engage the reader'.
   c) To persuade. E.g. 'because the writer uses a rhetorical question to encourage the reader to agree with their argument'.

Page 16 — Exam-Style Questions

1) Any four correct facts about George, either paraphrased or directly quoted from the text. For example:
   • George has a nasal voice.
   • George is wearing a "garish purple suit".
   • George has an "elaborate hairstyle".
   • George brings a bottle of wine to the party.
   • George has "greasy" hands.
   • George is wearing several rings.
   • George likes whisky.

2) All your points should use relevant examples and terminology, and comment on the effects of the language used. Here are some things you could mention:
   • Opening rhetorical question ("But Who Do I Vote For?") suggests that the writer is on the reader's side.
   • Casual style to make the reader comfortable, e.g. "Unless you've been living under a rock for the past month".
   • Use of the imperative form ("don't panic", "have a look") to give clear guidance to the reader.
   • Minimal technical language to avoid intimidating or confusing the reader.
   • Introductory / concluding paragraphs create a clear structure and summarise the information to make it easier for the reader to understand.

Page 23 — Exam-Style Questions

1) Answers should clearly compare the different ideas and techniques in each text, using quotations to support points. Here are some things you could mention:
   • In Source A, the writer illustrates their dislike of a new art style using hyperbole ("nothing short of an abomination"). In Source B, the writer expresses their admiration for a new art style, also using hyperbole ("They're revolutionaries").
   • Both sources use formal language, e.g. "I read with concern" in Source A, "progression in the medium" in Source B. This makes their opinion seem more important / authoritative.
   • Source B makes the restrictions of traditional art seem negative using a metaphor, "the iron shackles of 'traditional art'", whereas Source A thinks that the rules of traditional art are good: new artists should have "learnt from" older examples.

2) Your answer should offer an opinion on the statement. It should comment on the techniques used to describe both characters, using relevant examples and terminology to support each point. Here are some things you could mention:
   • I agree that you can identify with both characters, because dialogue is used to give an insight into each character's mindset, such as Annie: "Don't be ridiculous." and Lucas: "They'll kill me." This indicates that Annie is calmer and less prone to being overdramatic in comparison to Lucas.
   • The cumulative use of short sentences in Lucas's speech also emphasises his stress and helps the reader to identify with his panic, e.g. "I've looked everywhere. It's lost. They'll kill me."
   • The contrast between the two characters makes each character's personality stand out more and their individual perspective seem clearer. E.g. the adjectives used to describe Lucas's actions ("frantic", "manic") contrast with the adverbs used to describe Annie's actions, which are carried out "cautiously" or "calmly".

Section Three — English Language: Style and Techniques

Page 28 — Warm-Up Questions

1) a) Detached
   b) Upbeat
   c) Sentimental

2) Sentence a)

3) E.g. 'The tone is conversational. The writer uses slang phrases such as "cheesed off", and contractions like "it's", as well as humour when describing the trip to "River C and Swamp D".'

4) a) E.g. 'Customers are advised that we do not accept credit cards.'
   b) E.g. 'It is essential to ensure you have the correct tools before proceeding.'

5) E.g. 'The word "whispered" suggests that the speaker and listener are working together, whilst "spat" suggests that the speaker doesn't like the listener.'

6) a) ii) money
   b) E.g. 'It suggests that the narrator is very motivated by money. They see their sibling's theatre show as an opportunity to "cash in" and talk about time as something you can "buy".'

7) E.g. 'The verbs are very violent, which creates the impression that the wind is powerful and destructive.'

Page 29 — Exam-Style Questions

1) All your points should use relevant examples and terminology, and comment on the effects of the language used. Here are some things you could mention:
   - An informal style that uses phrases like "up to your neck" and "bag loads of new skills", which encourage a young audience to connect with the writer and the holidays they're offering.
   - The inclusion of the sentence "There's nothing wrong with wanting a break." to show that the writer understands the mindset of young people, so that they are more inclined to trust the writer's claims.
   - The short, punchy sentences that make up the last paragraph create an excited tone, which engages the reader's interest.
   - Descriptive but simple adjectives ("incredible", "fantastic") emphasise how fun the activities are.

2) All your points should use relevant examples and terminology, and comment on the effects of the language used. Here are some things you could mention:
   - Words and phrases associated with cold to emphasise the woman's detached personality ("icily", "stone cold").
   - The adverb in the phrase "breath caught painfully" suggests that the man's fear is physically painful.
   - The simile "like a condemned man", which emphasises that the man feels resigned to his fate, and indicates that the woman is in a position of great power.

Page 38 — Warm-Up Questions

1) E.g. 'It suggests that the lake is something to be wary of.'

2) E.g. 'The second text compares the water to something that the reader is familiar with, to make it easier to visualise.'

3) a) Personification. E.g. 'It makes the computer seem like it's mocking the writer, which conveys the writer's frustration.'
   b) Onomatopoeia. E.g. 'It helps the reader to imagine the noise created by the students.'
   c) Alliteration. E.g. 'It makes the text more memorable.'

4) E.g. 'Sarcasm is nastier than irony, because it has a mocking tone that's often meant to insult someone.'

5) Yes. E.g. 'The text is sarcastic because the positive phrase "Ivan is a brilliant secretary" contrasts with the negative context "he keeps forgetting to bring a pen".'

6) a) Antithesis. E.g. 'It highlights the contrast between the writer's expectations and reality, which makes the reality seem more disappointing.'
   b) Parenthesis. E.g. 'It creates familiarity between the writer and the readers, so they are more likely to be persuaded.'
   c) Hyperbole. E.g. 'It emphasises how terrible the writer feels the rain would be.'

7) E.g. 'It gives the writer's opinion as fact ("By far the best hobby") and makes generalisations, such as claiming that all young people "adore" playing cribbage.'

8) E.g. 'The adjectives "blistering" and "burning" suggest that the weather is physically uncomfortable. The imagery "as if I were underwater" helps the reader to imagine the physical strain on the narrator, which is furthered by the descriptive verb "trudged".'

Pages 39-40 — Exam-Style Questions

1) All your points should use relevant examples and terminology, and comment on the effects of the language used. Here are some things you could mention:
   - The use of animal similes and metaphors to indicate how vulnerable the workers are — "like mice in a cage", "lambs" — in contrast to the soldiers, who are "wolves".
   - The use of a simile to suggest the officer speaks in a forceful way — "fired his orders like cannon balls." This is reinforced by the use of short sentences and imperatives to show his authority.
   - The use of the descriptive verbs "huddled" and "shivered" to suggest the workers' weakness. This contrasts with the verbs "trampled" and "marched", which are used to suggest that the soldiers are powerful and authoritative.

2) All your points should use relevant examples and terminology, and comment on the effects of the language used. Here are some things you could mention:
   - Alliterative phrases such as "labyrinth of lost lanes" to emphasise how confusing the writer finds Kuala Lumpur.
   - Personification of vehicles that "rumble past impatiently", which conveys the idea that everything in the city is animated and full of life.
   - Onomatopoeic verbs such as "whine" and "buzz" help the reader to understand the writer's attitude to Kuala Lumpur as a loud and confusing place.

3) Answers should clearly compare the different ideas and techniques in each text, using quotations to support points. Here are some things you could mention:
   - The writer of Source A has a fairly balanced viewpoint: they acknowledge positive aspects, like the room's size, as well as negative aspects, such as the "limited refreshment". This makes the writer seem more reasonable.
   - The writer of Source B has a more negative viewpoint than the writer of Source A — they instantly "doubted" that the bedding was clean, which, combined with a complete absence of positive points about the room, shows that the writer is quite biased.
   - Hyperbole is used in Source B to emphasise the writer's dislike of the hotel room — "hadn't been opened for about a century". The writer of Source A, however, uses discourse markers such as "Nevertheless" and "but" to show their more balanced viewpoint.

4) Your answer should offer an opinion on the statement. It should comment on the techniques used to describe the party, using relevant examples and terminology to support each point. Here are some things you could mention:
   - The cumulative effect of using several descriptive verbs together in "joking, laughing, making introductions", to convey a sense of action and excitement to the reader.
   - Onomatopoeic verbs such as "thumping" and "clinking" to help the reader to imagine what the party sounds like.
   - The focus on describing colours in the third paragraph, which appeals to the senses to help the reader to visualise the upbeat mood of the party.

Page 48 — Exam-Style Questions

1) All your points should use relevant examples and terminology, and comment on the effects of the structural features used. Here are some things you could mention:
- The shift in time that the extract uses — it starts in the present day, goes back to the past, then returns to the present. This allows the reader to become emotionally invested in Joan, so the ending has a greater impact.
- The progression from "she had already been looking forward to the next visit", to "there wouldn't be a next visit", which emphasises the sadness of the fact that Joan's life is drawing to a close.
- The motif of Joan looking at the sea, which is revisited in the first and last paragraph, and is contrasted by the way she "raced into the sea" in the second paragraph. This structure adds interest to the end of the story.

2) All your points should use relevant examples and terminology, and comment on the effects of the structural features used. Here are some things you could mention:
- The long, complex sentence in paragraph one, which helps to build the reader's interest in the show.
- The three consecutive short, simple sentences at the end of the second paragraph act as a cliffhanger, to create a sense of Mikhail's panic and worry.
- The writer gradually increases the tension towards the end of the extract, using direct speech such as "Sixty seconds to curtain" to create a sense of activity around the stage area.
- The perspective shifts from the stalls to backstage, so that the reader first experiences the general excitement of the audience, and then focuses specifically on Mikhail. This emphasises his importance to the scene, making his nerves appear more intense.

Section Four — English Language: Writing

Page 58 — Warm-Up Questions

1) b) rhetorical questions and d) emotive language

2) E.g. 'Hiding away in the sleepy village of Lyttlewich, Howtonshire, is a true gem of English architecture that you can't afford to miss. Thousands of visitors flock to the ancient Lyttlewich Church every year to marvel at its truly stunning artwork. Isn't it about time you joined the crowd?'

3) a) E.g. 'Fertilisers provide things that plants need to grow.'
   b) E.g. 'The ear bones are some of the smallest in the body.'
   c) E.g. 'Roman soldiers used weapons to defeat their enemies.'

4) a) E.g. 'Money can be tricky to get your head around, so why aren't schools teaching us how to deal with it?'
   b) E.g. 'Before you start making your yummy cake, ask an adult to help you get everything you'll need.'

5) a) E.g. 'I took a deep breath and stepped onto the alien spaceship, ready for my next adventure.'
   b) E.g. 'The familiar sounds of the river rushing outside my window were all I needed to hear; I was finally home.'

6) a) E.g. 'First person, to give an insight into the character's thoughts and feelings.'
   b) E.g. '"Eerie", to make the forest seem scary and sinister. "Timid", to make the character seem afraid.'
   c) E.g. 'The wind howled through the trees like a wolf hungry for its prey.'

7) a) E.g. 'From the diving board, the swimmers below look like a shoal of brightly-coloured fish.
   b) E.g. 'The noises in the pool echo like whalesong.'
   c) E.g. 'I feel the roughness of the tiles under my bare feet.'
   d) E.g. 'The bitter chlorine catches in the back of my throat.'

8) Answers should include ideas for descriptive techniques that could be used to describe a family member. Here are some techniques you could include:
- Using all five senses to give a detailed description: "My uncle always smells strongly of fried bacon and soap."
- A simile, to help the reader imagine the person: "His clothes are made from coarse material that's as rough as sandpaper to the touch."
- Repetition to emphasise a prominent aspect of their appearance or personality: "He's always cheerful: when he wakes up in the morning; when he goes to bed; even when you interrupt his favourite TV programme.'

Page 59 — Exam-Style Questions

1) Answers need to be entertaining for an audience of adult regular readers. They need to use interesting language techniques to create a suitable tone and style. Writing needs to be structured and clear. Here are some techniques you could include:
- The five senses: 'The air smelt of damp vegetation.'
- Personification: 'The leaves whispered in the night.'
- A first-person narrator: 'I shivered with cold as a brisk winter breeze crept into our tent.'

2) Answers need to be entertaining for an audience of adults. They need to use interesting language techniques to create a suitable tone and style. Writing needs to be structured and clear. Here are some techniques you could include:
- Personification: 'The flowers in the fields blinked shyly in the moon's light.'
- An unusual character: 'The town's oldest resident, Agatha Hart, was a tiny lady who wore layers of colourful, clashing clothing, which made her look at least twice her diminutive size.'
- Direct address: 'You might think that nothing exciting could ever happen in a sleepy town like Drizzleford. You'd be wrong.'

3) Answers need to be entertaining for an adult. They need to use interesting language techniques to create a suitable tone and style. Writing should be structured and clear. Here are some techniques you could include:
- The five senses: 'The sun felt warm on Gráinne's face.'
- Metaphors: 'The rock was a formidable enemy, and Gráinne had conquered it.'
- Alliteration: 'The solid slate surface sat sturdily under her shoes.'

Page 68 — Warm-Up Questions

1) Purpose: to argue / persuade.
   Audience: people with an interest in cars.

2) a) First person
   b) E.g. 'You pretended to slip on a banana skin, cartwheeling your arms and legs in a manner so ridiculous that the audience couldn't help but laugh.'

3) E.g. 'After battling government cuts and unprecedented construction delays, Totwith General Hospital was today declared officially open by local MP Jan Clipper. With the first patients due to arrive on Monday, I'd say it's about time too.'

4) Leaflet

E.g. 'You can tell this text is from a leaflet because it uses bullet points to break up the information it gives about the restaurant. It also uses language techniques, such as the alliterative phrase "warm and welcoming", to grab the reader's attention.'

5) E.g. 'You can have the wildest adventures with us — just don't forget to buy your holiday insurance!'

6) E.g. '*The Candle-Maker's Request* is an interesting novel, but it's not one that I'd recommend you give to your kids — its dark tone and visceral descriptions make for a sometimes horrifying read. For adults, though, this book is undoubtedly one of the most gripping novels of the year — maybe even the decade. I simply could not put it down.'

7) E.g. 'Intro: introduce self and explain aims of speech.
   • Explain positive things about school — large size means lots of freedom, big range of subjects on offer, get to meet variety of new people.
   • Counter-argument: some people say our homework is too hard / there's too much of it, but it prepares you well for exams (give average results as evidence).
   • Tell them that there is lots of support and help available, which makes the hard bits easier.
   Conclusion: Secondary school is a big change, so choosing the right school for your child is important. Recap main reasons for choosing my school.

8) Familiar

E.g. 'The letter uses colloquial language like "yonks", and an exclamation mark. These create an informal style that suggests the writer is familiar with their audience.'

Page 71 — Exam-Style Questions

1) Answers need to create an appropriate tone and style using suitable vocabulary and language techniques. Writing needs to be well-organised, clear and technically accurate. Here are some techniques you could include:
   • Onomatopoeia: Their only memory of childhood will be the dull buzz of yet another message notification.
   • Complex sentences: As time goes on, we will witness our children becoming steadily more housebound; this cannot be allowed to happen.
   • Antithesis: As smartphones get smarter, our children are becoming dimmer.

2) Answers need to reflect purpose and audience using suitable vocabulary and language techniques. Writing needs to be well-organised, clear and technically accurate. Here are some techniques you could include:
   • Rhetorical questions: Do you really care about TV more than your health and wellbeing?
   • Lists of three: The more sleep you get, the happier, healthier and brainier you'll be.
   • Emotive language: It's absolutely vital that you get enough sleep: your health and happiness depend on it.

3) Answers need to create an appropriate tone and style using suitable vocabulary and language techniques. Writing needs to be well-organised, clear and technically accurate. Here are some techniques you could include:
   • Descriptive adjectives: We should leap at the chance to swap humdrum, drizzly British life for something new.
   • First-person narrative: In Bermuda, I saw a sunset so beautiful that it brought tears to my eyes.
   • Analogy: "Trying to understand different cultures without going out and experiencing them is a little like trying to paint a portrait of something without ever seeing it: basically, you're bound to get it wrong."

4) Answers need to create an appropriate tone and style using suitable vocabulary and language techniques. Writing needs to be well-organised, clear and technically accurate. Here are some techniques you could include:
   • Formal language: Dear Madam, I write to express my support for the recent government proposal for new housing in Garlborough.
   • Anecdotal evidence: I have witnessed dozens of young people struggle to find appropriate, affordable housing.
   • Linking phrases: Moreover, as a country, our population is crammed disproportionately into cities and towns.

Section Five — English Literature: Prose and Drama

Pages 84-85 — Warm-Up Questions

1) a) setting
   b) characterisation
   c) theme
   d) writer's techniques

2) E.g.
   • examples of how fate affects the characters' lives
   • examples of decisions and choices that the characters make of their own free will
   • whether the outcome of those decisions would have been any different if they had decided differently
   • whether the events that are decided by fate have a greater or lesser influence on the outcome of the play than the events that are decided by free will.

3) Answer depends on chosen text.

4) Answers should focus on what the character is like, how the writer presents them and how this makes you feel about them. Here are some points you could consider:
   • Actions: What does the character do in the text? How does he or she treat other people? How do their actions make you feel about them?
   • Structure: Does the character change over the course of the text? Do they learn anything?
   • Language: How is the character described? How does the character speak? Does this make them likeable or not?

5) Answer depends on chosen text.

6) Answers should focus on what atmosphere the writer creates and how they create it. Here are some points you could consider:
   - Structure: Does the writer reveal what's happening gradually or suddenly?
   - Language: What words does the writer use? How do they make you feel? Does the writer use any techniques to create or add to the atmosphere (e.g. imagery)?
   - Form: Are the sentences long or short? Do they vary in length? What effect does this have?

7) Answers should focus on what the structural feature is and the effect it creates. Here are some points you could consider:
   - What is the feature? Why do you think the writer chose to use it at this point in the story?
   - Does it add to your enjoyment of the text? If so, how?
   - How would the text be different if the writer had not used this feature or had used a different structure?

8) a) E.g. "The conch shell represents democracy — it enables the boys to impose a fair system on their meetings that allows them all a chance to put their views across."
   b) E.g. "The old chestnut tree symbolises Jane's relationship with Mr Rochester. Just as the tree is split in two by lightning, Jane and Mr Rochester are separated by the revelation that he is already married."
   c) E.g. "Driving is a symbol for freedom. The students have little control over their lives, but they believe that driving would give them some freedom and a sense of being able to escape from their lives."

9) a) Answer depends on chosen text.
   b) Answer depends on chosen text. Here are some points you could consider:
      - How does the writer describe the setting?
      - Does it seem like a generally pleasant time in which to live or not? Why or why not?
      - Do you think it's a realistic description of life during this time? Why or why not?
   c) Answer depends on chosen text. Here are some points you could consider:
      - Are men and women treated differently? Do they have different opportunities?
      - How does social class affect people's lives?
      - Are some characters treated differently on the basis of their race, beliefs or background?

10) Answer depends on chosen text. E.g. for 'A Christmas Carol', you could have picked out the following themes:
    - Social responsibility
      It is implied that Scrooge helping the Cratchits at the end of the novel saves Tiny Tim's life. This shows how important social responsibility is — it can save lives.
    - Redemption
      The contrast between Scrooge's behaviour at the beginning and at the end of the novel. This emphasises that anyone, even someone as miserly and mean as Scrooge, can be redeemed.
    - Family
      The Cratchits are "happy, grateful, pleased with one another, and contented with the time", despite their poverty. This shows that family can bring comfort and joy to life, regardless of the hardships that people have to endure.

11) Answer depends on chosen text. E.g.
    - You might write that the message of 'Macbeth' is: 'Ambition and lust for power can drive the humanity out of a person.'
    - You might write that the message of 'Pride and Prejudice' is: 'Don't judge people on first impressions or superficial qualities.'

12) Paragraph a) shows better use of quotations, because it uses short quotations that are embedded into the text.

Page 86 — Exam-Style Questions

1) For this question, you're asked to focus on one scene. Make sure you pick one that you think shows your chosen character in an interesting light, so you'll have plenty of things to write about. You need to really get to grips with the language, and show how Shakespeare uses words to influence the reader's opinion of the character. This answer is for the character of Beatrice in Act 2, Scene 1 of 'Much Ado About Nothing', but it's worth reading even if you're studying a different play. Here are some things you could mention:
   - Act 2, Scene 1 of 'Much Ado About Nothing' starts with Beatrice criticising Don John because he is "too like an image and says nothing". This shows her to be judgemental and somewhat cruel in her assessment of others.
   - Despite this, however, she appears to be well-liked. Rather than telling her off for her cruelty, Leonato just reminds her that she will never find a husband if she continues to be so "shrewd of tongue". This shows that he is more concerned about the consequences of her behaviour than how rude she is being, which implies that he cares about her future and wellbeing.
   - The exchange between Beatrice and Leonato shows Beatrice's negative attitude towards men. She says that every man is "a clod of wayward marl", which compares men negatively to mud. This highlights her unfair dislike of men in general.
   - Beatrice's conversation with Leonato also highlights her wit. For example, she answers Leonato's hope that she will be "fitted with a husband" by arguing that "Adam's sons are my brethren, and truly I hold it a sin to match in my kindred." In this line, she plays on the biblical idea that all men are descended from Adam in order to emphasise her point. This shows her intelligence and ability to think quickly. Jokes about incest would have been considered shocking in Shakespeare's day, so this also shows the extent to which Beatrice flouts convention and ignores the rules of society.
   - When the questioning turns to Hero, Beatrice supports her by suggesting that Hero should have some say in who she marries: "let him be a handsome fellow, or else make another curtsey" and by advising Hero not to rush into marriage: "there is measure in every thing". This shows Beatrice to be loyal to her cousin, but the fact that she repeatedly answers questions addressed to Hero makes her seem over-bearing. This suggests that her intentions are good, but that she can be insensitive in her efforts to protect the people she cares about. Her tendency to talk too much links her with her own assessment of Benedick, "evermore tattling", and this hints to the audience that they may be destined for each other.
   - However, Beatrice's lack of awareness of how suitable Benedick is for her is highlighted by their exchange. Pretending that she does not know it is Benedick, she calls him "a very dull fool" and says that his only gift is "devising impossible slanders". This shows that she has a cruel gift for finding and playing on people's weaknesses, whilst being unaware of her own.
   - Benedick's reaction to Beatrice's taunts shows that she tends to go too far. He says "all disquiet, horror, and perturbation follows her", showing that he is hurt by her words. He also claims that he "would not marry her", showing that her sharp wit and cruelty have brought her close to losing the love of Benedick.
   - The more positive side of Beatrice's personality is shown by Don Pedro's reaction to her: he calls her a "pleasant-spirited lady", says she was "born in a merry hour" and jokingly proposes to her. This shows that, when she does not see men as a threat, Beatrice's wit is a real asset, and she is capable of being very charming.

2) For this question, you have to focus on a single passage from a prose text you're studying. You should focus on the way that the author has used language to create a feeling of tension or excitement. This answer is for Chapter 23 (or Volume 3, Chapter 6) of 'Frankenstein', from "It was eight o'clock..." to "I rushed into the room.", but it's worth reading even if you're studying a different novel. Here are some things you could mention:

- Imagery is used to create tension in the passage, as Frankenstein awaits the monster's revenge. For example, Frankenstein's anxiety is reflected in the personification of the "restless waves" and the simile of the clouds, which move "swifter than the flight of the vulture". This constant movement creates a feeling of unease in the reader, increased by the presence of the "vulture", which is often seen as an omen of death.
- Shelley uses the weather to reinforce this atmosphere of unease. There is a "heavy storm of rain" and the moon's rays have been "dimmed". This creates an atmosphere of restlessness and threat, which echoes the turmoil and danger that Frankenstein faces. The wind has also risen with "great violence", which foreshadows the violence that the monster is about to unleash on Elizabeth.
- Shelley uses hyperbolic language such as "a thousand fears" to emphasise the strength of Frankenstein's anxiety as he waits for the monster. This creates further tension and makes the reader fear what is to come.
- Repetition is used to give an insight into Frankenstein's state of mind. Frankenstein repeats the words "peace" and "dreadful" in his dialogue with Elizabeth; this pattern of repetition suggests his disordered, fearful thoughts and helps the reader to share his anxiety. The repetition of "dreadful" with an added intensifier in "very dreadful" also gives emphasis to the danger that he and Elizabeth face from the monster.
- Shelley uses a long sentence to create a pause in the action of the story before Frankenstein finds out the cause of Elizabeth's scream. This forces the reader to wait before finding out what the scream was about, which increases the sense of tension and anticipation in the passage. The detailed description of Frankenstein's physical reaction during the pause, such as the "blood trickling" in his veins, helps the reader to put themselves in Frankenstein's place and imagine his fear.

3) This question asks you to focus on a particular theme. Make sure you choose a theme that is relevant to the text you have studied. Focus on how the writer uses language, structure and form to present the theme. This answer is for the theme of social class in 'An Inspector Calls', but it's worth reading whatever play you're studying, because it'll give you an idea of the kind of things you should be writing about. Here are some things you could mention:

- The Birling family represent the middle classes. Priestley establishes them as selfish and arrogant. For example, at the beginning of the play Arthur gives Eric and Gerald some advice that hints at his selfish mentality, explaining to them that "a man has to... look after himself and his own". This suggests that Priestley is trying to portray a similarly negative image of the middle classes.
- Eva Smith is presented as a symbol of the suffering that the working classes are forced to undergo as a result of middle-class families — there are "millions of Eva Smiths and John Smiths", which suggests that her story symbolises the difficulties of the working classes as a whole.
- The play emphasises the power that social class can give — Sheila uses her "power" as the daughter of the well-known, well-off Mr Birling to have Eva/Daisy fired, and it's heavily implied that as a result Eva/Daisy is forced to turn to a life of prostitution. Although this event had a huge effect on Eva/Daisy's life, Sheila says that, to her, it "didn't seem to be anything very terrible at the time". Priestley shows that a relatively unimportant decision by a middle-class woman can prove catastrophic for a working-class woman such as Eva/Daisy.

- The Birling family believe the working classes to be inferior, which is reflected in the way Sybil refers to Eva/Daisy dismissively as a "girl of that sort". However, Eva/Daisy is shown to be morally superior to some of the middle-class characters, turning down Eric's stolen money even though she needs it. This suggests that Priestley thought that social class didn't define a person's character or moral values.
- Eva/Daisy is also used to suggest that the upper and middle classes do not see the working classes as real people — she is often referred to as "the girl" or "that girl" by the Birlings, suggesting that they don't want to give her a name or identity. This is reinforced by the way that she uses different names throughout the play (Eva Smith, Daisy Renton and Mrs Birling). This reflects how she has had her identity taken away from her by the actions of the other characters.
- The Inspector presents an alternative to the Birlings' class-obsessed perspective. He disagrees with Arthur Birling's selfish, characteristically middle-class beliefs — the Inspector says that people "are members of one body" who shouldn't ignore each other's needs, regardless of social class.
- The opinions of the Inspector reflect Priestley's own socialist views — he acts as Priestley's 'mouthpiece' in the play. This is made most clear during the Inspector's final speech, in which he warns the Birlings that the consequences of selfish, uncharitable behaviour like theirs will be "fire and blood and anguish". He's speaking to the Birling family, but rhetorical techniques such as repetition ("millions and millions and millions") and violent imagery ("fire and blood") make the speech stand out, as though he's speaking directly to the audience.

4) For this question, you need to focus on the context of the text you've chosen in your answer and link it to the language, form and structure of the text. This answer is for 'Pride and Prejudice', but it's worth reading whichever set text you're studying, because it'll give you an idea of the kind of things you need to pick out. Here are some things you could mention:

- The rigid class divisions in Regency England cause conflict in the novel. People were expected to marry within their social class, and behave according to society's rules. Darcy has a higher social standing than Elizabeth due to his income and family background, which forms part of his prejudice against her — he believes she is "beneath" him. Darcy's prejudice against Elizabeth is one of the major obstacles to their eventual marriage.
- Social rules placed limitations on how it was acceptable to meet new people. For example, Mrs Bennet claims it is "impossible" for her daughters to visit Mr Bingley until Mr Bennet has done so. Organised events such as balls and parties were the best way of meeting new people, including potential husbands and wives. In the novel, this is reflected in the way that Jane and Mr Bingley meet at the ball in Chapter 3, and then further develop their relationship during the ball at Netherfield in Chapter 18.
- Regency society treated women differently to men — it wasn't socially acceptable for upper- and middle-class women to have jobs, which meant they were unable to earn money for themselves. They often couldn't legally inherit property either. This happens to the Bennet sisters, whose home is entailed to Mr Collins, meaning that their financial futures are very uncertain, and that they need to marry well. This desire to find suitable husbands drives many of the actions of the Bennet family throughout the novel.
- Regency society's beliefs about social propriety for women also meant that Lydia's elopement with Wickham is viewed as a very serious problem. It destroys her reputation: Mary says that Lydia's virtue is now "irretrievable", and Mr Collins claims

that Lydia's death would have been a "blessing" in comparison. Mr Collins also writes that Lydia's actions will have an "injurious" effect on the reputation of her entire family, while Elizabeth believes that her love for Mr Darcy must now be "in vain", as he will not marry her following the scandal. This highlights how seriously society views Lydia's actions.

- Society's views on women also affect the way characters perceive Elizabeth's behaviour. For example, the Bingley sisters criticise her for walking to visit Jane at Netherfield: Miss Bingley describes it as "an abominable sort of conceited independence", which highlights scorn of Elizabeth's breach of decorum. However, Mr Bingley defends Elizabeth's behaviour, and because he is presented as a more likeable character than either of the Bingley sisters, the reader is more likely to agree with his opinions. This hints that Austen believed the rules of Regency society could often be too strict.

Section 6 — English Literature: Drama

Page 96 — Warm-Up Questions

1) E.g. In 'An Inspector Calls', Priestley uses stage directions to help create an atmosphere of stately formality. For example, the furniture is described as "solid" and the room as a whole appears "substantial", but "not cosy and homelike".

2) Monologue — e.g. one person speaking alone for a long period of time. Example depends on chosen text.
Aside — e.g. a short comment that reveals a character's thoughts to the audience, but not to the other characters. Example depends on chosen text.
Soliloquy — e.g. when one character speaks their thoughts aloud for a long time, but no other character can hear them. Example depends on chosen text.

3) Answers depend on chosen text.

4) E.g. In Act 2, Scene 4 of 'Romeo and Juliet', Mercutio mocks people who swordfight for being pretentious, calling them 'lisping' and 'fashion-mongers'. This gives the scene a light-hearted tone that reflects the events of the play at this point — Romeo is in love with Juliet and they are due to be married. The humour here suggests to the audience that all is well and things will have a happy ending. This makes the following scenes even more tragic because the audience has been misdirected into thinking the play could end happily.

5) Answers should focus on how the passage makes you feel and how Shakespeare achieves this. Here are some points you could consider:
- How do you feel when you read the passage?
E.g. Is it funny, sad, exciting or frightening?
- How does Shakespeare convey the characters' feelings? Look at what they say and how they speak.
- What has happened directly before the passage and what happens next? Does the position of the passage in the text enhance its effect or affect your reading of it?

6) a) Don Pedro's speech — blank verse
The lines are written in iambic pentameter but they don't rhyme.
Prince's speech — verse.
The lines are written in rhymed iambic pentameter.
Feste's speech — prose
The start of each line doesn't begin with a capital letter.
b) The Prince's speech is written in iambic pentameter, and the regular rhythm emphasises the feeling of sorrow. It has an ABAB rhyme scheme, which makes it sound serious and important.

Page 99 — Exam-Style Questions

1) For this question, you can choose which play you write about, so make sure you go for the one you know best. You have to write about fate and free will, so you need to pick out bits of the play where the characters seem to be controlled by fate or acting of their own free will, and explain how each bit you write about relates to the question. Remember, you also need to come to a decision about whether fate or free will is stronger. This answer is for 'Romeo and Juliet', but it's worth reading whichever of Shakespeare's plays you're studying. Here are some things you could mention:

- The conflict between fate and free will is evident from the beginning of the play. In the prologue, Romeo and Juliet are referred to as "star-cross'd lovers", implying that their lives are controlled by fate, not by their own choices. The prologue also states that their death is the only thing that can "bury their parents' strife", or end the feud between the Montagues and the Capulets, suggesting that there is a purpose to their deaths. In this way, Shakespeare introduces the audience to the idea that Romeo and Juliet's deaths are unavoidably fated.

- The language in the prologue echoes this theme of fate: it is written in rhyming verse, which gives the feeling of a pattern long established, which cannot be changed.

- Having established that Romeo and Juliet are destined to die, Shakespeare gives the audience several reminders throughout the play, which strengthens the sense that their lives are controlled by fate. For example, Lady Capulet wishes that Juliet "were married to her grave" and Juliet sees Romeo "As one dead in the bottom of a tomb", foreshadowing their eventual suicides.

- The characters also seem to recognise the power of fate. For example, Romeo predicts that the Capulets' ball will lead to his death, when he says that the night will "expire the term / Of a despisèd life closed in my breast". He chooses to go to the ball despite this, suggesting that he does not believe he can change his destiny. However, the fact that Romeo refers to his life as "despisèd", suggests that he is filled with misery and self-hatred because of Rosaline's rejection and that, on some level, he no longer wants to live. He might therefore go to the ball of his own free will, hoping to die. Ironically, his death wish ends when he meets Juliet, but meeting her sets in motion the events that will end both their lives.

- Instead of a fate that originates "in the stars", Romeo and Juliet's lives could be seen to be controlled by their character flaws, which pre-determine the way that they will behave. For example, Romeo is very impulsive, and it is this that causes him to kill Tybalt, resulting in his own exile. He also kills himself on impulse, despite noticing that Juliet does not appear dead: "death's pale flag is not advanced there"; if he had waited, he would have saved both their lives. Similarly, Juliet's dishonesty and cowardice prove her undoing when her parents tell her she must marry Paris — instead of confessing that she is already married and facing her parents' anger, she instead goes along with Friar Lawrence's plan to fake her death.

- Although there is strong evidence that fate plays a significant part in the events of 'Romeo and Juliet', the importance of free will should not be underestimated. For example, it could be argued that because the characters often seem to know in advance what consequences their actions will have, they could simply act differently. This is illustrated when Romeo kills Tybalt — before he fights him he realises that killing Tybalt "begins the woe others must end." In other words, he knows that Tybalt's death will have repercussions, yet he still chooses to fight. When he kills Tybalt, he calls himself "fortune's fool", suggesting that he wants to blame fate for what he has done, and that he is simply pretending to have no other choice.

- Throughout the play, the characters are guided by their own desires and act according to their own wills, rather than what society expects of them. For example, Juliet is offered a chance to change her fate when her parents tell her that she is expected to marry Paris. Her Nurse advises her to think of herself as a widow: "Your first is dead" and go along with the wedding, but Juliet rejects this.

- There is strong evidence to suggest that Romeo and Juliet are indeed "star-cross'd", such as the coincidences that lead to Romeo being at the Capulets' party, and the sequence of events that prevents Friar Lawrence from warning Romeo of his plan to fake Juliet's death. However, each of the characters could have chosen a different path, so ultimately their ending is as much down to free will as it is fate.

2) For this question, you'll need to pick out specific examples to illustrate Shakespeare's use of comedy in the scene you've chosen, and then explain them in detail. This answer is for 'Twelfth Night', but have a read of the points anyway to get a feel for the kind of things you need to write. Here are some things you could mention:

- 'Twelfth Night' uses lots of traditional comic devices, including disguise, mistaken identity, comic characters, mistreatment of unsympathetic characters, and word play. Act 3 Scene 4 contains examples of each of these devices, making it one of the funniest scenes in the play. Throughout the scene, Shakespeare's humour works on two levels. The first is visual, for example how the characters look and their reactions to one another, and the second is language-based, for example puns, asides and the way that lines are delivered.

- At the beginning of the scene, Olivia sends for Malvolio, believing that his "sad and civil" character will match her own melancholy mood. This immediately creates dramatic irony for the audience, because we know from recent events that Malvolio will not be "sad and civil" when he arrives, whereas Olivia has no idea. This builds expectation in the audience, making Malvolio's entrance particularly comical.

- Malvolio is presented throughout the play as prudish, self-righteous and miserable. Because of this, the audience feels little sympathy for him, which makes his inevitable downfall more comical than if he had been a sympathetic character. Because he has previously prided himself on being sensible and respectable, his transformation into a dandy, wearing yellow stockings, is very funny. The comedy is heightened by his referring to them as though the others might not have noticed: "Not black in my mind, though yellow in my legs". Similarly, Malvolio's bawdy pun "To bed? Ay, sweetheart, and I'll come to thee" is funny because it is so out of keeping with his character.

- Sir Toby treats Malvolio like a chicken by calling him "my bawcock" and "chuck". This is funny because it is completely out of keeping with the way he normally addresses Malvolio, and also because Malvolio believes that he will soon be master of the house, so he deserves respect.

- Some of the jokes in this scene about Malvolio being "mad" or "possessed" are quite dark, for instance Sir Toby's idea that they put Malvolio "in a dark room and bound". Shakespeare is able to use sinister jokes like these because the audience is aware that the play is a comedy and will therefore end happily.

- Fabian's line "If this were played upon a stage now, I could condemn it as an improbable fiction" is funny for the audience, because it echoes their own thoughts about how improbable the plot is and creates sympathy for the characters who are trapped in such a ridiculous sequence of events. The actor could create more humour by talking directly to the audience, showing his ironic awareness that it is being "played upon a stage".

- Mistaken identity is one of the recurring themes of the play, and it is used to great effect in this scene. Sir Andrew mistakes Viola for Sebastian, which could be amusing for the audience if the two actors don't look particularly alike. Sir Andrew is therefore challenging a woman to a duel, which creates a humorous irony — by trying to protect his honour, Sir Andrew acts very dishonourably in trying to fight a woman.

3) This question requires you to think carefully about the importance of a single central character and how they're presented in the play, so all your points need to be clearly about that character. This answer is for the Inspector in 'An Inspector Calls', but it's worth reading whatever play you're studying, because it'll give you an idea of the kind of things you should be writing about. Here are some things you could mention:

- The Inspector in 'An Inspector Calls' serves a variety of functions within the play. He makes the Birlings recognise their faults and the consequences of their actions, highlights the importance of people taking responsibility for one another, and also serves as an all-seeing, God-like figure, giving the impression that we will be brought to justice for our crimes, even if we think nobody else is aware of them.

- One of his most important functions is to highlight problems within the Birling family and, by extension, within the class-obsessed social system of the early twentieth century. This is illustrated by the stage directions. When the Inspector arrives, the lighting changes from "pink and intimate" to "brighter and harder", suggesting that the Inspector will shine a light on the true nature of the Birling family and shatter the illusion of the 'perfect' family.

- The Inspector highlights how wrong class-based prejudice is. He shows compassion for Eva Smith, and gives her an identity, something which the Birlings fail to do. For example, Mrs Birling repeatedly refers to Eva as "the girl", as if she cannot bear to mention her name, and talks about "Girls of that class", showing that to her the working class are not individuals and are incapable of "fine feelings and scruples". The contrast in the way Mrs Birling and the Inspector talk about Eva makes Mrs Birling appear narrow-minded and shows the audience that it is wrong to look down on the working classes and treat them as though they are less important than other classes.

- On a broader scale, the Inspector promotes Priestley's socialist message: that we should all take responsibility for one another. This is shown most clearly at the end of the play, when the Inspector says "We are members of one body. We are responsible for each other". The repetition of "we are" includes both the other characters and the audience, making it clear that this is how everyone should behave. This contrasts directly with Birling's belief that a man has to "look after himself and his own", and highlights the selfishness and cruelty of the some middle-class attitudes at the time.

- The Inspector seems to know everything about the Birlings' treatment of Eva, which allows him to drive the action forward and always be one step ahead of the other characters. In this way, he has an almost God-like quality, which makes his pronouncements about how we should behave much more powerful, particularly when he talks about "fire and blood and anguish", creating an image of Hell and implying that people who do not care for others will be damned. The Inspector's final speech is out of keeping with the rest of his language in the play, indicating that the audience is supposed to view him as a dramatic device, rather than a convincing character.

4) For this question, you need to pick out specific examples of supernatural elements in the play you've chosen, and then explain them in detail. This answer is for 'Macbeth', but it's worth reading whatever play you're studying, because it'll give you an idea of the kind of things you should be writing about. Here are some things you could mention:

- The Witches are the first characters to appear on stage, which highlights their importance. They are accompanied by "thunder and lightning", which makes them seem more threatening, increasing the audience's perception of the supernatural as something powerful and dangerous.
- The Witches are the most notable supernatural presence in the play. Shakespeare presents their supernatural powers of prediction as a very powerful force, which drives the play forwards and influences Macbeth to commit terrible crimes, such as murdering Duncan.
- The three Witches are portrayed as unattractive and unnatural — they are "so withered and so wild" that they look scarcely human, and they curse a sailor to sleep "neither night nor day", which emphasises their cruelty. This hints at the negative way that society in Shakespeare's time, and especially the reigning monarch, King James I, viewed witchcraft.
- The Witches, Hecate and the apparitions all speak in verse. This emphasises the fact that they are different to the other characters — they exist outside the natural order of the world, so they speak unnaturally. The rhyme and rhythm they use makes their speech sound like a chant, which gives it a magical, spell-like quality.
- Lady Macbeth uses supernatural imagery — she calls on "spirits" to help her, which links her with the Witches and the supernatural. This helps the audience to recognise how far she will go to gain power and understand that she is a morally corrupt character.
- The supernatural elements in the play are often ambiguous — the appearance of Banquo's ghost, the dagger and the blood on Lady Macbeth's hands could all be figments of the characters' imaginations, or they could be genuine supernatural occurrences. This ambiguity adds to the complexity of the characters of Macbeth and Lady Macbeth — the reader is left wondering whether they are truly seeing supernatural visions, or if they have been driven mad by their guilty consciences. It also reinforces the fear that the supernatural causes in the play, as the visions inspire very strong feelings of horror in Macbeth and Lady Macbeth.

5) For this question, you need to write about the relationship between two characters over the course of a whole play. This means you need to pay particular attention to the changes that occur between the two characters as the play progresses. This answer is for 'Blood Brothers', but it's worth a read even if you haven't studied the play. Here are some things you could mention:

- Mickey and Edward become best friends and "blood brothers" almost as soon as they meet. This highlights their youthful innocence at that point in the play, as well as the immediate, instinctive bond between them. In contrast, at the end of the play Mickey uses the recurring motif of "Blood brothers" to express his sense of betrayal and anger. This emphasises how much the characters' relationship has changed since their first meeting as children.
- Just before Edward departs for university, Russell uses a montage to illustrate the continuing happiness of the relationship between Mickey and Edward as teenagers. The stage directions say that both characters "smile" frequently, which emphasises the joy and freedom of youth and their pleasure in each other's company. This contrasts with the characters' actions and emotions immediately after Edward

returns from university: the stage directions say that Edward "laughs" and jokes, but Mickey is "unamused" and denounces their blood brother bond as "kids' stuff". This contrast highlights the turning point in their relationship — Mickey has come to view Edward as "still a kid", and resents that he himself has had to grow up too quickly. Their relationship continues to deteriorate until the end of the play.

- The balance of power in the relationship between Mickey and Edward changes as time goes on. As children, Mickey has the power in the friendship. He has knowledge that Edward wants, and behaves in a way that Edward admires. When Edward shouts at Mrs Lyons, "you're a fuckoff!", it is clear that he's already strongly influenced by what Mickey says, even when he doesn't know what it means. As adults, Edward holds the influence in Mickey's life — he gets Mickey a house and a job. Mickey resents this, feeling that he "didn't sort anythin' out" for himself, and this contributes to the final confrontation between the brothers.
- The changing relationship between the two boys as they enter adulthood, and their eventual deaths, could be interpreted as a comment on the divisions between social classes in 20th-century Britain — even a bond as strong as Mickey and Edward's can be destroyed. In his final speech, the narrator asks whether "class" was to blame for the deaths of the two brothers, suggesting that this is part of Russell's message in the play.

Section Seven — English Literature: Prose

Page 106 — Warm-Up Questions

1) Answer depends on chosen text. Here are some points you could consider:
   - The writer's choice of language — is it formal and written in Standard English, or more informal and written using slang or dialect words?
   - The sentence structures the writer uses — does the writer use long sentences to describe something in detail, or short, punchy sentences to create an exciting beginning for the reader?
   - The writer's tone — what is the overall feeling of the text in the first paragraph? Does it seem particularly cheerful, conversational or melancholy? How is this achieved?

2) Answers should focus on how the writer sets the scene and what effect the description has. Here are some points you could consider:
   - Where is the passage set? What is the place like?
   - How does the passage make you feel? Can you pick out any words or phrases that contribute to this effect?
   - Does the writer use techniques such as imagery to make the description more vivid? If so, what effect does it have?

3) For example:
   a) Elizabeth Bennet is the central character in Jane Austen's 'Pride and Prejudice'. She is important because she is involved in much of the action, and is portrayed as one of the wisest characters, so we trust her judgement. She has the strongest will of any of the Bennet sisters and she follows her own mind. Because of this, she is responsible for many of the novel's turning points.
   b) Elizabeth is a presented as sympathetic character, which helps the reader to identify with her feelings and decisions. She is presented as a caring, witty character, but her mistakes (e.g. misjudging Darcy and Wickham) make her seem like a real person.

c) Elizabeth's opinion of Darcy and her sister's suitor, Wickham, changes as she recognises that she has misjudged them. By the end of the novel she has realised that appearances can be deceptive, and that it is wrong to judge people on first impressions.

4) E.g. In 'Anita and Me', the narrator writes in the first person, as an adult looking back on the events of her childhood. This allows the reader to follow her thought processes and empathise with her. The use of a grown-up narrator gives an adult perspective on the events and emotions of childhood, which adds humour and pathos to the narrative.

5) a) For example: "most unfortunate affair", "much talked of", "useful lesson", "loss of virtue in a female is irretrievable", "one false step involves her in endless ruin", "reputation is no less brittle than it is beautiful", "she cannot be too much guarded in her behaviour".

b) For example: "Reputation was extremely important for women in nineteenth-century Britain. Women who damaged their reputation by behaving in an 'improper' way were regarded as having lost their "virtue", a situation that was judged "irretrievable". This shows that, once a woman's good reputation was lost, there was no way of getting it back — she would have been affected for life. Such women were used as a "useful lesson" to prevent other women from behaving in the same way."

Page 109 — Exam-Style Questions

1) For this question, don't try to pick out every point in the novel where prejudice occurs. Instead, you should pick a few key scenes and explain how the writer uses language, structure and events to portray prejudice. You should also consider other characters' reactions to it, and what effect the theme of prejudice has on the novel as a whole. This answer is for 'Anita and Me', but it should come in handy whichever novel you're studying. Here are some things you could mention:

- In 'Anita and Me', racial prejudice is often casual, such as Deirdre calling her dog "Nigger" because it's black, without realising it's offensive. This casual racism shows the ignorance of some of the residents of Tollington, who often don't realise the impact of their racism. This is reinforced later in the novel, when Sam says that he "never meant" Meena when he made racist comments.
- The novel highlights the role of education and the media in inadvertently encouraging racism — Meena says that all she learned at school about India was from "tatty textbooks" showing Indians as servants, or from "television clips" showing "machete-wielding thugs". This means that neither she nor her classmates are given a fair picture of the country on which to base their assumptions. It also makes Meena feel ashamed of her Indian heritage.
- The internalised prejudice that Meena initially feels against her own culture changes as the novel continues. This is reflected in Meena's language: she initially uses slang and an "authentic Yard accent" to impress Anita, which shows that she's willing to reject her cultural identity in order to be more like the people around her. However, later in the novel she learns Punjabi, which shows that she's embracing her Indian heritage.
- The racist attitudes of characters in the novel reflect the views of many British people in late 1960s and early 1970s, when the novel is set. For example, Sam Lowbridge makes his racist views public by shouting "If You Want a Nigger for a Neighbour, Vote Labour!" on television — this was the slogan used by supporters of a real Conservative MP who was elected in Smethwick (a town in the West Midlands) in 1964.

- Characters in the novel react differently to racial prejudice. Mama's reaction to racism is to try to disprove racial stereotypes — for example, she purposely speaks English "without an accent". In contrast, Papa tells Meena that she shouldn't accept racist abuse: "first you say something back, and then you come and tell me." The Kumars' mild, non-violent reaction to racism paints them in a much better light than the racist characters in the novel, and emphasises how unfair and illogical racial prejudice is.
- Racial prejudice is linked to the social situation of racist characters. For example, Sam Lowbridge is openly racist — he gets angry with his Uncle Alan for giving money away to "darkies we've never met", because he wishes more money was spent helping him instead. His racism acts as an outlet for his frustration over his lack of prospects.

2) This question asks you to talk about your chosen text in relation to a particular theme, so make sure the examples you choose are relevant to that theme. Remember to discuss how language, form and structure are used to present the theme. This answer is for 'Pride and Prejudice', but it should come in handy whichever novel you're studying. Here are some things you could mention:

- 'Pride and Prejudice' was written during the late eighteenth century, when class distinctions based on wealth and family connections were fairly rigid, and people were expected to marry within their own class. This expectation, and the struggle to overcome it, is one of the main themes of the novel.
- Most of the characters in 'Pride and Prejudice' are upper class — either aristocracy (like Lady Catherine) or gentry (like Darcy, the Bingleys and the Bennets). However, Austen presents social class with greater nuance than this — there are subtle differences in where each family sits in the class hierarchy, based on how rich they are, where their money came from, and how far back they can trace their family.
- Minor distinctions like these don't stop characters socialising, for example Lady Catherine has Elizabeth to dinner. However, social class does have an effect on marriage in the novel — 'marrying down' is strongly frowned upon. For example, Lady Catherine doesn't want Elizabeth to marry Darcy, and at first he also says it's a "degradation".
- The characters in the novel are all aware of the restrictions of class. For example, Elizabeth recognises that because of her mother's family background, she and Jane are not necessarily 'good enough' to marry Darcy or Bingley, and Darcy himself describes Elizabeth's family as "decidedly beneath" his own.
- Although Elizabeth is aware of the barrier that class creates between herself and upper-class characters like Darcy and Lady Catherine, she is never intimidated by them. For example, whilst Mr Collins is "employed in agreeing to every thing her Ladyship said", Elizabeth is not afraid to speak her mind and criticise Lady Catherine's behaviour, for example telling Lady Catherine that she has "no right" to interfere in her business. Austen uses Elizabeth to criticize the restrictions of the class system, suggesting that they don't need to be as strictly adhered to as some in Regency society might think.
- Despite his class consciousness, Darcy is attracted by Elizabeth's "impertinence" and "indifference to decorum", traits which are considered inappropriate by upper-class characters like Lady Catherine. This demonstrates that, while social class does have a strong influence on Regency society, it can be over-ridden by love.
- Austen satirises attitudes to social class using the character of Lady Catherine. Lady Catherine is so convinced that her upper-class status makes her superior that it does not occur to her that the other characters might not agree with her views. For example, she is "shocked and astonished" that Elizabeth won't promise not to marry Darcy.

- Lady Catherine is determined that Darcy will marry her daughter because they are "descended… from the same noble line", despite the fact that Anne is "pale and sickly" and "spoke very little", making it clear that she would not be a good wife for Darcy. This contains an implicit judgement of those who see social class as the most important factor in a happy marriage.
- Lady Catherine's arrogance and rudeness paint a very different picture of the upper classes from the "respectable, honourable" image that she is keen to portray, and in this way, Austen makes it clear to the reader that social class is separate from manners and decency. This is also shown by the Gardiners who, although they are of a much lower social class than Lady Catherine, are consistently presented as intelligent, charming and well-mannered, as demonstrated by Elizabeth's joy that "she had some relations for whom there was no need to blush."
- However, it is not only the upper classes who behave in a socially unacceptable way — Mrs Bennet, who has a middle-class background, also ignores the rules of polite society. For example, whilst dining with the Bingleys and Darcy, she comments that Charlotte Lucas is "very plain", and boasts about "Jane's beauty" in an obvious attempt to encourage Bingley to marry her. This confirms one of the key messages in the novel: that social class is not linked to respectability or manners.

3) This question asks you about the writer's methods, so you need to pay close attention to things like structure and language in your answer. Remember to pick out key events and quotations to illustrate your points, and make sure you relate your points to the historical context of the novel. This answer is for 'Animal Farm', but it's worth reading whatever your set text is, because it gives you an idea of the kind of things a good answer should mention. Here are some points you could include:

- The feeling that all is not well on Manor Farm is present from the beginning of the novel. In the first sentence we are told that Mr Jones is "too drunk" to do his job, showing that he does not have control over the farm. This impression is furthered by the fact that the meeting takes place at night and in secret, and involves Major's "strange dream", which makes it seem almost supernatural.
- Major talks about the "hideous cruelty" of slaughter, uses emotive language such as "slavery" and repeatedly refers to humans as the "enemy". This builds the sense that something is about to happen, so the reader feels the same suspense as the animals, because they know that they are plotting a rebellion that could lead to failure and death. Fear of the evil in man is heightened at the end of Chapter One, when Mr Jones begins indiscriminately shooting, giving a sense of how easily the animals can be killed.
- Following the rebellion, the pigs quickly establish themselves as superior to the other animals. The pigs help with the ploughing by "walking behind and calling out 'Gee up, comrade!' ", which instantly makes the reader think of humans doing the same. This foreshadows later events and creates a feeling of anxiety.
- The feeling of fear increases once we realise what Napoleon is capable of. The clearest example of this is when he violently expels Snowball from the farm, and it becomes clear that he has been planning this takeover for some time. We find out that Napoleon took the puppies that he uses to terrorise the other animals from their mother and "reared them privately", implying that he has been planning to seize power since the beginning.
- The dogs themselves add to the sense of fear. Although earlier in the novel the dogs are described as "clever", and are capable of singing 'Beasts of England', Napoleon's dogs do not seem to have any language. This distinguishes them from the other animals and makes them more threatening, because they seem like a force that cannot be reasoned with.

- Following Snowball's expulsion, the mood of fear and uncertainty grows. The scene in which Napoleon slaughters animals he believes are "in touch" with Snowball is terrifying because it shows his power over the other animals. This reminds the reader of Stalin's secret police in the Soviet Union, who tortured and executed politicians who were not loyal to Stalin.
- Perhaps the most horrifying image in the novel occurs right at the end, when the animals realise that they cannot distinguish between man and pig. The line "The creatures outside looked from pig to man, and from man to pig… but already it was impossible to say which was which" creates a real sense of fear, because it is a macabre and disturbing image which reminds the reader of fairytales where men are turned into the beasts that they resemble. The reader realises that the utopian society described by Major can never be achieved, and that the animals will never be free of tyranny and oppression. Again, this echoes events in the Soviet Union, where Stalin's expulsion and subsequent assassination of Trotsky effectively wiped out the possibility of a utopian communist society and resulted instead in fear and oppression.

4) For this question, you need to work out what the author's ideas about the nature of evil are, then explain how these ideas are presented. This answer is for 'Lord of the Flies', but it's worth reading if you're studying a different set text. These points give you some ideas of the kind of things you could include:

- The main message of 'Lord of the Flies' is that evil is present in everyone, that it is only the constraints of society that prevent people from committing evil acts, and that evil can be easily brought to the surface by fear. Golding served in the navy during World War II, and was shocked by the fact that civilians were bombed and by the way that prisoners in concentration camps were treated. It was this experience that made him believe that humans are essentially savage, and that outside of the boundaries of civilisation people are capable of great evil. The way that the boys quickly revert to a savage state symbolises the way that humans perform evil acts when there is no authority to prevent this.
- The pig's head, the "Lord of the Flies", symbolises evil and gives the sense that the island could be a hellish place. This is backed up by some of Golding's descriptions of the island. For example, "always, almost visible, was the heat." As heat is traditionally associated with hell, this foreshadows the boys' descent into savagery. Likewise, the boys are permanently ill with "stomach-aches and a sort of chronic diarrhoea", suggesting that the island is an unhealthy place, whilst "the skull-like coco-nuts" remind the reader of corpses, foreshadowing the later deaths.
- The boys don't realise that the evil is inside them, so they make it into a real being — "the beast" — which gives them something to "hunt and kill". This allows them to think of themselves as good, backing up Jack's statement that they are inherently capable: "We're English; and the English are best at everything", and building their belief that by hunting they are ridding themselves of evil. However, the more savagely they act and the more they hunt the beast, the stronger the evil inside of them grows and the more real the beast seems. The beast continually changes shape, from a "snake-thing", to something that "comes out of the sea" to "something like a great ape". In this way, Golding shows the reader that the beast is not real, and also demonstrates how evil continually changes shape depending on what the boys are most scared of.

- When Simon says of the beast that "maybe it's only us", the others laugh at him — they are unable to accept the idea that there could be evil in each of them. Simon's death therefore symbolises the end of reason and goodness. In the scene in which Simon is killed, the boys are nameless and act as a "single organism" which kills with "teeth and claws". This animal imagery shows how savage the boys have become, and how they are losing the final traces of civilisation. Even Ralph feels "a kind of feverish excitement" when he talks about Simon's murder, which shows how strong evil is and how it is present even in the characters that we consider 'good' and 'civilised'.

- The novel is set against the backdrop of a nuclear war: Piggy talks about the "atom bomb" and says "They're all dead." This, together with the appearance of the naval officer at the end, reminds the reader that the boys' evil is minor on the wider scale of human evil, and reinforces Golding's message that savage behaviour is man's natural state.

5) For this question, you can write about any prose text that you've studied, so make sure you pick one that you can think of plenty to write about. You need to write about the ways in which the main character has changed, and the ways in which they've stayed the same through the course of the novel. Pick out key events that illustrate your points and don't forget to back up everything you say with quotes from the text. This answer is for 'Great Expectations', but it'll give you an idea of the sort of points you need to make whatever text you're studying. Here are some things you could mention:

- The novel is a Bildungsroman, which means that it follows the progress of one character, in this case Pip, as he grows up. The novel is narrated by Pip, which means that the thoughts and actions of the younger Pip are seen through the eyes of the older Pip. This gives the reader a clear sense of how the character has changed, because the older Pip frequently makes fun of or judges the younger Pip, for example when he asks Joe about spelling "with a modest patronage". This shows how the older Pip is more mature, and recognises the tendency of his younger self to judge people and try to change them, rather than accepting them as they are.

- At the start of the novel, Pip is a young, naïve boy. His main aspiration is to be Joe's apprentice, and he has no ambition to better himself. This changes when he first sees Satis House and meets Estella, and begins to feel that his own home is "coarse and common". In much the same way, his home becomes a metaphor for his own character and he starts trying to improve himself. It is this struggle for education, social class and wealth that causes the first big change in Pip's character.

- This change is demonstrated by the way that Pip acts towards Joe. At the start of the novel, Pip says that he "was looking up to Joe in my heart." However, following his move to London, and once he feels that he has become a gentleman, Pip treats Joe coldly because Estella "would be contemptuous" of Joe. This shows how Pip is blinded by wealth and status, and how his 'rise' in society has made him a harder, more selfish person, who judges people by their social standing and is prepared to hurt his oldest friend in order to impress Estella.

- Pip eventually starts to understand that wealth and status do not bring happiness. This realisation is foreshadowed by Dickens' description of London, a place that in the 19th century was associated with wealth and status, as having "the most dismal trees in it, and the most dismal sparrows, and the most dismal cats, and the most dismal houses". Repetition of the word "dismal" shows how disappointed Pip is with London, and later with his own social advancement.

- A second great change in Pip's character occurs when he meets Magwitch for the second time. Pip's realisation that his wealth, education and social standing are the result of a convict's generosity, rather than a favour from Miss Havisham, challenges his views about the social hierarchy he believes in, and makes him recognise his own "worthless conduct" towards Joe. This is a major turning point in Pip's character, as it makes him realise that social class and status are very different from generosity and goodness of heart, and that the latter qualities are more important.

- Dickens uses the character of Pip to represent the failings of a society that believed happiness could be attained through social climbing and wealth. By having Pip recognise the error of his ways, Dickens showed that he believed people were capable of altering their views and placing greater importance on decency, loyalty and hard work than on money and status.

Section Eight — English Literature: Poetry

Page 117 — Warm-Up Questions

1) a) A word that sounds like the noise it's describing, e.g. splash, creak.
   b) A pause or break in a line, often marked by punctuation.
   c) A sentence that runs over from one line to the next.

2) "the fizzy, movie tomorrows / the right walk home could bring."
   E.g. "The onomatopoeic word "fizzy" sounds lively and bubbly, emphasising the feeling of excitement about the future."

   "They accuse me of absence, they circle me."
   E.g. "Sibilance creates a hissing sound, which highlights the menacing tone."

   "a blockade of yellow bias binding around your blazer."
   E.g. "The alliteration causes hard 'b' sounds to dominate the line, creating a harsh tone which suggests the narrator is distressed."

   "All the alleyways and side streets blocked with stops"
   E.g. "The assonance of the short 'o' sounds in "blocked with stops" suggests that the narrator feels trapped."

3) Your answer should consider how dawn is personified in the extract and what this tells the reader about the speaker's feelings (e.g. lonely, scared, depressed). Here are some things you could mention:
   - Dawn is personified as an "army". This reminds the reader of soldiers preparing to attack, and suggests that the speaker dreads the coming day.
   - Dawn is normally a positive symbol, associated with light and new beginnings. The speaker views it negatively, suggesting that he has lost hope.
   - Dawn is described as "melancholy" — this reflects the feelings of the soldiers in the trenches. They are weary and depressed rather than energised and ready to fight.
   - The words "once more" show that the attack continues with no respite, and creates a sense that there will be no end to the war or to the soldiers' suffering.

4) a) E.g. "The strict rhyme scheme uses rhyming couplets (AABB etc.) to emphasise the Duke's obsessive need for order and control."
   b) E.g. "The direct address brings the narrator to life, making his presence a dominant feature of the narrative."
   c) E.g. "The Duke's speech often runs on from one line to the next, which creates the impression that he doesn't give his visitor a chance to speak, and shows his desire to dominate the conversation."

Section Nine — English Literature: Poetry Anthology

Page 125 — Warm-Up Questions

1) E.g. 'War Photographer' by Carol Ann Duffy has a regular rhyme scheme — it is "set out in ordered rows" like the photographer's spools. This helps to emphasise the care that the photographer takes over his work.

2) E.g. In 'She Walks in Beauty', the narrator uses the third person to describe a woman. This makes her more difficult to empathise with, because there is no insight into her thoughts or feelings, which creates distance between her and the reader. In contrast, in 'The Manhunt', Armitage uses the first person to explore the experience of the wife of a traumatised soldier returned from war. The first-person perspective allows an intensely personal description of her husband's scarred body and mind, which makes it easier for the reader to empathise with the speaker.

3) a) E.g. "'Forward, the Light Brigade!' / Was there a man dismay'd?"
(Charge of the Light Brigade, Alfred Tennyson)
Effect: End-stopping imposes order on the poem, reflecting the way that the soldiers' actions are controlled by the officers.
   b) E.g. "My father spins / A stone along the water. Leisurely"
(Eden Rock, Charles Causley)
Effect: This caesura slows the pace of the poem, which emphasises the feeling of peace.
   c) E.g. Porphyria's Lover, Robert Browning
Effect: It emphasises the sense of the narrator's control over Porphyria, because his is the only perspective the reader hears.
   d) E.g. "spits like a tame cat / Turned savage."
(Storm on the Island, Seamus Heaney)
Effect: Enjambment places emphasis on the word "Turned", which highlights how suddenly the storm arrives.

4) E.g. Tennyson uses form to convey a sense of order in 'Charge of the Light Brigade'. For example, end-stopping in the lines "'Forward, the Light Brigade!' / Was there a man dismay'd?" creates a controlled rhythm that reflects the way that the soldier's actions are controlled by the officers. In contrast, in 'Storm on the Island' Heaney uses enjambment to describe the storm: for example, he says that it "spits like a tame cat / Turned savage." Here, enjambment is used to emphasise the word "Turned", which highlights how suddenly the storm arrives, and how little power the islanders have against nature.

5) a) E.g. "I struck and struck again"
(The Prelude: Stealing the Boat, William Wordsworth)
Effect: The repetition of "struck" emphasises the narrator's fear and desperation to get away.
   b) E.g. "The slap and plop were obscene threats."
(Death of a Naturalist, Seamus Heaney)
Effect: The onomatopoeic words help the reader to vividly imagine the sounds of the frogs.
   c) E.g. "With sidelong flowing flakes that flock"
(Exposure, Wilfred Owen)
Effect: Alliteration emphasises the relentlessness of the snow.
   d) E.g. "a green-blue translucent sea"
(Kamikaze, Beatrice Garland)
Effect: The smooth, long 'u' sound makes the sea seem appealing.

6) E.g. 'Kamikaze' uses assonance to emphasise the beauty of nature. For example, the repeated long 'u' sound in the phrase "green-blue translucent sea" creates a smooth sound that emphasises the beauty of the sea. This highlights the pilot's appreciation of the natural world and hints that it influenced his decision to return home. In contrast, 'Exposure' uses alliteration to emphasise the terrible conditions the soldiers are experiencing: the snow is described as "flowing flakes that flock", which makes it sound relentless and overwhelming. This adds to the cumulative sense of threat in the stanza, which reflects Owen's negative depiction of war overall in the poem.

7) E.g. In 'Follower', Seamus Heaney uses nautical imagery to emphasise the father's strength and skill. One effective image in the poem is the description of the father's shoulders as "globed like a full sail strung". This simile likens the father to a ship, which creates an image of strength and power in the reader's mind.

Page 128 — Exam-Style Questions

1) For this question, you have to think about the way that the poets use form, structure and language to describe feelings towards another person, so make sure you choose poems that have plenty to write about on the subject. Comparing them means writing about the similarities and differences, so make some links between the poems in your answer. This answer is for 'Sonnet 29' by Elizabeth Barrett Browning and 'Love's Philosophy' by Percy Bysshe Shelley, but it gives you an idea of the kind of things you need to write whichever poems you're analysing. Here are some points you could make:

- Both poets use form to help convey a sense of longing for another person. In 'Love's Philosophy', the final line of each stanza is shorter than the other lines, which makes it stand out. This adds weight to the rhetorical question in each stanza, which emphasises the narrator's desire to be with his lover. The short lines also slow the pace of the poem — this creates a sense of wistfulness, which emphasises the narrator's yearning for his lover. In contrast, 'Sonnet 29' uses the sonnet form to link the narrator's feelings to a tradition of love poetry. However, whereas in a standard sonnet the solution often arrives in line 9, in 'Sonnet 29' it arrives early: "Rather, instantly / Renew thy presence" appears in line 7, hinting that the narrator cannot wait for her lover's arrival. The enjambment of these lines emphasises the words "instantly" and "Renew", which further underscores the narrator's eagerness to see her lover.

- 'Love's Philosophy' has a regular ABAB rhyme scheme, reflecting the constancy of the narrator's feelings towards his lover. However, half-rhymes such as "river" / "ever" create a note of discord, emphasising the narrator's sorrow at the fact that he and his lover are not together. This half-rhyme also emphasises the words "for ever", which underscores the narrator's desire for an eternal connection with his loved one. 'Sonnet 29' also has a strong rhyme scheme, with half the lines ending with the same sound, for example "tree" / "see". This helps to drive the poem forward, reflecting the narrator's impatience to be reunited with her lover. The end-rhyme "thee" is repeated four times, which emphasises the narrator's obsession with her lover and longing for him to return.

- 'Love's Philosophy' and 'Sonnet 29' both use natural imagery to emphasise feelings of longing for another person. In 'Love's Philosophy', Shelley personifies nature, for example "the mountains kiss high heaven", to suggest that all of nature craves intimacy. This adds weight to the narrator's argument that he and his lover should be together. Similarly, Barrett Browning's narrator compares her thoughts to "wild vines" to show that her longing for her lover is uncontrollable. The natural metaphor extends to her lover, who she likens to a "strong tree" about which she grows. This suggests that she yearns for his support.

- The narrator of 'Love's Philosophy' uses rhetorical questions, such as "Why not I with thine?", to make his lover question her refusal to be with him. This gives the poem a pleading tone, which emphasises the narrator's longing and helps the reader to empathise with him. In contrast, Barrett Browning uses imperatives such as "Renew" to express her impatience for her lover's return. She suggests that his presence will cause her thoughts to "Drop heavily down", suggesting that she feels burdened by her reflections when he is not there.
- Both 'Love's Philosophy' and 'Sonnet 29' use physical language to underscore the desire the narrators feel for their loved ones. Shelley repeats physical words associated with lovemaking, such as "kiss" and "clasp", to emphasise the relationship the narrator longs for. By suggesting that powerful entities such as mountains and the sun "kiss" and "clasp", Shelley implies that even the mightiest beings rely on physical union, which strengthens his argument that he and his lover should be together. Conversely, Barrett Browning uses violent language such as "burst" and "shattered" to describe the effect the lover's presence has on the narrator's thoughts. Such words emphasise the intensity of her passion and the suddenness with which her thoughts are eliminated when her desire is fulfilled. The plosive sounds create the impression that her thoughts are exploding, which conveys to the reader the sense that she is unable to contain her excitement.

2) For this question, you have to think about the way that the poets use form, structure and language to present time, so make sure you choose poems that have plenty to write about on the subject. Remember, you're comparing the two poems, so you need to think about similarities and differences between them. This answer is for 'The Emigrée' by Carol Rumens and 'War Photographer' by Carol Ann Duffy, but it gives you an idea of the kind of things you need to write whichever poems you're analysing. Here are some points you could make:

- Both 'The Emigrée' and 'War Photographer' use form to emphasise the changes in the main characters' circumstances that have occurred over time. 'War Photographer' is made up of four equal-length stanzas, and it has a regular rhyme scheme, which reflects the safety and security of the photographer's present situation. This contrasts with phrases such as "running children in a nightmare heat", which describe the chaos the photographer has witnessed in the past. This contrast between the poem's form and language emphasises how the photographer's past is very different from the life he currently leads. 'The Emigrée' also uses form to emphasise the differences between the narrator's past and present. The first two stanzas use lots of enjambment, but the final stanza includes more end-stopped lines. This underscores the contrast between the freedom of the narrator's past and the confined "city of walls" that characterises her present life.
- In 'The Emigrée', time is presented as a destructive force using a war metaphor: "time rolls its tanks / and the frontiers rise between us". By comparing time to an army, and suggesting that it has created the "frontiers" between herself and the past, the narrator suggests that time is responsible for the fact that she is unable to return. Similarly, in 'War Photographer' the influence of the past is presented as something that is personally destructive to the photographer. This is shown by the "tremble" of his hands as he develops the photographs, which is linked to the events of the past by the references to both "then" and "now" in the stanza.
- In both poems, time brings about a change in the main character's situation or circumstances, but it cannot destroy their memories. In 'The Emigrée', this is presented in a positive way. The narrator's memories of her past are described as "sunlight-clear" and "bright"; Rumens's use of light imagery in these phrases emphasises that the narrator remembers her old city with fondness. In contrast, in 'War Photographer' the photographer's memories of the past are presented as painful, using emotive words such as "cries" and "blood". This sensory imagery shows that his memories are still very vivid, showing that he can't move on from the events that he has witnessed.

- Both poems present time as incapable of healing emotional wounds. In 'The Emigrée', present-tense verbs, such as "takes" and "hides", combined with personification, describe the city of the narrator's past. This indicates that she has not been able to move on from the past, which is reinforced by the accusations of "absence" from her new life. Similarly, in 'War Photographer' Duffy uses the metaphor of a "a half-formed ghost" to imply that the photographer is being 'haunted' by his past. Even though he is "Home again", far away from the place and time in which the events took place, they still have a strong negative influence on his life.
- The main characters in both poems are symbolically taken back through time at the end of their narratives. In 'The Emigrée' this is presented positively: although the narrator says that there's "no way" for her to physically return to the old city, a personified version of her old home appears to her and takes her "dancing". This hints that her memories of the past are strong enough to overcome her present unhappiness. 'War Photographer' ends with the suggestion that the photographer is flying to another war zone, showing that the past is repeating itself. The final rhyming couplet makes his return seem unavoidable; because of his job, the photographer has no choice except to return to another version of the past that haunts him.

3) For this question, you have to think about the way that the poets use form, structure and language to present the effects of conflict, so you need to choose two poems that you think show the consequences of a conflict clearly. Remember, you're comparing the two poems, so you need to think about similarities and differences between them. This answer is for 'Dulce et Decorum Est' by Wilfred Owen and 'The Manhunt' by Simon Armitage, but it gives you an idea of the kind of things you need to write whichever poems you're analysing. Here are some points you could make:

- Both poems use narrative viewpoint to convey their messages about the effects of war. 'Dulce et Decorum Est' focuses on the effects of war on the soldiers who fight in it. The use of the first-person collective viewpoint in the first and second stanzas emphasises that war is a shared experience. The subsequent switch to the first-person singular at the end of the second stanza then highlights the impact of war on each individual who participates in it. In contrast, 'The Manhunt' uses the first-person singular throughout, which emphasises the effects of war on the individual. However, in this case, the speaker is the wife of a soldier, which emphasises that the effects of war are widespread and not just limited to those who fight.
- The first three stanzas of 'The Manhunt' are written in rhyming couplets, echoing the narrator's feeling that now her husband is back everything will return to normal. However, the rhyme scheme breaks down after this, which suggests that the woman has come to realise that her husband is still deeply affected by what he went through. In contrast, 'Dulce et Decorum Est' has a regular ABAB rhyme scheme. In the first stanza, this emphasises words like "trudge" and "sludge", to show how exhausting and tedious some aspects of war can be. Then, in the final stanza, the rhyme scheme emphasises words and phrases like "sin", "blood" and "desperate glory", which makes the narrator sound angry. This hammers home Owen's message that the real effects of war are very different from "The old Lie", and in fact it is not "Dulce et decorum", or sweet and right, to die for your country.
- Both poets use powerful imagery to convey the physical effects of war. Owen uses images of illness, like "Obscene as cancer" and "vile, incurable sores", which give the impression that the effects of war are similar to the effects of disease. This makes war sound unnatural and like something that could affect anybody. Similarly, Armitage uses metaphors to illustrate the

damage that war can do. He compares the soldier's body to a "blown hinge" and a "fractured rudder". This presents parts of the body as things that were once useful, but have been made useless by war.

- Both Owen and Armitage also mention the psychological effects of war. Owen's narrator dreams that the dead soldier "plunges at me, guttering, choking, drowning." This string of verbs shows that, even once the gas attack is over, it haunts the survivors and will not let them live peaceful lives. Similarly, the narrator of 'The Manhunt' mentions the "sweating, unexploded mine / buried deep in his mind", suggesting that her husband's problems are psychological as well as physical, and that his memories of war still cause him a great deal of distress.

4) For this question, you have to think about the way that the poets use form, structure and language to describe a particular place. You could choose to analyse poems that use different language to describe a similar place, or poems that describe very different places — just make sure you can think of plenty to say about the similarities and differences between the poems. This answer is for 'London' by William Blake and 'The Prelude: Stealing the Boat' by William Wordsworth, but it gives you an idea of the kind of things you need to write whichever poems you're analysing. Here are some points you could make:

- Both poems use form to help create a sense of place. 'London' uses an unbroken ABAB rhyme scheme, which echoes the relentless misery of the city, and contributes to the sense that London is a place full of pain and sorrow. In contrast, the extract from 'The Prelude' uses blank verse. The regular, unrhymed iambic pentameter of the poem makes it sound serious and important, which emphasises the power of the looming mountains.
- In 'London', the city is presented as being full of people. Blake repeats the phrase "I hear", which emphasises the noise of the city, and he refers to numerous people, such as the "soldier" and the "harlot", to create the impression that London is a crowded place. In contrast, Wordsworth notes that there is "nothing but the stars and the grey sky" above the narrator, which emphasises the vastness and emptiness of the place that he is in.
- The places described in both poems are presented as confining and inescapable. In 'London', Blake repeats the word "chartered", meaning 'legally defined' or 'mapped out', even using it to describe the River Thames. This makes it seem like natural features are controlled by human rules, which emphasises the power that authorities such as the monarch and the ruling classes have over the physical place and make the city seem oppressive. In contrast, Wordsworth uses repetition to make nature seem powerful and uncontrollable: in the phrase "a huge peak, black and huge", the word "huge" is repeated, which emphasises the sheer size of the mountain. This highlights that it dominates the narrator's view and makes it seem like he can't escape from it.
- Blake uses sensory imagery to present London as a place that is full of sadness and pain. For example, the emotive image of the "chimney-sweeper's cry" appeals to the reader's sense of hearing, which helps them to imagine the chimney sweeper's misery at the dangerous work he has to do. Wordsworth also uses sensory imagery to appeal to the reader's sense of hearing: he twice uses the word "silent" to describe the waters of the lake, which helps the reader to imagine the sense of quiet in the narrator's surroundings.
- The sense of place that Blake creates in 'London' is very personal: he uses a first-person narrative, and the poem loosely follows the narrator's journey on foot through London. This suggests that his view of London is linked strongly to his own emotions and feelings, emphasising the personal links that a person can have with a place. The extract from 'The Prelude' is also written in the first person. This has the effect of allowing the reader to see the narrator's changing perception of the place he describes. At the start of the extract, words such as "sparkling" and "glittering" create a beautiful, magical image of the lake. However, after seeing the scene around him in its entirety, he describes the scenery using negative adjectives such as "grim". This emphasises how much a person's sense of a place can change.

5) For this question, you have to think about the way that the poets use form, structure and language to present the power of humans in the poems you choose. Remember, you're comparing the two poems, so you need to think about similarities and differences between them. This answer is for 'Ozymandias' by Percy Bysshe Shelley and 'Checking Out Me History' by John Agard, but it gives you an idea of the kind of things you need to write whichever poems you're analysing. Here are some points you could make:

- Both poems examine the power of an individual. In 'Ozymandias', the individual (Ozymandias) was extremely powerful during his lifetime — he was a "king of kings" — but now he is reduced to the "colossal wreck" of a statue in the middle of a desert, showing that he is completely powerless. Conversely, in 'Checking Out Me History', the narrator had little power in the past: he repeats the phrase "Dem tell me" to highlight how little control he had over his own education and therefore his "identity". However, by the end of the poem he has taken power from the authorities: he says that he is "carving out" his own identity. 'Ozymandias' hints that striving for power is ultimately pointless because power doesn't last; in contrast, 'Checking Out Me History' suggests that it is vital in order to overcome injustice.
- The poets both use form to emphasise their message about striving for power. Agard uses a mixture of stanza forms, non-standard English, and no regular rhyme scheme. This indicates a rebellion against the formal structures of poetry and spelling that he would have been taught in school and shows that he is in control of his own education now. On the other hand, 'Ozymandias' is written in sonnet form, but it doesn't follow a regular sonnet rhyme scheme. This reflects the way that human power and structures can be destroyed by time and nature.
- The poems' structures also emphasise their messages about striving for power. In 'Ozymandias', the ruined statue is described by an anonymous "traveller". This second-hand account creates distance between the reader and Ozymandias and makes it seem like his power has had little lasting effect on the world. In 'Checking Out Me History', on the other hand, Agard structures the poem using repeated references to figures who fought injustice, such as "Toussaint L'Ouverture" and "Nanny de maroon". This brings these figures to prominence and reinforces the importance of striving for power against oppressive forces.
- Both poets use strong, aggressive language to show that those in power can be brutal. For example, in 'Ozymandias' the statue's "wrinkled lip" and "sneer" hint at his cruelty and lack of care for his subjects. There is no mention of Ozymandias's subjects rebelling against him, but by emphasising the ruler's brutality, Shelley may be hinting that such an attempt to gain power may be justified. In 'Checking Out Me History', violent verbs such as "Blind me" show the damage the narrator feels the authorities have done to him, emphasising their lack of concern for his wellbeing. In both poems, the use of strong, violent language may hint that striving for power over oppressive regimes is justified.

Section Ten — English Literature: Unseen Poetry

Pages 136 — Warm-Up Questions

1) E.g. It's about the narrator's sense of loss after someone she loves dies.

2) E.g. The narrator means that she and her lover never got the chance to live together and make a home, because he died.

3) E.g. The descriptions of spring are vivid and life-like, which contrasts with the narrator's dead lover. Phrases like "the violets peer" and "Every bird has heart to sing" describe the beauty and joy of spring and rebirth. At the same time, the final line of each stanza describes the narrator's feelings — she is unable to appreciate the beauty around her, and feels only loss and regret, rather than joy.

4) E.g. The rhyme scheme is ABAB. This gives the poem a simple rhythm, which emphasises the sadness of what the narrator is saying.

5) The final line is missing four syllables compared to the other lines. This emphasises the last line and makes it feel like it finishes too soon, which reflects the relationship between the narrator and her lover — it ended too soon, and now something is missing.

Page 137-138 — Exam-Style Questions

1) For this question, you have to think about what the poet is saying about loneliness and solitude, and how she says it. Make sure you comment on how form, structure and language are used to present feelings and ideas in the poem. Here are some points you could make:

- The poem has a nightmarish quality — the woman is alone, waiting nervously for her husband's safe return. The atmosphere is tense, as if something bad may be about to happen. The second stanza deals with the woman's actual nightmare, and the alliterative words "coming", "climbing" and "creeping" make the sea feel very menacing and hostile. It's like someone creeping in and stealing her lover. She wakes up, but with the "screaming gulls" and the sea "chill in her arms" it still feels as if she's in a nightmare.

- The main feeling of the first stanza is boredom — she has "nothing to do now he's gone". She needs to keep busy, so she cleans the house. But the cleaning is futile; the broom "leaves a trail of grit". This could show that the act of cleaning can't cleanse her mind of her fear and anxiety.

- The first stanza contains lots of 's' sounds — "dusts", "sweeps", "sand", "step", "sprinkling" and "hangs". This makes the stanza feel longer, reflecting the woman's feelings about how time slows down whilst she's alone. The sibilance also sounds like the sea, so it's a constant reminder of the woman's enemy.

- The second stanza describes the woman going to bed. She "sleeps downstairs", perhaps because she can't bear to be alone in their shared bed. This shows how even small things can be a painful reminder of the person you're missing. She also uses a "coat for a pillow" — the coat could well be her partner's, and by sleeping with it she may feel closer to him.

- In the third stanza, the onomatopoeic "screaming gulls" creates a vivid image. It's also a stark contrast to the silence of the rest of the poem, where the only sounds are the sweeping of the broom and the sibilance of the sea creeping closer. The screaming gulls might also be reminiscent of the screams of drowning sailors, highlighting the woman's fear that her partner will die at sea.

- His shirts are hanging on the washing line, which is a reminder that he's coming back, and feels homely and hopeful for a moment. But the final two lines, "and the high tide's breakers' / chill in her arms", immediately recall the sea and the woman's constant fear that her partner will never return. The "chill" of the waves in the woman's arms seems like a forewarning of death — as if she's holding her partner's cold, drowned body in her arms.

- The structure of the poem, broken into three stanzas, mimics the structure of the woman's life whilst her partner is away — it's divided into day, night, day. There's no rhyme, which reflects her slightly panicky state of mind. The final stanza is heavily enjambed, which creates a feeling of time moving faster, of disorder and confusion. The final stanza is also a line shorter, possibly reflecting her partner's early death.

2) For this question, you have to think about how the power of the sea is presented in the two poems. Make sure you comment on how form, structure and language are used to present feelings and ideas in the poem. You're comparing the two poems, so you need to think about similarities and differences between them. Here are some points you could make:

- Both poems present the sea as something dangerous and powerful. The subject of 'At Sea' fears that her partner will die at sea, while 'The Sands of Dee' describes the death of a girl who is drowned by 'The western tide'.

- Both poets use language to convey the sounds of the sea. In 'The Sands of Dee', the use of repetition (e.g. "o'er and o'er", "round and round") mirrors the sound of the waves and creates a sense of the relentless, unstoppable power of the sea. Similarly, in 'At Sea', the sibilance in the first stanza (e.g. "she dusts the house, / sweeps") echoes the sound of the sea and suggests its inescapable presence.

- The poets both create a tense, frightening atmosphere through the imagery they use. For example, the onomatopoeic image of "screaming gulls" in 'At Sea' creates tension and anxiety by suddenly breaking the silence of the poem with a sound that suggests fear and suffering. In 'The Sands of Dee', the imagery of the "rolling mist" and the alliterative description of the "wild" "western wind" creates a sense of danger and of the power of nature.

- The two poets personify the sea in similar ways. Kingsley describes it as "cruel, crawling" and "hungry", while Copley depicts it "coming", "climbing" and "creeping". In both cases, the imagery the poets use and the harsh alliterative 'c' sounds make the sea sound menacing and unstoppable.

- The form of the two poems is very different, and is used to create different effects. 'At Sea' is written in free verse, with variable line lengths and no rhyme, which makes it seem unstructured and chaotic. This reflects the way the sea affects the woman, mirroring the lack of structure in her life when her partner is away at sea. In contrast, the form of 'The Sands of Dee' reflects the movement of the sea. Unlike 'At Sea', Kingsley's poem has a regular rhyme scheme, AAABAB, which creates a strong rhythm, mirroring the relentless movement of the waves.

Section Eleven — Spelling, Punctuation and Grammar

Page 149 — Warm-Up Questions

1) E.g. 'Standard English is English that uses a formal style. It doesn't use any slang or local dialect words.'

2) The purpose of punctuation is to make writing clearer. Written language lacks the pauses and changes of tone that help the listener hear the differences between words, clauses and sentences. Without punctuation, it's possible for ambiguities and confusion to creep in. Who knows what you could accidentally say if you don't punctuate?

3) a) I'd like you to buy some groceries: milk, bread, frankfurters and anything else you fancy.
   b) He was the bravest of men, the greatest of men; they called him Keith.

4) a) The lollipop lady's lollipop had been stolen.
   b) The girls' faces fell as they saw what the homework was.
   c) It's a sale bonanza aboard the Shoe Ship this weekend — everything's half price in the world's only floating shoe shop!

5) "I just don't believe you", said Mark.
   "But I've never told a lie before", replied Jenny.
   There was a silence before Mark muttered, "Not a lie I've found out about at least."
   Jenny pretended not to hear him, and asked, "So what did you do last weekend, then?"

6) a) Dave wasn't sure **where** to park his car.
   b) Felicity spent two hours deciding what she should **wear** to the party.
   c) The chilli flakes had a horrible **effect** on the cake's flavour.
   d) Nathan was determined to **practise** his spelling every day.
   e) The twins celebrated **their** birthday together every year.

7) E.g. Compound: "It rained every day for two months, and the continual rain made Martha grumpy."

   Complex: "It rained every day for two months, which made Martha grumpy."

8) E.g. 'My Grandma is usually as gentle as a kitten, but when she gets angry, she's like a hurricane; she shouts as loudly as a foghorn and stomps around the house like an elephant.'

Practice Papers — English Language

Pages 154-157 — English Language: Paper 1

1) 1 mark for each valid response given, up to a maximum of four marks. Answers might include:
   • There are big bush-covered hills at the back
   • There are paddocks
   • There are bungalows
   • There's a sandy road
   • There are white dunes covered in reddish grass
   • There are fuchsias / nasturtiums / toi-toi grass
   • The bungalows have gardens with colourful plants

2) All your points should use relevant examples and terminology, and comment on the effects of the language used. Here are some things you could mention:
   • Descriptive verbs such as "huddled" are used to suggest that the sheep are fearful. This is reinforced by the words used to describe their movements: the sheep "trotted along quickly" as if in fear.
   • In contrast, the writer presents the dog as unafraid and even nonchalant. It runs along "carelessly" suggesting that it is "thinking of something else". This makes the roles of the animals clear: the dog is a working pet, whilst the sheep are animals in captivity.
   • The writer uses imagery to give really fine details of how the shepherd looks: his coat is "covered with a web of tiny drops". This detail helps to give the reader a clear picture of the shepherd, but also to help them feel the cold, wet conditions. The entrance of the shepherd is described using a shorter, less detailed sentence than the ones that surround it ("And then in the rocky gateway the shepherd himself appeared."). This helps to make his entrance seem dramatic, which emphasises his character's importance.

3) All your points should use relevant examples and terminology, and comment on the effects of the structural features used. Here are some things you could mention:
   • The writer starts the text using short statements to give the reader the broadest facts about the scene, it is "Very early morning" and "The sun was not yet risen". This then progresses to much longer sentences to build the fine details of what the bay looks like. However, these are still broken up by a further short statement, "A heavy dew had fallen". In this way the writer manages to build detail, whilst emphasising the most important points so the reader feels how chilly, early and damp it is.
   • The focus then moves from the bay, "Round the corner" and begins to describe the animals and the shepherd. The descriptions given at this point are short, giving small insights: the sheep-dog is "old" and the shepherd is "a lean, upright old man". They act as introductions to the characters, drawing the reader further in to the scene.
   • In the long, final paragraph, the writer brings together the misty scene she has described with the characters she has introduced. The reader is taken on a short journey along the "sandy road" which continues to emphasise the "shadowy" early morning.
   • The paragraph ends with the revelation of the mist rapidly rolling away, revealing everything that was hidden in the first paragraph. This makes it feel to the reader as if the day has begun, and the opening of the story is now over.

4) Your answer should offer an opinion on the statement. It should comment on the techniques the writer uses to make the text detailed and interesting, using relevant examples and terminology to support each point. Here are some things you could mention:
   • I agree in some ways that it is like watching a film. Phrases such as "came into view" and "in the direction of the sea" create a cinematic effect for the reader, directing the reader's focus in the way that a camera might. In this section of the text it is effective as it allows the reader to see what the shepherd is seeing, drawing them into the scene with him.
   • However, the writer adds more detail than you would normally be able to experience in a film. She appeals to the senses as she describes the "whiff of eucalyptus" and the shepherd's "wet beard", which adds to the richness of the description and allows the reader to feel even more like they are inside the scene.

5) Whether your answer is a story or a description, it needs to use an appropriate tone, style and register to match the purpose, form and audience. Writing needs to be well-organised, clear and technically accurate. Here are some techniques you could include:

In a description:
- Figurative language: A faint curtain of mist rose off the lake, swathing everything in a sheet of fine white cloud.
- Similes: Just past the end of the jetty, waiting like a promise, was the little red boat.
- Unusual descriptive words and phrases: Tendrils of gelatinous pond weed emerged from the water's edge.

In a story:
- Descriptive language that sets the scene: The mist had emerged a few hours ago, curling slyly around the trunks of the gnarled old oaks in the wood.
- Direct address to the reader: If you'd seen what I saw in the lake on that cold October evening, you'd have done the same thing.
- A dramatic, unexpected event: The storm appeared too suddenly for them to avoid it.

Pages 158-162 — English Language: Paper 2

1) 1 mark for shading each of the following statements:
   A Monica Albelli thinks being a nanny is a difficult job.
   D Lesley and Brian are both professionals of a similar age.
   E Lesley and Brian are affectionate parents.
   H Lesley and Brian sometimes gave Monica conflicting instructions.

2) Answers should use relevant quotes from both texts to summarise several differences between the two people. Here are some things you could mention:
- Mrs Sidgwick and Lesley are very different people, particularly in their attitude towards the people they employ. Mrs Sidgwick does not treat her governess as if she's a person; it is thanks to Mrs Sidgwick that Charlotte feels as if she is "not considered as a living and rational being". In contrast, Monica hints that, to an extent, Lesley treated her as a friend: for example, she "confessed" to Monica about her insecurities regarding her children.
- Lesley seems to care more about other people's feelings than Mrs Sidgwick. Lesley doesn't tell Monica the "real reason" that she was fired, suggesting that she might be trying to save Monica's feelings. In contrast, Charlotte writes as if Mrs Sidgwick does not consider Charlotte's wellbeing; Charlotte has "never" been so "fully" occupied before, which makes her so tired that she "can write no more".
- Mrs Sidgwick does not seem to take an interest in her children's education. Charlotte maintains that Mrs Sidgwick "does not intend to know me", even though the children are with her "constantly". This implies that she is distanced from her children and their well-being. Lesley, however, has strong views concerning Albelli's role, wanting her to create "responsible and hard-working individuals". Although Lesley also becomes distanced from her children, she views this development negatively; she feels "jealous" and "threatened" by Albelli, and replaces her.

3) All your points should use relevant examples and terminology, and comment on the effects of the language used, focusing on how it is used to influence her sister. Here are some things you could mention:
- Brontë uses a combination of formal and informal language in order to influence her sister. She uses polite, formal language in places, such as the phrase "I am most exceedingly obliged". This is a courtesy that would make her sister feel pleased. This formal language is then combined with familiar terms like "papa" and informal phrases, such as "Love to all" to appeal to the relationship between Brontë and her sister, making Brontë more likeable. This in turn would make her sister more inclined to agree with Brontë's viewpoint.
- Brontë also uses persuasive language to express her viewpoint. For example, she uses a list of three, describing the children she takes care of as "riotous, perverse, unmanageable". The cumulative effect of these negative adjectives helps to emphasise Brontë's displeasure with her current situation, which encourages her sister to sympathise with her difficulties.
- Brontë employs metaphors to stress the extent of the hardships she is facing, for example, "she overwhelms me with oceans of needlework". The word "oceans" implies that she feels her work is vast and never-ending, and "overwhelms" makes Brontë seem vulnerable. This helps to encourage feelings of tenderness and sympathy in her sister.

4) Answers should clearly compare the different attitudes and techniques in each text, using quotations to support points. Here are some things you could mention:
- Brontë's letter suggests that she feels limited and confined by the duties involved in looking after other people's children. She refers to her wards as being "constantly" with her. Brontë's choice of adverb suggests that she gets no respite from the children; it also indicates that she resents this constant imposition.
- Albelli indicates a similarly close proximity to her wards: the image of the young boy "curled" around her leg is a symbol of the closeness between them. However, she uses rhetorical questions to suggest that this closeness is desirable, which challenges negative attitudes such as Brontë's. She questions "How can Mary Poppins be indifferent?", to suggest that nannies should aim to be close to children in their care, even whilst maintaining some degree of professional detachment.
- Brontë suggests that the expectations of her role as a nanny are unattainable. She states that she cannot do what Mrs Sidgwick demands; "to love her children and be entirely devoted to them". Emotive language used throughout the extract supports this, with verbs such as "overwhelms" and "squeezed" implying that she is over-exerted. In contrast, Albelli highlights the danger of nannies surpassing expectations and fulfilling the role of a mother, as Lesley feels "threatened" by her success with the children. This implies that Albelli feels the problems faced by parents over childcare are greater than the problems experienced by nannies.

5) Answers need to use an appropriate tone, style and register to match the purpose, form and audience. Writing needs to be well-organised, clear and technically accurate. Here are some techniques you could include:
- Direct address: Our parents are trying their best to help us succeed, but they need to understand that putting us under so much pressure will ultimately be counterproductive.
- Repetition: Working hard isn't always a negative thing: it creates a sense of achievement, a sense of ambition and a vital sense of purpose.
- Facts and statistics: Some of the most academically successful education systems have the highest rate of student dissatisfaction.

- Satirical language: Draining the joy from a young person's life with constant chores and homework is, of course, one of the hallmarks of good parenting.
- Rhetorical questions: Should children look back on their childhood and struggle to remember anything but homework and chores?

Practice Papers — English Literature

Pages 164-165 — English Literature — Paper 1: Section A (Modern Texts)

1) This question requires you to think about a single central character, so all your points need to be about that character. You need to write about how Priestley presents Arthur Birling, so make sure you mention the techniques that he uses. These points give you some ideas of the kind of things you could include:

- Arthur Birling is initially presented as the character with the most authority in the play. He dominates the beginning of the play, giving long speeches and insisting that the other characters listen when he is speaking. For example, he asks "Are you listening, Sheila?" when it's not clear if he has her attention, and she apologises: "I'm sorry, Daddy." This shows the authority he has over her. By the end of the play, however, Birling's authority has been undermined. Sheila challenges him, saying that she "can't listen" to anything else he says, which shows that she's willing to disagree with Birling and no longer respects his authority. This decline in Birling's power could reflect Priestley's own views about the declining influence of the middle classes.
- Priestley presents Birling as very confident character, who is comfortable expressing his opinions: he often ends his own sentences with "of course", which indicates that he is very secure in his beliefs. Priestley uses dramatic irony to emphasise that Birling's confidence is misguided, and that he doesn't know as much as he thinks he does. The audience know that many of Birling's beliefs are wrong, because he references famous events that hadn't occurred in early 1912, when the play is set, but which the play's first audiences in 1945 would have known about. For example, he says that "there isn't a chance of war" with Germany, and that "the *Titanic*" is "absolutely unsinkable". This makes Birling seem over-confident, arrogant and foolish.
- Birling lacks social conscience: he doesn't feel any responsibility to society as a whole. For example, he tells Eric and Gerald that a man has to "look after himself and his own". The fact that he is presented as an unlikeable character who makes false statements about other things implies that he's wrong about this too. This also helps to strengthen Priestley's message in the play that the ruling classes should act more selflessly and do more to help those around them.
- Birling places great importance on reputation and connections. For example, he believes that his friendship with the "Chief Constable" will intimidate the Inspector, and he later claims that he would "give thousands" in a bribe to avoid a scandal. This shows that he is concerned with the way the rest of society perceives him, and that he will do almost anything, including breaking the law, to preserve his reputation.
- Birling is characterised by his interest in industry, something that is established when he defines himself as a "man of business" in the opening scene of the play. His preoccupation with business is reinforced by his use of language that is linked to money: for example, he hopes Sheila's marriage will bring "lower costs and higher prices" for his company. This suggests that money is more important to him than his daughter's happiness.

- Shortly after the Inspector leaves, Birling moves "hesitatingly", which suggests that he is shaken and contrasts with his confidence earlier in the play. However, when Gerald reveals that the Inspector was a "hoax", Birling decides that the family's problems are "All over now". This shows that he wasn't upset because he and his family had acted in a way that was morally wrong, but because of the "scandal" that the information could have caused and the damage it would have done to his reputation. It also shows that the Inspector's visit hasn't made him reconsider his selfishness and lack of social conscience, which highlights that he is incapable of change.

2) For this question, you're asked to write about the author's ideas about friendship, so all your points need to be about that theme. You need to write about how Syal presents friendship, so make sure you mention the techniques that she uses. These points give you some ideas of the kind of things you could include:

- Syal portrays two types of friends in the novel: false friends, like Anita, and true friends, such as Robert. Meena's realisation that Anita isn't a true friend is a key part of her character development throughout the novel.
- Initially, Meena values and is heavily influenced by Anita's friendship. She feels "privileged" to be her friend, thinks of her as a "kindred spirit", and tries to emulate Anita's behaviour, using coarse language such as "shag the arse off it". Because she values Anita's friendship, she is a good friend to her: for example, she tries to stop Anita finding out about the relationship between Deirdre and Dave, because she knows that Anita would feel hurt if she found out.
- In contrast, it is clear to the reader that Anita doesn't value Meena's friendship. Meena explains that "Anita talked and I listened", and Anita abuses her trust by trying to steal her belongings. This suggests that, instead of trying to engage with Meena's life and form a meaningful relationship with her, Anita just wants to exploit Meena for her own personal gain. This emphasises the unhealthy, unbalanced nature of their friendship.
- Eventually, Meena comes to feel "pity" rather than "love" for Anita, and to understand that Anita has been using her, so she decides to "erase" her from her mind. This is an important turning point for Meena, as she starts to appreciate her own value and potential instead of trying to become someone she's not. Her realisation that her friendship with Anita wasn't healthy or fair is linked to the development of her identity and personality.
- Anita's other friendships in the novel are also very unequal. She tries to control Fat Sally and Sherrie; for example, at the fair, she tells them, "I'm having the tall one, roight?" These friendships turn out to be fragile and easily broken: for example, Anita's friendship with Sally ends because she's going to a different school to Anita. This emphasises Syal's message that a friendship built on unequal terms is not healthy and cannot last.
- Syal presents examples of healthy friendships in the novel in order to highlight the inequality of Anita's relationships. For example, the Kumar family have close friendships with other people who have left India for England. Their friends are presented as a valuable source of love and support: Uncle Amman helps Shyam to find a job, and the Kumars rush to hospital to support Uncle Amman after he has a heart attack. This contrasts directly with Anita, who doesn't visit Meena at all when she's in hospital.
- Meena's friendship with Robert is presented as another contrast to her friendship with Anita. The relationship between Meena and Robert is equal: they support each other while they are in hospital, and they both have to make the effort to communicate through the window between them. As a result, their friendship brings them both pleasure: Robert's parents thank Meena for making him "so happy", and after leaving the hospital, Meena says that she was "still smiling" on her arrival back in Tollington. Syal makes it clear that, when a relationship is equal, it can bring happiness to both people involved.

3) For this question, you're asked to write about the author's ideas about fear, so all your points need to be about that theme. You need to write about how Golding presents fear, so make sure you mention the techniques that he uses. These points give you some ideas of the kind of things you could include:

- There are many different types of fear in 'Lord of the Flies'. Over the course of the novel, the boys' fears shift from fear of remaining stranded on the island to fear of the unknown and finally to fear of each other. Fear is also crucial to Golding's message, which is that evil exists inside everyone; through the events of the novel he shows how evil can be brought to the surface by fear.

- The events of the novel take place against a backdrop of fear in the form of nuclear war. Piggy suggests in the first chapter that they will never be rescued because of "the atom bomb" which means their potential rescuers are "all dead". We are reminded again about this war at the end of the novel when the naval officer arrives and behind him "another rating held a sub-machine gun." This backdrop of fear serves to remind us that fear and evil are not confined to life on the island, but exist all over the world.

- Fear of the unknown is first shown by the littluns' nightmares. They "suffered untold terrors in the dark" and Jack and Ralph agree that building shelters is important so that the littluns feel they have some sort of 'home'. At this point in the novel, the boys are trying to fight their fear of the unknown by recreating something familiar — the comforts of civilised society. The boys' feeling that creating a society can fend off fear continues throughout the novel. For example, Ralph and Piggy are drawn to the "partly secure society" of Jack's tribe, because it "hemmed in the terror and made it governable."

- The fear of the unknown gradually shifts and becomes fear of the beast. The beast changes form during the novel — it starts off as a "snake-thing" and then the dead airman is mistaken for "something like a great ape". These changes in form indicate to the reader that the beast only exists in the boys' imaginations, although they become increasingly afraid of it: "Course I'm frightened. Who wouldn't be?" Jack uses the boys' fear of the beast to control them, such as when he taunts Ralph by saying "I'm going up the mountain to look for the beast – now... Coming?"

- To start with, the boys try to conquer their fear of the beast by leaving offerings for it, and then by trying to hunt it down. However, they end up becoming even more afraid, and as their fear intensifies, so does their tendency to behave savagely. In turn, this makes them more frightened, because it seems to them that the beast is getting stronger. In chapter nine, when Jack's tribe dance, Golding describes them as "a single organism," which reflects the fact that the boys themselves have become beast-like. This is confirmed when they kill Simon with "the tearing of teeth and claws", showing how the boys' fear has made them behave like wild animals.

- Only Ralph and Simon understand that the "beast" is the evil inside them, such as when the Lord of the Flies says to Simon, "You knew, didn't you? I'm part of you?" They realise that believing in the beast gives the boys a way of focusing their fear of the unknown and of each other. Ralph recognises the evil inside himself and is terrified of becoming savage, but he has little choice when he is hunted like an animal. This makes his terror when he is being hunted all the more harrowing for the reader, and Golding emphasises this by saying he "became fear," showing that he has been completely overwhelmed by fear and is no longer really human.

4) This question requires you to think about a central character and how they change throughout the play, so all your points need to be about that character. You're asked to write about how Mickey is presented, so make sure you write about the techniques Russell uses. These points give you some ideas of the kind of things you could include:

- As a child, Mickey is friendly, and he easily bonds with Edward: he suggests that they become "blood brothers" and promise to "always defend" each other only a short time after they first meet. As the play goes on, he starts to push away the people he loves: he denounces his bond with Edward as "kids' stuff" and refuses to listen to Linda's concerns about his medication, repeatedly telling her to "leave me alone". His desire to break these bonds reflects the fact that he feels isolated by his circumstances, and emphasises that he has been let down by society.

- Mickey loses his innocence and sense of hope for the future over the course of the play. As a child, he longs to be older because he can "go to bed dead late" and "play with matches", but later in the play he bitterly tells Eddie that he "grew up" because he had to, and he can't be a child any more, however much he might now "wish" he was. This shows that he has come to believe that adulthood doesn't bring freedom, but rather pain and loss.

- At the start of the play, Mickey is presented as a sensitive character. He is "visibly shaken" when the other children all gang up on him after he uses the "'F' word", and he relies on Linda to "protect" him from the other children. This sensitivity as a child develops into insecurity as Mickey grows older: as a teenager, he is worried about how other people see him. For example, he self-consciously complains about his "ears that stand out" and hair that is "the colour of gravy". His insecurity worsens when he is an adult: he tells Linda that he wants to be "invisible", which suggests that he no longer wants to be a part of society.

- As a child, Mickey is childishly excited by naughty behaviour: he admires Sammy when he "wees straight through the letter box". This contrasts with his attitude towards the robbery he participates in later in the play: Sammy has to persuade him to take part, and he eventually only agrees to do so because of his desperate need for the "fifty notes" that Sammy promises him. This shows that as an adult, Mickey has no appetite for crime or breaking rules; it is only desperation that forces him to take part in criminal activity.

- Mickey's changes in personality are caused by the lack of opportunities that his low social class affords him: he has a menial, insecure job from which he is fired, and this leads to his criminal behaviour, imprisonment, depression and eventual death. Even though he tries hard to find another job after he is fired — he says he's been "walking around all day, every day, lookin' for a job" — he is unable to. This emphasises that he has few options, linking him to the millions of unemployed working-class men in the UK in the 1980s and reinforcing Russell's message about the unfairness of the class divide.

5) For this question, you need to discuss the author's ideas about education and learning, then explain how these ideas are presented and how they are important to the novel. These points give you some ideas of the kind of things you could include:

- Education is related to power in the novel: for example, the pigs are "the cleverest of the animals", so they "naturally" take over the running of the farm. The ability to read, write and reason allows the pigs to persuade the other animals that the pigs are superior to them. The less-educated animals lack the intelligence to challenge the pigs' authority, leaving them powerless.

- The pigs' intelligence and education allows them to use language to repress the working classes. For example, Squealer uses rhetoric to convince the other animals that Napoleon is a great leader. Orwell says that Squealer "spoke so persuasively" that the other animals believed him without question, even though they were "not certain what the words meant". In Chapter 2, we are told that Squealer could use words to "turn black into white" and later he uses confusing, meaningless statistics to persuade the animals that life is getting better under Napoleon. This shows how Squealer uses his intelligence and knowledge to brainwash the other animals, in the same way that Stalin created a 'cult of personality' to convince people in Russia that he was a good leader.

- The way the Seven Commandments are changed to suit Napoleon's aims is another example of the pigs using language to control the less educated animals. The pigs have power because they can "read and write perfectly", and therefore change the commandments to suit their own purposes. For example, the sixth commandment is changed so that it reads, "No animal shall kill any other animal *without cause*" to defend Napoleon's "execution of traitors". This reflects the way Stalin used propaganda to control the people of Russia and relates to the Great Purge, the killing of people thought to be traitors to instil fear in others. Because the other animals have not learned to read, they don't immediately notice when the commandments are changed, and when they do notice, they can't prove it.

- Snowball attempts to teach the other animals to read, though his attempts are frustrated because the other animals lack the intelligence or motivation to learn – most of the animals on the farm are unable to "get further than the letter A." Snowball's attempt to teach the animals to read shows that he believes that educating the masses is the only way to make the revolution work, because then the commandment, "All animals are equal", would be fulfilled. In contrast, Napoleon chooses to concentrate his teaching on a select few, such as the puppies, who he trains to attack anyone who objects to him. He only teaches the puppies what they need to know to be useful to him, which contrasts with Snowball's attitude to education. Napoleon also teaches the sheep to loudly repeat the phrase "Four legs good, two legs bad" whenever they are agitated, which effectively "put an end to any chance of discussion." The little education that they receive makes them a powerful tool for Napoleon, showing how he educates selectively in order to continue the oppression. They use the words without understanding what they mean, which shows how the less-educated animals simply accept the terms of the revolution and their own repression.

- The lack of education in the "lower animals" means that they are unable to protest, because they cannot articulate why the pigs are acting unfairly. We are told that the animals "would have protested" about Napoleon cancelling Sunday meetings "if they could have found the right arguments." Even when the animals eventually become aware of their own repression, their lack of education means that they are powerless to challenge the pigs.

6) For this question, you need to discuss the author's ideas about education, and explain how these ideas are presented. These points give you some ideas of the kind of things you could include:

- The character of Hector represents the belief that education should be well-rounded and not constrained by examinations, which he describes as "the enemy of education". He also thinks that all learning is "precious" even if it doesn't have "the slightest human use", which reflects his belief that education and knowledge is valuable in its own right, rather than being merely a means to an end.

- Hector is presented as a likeable, if flawed, character. His actions in the first scene are described as an "elaborate pantomime", showing that he tried to entertain the boys and make learning enjoyable. After his death, Akthar says that there was a "contract" between Hector and his class, which also hints at their strong bond with him. Hector's likeability encourages the audience to sympathise with his views on education and learning.

- Hector's students are clearly influenced by his teaching style: when they are in lessons with Irwin, they behave as if they were in a lesson with Hector, quoting poetry and re-enacting a scene from "Brief Encounter". Later, the boys are seen to have been similarly influenced by Irwin: for example, Scripps describes truth as "relative". This shows how impressionable the boys are and emphasises the responsibility that a teacher has towards their students.

- The Headteacher's views on education contrast with Hector's. Like Hector, he thinks that wider education is important, but for different reasons: he tells Mrs Lintott that "something more" than good grades is required, but only in order for the boys to get places at a good university. His motivations are shallow: he is interested in how the boys' achievements will affect "league tables", which shows that he is primarily motivated by his desire to improve the reputation of the school. This makes his perspective on education seem short-sighted, in contrast to Hector, who is trying to prepare the boys for "Grief. Happiness." and even "dying": he wants their education to equip them for life outside of formal education.

- After Hector's death at the end of the play, the Headteacher speaks positively about Hector's teaching: he uses figurative language to describe the "bank of literature" in which Hector's pupils have become "shareholders". This suggests that the events of the play have caused him to re-evaluate his stance on Hector's value as a teacher. However, his choice of language indicates that he still doesn't understand Hector's perspective: the analogy he chooses is linked to money and profit, which shows that he still sees education as a tool that should be used to achieve wealth and success.

- Irwin's teaching style involves disregarding the truth in order to achieve an academic objective. He uses analogies to explain to the boys that an interesting opinion is more important than the facts: he says that truth in an exam is as unimportant as "thirst at a wine-tasting or fashion at a striptease". These activities are frivolous and unimportant, which highlights Irwin's dismissive attitude towards the truth. At some points during the play, there are hints that Bennett disagrees with Irwin's views. For example, when Dakin suggests that Nazi "death camps" have to be "seen in context", Irwin's view is that this is "inexpedient", as opposed to Hector's more humane, compassionate view that they were an "unprecedented horror". This gives the audience more perspective on Irwin's claims, making them lose sympathy for his views, and thereby strengthening their support for Hector's approach.

- Bennett uses Hector's death to suggest that Hector's ideas about education are dying out. This is emphasised by Irwin's comment at Hector's funeral: he says that there is no "time" for Hector's "kind of teaching" any more. However, Scripps contradicts Irwin, stating that Hector's teaching is "the only education worth having". These are the last words that any of the students say in the play, which highlights their importance to Bennett's central message, as well as providing some hope for the audience: if Hector's pupils believe in his ideas about education, perhaps they will not be forgotten entirely.

Pages 166-167 — English Literature — Paper 1: Section B (Poetry Anthology)

1) For this question, you have to think about the way that the poets use form, structure and language to describe nature, so make sure you choose a second poem that has plenty to write about on the subject. Comparing them means writing about the similarities and differences, so make some links between the poems in your answer. This answer compares 'The Prelude: Stealing the Boat' by William Wordsworth with 'Storm on the Island' by Seamus Heaney, but it gives you an idea of the kind of things you need to write whichever poems you're analysing. Here are some points you could make:

- 'The Prelude: Stealing the Boat' and 'Storm on the Island' both present nature as a powerful force, which can have a profound effect on humans. In Wordsworth's poem, the narrator experiences nature's "power" when he sees a "huge" mountain while rowing on a lake, which causes a "darkness" to hang over his thoughts for "many days" afterwards. Meanwhile, in Heaney's poem an island community experiences the violent power of nature in the form of a storm that "pummels" them. Both poems present nature as having power over humans — in Heaney's poem the impact of this power is physical, whereas in Wordsworth's poem it is psychological.

- Wordsworth and Heaney both use personification to present nature as a conscious force that can threaten humans. Wordsworth's narrator uses personification to describe how the mountain "Strode after" him with "measured motion". The word "measured" and the use of alliteration in this phrase suggest that the mountain is chasing the narrator, enabling the reader to share in his fear. Heaney also personifies nature, using language usually associated with war, such as "strafes" and "bombarded", to compare the actions of the wind to those of a fighter pilot. The use of such violent imagery emphasises the power of the storm, and suggests that the wind is deliberately attacking the island. This highlights how destructive the storm could be, which helps to clarify the islanders' fear.

- In both poems, the sense of threat created by nature is heightened by the use of contrasting imagery. In Wordsworth's poem, the "grim shape" of the mountain contrasts with beautiful images such as "sparkling light", which are used to describe nature in the first twenty lines. This contrast emphasises how varied and therefore unpredictable nature can be, which hints at the danger it can pose. Heaney also uses contrast to create a sense of nature's dangerous unpredictability. For example, the simile comparing the stormy sea to "a tame cat / Turned savage" juxtaposes a safe image with a violent one to show that the storm has the power to change rapidly from familiar to frightening. The enjambment across these lines places emphasis on "Turned", making this transformation seem even more sudden and shocking.

- Both poems have a distinct turning point, which heightens the presentation of nature as changeable and dramatic. In 'The Prelude: Stealing the Boat', the volta in line 21 represents the moment when the narrator first encounters the "huge peak", and at this point the mood of the poem shifts from confidence to fear. The "craggy ridge" in line 14 poses no threat to the narrator, who is able instead to focus on the equally harmless "stars and the grey sky". However, by line 24 nature has become much more threatening, with the

mountain described as having "Upreared its head" — this is an ugly image of nature that gives a clear impression of the narrator's fear. The suddenness of this shift from confidence to fear reflects the dramatic impact that nature can have, and its ability to change without warning. Similarly, in 'Storm on the Island', the volta in line 14 represents the sudden arrival of the storm. The language used after this, such as "We just sit tight", emphasises the islanders' lack of power and their passivity, which contrasts with the dramatic activity of nature. The poem's tone is subsequently transformed by the storm's arrival — the confident opening statement, "We are prepared", now sounds empty, as the island community is powerless in the face of the storm. As in Wordsworth's poem, this change of tone reflects how changeable nature can be, and emphasises how unsettling this changeability can be for humans.

- Both poems emphasise the physical presence of nature. In 'The Prelude: Stealing the Boat', Wordsworth repeats the word "huge" in the phrase "a huge peak, black and huge" to emphasise the mountain's size, suggesting that its physical appearance seems overwhelming to the narrator. The consonance of the harsh 'k' sound in "peak" and "black" further emphasises the stark power of nature, hinting at the threat the narrator feels from it. In contrast, in 'Storm on the Island', Heaney focuses on the invisibility of the winds that seem to attack the island — "We are bombarded by the empty air". This paradox of the storm's violent but invisible physical power highlights that it is impossible for the islanders to fight back against the "huge nothing" that assaults them. This presents nature as an unstoppable physical force.

2) For this question, you have to think about the way that the poets use form, structure and language to present ideas about freedom and constraint, so make sure you choose a second poem that has plenty to write about on the subject. Comparing them means writing about the similarities and differences, so make some links between the poems in your answer. This answer compares 'London' by William Blake with 'Hawk Roosting' by Ted Hughes, but it gives you an idea of the kind of things you need to write whichever poems you're analysing. Here are some points you could make:

- 'London' and 'Hawk Roosting' offer two very different perspectives on freedom and constraint. Blake depicts the city of London as constricting, and the people who live in it seem to be trapped in their lives of misery. In 'Hawk Roosting', on the other hand, Hughes emphasises the freedom of the hawk due to its immense power and ability to hunt.

- Both poets use a first-person narrative to create a sense of the narrators' freedom. 'London' is a first-person dramatic monologue, which allows an insight into the narrator's thoughts and feelings as he walks around the city. The poem shifts through images of other people, which creates the sense that the narrator is the only person free to move around a city full of people who are trapped by their circumstances. Although the narrator also seems constrained by London's "chartered" streets, his relative freedom emphasises the constraint that has been forced upon the other people he sees. 'Hawk Roosting' also uses a first-person narrative, which enables Hughes to personify the hawk. Phrases such as "it is all mine" emphasise the power that the hawk feels over nature, which helps the reader to understand the freedom it has to fly and hunt.

- The form and structure of both poems allows the poets to emphasise a sense of freedom or constraint. Most of the lines of 'Hawk Roosting' are unrhymed, reinforcing the idea that the hawk is free to exist without constraint. However, the rest of the form is more rigid — there are six stanzas of equal length, and most of the lines are end-stopped. This could reflect the constraint that the hawk tries to force on its environment, linking it to human tyrants who want to "keep things like this". Alternatively, the rigid form could hint that the hawk is not as free as it believes, as it is trapped by its own nature. 'London' also has regular four-line stanzas, but unlike 'Hawk Roosting' it has a fixed ABAB rhyme scheme. These two elements combine to make the poem seem restrictive and inflexible, which contributes to the overall sense of constraint.

- Both poets use imagery to emphasise the sense of freedom, or lack of freedom, in the poems. In 'Hawk Roosting', imagery is used to emphasise the vastness of the hawk's environment: Hughes refers to "the earth's face", the "high trees" and "the sun's ray"; these images emphasise the huge area that the hawk can see. In contrast, the imagery in 'London' helps to emphasise the sense of constraint in the poem. For example, the image of the "mind-forged manacles" likens the Londoners to prisoners and makes their suffering seem permanent. This reinforces how trapped the residents of London are.

- Repetition is used in 'London' to make the reader feel that the city's residents can't escape the constraints of their environment. In the second stanza, the phrase "In every" is repeated at the beginning of the first three lines. This creates a sense of inevitability: regardless of the people's actions, they will continue to be trapped in poverty. In 'Hawk Roosting', on the other hand, repetition is used to emphasise the hawk's power and freedom. In the poem's third stanza, the word "Creation" is repeated twice. This links the hawk's power to that of a god, which emphasises its freedom to act as it wishes.

3) For this question, you have to think about the way that the poets use form, structure and language to present the breakdown of a relationship, so make sure you choose a second poem that has plenty to write about on the subject. Comparing them means writing about the similarities and differences, so make some links between the poems in your answer. This answer compares 'Neutral Tones' by Thomas Hardy with 'When We Two Parted' by Lord Byron, but it gives you an idea of the kind of things you need to write whichever poems you're analysing. Here are some points you could make:

- The two poems have a similar subject matter — the end of a romantic relationship — and they use similar narrative voices to present this. Both poems are written in the first person, which gives the reader an insight into the thoughts and feelings of the narrators. Both narrators also use second-person pronouns, such as "thee" and "your", throughout the poems, which indicates that they are addressed directly to their former lovers and emphasises the fixation that both narrators have on the women they address.

- However, the two narrators express different emotions towards the breakdown of their relationships. In 'Neutral Tones', there is a time jump at the end of the third stanza, which is introduced by an ellipsis. This creates a sense of distance between the events of the past and the narrator's present-day life: although he is still haunted by the loss of his lover, he seems calm about it. The emotions that the narrator expresses in 'When We Two Parted', on the other hand, seem stronger and less controlled. For example, in line 20 he uses a rhetorical question, asking "Why wert thou so dear?" This emphasises his sense of desperation and shows how upset he is at the loss of his lover.

- Both poems have a cyclical structure that reinforces the narrator's sense of regret and loss. The final line of 'When We Two Parted' refers back to the poem's opening stanza by repeating the phrase "silence and tears". This emphasises that the breakdown of the relationship has been a traumatic experience for the narrator, as well as suggesting that he is unable to move on from it. In 'Neutral Tones', the final two lines of the poem repeat the images of the "sun", "tree" and "pond" that are introduced in the first stanza. This reflects

the narrator's inability to forget the pain that his former lover inflicted on him. The return of the 'A' rhyme in the ABBA rhyme scheme reinforces this sentiment, reflecting the way that the narrator's memory of the break-up returns to affect him.

- Both poems use references to death to create a sense of hopelessness. In 'Neutral Tones', Hardy uses washed-out colours, such as "white" and "grey", to make the scene seem lifeless, and he describes the lover's smile as "the deadest thing". This creates a sense of finality that reflects the death of their relationship. In 'When We Two Parted', on the other hand, Byron describes his lover as "Pale" and says that he "grieve[s]" for her, which makes it sound as if she has died. As in 'Neutral Tones', there is a sense that their relationship has been irrevocably destroyed, and there is no returning to the love they used to share. The word "grieve" also emphasises the strength of Byron's emotions: he is as upset as if his lover really had died.

4) For this question, you have to think about the way that the poets use form, structure and language to present ideas about power, so make sure you choose a second poem that has plenty to write about on the subject. Comparing them means writing about the similarities and differences, so make some links between the poems in your answer. This answer compares 'My Last Duchess' by Robert Browning with 'La Belle Dame Sans Merci' by John Keats, but it gives you an idea of the kind of things you need to write whichever poems you're analysing. Here are some points you could make:

- 'My Last Duchess' is a dramatic monologue. In phrases such as "not the first / Are you to turn and ask thus", the poem implies that the person the monologue is addressed to has spoken, but their words are not reported in the poem. The reader is not allowed to hear from anybody other than the narrator, which means that he dominates the poem; this shows the power that he is capable of asserting over others. In contrast, 'La Belle Dame Sans Merci' is in the form of a dialogue between two strangers. The knight requires prompts and questions from the stranger to be able to narrate his tale — he displays none of the power and authority that one would expect from a knight, and appears considerably less powerful than the Duke in 'My Last Duchess'. This hints that human power is a temporary attribute, which can be lost.

- The presentation of power in the poems is reflected by the poets' choice of metre and rhyme scheme. 'My Last Duchess' is tightly structured using rhyming couplets and iambic pentameter. This mirrors the tight control that the Duke exercises over others: he dictates exactly what his companion should look at in the gallery, and it is strongly suggested that the Duke's attempt to control his late wife resulted in her death: "I gave commands; / Then all smiles stopped together." 'La Belle Dame Sans Merci' also has a regular structure: it is divided into four-line stanzas, and it has a regular rhyme scheme and metre, which creates a sense of relentlessness that highlights the knight's ongoing distress. However, the last line in each stanza is shorter than the first three. This slows the pace of the poem and breaks up the rhythm, which hints at the knight's disordered state of mind and the woman's continuing power over him.

- Power is linked to beauty in both poems. In 'My Last Duchess', the Duchess's physical beauty gave her power over men — for example, one admirer gave her a "bough of cherries". It is clear that the Duke was jealous of her "approving speech" and "blush", showing that despite his domineering nature, the Duchess had some power over him because she was able to affect his emotions. Similarly, the knight in 'La Belle Dame Sans Merci' is so enthralled by the woman's looks that he sees "nothing else" and is prepared to follow her anywhere; this emphasises the power she has over him.

- Both poems explore ideas about where the characters' power comes from. In 'My Last Duchess', despite hints of the Duchess's power over the Duke, it is ultimately the Duke who is the most powerful. He declares that his name is "nine-hundred-years-old", showing that he is at the top of a class system and therefore holds power over those beneath him. This presents power as being derived from a person's wealth and status, and shows that it can be passed down through history. Like the Duke, the woman in 'La Belle Dame Sans Merci' possesses great power. She renders the "knight-at-arms", a traditionally powerful figure, powerless, and there are suggestions that she has a similar power over "warriors" and "kings, and princes" — other figures that are typically seen as powerful. This may suggest that she holds a power that is greater than earthly power.

5) For this question, you have to think about the way that the poets use form, structure and language to present attitudes to conflict, so make sure you choose a second poem that has plenty to write about on the subject. Comparing them means writing about the similarities and differences, so make some links between the poems in your answer. This answer compares 'The Charge of the Light Brigade' by Alfred Tennyson with 'Bayonet Charge' by Ted Hughes, but it gives you an idea of the kind of things you need to write whichever poems you're analysing. Here are some points you could make:

- 'The Charge of the Light Brigade' and 'Bayonet Charge' are both written about a battle, and the experiences of a soldier or soldiers who fought in it. Alfred Tennyson wrote 'The Charge of the Light Brigade' about the unnecessary deaths of the Light Brigade in the Crimean War, whilst Ted Hughes wrote 'Bayonet Charge' about the experiences of a nameless soldier in a battle in World War I.

- Both poets use the rhythm and structure of their poems to reflect the attitude to war of the soldiers who fight in it. 'The Charge of the Light Brigade' has a regular rhythm, which mirrors the steady advance of the cavalry and highlights their willingness to do their duty, even when they know it may well lead to their deaths. However, the irregular rhyme scheme disrupts this order, possibly hinting at the doubts and fears of the soldiers and suggesting that their attitude isn't as straightforward as it first appears. Similarly, 'Bayonet Charge' has no rhyme scheme, and it also has no regular metre, which creates a sense of chaos. Hughes stresses this feeling by emphasising the fear and confusion of an individual soldier, through which he displays the attitude that war is tumultuous and cannot be viewed in an ordered, objective way by those who are directly involved.

- 'Bayonet Charge' is a more personal narrative than 'The Charge of the Light Brigade'. In 'The Charge of the Light Brigade', the poet focuses on the fate of a whole brigade of men, who he only refers to as "the six hundred". In the first 36 lines of the poem, they act as a unit, who are not supposed to "make reply" or "reason why", only to act as commanded. This helps Tennyson to emphasise the idea that war can be tragic, as some of the soldiers do not return: they are "Not the six hundred" any more. In contrast, 'Bayonet Charge' focuses on the experience of a single soldier, which allows Hughes to convey the feelings that war can incite in those who fight, such as "alarm" and terror; this presents war as a strongly personal and emotional experience. It also emphasises the loneliness of war, and the way that individual soldiers can feel isolated despite the many other soldiers around them.

- Both poets refer to weapons to highlight the attitude that conflict can be unfair. Tennyson contrasts the Light Brigade's "sabres" with the "Cannon" and "battery-smoke" of the enemy around them. This hints that the narrator believes the Light Brigade should have been better equipped. Similarly, in 'Bayonet Charge' the narrator compares the soldier's rifle to a "smashed arm". This simile suggests that it is useless against the enemy's "rifle fire", suggesting that an individual soldier is powerless and largely defenceless. This emphasises the injustice of the "cold clockwork" that sends men to war.

- The narrator's voice in 'The Charge of the Light Brigade' is full of admiration for the men's bravery and sacrifice, but it is also tinged with regret for the loss of life, and both emotions can be seen in his emphatic use of exclamation marks, for example "O the wild charge they made!" This creates a tone of heightened emotion that emphasises the narrator's overall attitude that these men should be admired for their bravery in the face of almost certain death. Hughes more explicitly criticises the loss of life in war: he describes the soldier as still "Listening" for "the reason" that he is at war, but his doubt receives no answer or resolution, which implies that the soldiers' lives are being wasted unnecessarily.

- The poets present different attitudes regarding heroism and nobility in war. Tennyson uses phrases that have a very solemn tone, such as the repeated references to the "valley of Death", which is taken from the Bible. These phrases make the soldiers' actions seem meaningful and important, which emphasises the soldiers' heroism and presents war as momentous. In contrast, Hughes suggests that the concepts of nobility and heroism are useless in the face of the realities of war: he explains that "King" and "honour" are "Dropped like luxuries" in the heat of battle. This indicates his criticism of the reasons that soldiers are given to justify their going to war.

6) a) For this question, you have to think about the way that the poet uses form, structure and language to present ideas about love. This answer is about 'Sonnet 43' by Elizabeth Barrett Browning, but it gives you an idea of the kind of things you need to write whichever poem you're analysing. Here are some points you could make:

- 'Sonnet 43' takes the form of a Petrarchan sonnet: it has fourteen lines that consist of an octave followed by a sestet. Sonnets were traditionally used when writing love poetry. This links the narrator's love to an established literary tradition, which emphasises how important she perceives her love for the subject of the poem to be.

- The poem has a regular, unbroken rhyme scheme, which gives it a constant, unfaltering rhythm that reinforces the steadfastness of the narrator's feelings. This is emphasised by the poet's use of repetition: the phrase "I love thee" is repeated at the beginning of several lines throughout the poem; the phrase becomes a simple refrain that sticks in the reader's mind and emphasises the strength and constancy of the narrator's feelings.

- The poem links love to religion, as the narrator says that her love for the subject of the poem has replaced her "lost Saints". This highlights the impact that love can have on a person's life: for the narrator, it is so strong that it is equivalent in importance to religion. Nineteenth-century society was very religious, so this would have been a very strong sentiment when the poem was written.

- The narrator emphasises that love has taken over almost all aspects of her life: she uses a list to explain that she loves the person in the poem with "the breath, / Smiles, tears, of all my life!" This list makes it seem as though her love for the subject of the poem is all-encompassing. This is strengthened by the exclamation mark at the end of the phrase, which indicates the intensity of her emotions.

b) This question asks you to compare how love is presented in two poems, so make sure you choose a second poem that has plenty to write about on the subject. Comparing them means writing about the similarities and differences, so make some links between the poems in your answer. This answer compares 'Sonnet 43' by Elizabeth Barrett Browning with 'The Manhunt' by Simon Armitage, but it gives you an idea of the kind of things you need to write whichever poems you're analysing. Here are some points you could make:

- 'The Manhunt' offers a different perspective on love from 'Sonnet 43': the poem describes the damaging effects that war and injury have had on a couple's relationship, which contrasts with the purely positive portrayal of the narrator's love in 'Sonnet 43'.

- The poets both use structure to emphasise the narrators' feelings of devotion towards their lovers, although they approach this in different ways. 'The Manhunt' is structured in couplets, some of which rhyme, and some of which do not. The regularity of the two-line stanzas reflects the dedication with which the narrator attempted to reach her husband, while the irregularity of the rhyme scheme mirrors how difficult this was. This contrasts with the regular rhyme scheme and sonnet form of 'Sonnet 43', which hint that the narrator has an idealised view of love — the poem does not share the realism of 'The Manhunt'.

- The different ways in which the narrators express their love for another person reveal something of the nature of the corresponding relationships. In 'The Manhunt', the couple's relationship is illustrated through physicality and action: this is suggested by the poet's use of verbs such as "handle and hold", which emphasise the physical, tangible nature of their relationship. In contrast, the love of the narrator in 'Sonnet 43' is less physical and more idealistic; phrases such as "I love thee freely" focus on the perfection of the narrator's love, rather than illustrating how it applies in everyday circumstances. This makes her love seem romantic and less rooted in the realities of life than the portrayal of love in 'The Manhunt'.

- Both narrators use comparative language to emphasise their feelings. In 'The Manhunt', the narrator uses metaphors to compare parts of her husband's body to delicate objects such as "porcelain" and "parachute silk", which emphasises his fragility and the delicacy with which she cares for him. In 'Sonnet 43', on the other hand, Barrett Browning uses comparative language to describe her love, rather than to describe her loved one. She compares her love to a variety of abstract concepts to establish its quality: for example, she says she loves as "purely" as men "turn from Praise". This implies that her love is 'pure' because it does not require praise or reward.

7) a) For this question, you have to think about the way that the poet uses form, structure and language to present feelings for another person. Here are some points you could make:

- In the first half of the poem, Byron's description of the woman is dominated by her looks: he describes her "eyes" and "raven" hair. It is only after line 10 that he mentions elements of her personality. This suggests that her physical appearance is the strongest attraction for the narrator, and that it has defined his feelings towards her.

- Each stanza is composed of a single sentence, which is broken up over several lines that are often enjambed. This highlights the strength of the narrator's adoration by making his love seem overwhelming and excessive. The sentence in the final stanza then ends with an exclamation mark rather than a full stop: the poem builds towards a final, dramatic expression of emotion. This reflects the excitement that the narrator experiences as he thinks and writes about the woman.

- The narrator focuses on individual parts of the woman's body, such as her "eyes" and "cheek". This creates the impression that he is picturing her in great detail as he writes, which emphasises the obsessive nature of his feelings towards her.

- The subject of the poem is never named: she is only ever referred to as "she". This creates a sense of mystery surrounding the woman, giving her an almost mystical quality that elevates her above other women and reinforces Byron's idealised view of her looks and personality.

b) This question asks you to compare how feelings for another person are presented in two poems, so make sure you choose a second poem that has plenty to write about on the subject. Comparing them means writing about the similarities and differences, so make some links between the poems in your answer. This answer compares 'She Walks in Beauty' by Lord Byron with 'Valentine' by Carol Ann Duffy, but it gives you an idea of the kind of things you need to write whichever poems you're analysing. Here are some points you could make:

- Both poems use form to help convey the narrator's feelings for another person. For instance, 'She Walks in Beauty' has a very regular rhythm and form: it has three equal, six-line stanzas, an alternating ABAB rhyme scheme and is written in regular iambic tetrameter. This precise form reflects the perfect beauty and character that the narrator feels the woman in the poem possesses. In contrast, 'Valentine' doesn't conform to a formal structure or regular rhythm. This emphasises the narrator's desire to present her feelings for her lover in an uncontrived, "truthful" way.

- Both narrators use strong adjectives to portray their powerful feelings for the subjects of the poems. In 'Valentine', Duffy uses "fierce" and "Lethal" to convey the idea that the narrator's love is potent and forceful. Similarly, in 'She Walks in Beauty' the narrator's feelings are emphasised by the repetition of the word "So" in line 14, which places stress on the adjectives "soft" and "calm" used to describe the woman, and highlights his feelings of awe and adoration.

- The narrator of 'She Walks in Beauty' presents an idealised picture of the woman he loves, using hyperbole to describe her "pure" mind and "innocent" heart. This makes his love for her seem unrealistic, because he does not see any flaws in her personality. In contrast, in 'Valentine' Duffy presents a more realistic idea of the narrator's love for another person: she mentions the "tears" and "grief" that love can cause, which shows that she is not shying away from the more negative feelings that love can bring.

- Both poets use analogy to describe their feelings towards the people they love. Duffy compares her love to an "onion", which she contrasts with the traditional trappings of Valentine's Day: "a red rose" and "a satin heart". This emphasises how different the narrator's love is compared to traditional romantic stereotypes. She then compares the onion to "a moon", which suggests that whilst her love is unconventional, it is still beautiful. In contrast, the narrator in 'She Walks in Beauty' compares the woman he loves to "cloudless climes and starry skies". This natural imagery emphasises the woman's beauty. Byron's analogy is more conventional; it emphasises the strength of the narrator's feelings by linking his feelings to a tradition of love poetry.

8) For this question, you have to think about the way that the poets use form, structure and language to present ideas about the reality of war, so make sure you choose poems that have plenty to write about on the subject. Comparing them means writing about the similarities and differences, so make some links between the poems in your answer. This answer is for 'Exposure' by Wilfred Owen and 'Remains' by Simon Armitage, but it gives you an idea of the kind of things you need to write whichever poems you're analysing. Here are some points you could make:

- In 'Exposure', Owen uses a regular rhyme scheme (ABBAC), which reflects the monotonous nature of the men's experience of war, but the rhymes are often half-rhymes (for example "snow" and "renew"). The rhyme scheme offers no comfort or satisfaction — the jagged rhymes reflect the confusion and fading energy of the soldiers. In contrast, 'Remains' has no regular rhyme scheme; this contributes to the conversational tone of the poem, which highlights the involvement of ordinary individuals in war and helps the reader to relate to the narrator of the poem.

- Both poets use the experience of soldiers in war to convey a message about the violent, but often monotonous, reality of conflict. This is partly conveyed in both poems through the use of structure. 'Remains' has a repetitive structure: the events recounted in the first half of the poem are repeatedly mentioned in the second half. This highlights the traumatic impact of war on those who fight in it, as it shows that the narrator has flashbacks to the death of the looter even when he is "on leave". In 'Exposure', on the other hand, a repetitive structure is used to emphasise the static, hopeless nature of war. All of the stanzas end with half-lines, and in four of them the phrase "But nothing happens" is used. This simple half-line highlights the lack of change or hope for the men in the trenches, and makes clear that for them the war seems endless and inescapable.

- Both poets use alliterative techniques to emphasise the danger that soldiers are exposed to as part of war. In line 4 of 'Exposure', sibilance is used to mimic the sound of the sentries' "whisper", which creates a sense of ominous quiet that helps the reader to understand the tense atmosphere. Then, in the fourth stanza, alliteration is used to create a sense of chaos and danger in the phrases "sudden successive flights of bullets" and "flowing flakes that flock". This emphasises the danger that the soldiers face, not just from "bullets" but from the "deathly" winter weather. In 'Remains', Armitage also uses sibilance to create a sense of the difficult conditions the soldiers must live in. The phrase "sun-stunned, sand-smothered land" emphasises how hot and dusty the desert is, and places emphasis on the violent verbs "stunned" and "smothered", which indicate the violent nature of the conflict.

- Both poets explore the reality of war in relation to the soldiers' lives at home. In 'Exposure', Owen uses personification to describe the "kind fires" of home and the "smile" of the sun, which makes the soldiers' home seem pleasant and appealing. This contrasts with the poor conditions, such as the "merciless" winds, that the soldiers experience whilst at war, and helps to emphasise the harsh realities of conflict. In 'Remains', on the other hand, the writer focuses on how the trauma of war disrupts the narrator's home life. All the narrator has to do is "blink" for the memories to return to haunt him; this emphasises the long-term psychological impact that the realities of war can cause.

9) For this question, you have to think about the way that the poets use form, structure and language to present ideas about childhood, so make sure you choose poems that have plenty to write about on the subject. Comparing them means writing about the similarities and differences, so make some links between the poems in your answer. This answer is for 'Follower' by Seamus Heaney and 'Before You Were Mine' by Carol Ann Duffy, but it gives you an idea of the kind of things you need to write whichever poems you're analysing. Here are some points you could make:

- In both poems, the narrators write about their impressions of a parent. The narrator in 'Follower' recalls his childhood memories of his father and reflects on how their relationship has changed over time, whereas in 'Before You Were Mine' the narrator uses memories from her childhood to inform her description of her mother's life before she was born.

- Both poems have a regular form; these careful frameworks emphasise how precious the narrators' memories are to them. 'Follower' has six four-line stanzas, and 'Before You Were Mine' consists of four five-line stanzas; in both poems, this creates an unhurried, steady rhythm that reflects the narrators' considered presentation of their memories. This highlights the importance of these childhood memories and implies that both narrators consider the day-to-day activities of their childhoods to have been significant and formative, even if they were just ordinary events at the time.

- Both poets use imagery to describe the parent in the poem, and to hint that the narrator idolised them as a child. In 'Follower', Heaney uses nautical imagery to emphasise the power and strength of the father, comparing his shoulders to a "full sail strung". In contrast, the narrator in 'Before You Were Mine' describes her mother as "Marilyn", in reference to Marilyn Monroe. By using the metaphor of a Hollywood film star to describe her mother, the narrator highlights the way that children idolise their parents, and illustrates how central a role parents play in their children's lives.

- Both poems use lists of verbs to create vivid descriptions. In 'Before You Were Mine', the phrase "sparkle and waltz and laugh" makes the mother seem playful and fun, which further emphasises how the narrator idolises her. In contrast, the narrator in 'Follower' describes himself as "tripping, falling, / Yapping". This highlights the active, clumsy nature of his childhood self, and contrasts with verbs such as "Mapping" and "angled" that are used to describe the measured, skilful actions of the narrator's father. These positive descriptions of their parents used by both narrators present the parents as figures that the narrators aspire to be like.

- Both poems explore this idea of children taking on characteristics of their parents as they grow older. In 'Follower', this happens in the final two lines of the poem, which indicates its significance. The father, in whose "wake" the son once followed, is now "stumbling / Behind" the narrator, whilst the narrator is now the one who leads. This reflects the way that the roles between the narrator and his father have been reversed since his childhood. The narrator in 'Before You Were Mine' also takes on the role of a parent, asking "whose small bites on your neck, sweetheart?" The word "sweetheart" makes it sound as if the narrator is affectionately mimicking the voice of a parent. In this way, Duffy presents childhood as having an inevitable endpoint, after which the child begins to acquire the traits of their parent. It also creates a sense of nostalgia, hinting that the narrator's childhood was a happy time that she is keen to relive.

As adults, both narrators seem to feel a sense of guilt at holding their parent back. In 'Follower', the narrator describes himself as a "nuisance" to his father, whilst in 'Before You Were Mine' the narrator describes her "possessive yell" and suggests that the time before her birth was "the best one" for her mother. However, both narrators seem to be unaware of the negative effect they have on their parents until they are older; this suggests that childhood is a time of innocence and unquestioning acceptance of a parent's love and attention.

Pages 168-169 — English Literature — Paper 1: Section C (Unseen Poetry)

1) For this question, you have to think about what the poet is saying about the speaker's attitude to parenthood and how she presents this attitude. Make sure you comment on how form, structure and language are used to present feelings and ideas in the poem. Here are some points you could make:
- 'For a Five-Year-Old' is about the relationship between a mother and a child, and the responsibility that the mother feels for her child's upbringing. This responsibility is emphasised using the form of the poem: it is mostly written in iambic pentameter, which creates a steady rhythm that reflects the narrator's dedication and commitment to her child.
- The poem's narrator addresses the narrative directly to the child, repeating the pronouns "you" and "your" throughout. This reflects the narrator's constant awareness of how her actions affect her child's development, and emphasises the idea that parenthood affects every aspect of a parent's life.
- The poem is structured using two distinct stanzas. In the first stanza, the narrator describes a specific interaction with the child, and then in the second stanza she describes some of the unkind things she has done at other times in her life. The child's "careful hand" in the first stanza contrasts with violent verbs such as "trapped", "shot", "drowned" and "betrayed" in the second stanza. This makes it clear that the narrator behaves differently around the child in order to set a good example, and emphasises her belief that it is important to teach children the correct lessons in life, regardless of one's personal experience.
- The end of the poem is structured to reflect the responsibility that the narrator feels. The caesura in line 15 separates the events of the past from the present and emphasises that, despite the unkind things the narrator has done in the past, she understands that she needs to set a good example for her child. The poem ends with the statement that "we are kind to snails"; the simplicity of this assertion suggests that the narrator believes it is important to simplify the complexities of adult life for children.
- The poem has an unusual rhyme scheme: although it is mostly composed of rhyming couplets, the first and last lines of each stanza rhyme. This creates a sense of completeness, and mirrors the mother's belief that a parent should shield their child from the harsh realities of adult life. The return to the snail motif in the final line also creates a cyclical structure that highlights the narrator's dedication to teaching the child kindness.
- The snail could be seen to symbolise the child; the care and delicacy with which the narrator teaches her child to handle the snail reflects her belief that the responsibilities of parenthood must be carried out with similar care and delicacy. In the first stanza, the snail is presented as fragile using the alliterative phrase "carry it outside, with careful hand". This makes the word "careful" stand out to the reader, which shows the care and attention that the child pays to the snail, and hints at the snail's fragility. In the second stanza, the narrator refers to the child's "gentleness" and her own ability to 'mould' the child. This suggests that, like the snail, the child is fragile, and highlights the responsibility that the narrator feels to make sure that the child is treated with the same kindness and care that they show to the snail.

2) For this question, you have to think about what the poet is saying and how she says it. Make sure you comment on how form, structure and language are used to present feelings and ideas in the poem, and how the poem makes you feel. Here are some points you could make:
- 'For a Five-Year-Old' is about the relationship between a mother and a child, and the responsibility that the mother feels for her child's upbringing. This responsibility is emphasised using the form of the poem: it is mostly written in iambic pentameter, which creates a steady rhythm that reflects the narrator's dedication and commitment to her child.
- The poem's narrator addresses the narrative directly to the child, repeating the pronouns "you" and "your" throughout. This emphasises to the reader how central the child is to the narrator's life, emphasising the idea that parenthood affects every aspect of a parent's life.
- The poem is structured using two contrasting stanzas. The child's "careful hand" in the first stanza contrasts with violent verbs such as "trapped", "shot", "drowned" and "betrayed" in the second stanza. This makes the narrator's former actions more shocking for the reader, and creates a strong contrast between the innocence of childhood and the reality of adulthood.
- The poem has an unusual rhyme scheme: although it is mostly composed of rhyming couplets, the first and last lines of each stanza rhyme. This creates a sense of completeness, and mirrors the mother's belief that a parent should shield their child from the harsh realities of adult life.
- The snail could be seen to symbolise the child; the care and delicacy with which the narrator teaches her child to handle the snail reflects her belief that the responsibilities of parenthood must be carried out with similar care and delicacy. In the first stanza, the snail is presented as fragile using the alliterative phrase "carry it outside, with careful hand". This makes the word "careful" stand out to the reader, which shows the care and attention that the child pays to the snail, and hints at the snail's fragility. In the second stanza, the narrator refers to the child's "gentleness" and her own ability to 'mould' the child. This creates the impression that, like the snail, the child is fragile, and highlights the responsibility that the narrator feels to make sure that the child is treated with the same kindness and care that they show to the snail.

3) For this question, you have to think about how the relationship between an adult and a child is presented in the two poems. Make sure you comment on how form, structure and language are used to present feelings and ideas in the poems. You're comparing the two poems, so you need to think about similarities and differences between them. Here are some points you could make:
- Adcock and Pugh both write about the process of a child learning about the world around them. Both poems are written in the first person, which allows the reader an insight into the narrators' thoughts and feelings and makes their descriptions of their relationship and experience feel more personal.
- Both poems contain characters who feel responsible for a child's moral education. In 'For a Five-Year-Old', the narrator understands that her child's "gentleness" is "moulded" by her own words; the verb "moulded" emphasises the patience and care that goes into such teaching. In 'The Beautiful Lie', the child's grandmother asks the boy, "Did you do that?", in order to teach him that his actions are wrong. The plosive 'd' and 't' sounds in this phrase make the grandmother sound harsh and angry. This increases the reader's pleasure in the unexpected side-effect of her words: they "showed him" he had the "choice" of lying.

- Although both poems are about the joy of watching a child learn, the poets present different messages about what it is important for a child to learn. Adcock focuses on the innocence of the child, and the mother's pleasure in preserving this innocence. In contrast, Pugh's narrator takes pleasure in observing a small loss of innocence, as the child learns how to lie.
- The poets reinforce their messages using their rhyme schemes. The middle six lines of each stanza of 'For a Five-Year-Old' use rhyming couplets; this careful use of form highlights the care and attention with which the narrator tries to preserve the child's "gentleness". In contrast, 'The Beautiful Lie' has no rhyme scheme and an irregular rhythm. This reflects the freedom that the narrator believes the boy gains by learning how to "*tell a story*": the realisation that he is able to lie opens up a world of imagination. The poem presents this as a "moving" and "momentous" occasion for the narrator, showing how an adult can experience the world afresh through a child, and hinting at how, for an adult, the achievements of a child they love can be more important than their own accomplishments.
- Both poets create a gentle rhythm that reflects the relationship between an adult and a child. In 'The Beautiful Lie', Pugh uses enjambment and caesurae to create a slow rhythm and sense of calm, which reflects the narrator's gentle love for the boy. In 'For a Five-Year-Old', Adcock uses iambic pentameter to create a gentle, regular rhythm that sounds conversational. This highlights the love and attention that the narrator gives to the child, and the care that she must exercise in teaching the child to be "kind".
- Both poems emphasise the sense of wonder that the narrator has towards the child. In 'The Beautiful Lie', the narrator is fascinated by the signs that the boy is growing up and learning. This is shown through the use of natural imagery such as the "northern lights" and "the unreal sea", which suggests that the child is expanding into new and undiscovered territory and evokes ideas of adventure and exploration. Similarly, in 'For a Five-Year-Old', the narrator seems awed by the gentle personality of her child, despite her own past: this is shown by the repetition of the phrase "from me" in lines 11 and 12. This repetition emphasises how surprised the narrator is that, despite her actions in the past, she has taught her child "gentleness" and "faith".

4) For this question, you have to compare the way that both poets use form, structure and language to convey their viewpoint to the reader. Comparing them means writing about the similarities and differences, so make some links between the poems in your answer. Here are some points you could make:
- Adcock and Pugh both write about the process of a child learning about the world around them. Both poems are written in the first person, which allows the reader an insight into the narrators' thoughts and feelings and makes their descriptions of their relationship and experience feel more personal.
- Although both poems are about the joy of watching a child learn, the poets present different messages about what it is important for a child to learn. Adcock focuses on the innocence of the child, and the mother's pleasure in preserving this innocence. In contrast, Pugh's narrator takes pleasure in observing a small loss of innocence, as the child learns how to lie.
- The poets reinforce their messages using their rhyme schemes. The middle six lines of each stanza of 'For a Five-Year-Old' use rhyming couplets; this careful use of form highlights the care and attention with which the narrator tries to preserve the child's "gentleness". In contrast, 'The Beautiful Lie' has no rhyme scheme and an irregular rhythm. This reflects the freedom that the narrator believes the boy gains by learning how to "*tell a story*": the realisation that he is able to lie opens up a world of imagination. The poem presents this as a "moving" and "momentous" occasion for the narrator, showing how an adult can experience the world afresh through a child, and hinting at how, for an adult, the achievements of a child they love can be more important than their own accomplishments.

- Both poets create a gentle rhythm that reflects the relationship between an adult and a child. In 'The Beautiful Lie', Pugh uses enjambment and caesurae to create a slow rhythm and sense of calm, which reflects the narrator's gentle love for the boy. In 'For a Five-Year-Old', Adcock uses iambic pentameter to create a gentle, regular rhythm that sounds conversational. This highlights the love and attention that the narrator gives to the child, and the care that the narrator must exercise in teaching the child to be "kind".
- Both poems explore the theme of lying. In 'The Beautiful Lie', Pugh uses a series of images to indicate that a child's first lie is a fundamental and positive part of growing: she compares it to "the first time a baby's fist clenches" a finger, and "the first / taste of fruit". These images appeal to the reader's senses of touch and taste respectively, which helps the reader to understand how vivid and important an experience a child's first lie is. In 'For a Five-Year-Old', on the other hand, it is not the child who lies: it is the mother, who teaches the child to be "kind" to animals without mentioning that she has previously killed "mice", "birds" and "kittens". The poem suggests that it is necessary for parents to lie to their children: in the narrator's case, lying about her past actions helps her to bring her child up to be "kind" and to protect them from the harsh truths of adulthood.
- Both poems emphasise the sense of wonder that the narrator has towards the child. In 'The Beautiful Lie', the narrator is fascinated by the signs that the boy is growing up and learning. This is shown through the use of natural imagery such as the "northern lights" and "the unreal sea", which suggests that the child is expanding into new and undiscovered territory and evokes ideas of adventure and exploration. Similarly, in 'For a Five-Year-Old', the narrator seems awed by the gentle personality of her child, despite her own past: this is shown by the repetition of the phrase "from me" in lines 11 and 12. This repetition emphasises how surprised the narrator is that, despite her actions in the past, she has taught her child "gentleness" and "faith".

Pages 171-174 — English Literature — Paper 2: Section A (Shakespeare)

1) a) For this question, pay close attention to how the characters behave in the extract, and what their behaviour shows about them and their relationship. Look closely at the language each character uses and what it suggests about how they feel. Here are some points you could make:
- The extract is a comic scene between Benedick and Beatrice which presents the characters as witty and likeable, even though they're exchanging insults. Although this is the first time that the audience sees the two characters meet, there are hints that they had a close relationship in the past. For example, Beatrice says, "I know you of old", which suggests that she has known Benedick for a long time, and her comment that he always ends with "a jade's trick" may hint that he has treated her badly in the past. This increases the tension of the scene, as the audience is unsure whether their insults are genuinely playful or motivated by past events.
- Beatrice and Benedick are presented as unafraid of insulting each other's appearance and character. Benedick calls Beatrice "Lady Disdain", which attacks her sharp, cynical wit. Beatrice later retorts that scratching Benedick's face "could not make it worse". This shows that both characters are outspoken and feisty. This is particularly true of Beatrice, whose strength of character contrasts with the Elizabethan stereotype of the meek, respectful woman represented by Hero.

- Both characters use wordplay, which emphasises their wit. Between them, they cleverly develop the same extended metaphor using animal imagery. Benedick insults Beatrice by calling her a "parrot-teacher", which implies that she talks incessantly and repetitively, like someone repeating a phrase for a parrot to learn. In return, Beatrice replies, "A bird of my tongue is better than a beast of yours." She suggests that she is cleverer than Benedick by linking his intelligence to that of a "beast" that cannot speak. This interplay shows that they are equally matched in wit, and may hint to the audience that they are destined to be together.
- Both characters, despite their disagreement on most things, agree that they have no desire to marry. Benedick says, "truly, I love none" and Beatrice says "I had rather hear my dog bark at a crow than a man swear he loves me." It's ironic that the only thing they agree on is that they don't love anyone, as Shakespeare hints that despite their protestations, they'll probably fall in love later in the play. Even here, with Beatrice and Benedick both rejecting love, the audience is likely to be persuaded that they are perfectly matched in character and intelligence, and to hope they'll change their mind about love. This is reinforced by the audience's prior expectations of the play: based on Shakespeare's other comedies, they'll be expecting a happy ending.

b) In this question, you need to think about the play as a whole, and how Hero and Claudio's relationship changes during the course of the play. Here are some points you could make:
- Claudio first mentions his love for Hero when he speaks to Benedick in Act 1, Scene 1. He says "I love her, I feel", although he himself admits that his love "might too sudden seem," suggesting that it might not be completely genuine. He describes Hero as the "sweetest lady that ever I looked on", which suggests that his love is based on her beauty, and he also uses traditional romantic imagery to describe her as a "jewel". However, this image is also linked to money and reminds the audience of Hero's wealth, which could be seen as a motive for Claudio's love.
- Hero and Claudio quickly become engaged. Hero is silent when the lovers meet, only whispering in Claudio's ear that "he is in her heart." Hero's silence shows that she is playing the traditional role of the young, shy virgin. From this point, Claudio becomes a typical courtly lover, showering Hero with gifts and love poems. Hero and Claudio both follow the traditional rules of courtship in Elizabethan society. This contrasts with Beatrice and Benedick, who insult each other at the start of the play, showing that they have an unconventional relationship.
- When Hero is accused of being unfaithful, Claudio accepts Don John's 'proof' immediately, instead of trusting Hero. Despite his previous love for her, he cannot get past his belief that she "knows the heat of a luxurious bed". Just as Claudio was hasty to fall in love, he is also quick to fall out of love again, showing him to be fickle and shallow. Claudio rejects Hero because he believes that her honour and virginity, both valuable assets in Elizabethan society, have been ruined. This shows that Claudio's love for Hero was based on her reputation and beauty rather than knowledge of her personality. In contrast, Hero's love for Claudio is presented as strong and steadfast: despite being cruelly shamed in public by Claudio, Hero doesn't stop loving him.
- Both Claudio and Hero are presented as young and inexperienced: Claudio says that it is only since he has returned from war that he has had the "soft and delicate desires" of a lover. As Claudio declares his love for Hero the first time he sees her, he has no basis for judging her moral character. In addition, Claudio makes the mistake of being led by Don John and choosing social propriety over trust. This shows that he is easily led by other characters and hasn't yet learnt to follow his own judgement.
- Likewise, Hero's quick acceptance of Claudio, despite his cruel treatment of her, can be explained by her youthful inexperience. She marries him because this is what is expected of her by society, rather than challenging him for his lack of trust in her, as we imagine that Beatrice would have done in the same situation.
- When Hero reveals herself again at the end of the play, Claudio declares that she is "Another Hero!" and Hero says that in the past Claudio was her "other husband." This suggests that their relationship has been renewed and strengthened by the difficulties they have overcome, since now they are like different people.

2) For this question, you have to write about masculinity, so you need to pick out important bits of the play where Shakespeare addresses this theme, and explain how each bit you write about relates to the question. Don't forget to write about the extract in detail as well as the rest of the play. Here are some points you could make:
- In Act 1, Scene 7, Lady Macbeth links the idea of masculinity to bravery and violence. She bullies her husband into killing Duncan by questioning his masculinity: "When you durst do it, then you were a man". From Lady Macbeth's perspective, the ability to commit violent acts is a key element of masculinity.
- Macbeth's view of masculinity in the extract contrasts with that of Lady Macbeth. He explains that to kill his king would not "become" a man, and that if he commits the murder he is "none": not a man at all. Macbeth incorporates concepts of honour and loyalty into his ideas about masculinity, which shows that he is morally more principled than Lady Macbeth.
- However, as the scene progresses, Lady Macbeth persuades Macbeth to change his mind, and he decides once again that he will kill the king. It is clear that Lady Macbeth's attacks on his masculinity have influenced him, as he tells Lady Macbeth that due to her "undaunted mettle" (bravery) she deserves to "Bring forth men-children only". This shows that, like Lady Macbeth, he has come to associate masculinity with the desire to commit violent acts, regardless of whether or not it is the moral thing to do.
- Shakespeare challenges this view of masculinity by presenting Macbeth and Lady Macbeth's actions as cowardly. They kill Duncan in his sleep, and they pin his murder on his innocent servants. Audiences at the time would have considered Macbeth's actions to be unmanly and dishonourable. His lack of honour and unmasculine behaviour sets the scene for his eventual downfall.
- Lady Macbeth's influence on Macbeth's view of masculinity is emphasised later in the play, when Macbeth uses her tactics to persuade the murderers to kill Banquo. He suggests that, if the murderers refuse to kill Banquo, they are in the "worst rank of manhood". This is ironic: Macbeth is suggesting that the men are less masculine because they are reluctant to kill Banquo, but Macbeth has made the decision not to kill Banquo himself. This cowardly behaviour contrasts with his behaviour at the beginning of the play, where he is described as "brave" after killing Macdonald in battle. As the play progresses, Macbeth becomes less willing to commit 'masculine' acts of violence; instead he acts like Lady Macbeth, manipulating other people to achieve his own ends. This suggests that he is moving away from the "brave" warrior of Act 1, which was the masculine ideal of the Middle Ages, when the play is set.

- Shakespeare's presentation of violent but noble masculinity can also be seen elsewhere in the play, particularly in Act 4, Scene 3, when Macduff discovers that his wife and children have been killed. Malcolm's reaction to the news is to incite Macduff to "great revenge"; he links this to Macduff's masculinity by saying that Macduff must "Dispute" the matter violently, "like a man". This suggests that the association between masculinity and violence was a commonly held view at the time.

- However, Macduff's idea of masculinity is less limited: he explains that while he intends to fight Macbeth, he must also "feel" his grief as a "man" should. This shows that Macduff sees the ability to feel emotion as an important part of his masculinity, alongside notions of bravery and aggression. Macduff is not constrained by the idea that to be a man, he must be unfeeling or mindlessly violent; this sets the scene for him to be a worthy victor over Macbeth at the end of the play.

3) a) For this question, you'll need to look carefully at the language used in the extract, but keep in mind where the extract fits into the play too. Remember to refer to the plot and characters in your answer, and back your points up with quotes. Here are some points you could make:

- Romeo compares Juliet to the sun: "what light through yonder window breaks?". This makes it seem as though he feels that the world is lit up by Juliet's presence. He goes on to say that the moon is jealous of her, "pale with grief / That thou... art far more fair than she." This metaphor suggests the power of Romeo's feelings and his sense of awe at her beauty. The comparison seems particularly dramatic given that the two have just met, which emphasises Romeo's ability to fall in love very quickly.

- Romeo is clearly desperate to talk to Juliet. This is shown by the fact that when he sees her he says "She speaks, yet she says nothing." This sounds as if he is caught between being encouraged and discouraged by the way he feels. He is desperate to talk to her, but he is still unsure of himself. This is also shown in his indecisiveness — "Her eye discourses, I will answer it. / I am too bold." This sense of uncertainty is emphasised in the lines "It is my lady, O it is my love! / O that she knew she were!" Romeo has fallen in love with Juliet, but he hasn't told her yet and doesn't know if she feels the same way — this creates tension, as both he and the audience are unsure of what will happen.

- There is a strong sense of physical attraction in this scene, as Romeo enjoys looking at Juliet and imagining being with her: "See how she leans her cheek upon her hand. / O that I were a glove upon that hand". Shakespeare shows that Romeo physically desires Juliet, and hints that Romeo's feelings for Juliet at this stage in the play are relatively shallow and rooted in lust rather than true affection.

b) For this question, you'll need to look at the play as a whole, and pick out bits where the audience might feel particularly sympathetic towards Juliet. Remember to refer to the plot and characters in your answer, and back your points up with quotes. Here are some points you could make:

- The audience are led to feel sympathy for Juliet at the end of Act 1, Scene 5, when she learns that Romeo, with whom she has just fallen in love, is "The only son" of her "great enemy". Shakespeare uses antithesis to emphasise how upset Juliet is at this revelation: the phrase "My only love sprung from my only hate" emphasises her confusion and the strength of her two contrasting emotions.

- Shakespeare's use of foreshadowing throughout the play makes the audience feel sympathy for Juliet even when she is happy or excited. For example, she says that she would "kill" Romeo with "much cherishing" in Act 2, Scene 2, while in Act 3, Scene 5 she has a premonition of seeing him "dead in the bottom of a tomb". These constant references to death remind the reader of the play's prologue, in which it is made clear that Romeo and Juliet are destined to "take their life". This makes Juliet's moments of happiness with Romeo seem bittersweet, as they are doomed to end in tragedy.

- Act 5, Scene 3 is perhaps the scene where the reader feels most sympathy for Juliet. When she first wakes up she asks "where is my lord?" and then repeats her question: "Where is my Romeo?". This makes her seem eager and excited to see Romeo again; there is dramatic irony here as the audience know that Romeo is dead. This knowledge makes the audience feel sympathy for Juliet, as she is about to discover the truth.

- When Juliet subsequently finds out that Romeo is dead, her language increases the sympathy that the audience feels for her. She describes the "happy dagger" with which she will kill herself; this indicates that Romeo's death has destroyed her so completely that she is happy to die, which shows the strength of her love.

4) For this question, you have to write about justice and mercy, so you need to pick out important bits of the play where Shakespeare addresses these themes, and explain how each bit you write about relates to the question. Don't forget to write about the extract in detail as well as the rest of the play. Here are some points you could make:

- Portia's speech in Act 4, Scene 1 explores in detail the two related themes of mercy and justice. The speech is written in blank verse, which makes it seem more important than if it were written in prose. This emphasises that these are key themes in the play.

- The speech presents the concepts of mercy and justice as two very different things. Portia links justice with the laws of Venice: if Shylock follows his "plea" for "justice", then the "strict court" of Venice will be forced to sentence Antonio. Mercy, on the other hand, is presented as a human quality that can be used to "mitigate" the law; in this speech, Portia asks Shylock to consider abandoning his case against Antonio in the name of "mercy", even though "justice" would convict him.

- Portia's speech hints at a negative portrayal of justice that is reinforced throughout the play. Many of the characters associate justice with the character of Shylock, who is obsessed with "justice and his bond." His cruel quest for revenge on Antonio relies on the justice of the court, which shows that Venetian justice is unreliable and can lead to unfair consequences.

- In contrast, the portrayal of mercy in Portia's speech is strongly positive. She calls mercy an "attribute to God" that comes from "heaven", and says that if justice alone were followed then nobody would "see salvation". This suggests that mercy is a divine attribute, which is required in order to reach heaven. This would have resonated strongly with the predominantly Christian audiences of the Elizabethan era, who would have understood mercy as an important quality of a good Christian person.

- The idea that showing mercy is the right thing to do under any circumstances is reinforced throughout the play. Despite Portia's speech, and Bassanio's offer of money, Shylock refuses to show mercy to Antonio, insisting that "no power in the tongue of man" can persuade him to change his mind. His insistence on justice and refusal to be merciful condemns him: Portia twists the rules of the court so that justice no longer works in his favour, and he can no longer harm Antonio; furthermore, Shylock's own life and fortune are forfeit.

- However, Shylock's life is saved by the "mercy" of the Duke. Even though the Duke wants to punish Shylock, he refrains from sentencing him to death because he wants to prove the "difference" between his "spirit" and Shylock's. It is ironic that Shylock is saved by the very mercy he refused to show.

- Shylock's reprieve also creates a sense of satisfaction for the audience. Despite Shylock's actions, Shakespeare creates some sympathy for him; for example, in Act 1, Scene 3 Shylock describes the abuse that he has previously received from Antonio: he has been "spit" upon and "rated" (verbally abused). Because of this, it would seem unjust in the wider morality of the play to kill Shylock; as it is, he receives less harsh punishments that still force him to pay for his cruelty.
- Antonio's final request as part of Shylock's punishment is to insist that he "become a Christian". Audiences in Shakespeare's time would have associated Christianity with mercy, so it is appropriate that Shylock's final punishment is to be forced to embrace the ideals of mercy and forgiveness that he previously rejected.

Pages 175-180 — English Literature — Paper 2: Section B (19th-Century Prose)

1) For this question, you have to write about poverty, so you need to pick out important bits of the novel where the writer addresses this theme, and explain how each bit you write about relates to the question. Don't forget to write about the extract in detail as well as the rest of the novel. Here are some points you could make:

- Scrooge's encounter with Ignorance and Want at the end of Chapter 3 represents a turning point for his character, as he has a strong reaction to the way they look and begins to understand the effects of his attitude towards the poor. Ignorance and Want look like starving children: they are "ragged" and "wretched", which causes Scrooge to feel "appalled". His emotional reaction contrasts with the portrayal of him as unfeeling at the beginning of the story, which shows that the reality of poverty, observed first-hand, is shocking enough to persuade even the most uncompassionate person to change.
- Dickens also uses the characters of Ignorance and Want to convey a wider message to his audience. The Ghost of Christmas Present explains that the children are a result of "Man's" neglect, which reflects Dickens's belief that Victorian society was to blame for the lack of education (Ignorance) and basic amenities such as food (Want) among poor children. The spirit explains that ignoring the problems of poverty will lead to "Doom", which suggests that Dickens thought upper- and middle-class attitudes to poverty would have negative repercussions for the whole of society.
- Despite their sympathetic attributes, Ignorance and Want are also described as "devils" and "monsters". This suggests that poverty can corrupt the innocence of childhood, which hints at how powerful an evil it is.
- The Ghost of Christmas Present reminds Scrooge of his words earlier in the novel: "Are there no prisons?", showing that, at the start of the novel, Scrooge regards poverty as a crime. This is in keeping with the attitudes of many people in Victorian society: people in debt could be thrown into 'debtor's jail', and they were not released until they repaid their debts. By presenting Ignorance and Want as children, Dickens reinforces the message that the poor are not to blame for their situation, and that they should be helped rather than punished.
- Dickens uses Scrooge's character to attack the mentality that Victorian society had towards the poor. Scrooge initially represents selfish members of the middle and upper classes in Victorian society. He refuses to give to charity, and he calls poor people "surplus population", saying it would be better if they died. The description of Scrooge as a "sinner" shows that his attitude to the poor is ungodly and morally wrong.

- As the book continues, Scrooge learns to reject his selfish views: in the final chapter, he buys the Cratchits a "prize Turkey", and he makes a large donation to a charity that helps the poor. Helping those less fortunate makes him happy: he greets everyone with a "delighted smile" and repeatedly acts with a "chuckle". Scrooge's happiness at the end of the novel shows that it can be satisfying and enjoyable to help the poor. His actions also have a dramatic effect on the Cratchit family, as Tiny Tim survives thanks to Scrooge's financial help. Dickens highlights the ability of the middle and upper classes to have a huge effect on the lives of those in poverty.
- Dickens presents the Cratchit family in an idealistic way. Despite their poverty, they are a cheerful, loving family: they greet their meagre Christmas dinner with "universal admiration", and they try to stay "cheerful" for each other's sake after Tiny Tim dies. Dickens presents the Cratchits as a perfect family, which emphasises how tragic and unfair it is that they suffer from the effects of poverty, as well as challenging the commonly held Victorian belief that poor people were morally deficient.

2) For this question, you have to write about morality, so you need to pick out important bits of the novel where the writer addresses this theme, and explain how each bit you write about relates to the question. Don't forget to write about the extract in detail as well as the rest of the novel. Here are some points you could make:

- The novel emphasises the internal conflict that can be caused by immoral desires. This can be seen in the extract, as Jekyll says that he has "called" Hyde from his "own soul". This highlights the link between them, and reinforces the idea that Hyde's "depravity" represents the dark side of Jekyll's personality. Elsewhere in the novel, Stevenson uses the language of battle to make it clear that it is a struggle for Jekyll to suppress this dark side: there is a "war" within Jekyll, and the "two natures that contended in the field" of his mind sound like two forces meeting on a battlefield. Jekyll claims that this struggle applies to all of mankind: he says that "man is not truly one, but truly two". This reflects Stevenson's message that all humans have an immoral side.
- In the extract, Jekyll makes it clear that he understands his actions as Hyde are morally wrong: he describes Hyde's "depravity", and even calls his actions "bestial", which suggests that they are inhuman and animalistic.
- However, Jekyll does not feel guilt over Hyde's actions: he says it is "Hyde alone" who is to blame, and his own "conscience slumbered", which makes him sound passive and unaffected by the chaos and destruction that Hyde has caused. In Jekyll's view of morality, he has done nothing wrong, despite the fact that he is the one who has created Hyde and is therefore responsible for him.
- Jekyll's language in this extract hints at his ambiguous morality: he describes Hyde's behaviour using some positive language, which suggests that he cannot bring himself to entirely condemn Hyde's actions. Whilst he claims to be "aghast" at Hyde's behaviour, he also describes the "sea of liberty" that Hyde brings him, and he reacts to Hyde's "depravity" with "a kind of wonder". This hints at the conflict between how Victorian ideas of morality dictate that Jekyll should feel and how he actually feels: whilst he feels forced to condemn Hyde's actions in writing, there is a sense that underneath he envies and almost admires him.
- Stevenson also uses other characters in the novel to illustrate the flaws in Victorian views of morality. Victorian society had a rigid set of moral values, so to maintain a good reputation, people had to repress many of their true feelings and desires in public. For the characters in the novel, preserving a good reputation appears to be more important than actually acting morally. For example, Utterson is more concerned about preserving Jekyll's reputation than bringing Hyde to trial: after Carew's murder, he says to Jekyll, "If it came to a trial, your name might appear." This shows his concern for Jekyll's reputation, and emphasises that he prioritises it over the pursuit of justice.

- Characters in the novel are often unwilling even to discuss anything that is not respectable or morally right. For example, Utterson is wary of gossip, which he avoids in case it reflects badly on him or his friends. He and Enfield agree never to talk about Hyde, and believe in not asking questions if something "looks like Queer Street". Jekyll is similarly reluctant to talk about Hyde: he tells Utterson that it is a "private matter", and Utterson respects his request for privacy and drops the subject. This behaviour increases the sense that morality in the novel is flawed: the characters are willing to ignore their moral concerns in order to maintain their respectability.

- The novel suggests that evil is ultimately more powerful than moral behaviour. Hyde grows stronger as the novel progresses, and eventually he overpowers Jekyll, and causes his death. This highlights Stevenson's message that trying to hide immoral desires beneath a civilised, moral exterior is very dangerous.

3) For this question, you need to pick out key events in the novel that show the relationship between the two characters, so it's important to know the text well. If you can, try to find scenes which show different aspects of the relationship so that you have plenty of things to talk about. Here are some points you could make:

- Mr and Mrs Bennet's relationship is established at the beginning of the novel, when they discuss Mr Bingley's arrival at Netherfield. Mr Bennet mocks Mrs Bennet's vanity by suggesting that "Mr Bingley may like you the best of the party." This shows that Mr Bennet is more intelligent and witty than Mrs Bennet, and does not regard her as an equal, but rather makes fun of her, realising that she won't understand the joke. His behaviour is quite cruel, which also reveals his lack of affection for her. The fact that she does not appear to be offended by his teasing and lack of respect for her may be due in part to the fact that society in the early nineteenth century would not have allowed a woman like Mrs Bennet to earn a living, so she would have been entirely dependent on Mr Bennet, and could not afford to drive him away.

- Mrs Bennet switches between berating her husband for not doing as she asks, and treating him affectionately when he does what she wants. For example, in the extract she is angry and resentful when he refuses to visit Bingley, and says "You take delight in vexing me", but when she later learns that he has visited Bingley, she is delighted and immediately forgives him: "What an excellent father you have, girls". The speed with which her attitude to Mr Bennet changes shows how shallow her feelings towards him are. This highlights that their marriage isn't based on deep feelings of love, respect or equality, which reinforces the idea that they are not particularly happy in their relationship.

- It is clear that Mr Bennet has distanced himself from his marriage; he spends a lot of his time alone in his library, and seems to take little pleasure in being with his wife, apart from the fun of teasing her. Because of his jokes at Mrs Bennet's expense, Elizabeth believes that Mr Bennet is to blame for "exposing his wife to the contempt of her own children", showing that she believes he should have tried to set a good example for his wife, or correct her behaviour, rather than mocking it.

- Mr and Mrs Bennet are both largely comic characters, Mr Bennet because of his quick, dry wit, and Mrs Bennet because of her ignorance and lack of decorum. However, their relationship has more serious undertones; it is clear that the marriage was a mistake and they are fundamentally unsuited to one another. For example, Mr Bennet is described as "a mixture of quick parts", whereas Mrs Bennet is "a woman of mean understanding", which illustrates the difference in their intellect. We are told that Mr Bennet was initially "captivated by youth and beauty", showing that his feelings were superficial, and all "Respect, esteem, and confidence" for his wife were quickly lost. This illustrates one of Austen's messages: that it is important to select a partner on the basis of intellect, compatibility and love, rather than on the basis of wealth or sexual attraction.

- The Bennet's unhappy marriage is echoed in other marriages in the novel that are motivated by financial or superficial reasons, namely Charlotte and Mr Collins, and Lydia and Mr Wickham. In this way, Austen uses Mr and Mrs Bennet as a way of foreshadowing what will become of these couples, and as a way of emphasising that the cycle of unhappy marriages will never be broken until people realise that the only good reason to marry is for love.

4) This question requires you to think carefully about the importance of a single central character and how they change throughout the novel, so all your points need to be clearly about that character. Don't forget to write about the extract in detail as well as the rest of the novel. Here are some points you could make:

- The character of Mr Rochester undergoes a series of dramatic changes over the course of the novel. In the extract, he describes his younger self as "stiff-necked" and "proud", a judgement that is supported by Jane's early encounters with him. The extract takes place after Jane has been absent from his life for some time; when she returns, he is presented as a changed man. The hardships he has gone through have made him understand and overcome the flaws in his character, and he has learned "humility".

- The most obvious change in his character that the extract reveals is his newfound respect for and worship of God: he admits that he initially "almost cursed" the fate that had taken Jane away, but believes that the hardships he went through were "chastisements" from God, which re-establish his faith in a "beneficent" God who "sees... far clearer" and "judges... far more wisely" than man. For the novel's 19th-century audience, Rochester's newfound piety would have been a sign of his virtue and goodness. Later, he regains his sight in one eye, which Jane describes as a sign of God's "mercy". This indicates that Rochester has earned forgiveness for his past sins, and has become a virtuous man.

- This newfound virtue manifests itself in Rochester's actions. Earlier in the novel, Rochester calls his younger self a "trite, commonplace sinner" for his relationship with Céline Varens. His treatment of his wife, Bertha Mason, could also be seen as sinful: he locks her in an attic and denies her existence. However, by attempting to rescue her from the Thornfield fire, Rochester demonstrates that he has already begun to change for the better. This hints that Jane's departure is a necessary step that allows him to re-evaluate his past behaviour and atone for his mistakes.

- Rochester is also presented as truthful in the extract: he offers "very sincere" prayers of repentance, and he openly discusses the strength of his feelings for Jane. This is significant because, earlier in the novel, Brontë presents Rochester as being prepared to deceive others to achieve what he wants: for example, he dresses up as a gipsy, an act which Jane describes as "scarcely fair", to tell Blanche that he is not rich and to question Jane about her feelings. This shows how, at this earlier stage in his life, he tried to control people. It also suggests that he had little respect for people's feelings, which contrasts markedly with his real "remorse" and recognition of the "guilt" he would have caused Jane if he had married her bigamously.

- Rochester also undergoes a dramatic transformation in terms of appreciating goodness and sincerity in others. During Jane's time at Thornfield, he surrounds himself with "fine, fashionable people" such as Blanche Ingram, who is shown to be superficial and "not good-natured". In contrast, Jane's absence makes him recognise that she is his "alpha and omega", and that only in her presence can he experience "bliss and peace". This shows that he has learnt to value the company of people who are kind, honest and moral, rather than those who are elegant and fashionable.

- Rochester is "humbled" by his experiences, and this is also reflected in his attitude towards wealth and material possessions: when he and Jane first become engaged, he is excited to "pour" jewels into her lap and dress her in "satin and lace". However, when Jane finds Rochester at Ferndean he is no longer interested in "fine clothes and jewels"; instead Jane is described as "the most precious thing he had". This progression of character shows that he has come to understand what is truly valuable in life, and to reject the shallow obsession with wealth and status that characterises the upper classes in the novel.
- By the end of the novel, Rochester has overcome his flaws, and the reader sees that he is now worthy of marrying Jane. This makes the novel's resolution satisfying for the reader, who sees that the characters have received the outcome they deserve.

5) This question requires you to think carefully about the importance of a single character, so all your points need to be clearly about that character. Don't forget to write about the extract in detail as well as the rest of the novel. Here are some points you could make:

- In the extract, Dickens introduces the character of Miss Havisham in a highly descriptive way. The "satins, and lace, and silks" of Miss Havisham's bridal clothing contrast sharply with her "withered", "sunken" body; this creates a vivid image of her that is memorable for the reader, and makes them want to find out more about the character.
- Dickens's use of Pip as a first-person narrator emphasises how intimidating Miss Havisham appears. He compares her to a "ghastly waxwork" and a "skeleton"; these frightening images suggest that Miss Havisham is almost inhuman in her appearance, and reflect Pip's sense of fear.
- Dickens uses strong imagery to show how obsessed Miss Havisham is with her own despair: for example, she keeps her mouldy wedding cake, despite the fact that it is covered with insects and "black fungus". This indicates that she hasn't been able to move on from the past, and the unpleasant image suggests that her obsession is dangerous and unhealthy.
- Miss Havisham is manipulative: she has raised Estella to "wreak revenge on all the male sex", which the reader sees when she deliberately directs Pip's attention to Estella's beauty in order to manipulate him into falling in love with her. This love hurts Pip emotionally: he says that he is "as unhappy" as Miss Havisham could "ever have meant" him to be. This makes her seem cruel and uncaring, as she purposely intended Pip to be hurt by Estella.
- However, Miss Havisham's past allows the reader to begin to understand her cruel actions. Herbert describes her treatment at the hands of Arthur as "cruel mortification", which makes the reader begin to understand her personality. Later, when Magwitch is revealing more about Miss Havisham's story, he only refers to her in passing as "a rich lady". This hints at the callous way in which Compeyson treated Miss Havisham as disposable, and presents her as a victim of a crime, which makes the reader feel more sympathetic towards her.
- Dickens also creates sympathy for Miss Havisham using her relationship with Estella. After purposefully training Estella to be "hard", "proud" and incapable of love, she realises that Estella cannot love her. This upsets her: Dickens describes how she "shrieked" and "moaned", which indicates her distress. Her desire for revenge has damaged Estella as well as Pip, and has meant that she ends up alone and unloved; this makes the reader feel sympathy for her.
- By the end of the novel, Miss Havisham begins to feel regret over her past cruelty. She regrets her past actions, particularly regarding Estella, repeatedly asking Pip "What have I done!" She becomes a weak, pitiable creature who begs Pip for forgiveness "on her knees" and is desperate to do "something useful and good". Her regret makes the reader feel even more sorry for her, rather than blaming her for her actions.

6) For this question, you have to write about revenge, so you need to pick out important bits of the novel where the writer addresses this theme, and explain how each bit you write about relates to the question. Don't forget to write about the extract in detail as well as the rest of the novel. Here are some points you could make:

- Frankenstein's language in the extract presents revenge as a powerful and violent force: he uses emotive, visceral phrases such as "drink deep of agony" to show the strength of his anger and indicate his desire to do real harm to the monster.
- Shelley makes it clear that Frankenstein's quest for revenge has affected his sanity. In the extract, he talks about the "spirits of the departed" as if they are really there, and his hyperbolic language as he describes his "deep and eternal grief" and swears an oath to "the spirits" emphasises that his behaviour is irrational. This shows the reader that he has been emotionally destroyed by the suffering he has faced, and helps them to understand his motivation in setting out on a fatal quest for revenge on the monster.
- The idea that revenge is something unhealthy and harmful is established early on in the novel. After William's death, Alphonse begs Frankenstein to avoid "brooding thoughts of vengeance", as they will end up "festering, the wounds" of his mind. The use of the word "festering" suggests that revenge is like a disease, which hints at the harm it will cause in Frankenstein's life.
- Alphonse's words eventually prove true: both Frankenstein and the monster seek revenge on each other, and this becomes a damaging cycle that destroys both of their lives. Revenge isolates Frankenstein permanently from society, and drives him to the Arctic, eventually leading to his death; meanwhile, the monster is made miserable, describing his quest for revenge as "deadly torture".
- The monster's idea of revenge is more complicated than Frankenstein's. Frankenstein has one goal: to kill the monster in order to avenge the deaths of his family. In contrast, the monster's revenge is more calculated: he kills Frankenstein's loved ones first, in order to inflict on Frankenstein the kind of loneliness he has suffered. This shows that his thirst for revenge has made him cruel and scheming.
- The monster and Frankenstein are linked by their desire for revenge. This can be seen in the similarities between their language as their quests for revenge continue. Frankenstein's language towards the end of the novel is violent and uncontrolled: he describes his "unspeakable" rage and "devouring" desire to exact revenge. Similarly, the monster often speaks violently: for example, he promises to bring about Frankenstein's "destruction", when he initially refuses to create a female companion. This highlights how both characters' desire for revenge causes them to become cruel and violent.
- Shelley makes it clear that revenge is an ultimately unsatisfying endeavour. Even though the monster achieves the destruction he wants, he is still "miserable" because he has been "polluted" by his crimes, so he decides that the only option is to kill himself. This suggests that he has been irrevocably tainted by the murders he has committed, and shows that even though he has been able to fulfil his revenge, it is not satisfying enough to overcome his sense of guilt and shame.

Glossary

alliteration	When words that are <u>close together</u> start with the <u>same sound</u>. E.g. "the <u>b</u>eat of the <u>b</u>and".
ambiguity	Where a word or phrase has <u>two or more</u> possible <u>interpretations</u>.
analogy	A <u>comparison</u> to show how one thing is <u>similar</u> to another, which makes it easier to <u>understand</u> or more <u>memorable</u>. E.g. "the human brain is like a super-computer: complex and powerful."
antithesis	A <u>rhetorical technique</u> where <u>opposing</u> words or ideas are put <u>together</u> to show a contrast.
aside	When a <u>character</u> in a play makes a <u>short comment</u> that reveals their <u>thoughts</u> to the <u>audience</u>, and no other character can hear it.
assonance	When words share the same <u>vowel sound</u> but their consonants are different, e.g. "in this d<u>ee</u>p joy to s<u>ee</u> and hear th<u>ee</u>".
audience	The <u>person</u> or <u>group of people</u> that read or listen to a text.
autobiographical	Describing something that happened in the <u>writer's life</u>.
biased writing	Writing that gives <u>more support</u> to one point of view than to another.
blank verse	Lines from a play or poem that are written in <u>iambic pentameter</u> and <u>don't rhyme</u>.
broadsheet	A <u>formal</u> type of newspaper, which often focuses on more <u>serious</u> topics, e.g. *The Guardian*.
caesura (plural <u>caesurae</u>)	A <u>pause</u> in a line of poetry. E.g. the full stop in "Over the drifted stream. My father spins" in 'Eden Rock' by Charles Causley.
chronological	When events are arranged in the <u>order</u> in which they <u>happened</u>.
cinematic writing	Writing that makes the reader feel like they're watching a <u>film</u>.
clause	Part of a sentence that has a <u>subject</u> and a <u>verb</u>. <u>Main clauses</u> make sense on their own.
colloquial language	<u>Informal</u> language that sounds like ordinary <u>speech</u>, e.g. "with your pals".
commentary (newspaper article)	A type of newspaper article that expresses the <u>opinions</u> of the writer on a theme or news event. Also called a <u>column</u> or <u>opinion piece</u>.
complex sentence	A sentence that contains <u>one or more subordinate clauses</u>.
compound sentence	Two <u>main clauses</u> joined to make one sentence using a <u>conjunction</u> such as 'or', 'but' or 'and'. E.g. "The cat came in, <u>and</u> the dog left the room."
connotations	The <u>suggestions</u> that words can make <u>beyond</u> their obvious meaning. E.g. 'stroll' means 'walk', but it has connotations of moving slowly.
consonance	<u>Repetition</u> of a <u>consonant sound</u> in nearby words, e.g. "And fi<u>t</u> the brigh<u>t</u> s<u>t</u>eel-poin<u>t</u>ed sock".
context	The <u>background</u> to something, or the situation <u>surrounding</u> it, which affects the way it's understood. E.g. the context of a text from 1915 would include the First World War.
counter-argument	The <u>opposite</u> point of view to the writer's own view. This is useful when writing to argue or persuade — first give the counter-argument, then explain why you <u>disagree</u> with it.
direct address	When a narrator or writer <u>speaks directly</u> to another character or to the reader, e.g. "you might recall..."
double negative	A sentence construction that <u>incorrectly</u> expresses a <u>negative idea</u> by using <u>two</u> negative words or phrases, e.g. "I <u>don't</u> want <u>no</u> trouble."
dramatic monologue	A <u>form</u> of poetry that uses the assumed voice of a <u>single speaker</u> who is <u>not the poet</u> to address an <u>implied audience</u>.

Glossary

emotive	Something that makes you <u>feel</u> a particular <u>emotion</u>.
empathy	The ability to <u>imagine</u> and <u>understand</u> someone else's <u>feelings</u> or <u>experiences</u>.
end-stopping	Finishing a line of poetry with the <u>end</u> of a <u>phrase or sentence</u>, usually marked by punctuation.
enjambment	When a sentence or phrase runs over from <u>one line</u> or <u>stanza</u> to the <u>next</u>.
explicit information	Information that's <u>directly stated</u> in a text.
figurative language	Language that is used in a <u>non-literal</u> way to create an effect, e.g. personification.
first person	A <u>narrative viewpoint</u> where the narrator is one of the <u>characters</u>, written using words like 'I', 'me', 'we' and 'our'.
flashback	A writing technique where the scene shifts from the <u>present</u> to an event in the <u>past</u>.
foreshadowing	A literary device where a writer <u>hints</u> or <u>gives clues</u> about a <u>future event</u>.
form	The <u>type</u> of text (e.g. a letter, a speech) or poem (e.g. a sonnet or a ballad).
frame narrative	A narrative in which one story is presented <u>within</u> another.
free verse	Poetry that <u>doesn't rhyme</u> and has <u>no regular rhythm</u> or <u>line length</u>.
generalisation	A statement that gives an <u>overall impression</u> (sometimes a misleading one), without going into details. E.g. "children today eat too much junk food."
half-rhymes	Words that have a <u>similar</u>, but not identical, <u>end sound</u>. E.g. "plough" and "follow".
hyperbole	When <u>exaggeration</u> is used to have an <u>effect</u> on the reader.
iambic pentameter	Poetry with a <u>metre</u> of <u>ten syllables</u> — five of them stressed, and five unstressed. The <u>stress</u> falls on <u>every second syllable</u>, e.g. "And <u>full</u>-grown <u>lambs</u> loud <u>bleat</u> from <u>hilly</u> <u>bourn</u>".
imagery	Language that creates a <u>picture in your mind</u>, e.g. <u>metaphors</u>, <u>similes</u> and <u>personification</u>.
imperative verb	A verb that gives orders or directions, e.g. "<u>run</u> away" or "<u>stop</u> that".
impersonal tone	A tone of writing that <u>doesn't</u> try to directly <u>engage</u> with the reader.
implicit information	Information that's hinted at <u>without</u> being said outright.
inference	A <u>conclusion</u> reached about something, based on <u>evidence</u>. E.g. from the sentence "Yasmin wrinkled her nose at the lasagne", you could <u>infer</u> that Yasmin doesn't like lasagne.
internal rhyme	When two or more words <u>rhyme</u>, and at least one of the words <u>isn't</u> at the end of a line. The rhyming words can be in the <u>same</u> line or <u>nearby</u> lines. E.g. "The soft young <u>down</u> of her; the <u>brown</u>".
inversion	Altering the <u>normal word order</u> for <u>emphasis</u>, e.g. "On the table sat a hedgehog."
irony	When <u>words</u> are used to <u>imply the opposite</u> of what they normally mean. It can also mean when there is a difference between <u>what people expect</u> and <u>what actually happens</u>.
juxtaposition	When a writer puts two ideas, events, characters or descriptions <u>close to each other</u> to encourage the reader to <u>contrast</u> them.

Glossary

linear structure	A type of narrative structure that tells the events of a story in <u>chronological</u> order.
linguistic devices	<u>Language techniques</u> that are used to have an <u>effect</u> on an audience, e.g. onomatopoeia.
list of three	Using <u>three</u> words (often adjectives) or phrases together to create <u>emphasis</u>.
metaphor	A way of describing something by saying that it <u>is something else</u>, e.g. "his feet were blocks of ice".
metre	The arrangement of stressed and unstressed syllables to create <u>rhythm</u> in a line of poetry.
monologue	<u>One person</u> speaking alone for a long period of time.
mood	The <u>feel</u> or <u>atmosphere</u> of a text, e.g. humorous, peaceful, fearful.
motif	A <u>recurring</u> image or idea in a text.
narrative	Writing that tells a <u>story</u> or describes an <u>experience</u>.
narrative viewpoint	The <u>perspective</u> that a text is written from, e.g. <u>first-person</u> point of view.
narrator	The <u>voice</u> or <u>character</u> speaking the words of the narrative.
non-linear structure	A type of narrative structure that tells the events of a story in a <u>non-chronological</u> order.
objective writing	A <u>neutral</u>, <u>unbiased</u> style of writing which contains <u>facts</u> rather than opinions.
omniscient narrator	A narrator who <u>knows</u> the thoughts and feelings of all the characters in a narrative.
onomatopoeia	A word that <u>imitates</u> the sound it describes as you say it, e.g. 'whisper'.
oxymoron	A phrase which appears to <u>contradict</u> itself, e.g. "pale darkness".
pace	The <u>speed</u> at which the writer takes the reader through the events in a text or poem.
paraphrase	Describing or rephrasing something in a text <u>without</u> including a direct quote.
parenthesis	A <u>rhetorical technique</u> where an <u>extra</u> clause or phrase is <u>inserted</u> into a complete sentence.
pathetic fallacy	Giving <u>human emotions</u> to objects or aspects of nature, in order to create a certain <u>mood</u>. E.g. "The fog stretched its cold fingers stealthily towards us".
personification	Describing a non-living thing as if it's a <u>person</u>. E.g. "The sea growled hungrily."
phonetic spellings	When words are spelt as they <u>sound</u> rather than with their usual spelling, e.g. "yow" instead of "you". It's often used to show that someone is speaking with a certain <u>accent</u> or <u>dialect</u>.
plosive	A <u>short burst of sound</u> made when you say a word containing the letters b, d, g, k, p or t.
protagonist	The <u>main character</u> in a text, or the <u>leader</u> of a particular cause or movement, e.g. Pip is the protagonist in 'Great Expectations'; Lenin was a protagonist in the Communist movement.
purpose	The <u>reason</u> someone writes a text, e.g. to persuade, to argue, to advise, to inform.
register	The specific <u>language</u> used to <u>match</u> writing to the <u>social situation</u> that it's for.

Glossary

Glossary

rhetoric	Using language techniques (e.g. repetition or hyperbole) to achieve a persuasive effect.
rhetorical question	A question that doesn't need an answer but is asked to make or emphasise a point, e.g. "Do you think the planet is worth saving?"
rhyme scheme	A pattern of rhyming words in a poem, e.g. if a poem has an ABAB rhyme scheme, this means that the first and third lines in each stanza rhyme, and so do the second and fourth lines.
rhyming couplet	A pair of rhyming lines that are next to each other.
rhythm	A pattern of sounds created by the arrangement of stressed and unstressed syllables.
sarcasm	Language that has a scornful or mocking tone, often using irony.
satire	Text that makes fun of people or situations, often by imitating them and exaggerating their flaws.
second person	A narrative viewpoint that is written as if the reader is one of the characters.
sensory language	Language that appeals to the five senses.
sibilance	Repetition of 's' and 'sh' sounds, e.g. "a shrill whistle shattered the stifling silence".
simile	A way of describing something by comparing it to something else, usually by using the words 'like' or 'as'. E.g. "The apple was as red as a rose".
simple sentence	A sentence that is only made up of a single main clause.
slang	Words or phrases that are informal, and often specific to one age group or social group.
soliloquy	When a single character in a play speaks their thoughts out loud, but no other characters can hear them.
sonnet	A form of poem with fourteen lines, that usually follows a clear rhyme scheme.
standard English	English that is considered to be correct because it uses formal, standardised features of spelling and grammar.
stanza	A group of lines in a poem.
structure	The order and arrangement of ideas in a text. E.g. how it begins, develops and ends.
subject	The person or thing that performs the action described by the verb. E.g. in "Billy ate a sandwich", Billy is the subject.
syllable	A single unit of sound within a word. E.g. "all" has one syllable, "always" has two.
symbolism	When an object stands for something else. E.g. a cross symbolises Christianity.
syntax	The arrangement of words in a sentence or phrase so that they make sense.
tabloid	A less formal type of newspaper, which often focuses on more sensational topics.
third person	A narrative viewpoint where the narrator remains outside the events of the story, written using words like 'he' and 'she'.
tone	The feeling of a piece of writing, e.g. happy, sad, serious, light-hearted.
viewpoint	The attitude and beliefs that a writer is trying to convey.
voice	The characteristics of the person narrating a poem or text.
volta	A turning point in a poem, when the argument or tone changes dramatically.

Index

Index

Index

FHS45